BORN UNDER SATURN

Born under Saturn

The Letters of Samuel Loveman and Clark Ashton Smith

Edited by S. T. Joshi and David E. Schultz

Hippocampus Press

New York

Contents

Introduction

It would seem that Samuel Loveman (1887–1976) and Clark Ashton Smith (1893–1961) were destined to become close colleagues and correspondents. All apart from their mutual interests—chiefly in weird and Decadent poetry but also in the broader realms of art, aesthetics, and the life of the mind—they shared a striking number of literary colleagues, from George Sterling to H. P. Lovecraft to George Kirk to Donald Wandrei. It was Sterling—then the chief practitioner of "pure" poetry in the United States and the head of a group of "Bohemian" writers in Carmel, California—who put the two writers in touch in 1913, leading to an association that continued, at times intensely and at times sporadically, for at least the next three decades.

Smith led the more superficially uneventful life. Born on 13 January 1893, in Long Valley, California, he spent most of his life in nearby Auburn and never ventured out of the state. A prodigious autodidact, Smith pored over Webster's Unabridged Dictionary and began writing tales fashioned after the *Arabian Nights* as early as 1907. That same year, he discovered the work of Sterling, who in 1903 had published *The Testimony of the Suns and Other Poems,* and who had just attained notoriety by the publication of the fantasy epic "A Wine of Wizardry" in *Cosmopolitan* (September 1907), accompanied by a laudatory article by Ambrose Bierce, his mentor. The subsequent furor incited by the poem, and by Bierce's flamboyant praise of it, created a brief sensation, chiefly in California. Sterling went on to publish a second volume of poetry, *A Wine of Wizardry and Other Poems,* in 1909.

Smith sought Sterling's advice on poetry matters in early 1911, leading to a correspondence that did not cease until Sterling's suicide in 1926. Sterling acted as liaison between Smith and the San Francisco publisher A. M. Robertson, who issued Smith's *The Star-Treader and Other Poems* in August 1912. The book was an immediate sensation on the West Coast. On 14 May 1913, Sterling casually asked Smith to send a copy of *The Star-Treader* to Loveman—whom he described as "a young poet (22, I think) of whom I expect great things—after his own style."[1]

Loveman was in fact twenty-six at this time. He was born on 14 January 1887 and spent most of the first thirty-seven years of his life in Cleveland. He appears to have joined the National Amateur Press Association as early as 1902, although no publications prior to 1904 have been found. While

---

1. *The Shadow of the Unattained: The Letters of George Sterling and Clark Ashton Smith,* ed. David E. Schultz and S. T. Joshi (New York: Hippocampus Press, 2005), 88.

Loveman did publish some poetry and criticism in the amateur press at this time, he sought a wider market for his work in 1908 when he wrote to Ambrose Bierce, sending him his poem "In Pierrot's Garden" with the hope that Bierce could secure publication for it in a major magazine. Bierce—just as he had done with "A Wine of Wizardry"—sent the poem to a dozen or more magazines, all of which turned it down; but the effort led to a sporadic correspondence that lasted until the fall of 1913, when the aging journalist and satirist ventured from his residence in Washington, D.C., to Texas, and then across the border into Mexico, where he disappeared, never to be heard from again. Bierce had sent "In Pierrot's Garden" to Sterling in the fall of 1909, and Sterling dropped Loveman a line shortly thereafter.

It is understandable that poetry and poets should be the main topic of conversation between Smith and Loveman during the first decade or so of their correspondence, for neither writer had much interest in any other mode of expression at this time; if anything, Loveman's work was the more varied, although his approach to authorship frequently tended toward the casual, if not the careless.[2] Loveman had issued a slim volume of his *Poems* in 1911 and, although he occasionally worked on tales and even an entire novel (*Philip Heather,* never completed), he appears to have been more of an appreciator and critic of literature than a producer of it. And given that he had access to far more abundant literary and bibliographical resources in Cleveland than Smith had in Auburn, it is not surprising that Loveman would often pass along—either as loans or as outright gifts—an array of volumes for Smith's edification and enjoyment. These included obscure poets, on the borderline of the weird and fantastic, such as Thomas Lovell Beddoes and Francis Saltus,[3] as well as more standard nineteenth-century poets such as John Clare and Algernon Charles Swinburne. Loveman had a particular interest in Clare as well as John Keats, writing articles on these figures in little magazines in the 1910s and 1920s. He also encouraged Smith to read prose writers such as Walter Pater, George Meredith, and Joseph Conrad.

Loveman had abandoned the amateur press around 1910 but returned to it in 1917, thanks to his association with H. P. Lovecraft, who had admired Loveman's poetry and hoped he would write more. But the United States' entry into World War I in the spring of 1917 eventually caused a major disruption in Loveman's life, and in the summer of 1918 he was drafted and

---

2. It is well known that, during the 1920s, and especially during H. P. Lovecraft's stay in New York (1924–26), he would compel Loveman to recite his poems from memory to transcribe them, since Loveman himself could not be bothered to generate handwritten or typed copies.
3. Saltus was the half-brother of Edgar Saltus, a popular and critically acclaimed novelist of the later 19th century. In the early 1920s Loveman had written a treatise on Saltus that had been accepted by a publisher, but it never appeared.

compelled to leave for Camp Gordon, Georgia, where he stayed for about a year and attained the rank of sergeant. Smith's poor health at this time presumably exempted him from military service. Indeed, Smith's various maladies—which may have included tuberculosis as well as a bout with depression—hindered his own poetic output, and it was only through Sterling's influence that another volume of his work, *Odes and Sonnets,* appeared in 1918 under the prestigious imprint of the Book Club of California.

In 1920 Smith wrote his own fantasy epic, *The Hashish-Eater,* and sent it to Loveman. We have only a brief response from the other poet, wherein he states that Smith's work is "the greatest poem you have ever written—far greater than the 'Wine of Wiz.'" The poem was published in Smith's third poetry volume, *Ebony and Crystal* (1922)—whose publication by a local printer he was compelled to subsidize. In February 1921 Loveman undertook a long poem of his own, *The Hermaphrodite,* a gorgeous evocation of the spirit of classical Greece. Smith read some portions of it in the fall of 1922 and reacted enthusiastically (it "contains many of the loveliest verses that you have written"); but the work was not completed for years and would not be published until 1926. Meanwhile, Loveman was sending Smith individual sheets of his prose drama, *The Sphinx,* which similarly was completed many years later and published in 1944.

Smith's and Loveman's worlds were coming together through their increasingly frequent association with mutual colleagues. The Cleveland bookseller George Kirk visited Smith in California in 1920; in 1922 he issued Loveman's edition of *Twenty-one Letters of Ambrose Bierce.* In early 1921 Loveman first met the young poet Hart Crane and his circle of aesthetes, eventually becoming one of Crane's closest friends; Smith did not meet or correspond with any of these figures, but heard a great deal about them from Loveman.

But the two authors' relations with H. P. Lovecraft are of intense interest. In December 1919 Loveman sent Smith the manuscript of one of Lovecraft's stories, "Beyond the Wall of Sleep," to read. It was at this very time that Loveman served as the central figure in a weird dream that Lovecraft had, which he soon thereafter wrote up into the story "The Statement of Randolph Carter." But Smith did not get in touch with Lovecraft at this time. That only occurred in 1922. In April of that year, Loveman had made a trip to New York to look for work, and Sonia H. Greene—an amateur journalist living in Brooklyn who was courting Lovecraft and used Loveman's advent to the city as a means to draw the reclusive Lovecraft away from his hometown of Providence, R.I.—arranged for the two men to stay in her apartment while she stayed elsewhere. Loveman does not mention meeting Lovecraft in his extant letters to Smith at this period; but it was soon thereafter that he and George Kirk presented Lovecraft with copies of Smith's poetry volumes, leading to Lovecraft's enthusiastic letter to Smith of 12 August 1922, written during a visit to Loveman in Cleveland. Even so, Smith refers to the New Englander as "your friend Lovecraft" in his letter to Loveman of 2 November 1922.

One of the reasons Lovecraft was so taken with Smith, both as a poet and as a general aesthete, was the fantastic artwork that Smith began producing around 1920 and sent to Loveman. In the course of time Loveman amassed a collection of hundreds of Smith's paintings and drawings, showing them to Lovecraft when the latter visited him in Cleveland in August 1922. And although Lovecraft was corresponding regularly with Smith in the early to mid-1920s, his relations with Loveman would become still closer when he moved to Brooklyn in March 1924 after marrying Sonia Greene. Loveman became part of the "Kalem Club," a group of more than half a dozen devotees of literature who would meet weekly to discuss the burning issues of the day.

It is at this very juncture that the Smith–Loveman correspondence becomes considerably more sporadic and fragmentary. It is unclear whether this is because letters from this period simply do not survive or whether the two writers actually sensed a lessening of their intellectual and emotional bonds. Even though Smith, as early as 1915, had written, "I may write a few short stories myself," he did not begin writing fantastic fiction in earnest until 1929, following a few random attempts in the four preceding years. In the very few extant letters by Loveman during this period, he says nothing of Smith's fictional output. He himself at this time was firmly ensconced in the book trade in New York, working for Dauber & Pine and later establishing his own Bodley Book Shop. In 1936 he published a modest volume of his poetic output of the past three decades, *The Hermaphrodite and Other Poems.*

The last extant letter between the two writers is one from Smith to Loveman dated 25 November 1941—unless the undated postcard that Loveman sent to Smith from Venice is of a later date. Both men lived for decades beyond this time, and the total absence of letters must signal an eventual petering out of their association, even though they still seemed to share many mutual interests.

Nevertheless, what remains of the correspondence provides rich insight into the lives and minds of these two compelling figures. Their thirst for the obscurer corners of American, English, and world literature and art; their taste for the weird, Decadent, and fantastic; their scorn of conventional bourgeois life; their devotion to the intellectual and aesthetic stimulus to be found in books—all these things remain refreshing and serve to portray the distinctive characteristics that make each of them a figure of consuming interest.

—S. T. JOSHI
DAVID E. SCHULTZ

A Note on This Edition

This volume prints all known letters between Clark Ashton Smith and Samuel Loveman, all taken from extant manuscript sources. Letters by Loveman in the first few years of the two writers' association are in very short supply, presumably because Smith failed to preserve them or they were subsequently lost or destroyed. Smith did preserve a number of envelopes containing letters from Loveman; these have been conjecturally placed with extant letters (many of which are undated) or as separate items denoting lost letters. The letters have been thoroughly annotated, and the bibliography includes works by Smith, Loveman, and others that are discussed or alluded to in the letters.

The editors and publisher are grateful to the Bancroft Library, University of California, for permission to publish the letters of Clark Ashton Smith; to CASiana Enterprises, Inc., for permission to publish the letters and other works by Clark Ashton Smith; and to Brown University, John Hay Library, for permission to publish the letters of Samuel Loveman. We are also grateful to Steven Black, Derrick Hussey, and Darin Coelho Spring for their assistance in the preparation of this volume. Special thanks go to Martin Andersson for his proofreading.

—S. T. J., D. E. S.

Abbreviations used in the notes are as follows:

CAS	Clark Ashton Smith
GS	George Sterling
SL	Samuel Loveman
ALS	autograph letter, signed
ANS	autograph note, signed
TLS	typed letter, signed
AJ	*Auburn Journal*
CF	CAS, *The Collected Fantasies* (2006–2010; 5 vols.)
CP	CAS, *Complete Poetry and Translations* (2007–08; 3 vols.)
EC	CAS, *Ebony and Crystal* (1922)
H	SL, *The Hermaphrodite and Other Poems* (1936)
OS	CAS, *Odes and Sonnets* (1918)
S	CAS, *Sandalwood* (1925)
SP	CAS, *Selected Poems* (1971)
ST	CAS, *The Star-Treader and Other Poems* (1912)
SU	GS & CAS, *The Shadow of the Unattained* (2005)
WT	*Weird Tales*

Born under Saturn

[1]   [ALS]

Auburn, Cal.
June 2nd, 1913.

My dear Loveman:

Thanks for your good poems. I like all three, and can scarcely say if any one of them is the best. That's a fine idea of yours, to write poems on these dead and forgotten poets. Section IV of "In Pierrot's Garden," seems especially exquisite to me.

I'm glad you like my book.[1] You certainly pay it some conspicuous compliments. I'm pleased that "Nero" and "To the Sun" are among your favourites. Apropos of your remarks on my anti-Wordsworthian attitude, you may be interested to know that I've been particularly jumped on for that by the critics—both professional and non-professional. One reviewer spoke of the "vicious spirit animating this sonnet" ("Retrospect and Forecast") and called it "a libel on Life, which is given the character of a vampire."[2] I hold that there's more truth than poetry in that particular sonnet. Thank heavens, I've only seen about half-a-dozen reviews!

I had hoped to go to Carmel myself this summer, but it[']s all off, now, till Autumn, at least. You'd love the place. Pray stop off and spend a day with me, if you should come out to visit Sterling,[3] and can manage it. Auburn is on the Overland line of the S. P.,[4] by which you'd doubtless come. There's a few hundred miles of view from my hill-top here. The Sacramento valley looks simply enchanting—at my distance from it!

I am,
Very cordially yours,
Clark Ashton Smith

[Envelope postmarked Auburn, Cal., June 2, 1913.]

Notes

1. *The Star-Treader and Other Poems,* published November 1912.
2. John Jury, "The Star-Treader. A Book of Verse by Clark Ashton Smith—A Review," *San Jose Mercury and Herald* (8 December 1912): magazine section, p. 2. In Connors 46–50.
3. George Sterling (1869–1926), a prolific and leading Californian poet of the period, had been CAS's mentor since 1911. He wrote prefaces to CAS's *Odes and Sonnets* (1918) and *Ebony and Crystal* (1922).
4. The Southern Pacific Railroad, an enormous railroad network that operated in the western U.S. from 1865 to 1998.

[2]　　[ALS]

Auburn, Cal.,
Aug. 1st, 1913.

My dear Samuel Loveman:

I might have answered your letter thus: It's been lying around for a fortnight, I should say, and as I haven't been at all busy during that time, the neglect is a simple case of laziness.

I'd certainly like to see the Swinburne pamphlet,[1] if you can loan or secure me a copy. Swinburne's critics said a lot of unpardonably mean and stupid things, and some aren't through saying them yet. I've just started an Ode to Swinburne, but am not at all sure that it will turn out well. I've also planned one on Poe.[2] I shall put more variety into the structure of these odes than I did in my others, and shall make use of Alexandrines or even longer lines.

You ask if I've written anything lately. I've not been keeping up my usual pace, and what I have written is not likely to increase my popularity. "The Witch in the Graveyard" (my longest and perhaps most successful attempt at the weird and the ghastly),[3] "The Medusa of Despair", which seems easily my most terrific sonnet, and a prose-poem, "The Demon, the Angel, and Beauty," are perhaps the principal titles among my late productions.

New York must have been an experience. I should like to see the place, but I'm sure I'd not want to live there.

Thanks for your good quatrain. I shall love to see your "Triumph of Anarchy,"[4] which you speak of sending me.

Most Cordially Yours,
Clark Ashton Smith.

Notes

1. Possibly James Leatham, *Algernon Charles Swinburne: A Short Anniversary Study* (Cottingham, UK: Cottingham Press, [1913]; 8 pp.).
2. Neither poem was completed.
3. It is 67 lines. *The Hashish-Eater* (written years later) is considerably longer.
4. I.e., "A Triumph of Anarchy" (same as "The Mask of Anarchy" in letter 5).

[3]　　[ALS]

Auburn, Cal.,
Aug. 22nd, 1913

Dear Loveman:

Many thanks for the Swinburne pamphlet, which I've greatly enjoyed. It's full of fine invective and red-hot truth. But is it really worth while to do one's critics the honour of paying them so much attention? I refuse even to read *my* critics any more.

I agree with you that Swinburne is the greatest of the Victorians. Tennyson and Matthew Arnold are both great—much better poets than Browning, it seems to me—but neither is of the first rank. James Thomson, of the "City of Dreadful Night,"[1] is another major poet of the same period, who is too little known.

I think I'd like the poem you enclose better, if you'd add a few stanzas to it. It *is* "sketchy,["] as you say, and I'm not sure that I "get" the last stanza. There's quality in the poem, tho. (I hope you'll not mind my criticism.)

I haven't seen much of Alexander's work,—only a sonnet or two in the San Francisco papers. I liked one of them—a strong sonnet on "Life."[2]

I've seen but one English review of the "Star-Treader"—a rather skimpy mention by Stephen Phillips in the "Poetry Review."[3] And I shouldn't have seen *that* if Phillips hadn't had the gall to send me a copy.

I enclose a sonnet which you may have. It's the only extra copy of anything worth while that I have lying around. I'll try to send you something more next time. I do all my own typewriting, and hate the work like hell.

Very cordially yours,

Clark Ashton Smith

Notes

1. James Thomson (1834–1882), who wrote under the pseudonym Bysshe Vanolis or "B. V.," was a Scottish poet famous primarily for the long poem *The City of Dreadful Night* (1874), which expressed bleak pessimism in a dehumanized, uncaring urban environment.

2. Samuel John Alexander, author of *The Inverted Torch and Other Poems* (San Francisco: A. M. Robertson, 1912). CAS refers to "To Life," p. 157.

3. See "Voices from Overseas," *Poetry Review* 2, No. 4 (April 1913): 139–41. The unsigned review by Phillips (1868–1915), English poet, dramatist, and editor of *Poetry Review*, covered three books, by G. Herbert Gibson, Robert W. Service, and CAS.

[4]   [ALS]

Auburn, Cal.

Nov. 14th, 1913

My dear Loveman:

Please pardon my delay in acknowledging, and thanking you for, the copy of Bridges' poems.[1] I've more worries and distractions than you perhaps think: after reading the book, I quite forgot until to-day that I'd not acknowledged it.

I like Bridges, tho I think his vein a very slender one. Often (to my taste), his work seems almost wilfully commonplace—simple to an extent which strikes me as affected. But some of his things are full of a delicate beauty and melody. I greatly admire and respect him for his disregard of contemporary taste and standards.

There's no news here. I've neither written nor sold anything in months, but am planning more ambitious things than I've yet attempted. I've rather a tendency to overwork, and I think that the rest I'm taking is doing me a lot of good. I shall *have* to get to work before many months—either that, or run amuck, at the rate my vitality seems to be accumulating.

I think, too, of getting out of Auburn as soon as I can—which may not be for a year or two yet. I'll go to Carmel, of course (you couldn't hire me to live in a city) for the natural beauty of the place, and to be near my friend Sterling. I don[']t care much about the rest of the literary colony there— they're mostly third-rate magazinists; but even they are preferable to these indifferent or even hostile Auburnites.

Please write to me when you can. I'll close now, for I've nothing more that seems worth mentioning.

Cordially yours, Clark Ashton Smith

Notes

1. Robert Bridges (1844–1930), Poet Laureate of England from 1914 to 1930. CAS refers to his *Poetical Works*.

[5]   [ALS]

Auburn, Cal.,
Feb. 16th, 1914.

My dear Loveman:

I fear that I've left your last letter unanswered for an almost unforgivable length of time. I must have received it (with the poem) some time in December. And now it's mid-February, with the manzanita shrubs in bloom, and an occasional cyclamen or buttercup beginning to appear in lowly places. Ill-health, and sheer lack of subject-matter out of which to compose a decent epistle, have made me neglect my correspondence, scanty as it is, during these latter months.

I like the fragment of the "Mask of Anarchy," which you enclose, and would certainly urge you to finish the poem. Your jeu-de-esprit, "Adventure," is good of its kind. I'll try to send you something of my own with this letter, if I can find a poem or two that seem worth enclosing. With the exception of two prose poems, and a negligible sonnet, I've written nothing since last Summer. The stagnation and monotony of existence here, together with a dis-ordered digestion, have brought my work to a halt for the time, it would seem.

Sterling, who is going to New York in March, promises to spend a few days with me before he leaves. There's one rift in the clouds, at any rate.

You speak of leaving Cleveland in the Spring. Are you coming this way, by any chance? If you are, I'll expect you to stop off and pay me a visit. You spoke once of coming to California, if I remember rightly.

I've nothing more worth writing, so I'd best stop. Write me soon, if you can pardon my neglect.

Faithfully yours,
Clark Ashton Smith

[6]   [ALS]

Auburn, Cal.,
Apr. 11th, 1914

Dear Samuel:

You should be sufficiently familiar with my negligent and sloth-ful habits of correspondence by this time, to be not greatly surprised (nor, I trust, offended) at my remissness in acknowledging your photograph and last letter. In my present state of mental exhaustion and general inefficiency, I've been deferring my answer from day to day thro sheer dread of the effort in-volved in letter-composition.

My hearty thanks for the photograph! It's very attractive, and, save for the clipped locks, poetic. You've a peculiarly bright and sensitive look, if you don't mind my saying it.

I enclose the only picture of myself of which I happen to possess extra copies. It was taken about the time my book appeared (in 1912). I enclose also an old negative; neither of these is any too characteristic, but they may give you some idea of how I look. I'll send you a better photograph some day.

Sterling was here for a day, about the end of last month. He's somewhere in the Middle West now, on his way to New York, and is, if I remember rightly, to deliver [a] lecture on Californian poetry at Ann Arbor, about the 13th. You'd best address him (at present) in care of the Bohemian Club, San Francisco. His New York address will be the Lambs' Club.

You speak of writing a drama on the old theme of Oedipus.[1] The subject is tremendous enough (none more so!) but, speaking for myself, I'd scarcely care to attempt it, after Sophocles. Why not some less familiar theme from mythology, or better still, an original one of your own? I'm shy of these re-worked plots, myself. Unless one is a Shakespeare, he'd best leave them alone. The chief danger lies in the difficulty of avoiding imitation. I've a dra-matic lyric entitled "Satan Unrepentant," among my unpublished poems, which would be about the best thing I've done, if it weren't for the existence of Paradise Lost! But don't let anything that I've said discourage you, if you really feel impelled to write an "Oedipus,["] and are assured that you've a new view-point from which to treat the theme. That's the essential thing, after all. Do you think of employing the modern bugaboo, Heredity, in place of Fate, in your interpretation? There might be possibilities in *that*. But perhaps you've some other angle of treatment that's as good or better. There are necessarily many aspects to so huge a theme as "Oedipus."

Let me hear from you again before long. I may have something to send you the next time I write. I've several prose-poems in project, and may attempt to do something with them presently. Anything would be better for me than my present idleness and inertia.

As ever, your friend,

Clark Ashton Smith

Notes

1. SL's *Poems* (1911) contains *Oedipus at Colonus,* a short verse drama.

[7]   [ANS][1]

[Postmarked Cleveland, Ohio,
21 September 1914.]
Cleveland, O.
9-21-1914

Dear Clark,

This is to assure you that there will shortly come from me a letter of most mammoth proportions. Forewarned is forearmed. I've been very much under the weather all summer.

Sincerely,

Samuel Loveman

9208 Miles Park Ave., S.E.

Notes

1. *Front:* [Blank.]

[8]   [ALS]

Auburn, Cal.,
Jan. 11th, 1915.

Dear Sam:

Again I'm in your debt for a new poet worth knowing. The volume of Lionel Johnson arrived last week, and I've already run thro it, and picked my favourites. "The Dark Angel" is one of them. I had marked it before your letter came. I like also "The Precept of Silence," "A Stranger," and "Nihilism." I seem to have had a strange misconception as to the character of Johnson's poetry—I had thought him of the same ilk as Dowson and Symons; but the only poets whom he suggests at all, are Landor and Matthew Arnold.[1] His verse has the same cold, marmoreal quality as theirs, tho individual and different in many other respects . . . Mr. Pound's preface is a sort of Chinese puzzle to me—but then, I never read anything of Ezra's with the expectation of being able to understand it.[2] His dark, oracular logographs, and literary abracadabra, would be a source of confusion to the Sphinx. . . . Some of his poetry, as George once wrote to me, "would give a she-baboon the erysipalis."[3] Isn't that a delicious phrase?

I, too, will begin to write poetry again in the course of time—most poets, I imagine, have sterile periods of more or less length. The trouble with me is, that I'm growing too fond of my idleness. And I know all too well that I can't afford to be idle. I wish to the deuce I might be—I've worked a great deal in the past, and have had very little pleasure, outside of my books, and a friendship or two— of the platonic kind. One gets rather desperate under that sort of regimen . . . One can suffer as much from emotional starvation as from any other kind.

The weather is clear to-day, after two weeks of rain, fog, snow, sleet, drizzle, frost, wind and ice. It's still cold, tho, and I'm writing this with my overcoat on. Thursday (the 13th) will be my 23rd birth-day. It's only a week from that of Poe—the 19th. We were both born under Saturn, and the Sign Capricornus. So, too, I believe, was Verlaine.[4]

I may have something to send you in my next—probably a prose-poem, since I'm hardly in the mood for verse.

   Faithfully,

     Clark.

Notes

1. Ernest Dowson (1867–1900), English poet, novelist, and short story writer often associated with the Decadent movement; Arthur Symons (1865–1945), English poet, critic, and magazine editor; Walter Savage Landor (1775–1864), English writer and poet best known for the prose *Imaginary Conversations;* Matthew Arnold (1822–1888), English poet and cultural critic.

2. Lionel Pigot Johnson (1867–1902), *Poetical Works,* preface by Ezra Pound (London: Elkin Mathews 1915).

3. Actually, *erysipelas*, a bacterial infection of the skin's outer layers. See GS to CAS, 16 September 1913 (*SU* 96).

4. "I wonder that thou, being, as thou sayest thou art, born under Saturn, goest about to apply a moral medicine to a mortifying mischief." *Much Ado about Nothing* 1.3. Paul Verlaine was born 30 March, and thus was an Aries.

[9] [ALS]

                Cleveland, Ohio.

                   Feb. 5, 1915.

Dear Clark,

   Somehow, I half-hoped to hear from you in all these months, for lo! I, who have ever been the spirit of restlessness had fallen into a rut from which there seem'd no escaping. I've always been a lonely, submersive sort of a chap, but the experiences of the past year are over and done with, I hope, forever.

How has it been with you, brother? I have scann'd leagues of magazines for your work but not a thing have I ever found, saving two poems that glorified (along with Sterling's) an ancient number of that singularly misnomered affair, "Poetry."[1] Tell me about yourself—about your work—please. Your "Nero" and "Saturn" gave superlative promise for a sometime epic—at least so I hoped.

So far I have seen no reviews of George's new book,[2] but it doesn't matter. For sheer poetry—poetry that emphasises itself by a kind of breathless beauty along with an unshatter'd solitariness, the book stands supreme. There is no man alive who so nearly realizes that quality as does Sterling. Isolated he is, but great.

Clark, here's a jest—a good jest i' faith! Commend me for my insularity. I find in a recent purchase of Ambrose Bierce's works, exactly three years after publication, that the good man has given me a genuine send-off in the essay entitled "Thought and Feeling".[3] I have not thanked him either, and the old gentleman having departed for regions unknown (So. America, he wrote me in a strange note over a year ago) I am forced to forego my expression of gratitude. Who, tell me, is Emma Frances Dawson?[4] A California writer apparently, and he rates her very high in an appreciative essay.[5] Is her book (or books) still to be procured?

I've a novel started[,] "Philip Heather"—so different from the modern garbage. Would you care to read a chapter or two? You will like young Philip, I think. Have you had your visit to Carmel yet? I am going to try and make George forgive me my discreditable silence. Write soon.

    With kind regards

        Your friend

          Samuel Loveman.

9208 Miles Park Ave., S.E.,

Notes

1. "Remembered Light" and "The Sorrow of the Winds" by CAS. Three poems by GS—"At the Grand Cañon," "Kindred," and "A Legend of the Dove"—appeared in the December 1912 issue.
2. George Sterling, *Beyond the Breakers and Other Poems* (1914).
3. Bierce, "Thought and Feeling," *Collected Works* 10.274–77. Bierce's piece—originally published in the *New York American* (11 April 1903): 14 and the *San Francisco Examiner* (18 April 1903): 16—is actually about Robert Loveman.
4. Emma Frances Dawson (1839–1926), author of short stories and poems. Most of her fiction was gathered in *An Itinerant House and Other Stories* (San Francisco: Doxey's, 1897).
5. Bierce, "Emma Frances Dawson," *Collected Works* 10.166–71.

[10]   [ALS]

Auburn, Cal.,
Feb. 12th, 1915.

Dear Samuel:

Ever so many thanks for the book you send me! "Joseph and His Brethren"[1] (tho I've not yet read it to the end) seems to me to contain more genius than many a poem that's far better known, or even accepted as classic. I shall be delighted to seek a closer acquaintance with it when I've more time.

I'm really ashamed that I've waited so long for a letter from you, instead of writing, as my better self prompted me more than once. My only excuse, perhaps, is the sink of depression and semi-sickness in which I've lain for the last year or so. Even letter-writing has seemed an almost impossible effort to me. And as for the work that I'd hoped to do—it's all a heap of scraps and fragments and rough beginnings. I find myself in a mood of utter dissatisfaction with everything that I've written so far, and a state of incapacity to accomplish anything better. I've enough ideas, but lack the strength to hammer them into shape.

I heartily agree with you as to George's new book. He's inconceivably greater—especially in pureness of style and distinction of mood—than any other English-writing poet of the present with whose work I happen to be familiar. I wish I could hope that sometime, somehow, I might write a poem half as good as any one of the dozen best things that George has done. Beside them, my own poems are mazes of mixed metaphors, and thorn-thickets of consonantal words.

I confess that I've never even heard of Emma Frances Dawson. However, her work must be worth knowing, if Bierce has written an essay upon it.

Please send me the chapter (or chapters) of your novel, if you will. I feel sure that anything you write **will** be different from the "modern garbage", the reading of which I've entirely forsworn, these latter years.

I enclose a few sonnets, and other trifles. I've some longer things, together with a few prose poems, but not extra copies.

As ever, your friend,
Clark Ashton Smith

Notes

1. Charles Wells (1800–1879), English poet, author of *Joseph and His Brethren: A Scriptural Drama in Two Acts* (1824). The edition in question may be the reprint of 1908, with an essay by Swinburne and a reminiscence by Theodore Watts-Dunton.

[11]   [ALS]

Auburn, Cal.,

Feb. 28th, 1915.

Dear Samuel:

Thanks for your kind letter, and the chapters of your novel, and your munificent praise of my trifling poems! I like your "Philip Heather"; there's a charming atmosphere about the story, and not the least taint of the ultra-modern manner that I can detect. I'd love to see more of it, if I'm not putting you to excessive trouble ... I think you've a fine gift of character-delineation, and description: all the personages you have introduced are vivid, vital, and individual. One doesn't forget them.

I may write a few short stories myself; I've ideas for at least two; but I dare say they won't sell—one of the conceptions is exotic, and both are rather ghastly. I've eight or nine prose-poems on hand, most of them howling for revision; and shall probably write several more presently. They're utterly un-salable, like nearly all my work—the magazines seem to want nothing but lyr-ics of sentiment or "social uplift", and in these, as you know, I do not deal. I've about given up submitting anything to editors—the sample letters of re-jection which I enclose will give you some idea why. It's obvious that the edi-tors who see anything in my poems at all, are afraid to publish them—a certain testimonial to the originality of the work, at any rate. How easy it is for one to run counter with taboo-marks and fetiches of one kind or another! D—n all such! I'm in a mood to smash everything of the kind in sight, like Shelley and Swinburne and Baudelaire, and would if I had the strength. Noth-ing should be sacred but truth, and no one can possibly desecrate *that*.

I enclose a few things, including two prose-poems, "The Shadows", and a "Psalm to the Desert" in the Bible manner. The "Psalm to the Desert" was written since my last letter to you. It's pretty rough and scabrous, and I rather think some of the verses are too metrical, toward the end. However, you may find ideas in it.

Apropos of your projected act of "Lear", you may be interested to know that I once wrote an appendix to "Paradise Lost"![1] It may amuse you, so I'm sending a copy of it—also the letter with which the "Atlantic Monthly" rejected it. Read it in connection with "The Abyss Triumphant." As you'll doubtless have observed by this time, I've rather a penchant for ripping up the universe.

Here are a few titles from my notebook,[2] each of them representing an idea, or at least the hint of an idea, for a poem: "The Night-Fires,['] "The Veils of the Void," "The Immanence of Time,['] "The Blindness of Orion,['] "Chant of the Titans," "The Mummy,['] "The Avatars of Light," "The Voice of the Mote,['] "Psalm to the North," and "The Dragon-Worms." How I wish they were all written—the mere effort seems to tear me to pieces of late, and my last attempt at concentration gave me a horrible headache. However, one must be patient, I suppose. I may possibly get out a new book by 1917, if my publisher is willing. I've yet to write a title-poem, too, and I'd like to write some odes in honor of Poe and Swinburne to include in it. I shall include all my prose-poems in a separate section—they'll make a goodly part of the book.[3]

I've none of the three poets whom you mention,—Darley, Beddoes, and Blake.[4] My library contains little but the so-called "classics," which are easily obtained, and in cheap editions—a desideratum with me. I've read some of the poems of Blake and Beddoes, tho, and like both. The "Dream-Peddlery"[5] of the latter is a rare and beautiful poem.

Phraxanor is delightful—only a money-minded Jew could have been so churlish and ungentlemanly as to resist her, it seems to me. And, as you say, it is certainly surprising that a pre-Swinburnian poet should have conceived such a type.[6]

By the way, are you familiar with the work of John Davidson?[7] Such poems of his as I have seen are striking and admirable.

Write to me when you can, and believe me,

Sincerely, your friend,
Clark Ashton Smith

P.S. I enclose a few "snaps" of myself and my parents. They're not very good, but may give you some idea of my appearance. I'm close to 5 feet 10 in height, and weigh 125 pounds, more or less. I'll send you a good photograph of me some day—those that I have on hand are not half ugly enough.

Notes

1. "Satan Unrepentant."

2. Published as *The Black Book of Clark Ashton Smith*.

3. *EC* did not appear for another seven years and was not published by A. M. Robertson (1855–1934), San Francisco bookseller who published most of GS's poetry and also issued *ST*.

4. George Darley (1795-1846), Thomas Lovell Beddoes (1803–1849), and William Blake (1757–1827), all English Romantic poets.

5. Actually "Dream-Pedlary."

6. CAS probably refers to the character Phraxanor in Charles Wells's play *Joseph and Potiphar's Wife*.

7. John Davidson (1857–1909), Scottish poet, playwright, and novelist, best known for his ballads.

[12] [ALS]

Cleveland, Ohio.
March 5, 1915.

Dear Clark,

Merely a word to accompany the Jno. Davidson. Don't be offend-

ed—books go a begging in a place like Cleveland. Why, I have actually pur-
chas'd a Campion, a Crashaw and a Richd Lovelace[1] at the local dep't store for
only ten cents! Think of it—Campion, Crashaw, Lovelace! As for Davidson,
there's no doubt about his eminence, particularly in certain ballads. I'll write you
at length in a few days. I want to give you my candid opinion of the "Atlantic"—needless to tell you, it is not complimentary. It would be shriekingly funny—if it weren't quite so pathetic—their refusal of "Satan Unrepentant." But
more anon. I want to send you the remainder of the medieval tale in my next.

Your friend,
Samuel Loveman

9208 Miles Park Ave., S.E.

P.S. Had a card from George. He promises to write.

Notes

1. English poets Thomas Campion (1567–1620), Richard Crashaw (1612?–1649), and
Richard Lovelace (1617–1657). It is not clear which editions SL purchased at this
time. They may be these: Richard Lovelace, *Songs and Sonnets* (New York: R. H. Rus-
sell, 1901); *The Religious Poems of Richard Crashaw*, introduction by R. A. Eric Shepherd
(St. Louis: Herder, 1914); *Complete English Works of Thomas Campion*, ed. A. H. Bullen
(London: Sidgwick & Jackson, 1909 [orig. 1889]).

[13]   [ALS]

Auburn, Cal.,
March 19th, 1915

Dear Samuel:

   Ever so many thanks for the John Davidson volume, which I
have been wanting for a long time. As for Davidson's work, he seems to me
quite equal to any other of the latter Victorians—more even, on the whole,
than Francis Thompson,[1] tho doubtless not so pure a poet. The "Ballad of
Hell" is unquestionably great, tho personally I prefer certain of the others,—
"The Ballad of a Nun," and the one about Tannhauser—I forget its exact title.[2]

   I like your mediaeval story,[3] tho, frankly I doubt if you'll be able to sell it
to the magazines—which I mean for anything but dispraise. The tale is too
peculiar, both in style and conception, for the average reader, tho it's very
much to *my* taste, and seems to me unusually well-done.

   I return your letters of rejection, since I suppose you'll want to keep
them. Your "Pierrot," of which you sent me a copy once, is a beautiful
thing—much too beautiful and poetic for any magazine, especially the
"down-east" ones. As George once wrote to me on a similar occasion, "What
can you expect from a pig but a grunt?"[4]

   By the way, apropos of Bierce, have you heard the rumor to the effect that he has recently turned up in England, and is drilling a regiment for service in the war? I'm inclined to believe that it's true, even tho it's only a newspaper report. It sounds so much like the old gentleman—the very thing that one would expect him to do.

It's not impossible that I may use "Satan Unrepentant" as the title-poem of my next book—tho I'd like to have something better, and may have, by 1917. I'm glad you like the thing—most of my friends seem rather shy of it, and can't get over the idea that the poem is a Miltonic imitation—which shows you how much originality of discernment most people have.

I'm enclosing another of my evocations of shadow, since you liked the one I sent so well. I've half-a dozen more—"The Demon, the Angel, and Beauty," "The Crystals," "The Black Lake", "The Sun and the Sepulchre", and others, all of them highly fantastic, if nothing else. You'll note that these conceptions I'm working out in prose are of a character that would be peculiarly difficult to do in verse. I've some ideas that would be better than hasheesh-visions if properly worked out—but I dare say any ass can get ideas. The difficulty lies in putting them into anything like effective permanent form. By the way, do you find any musical quality at all in the thing I'm sending? I'd like to make my prose fairly pleasing to the ear, tho I can't be at all sure that I succeed. Ears differ greatly as to such matters, I think. My own is perhaps even super-sensitive, since it's so difficult for me to write anything that doesn't irk my ear for some reason or other. I resent the prevalence of the mutes and other harsh consonants in the words of the language. You'll note that I make considerable use of alliteration,—another thing that would doubtless help to condemn my work with the Boston magazines.

I enclose a rather good and characteristic picture of myself, clipped from an old newspaper. It may be a bit juvenile for me now—but not very much so, since I generally pass for being much younger than I am. My hair and eyes are dark-brown, and I dare say I show the old Celtic strain that I inherit from my father.[5] I've a touch of French blood, too, which may account for some of the tendencies of my work.

Write me soon, please, and believe me,
      Sincerely your friend,
            Clark Ashton Smith

Notes

1. Francis Thompson (1859–1907), English poet and mystic, best known for "The Hound of Heaven."

2. "A Ballad of Hell," "A Ballad of a Nun," and "A Ballad of Tannhäuser" are all found in Davidson's *Selected Poems* (1904).

3. Perhaps "A Hopeless Love," set in medieval France.

4. GS to CAS, 15 October 1912 (*SU* 68).

5. Timeus Smith (1855–1937).

[14]   [ALS]

Auburn, Cal.,

April 2nd, 1915.

Dear Samuel:

Your letter and the volume of Beddoes arrived in the same mail yesterday, and I must thank you for the book without delay. I've already run thro "Death's Jest-Book", and find it very much to my taste. It has all the best qualities of Webster,[1] with a quite unique and altogether unnameable quality which I've not met with elsewhere. Some of the songs, like the one about the crow, (as Victor Hugo said of the poems of Baudelaire) "create a new shudder."[2] There's no doubt of the author's greatness and genius, but I can readily understand that it's not a genius which would find popular favour. How many of the really poetic poets are "popular", anyway, in spite of their wide-spread reputation? And what's a reputation? One can't live in the opinions of others—opinions which are probably wrong, and certain to be capricious or more or less prejudiced.

Thanks for the revision of the story! The tale is very charming, delicate, and beautifully written—"the prose of a poet." I hope you'll write more of such things, when you feel in the mood for prose-composition.

I've done little enough myself, of late, except fill my note-books with titles, ideas, lines, and fragments. Some of my conceptions, if properly worked out, are warranted to make a pompadour of any natural locks possessed by the maiden-editors of Boston. "A Dialogue of the Dead", "Eclogue of the Five Devils", and "The Living Forest," are some of my possible titles. The last is to be a description of a forest of half-animal and carnivorous vegetation, all writhing and turning and ravishing about in the ghastly exuberant light of a vast green sun.

I enclose some more of my prose things, together with a brief dramatic fantasy entitled "The Witch in the Graveyard", which I've probably not sent you before. You'll like it, I think, tho some of the lines are pretty rough and scabrous. Fancy what the "Atlantic" would say to such a title! ... "The Demon, the Angel, and Beauty" was rejected by them as being "too esoteric". But I don't think *you* will find it so very obscure. For the life of me, I can't see why it should be, unless it's thro the sheer unusualness of the idea.

I may have something new to send you in my next. I've one new prose-poem begun, and may accumulate sufficient resolution to go on with it presently. The title is "The Mortuary"—a description of the light-effects in a graveyard, together with a vision of the chemistry of corruption (don't shudder, please!) There may be a good deal of weird beauty in the thing, if it works out as I desire.

The poems you quote are good work, especially the beautiful Wade sonnet,[3] which I had never read before. I've seen a little of Chivers,[4] tho not the verses which you give. The man seems to have been a sort of Poe run mad.

By the way, have you ever seen anything of the work of a poet named E. H. Visiak?[5] There are some lines of his, which I think would be difficult to surpass for concentrated horror:

"The Skeleton at the Feast

Dance in the wind, poor skeleton,
You that was my deary one,
You they hanged for stealing sheep,
Dance and dangle, laugh and leap:
To-morrow night, at requiem's bell,
I am to serve a sheep in hell,—
My lady's wedding. Lord love her,
Wait until they lift the cover!"

I'm glad to hear that your health is better. My own seems to fluctuate,—I feel quite well one day, and as nervous as a cat the next.

Write to me, and believe me,
　　Faithfully your friend,
　　　　Clark Ashton Smith.

P.S. Of course, I'd be very glad to have copies of the letters of which you speak, if I'm not giving you excessive trouble. . . . Like all good work, Wells' poem improves upon re-reading.

Notes

1. John Webster (1580?–1634?), English Jacobean dramatist best known for *The White Devil* and *The Duchess of Malfi*.
2. Victor Hugo wrote in a letter to Baudelaire dated 6 October 1859, "Vous créez un frisson nouveau" [You are creating a new shudder]. CAS refers to "The Carrion Crow."
3. Probably Thomas Wade (1805–1875), English poet and dramatist. The sonnet is unidentified.
4. Thomas Holley Chivers (1809–1858), American physician from Georgia turned poet. Best known for his friendship with Edgar Allan Poe and his controversial defense of the poet after his death.
5. E. H. Visiak (1878–1972), English writer, known chiefly as a critic and authority on John Milton; also a poet and fantasy writer. The poem quoted is from *The Phantom Ship and Other Poems* 30.

[15]   [ALS]

Auburn, Cal.,

Apr. 22nd, 1915.

Dear Samuel:

I'm answering your letter immediately, to thank you in advance for the books of which you speak, and for the fine lyric and the prose-essay. "Shadow-Love" is very much to my taste, and contains a quality which I don't remember to have met before in American poetry. There's a touch of Heine about it, I should think, as far as I can judge from the translations of his work. "Memoralia" is very good, only I wish it were longer. It rather tantalizes me as it stands—which isn't a bad effect in itself.

I'm so sorry to hear of your continued ill-health. I've had rather a relapse myself, after a few weeks of tolerable health, and everything is at a standstill. It's not altogether a matter of nerves, but rather, I fear, one of constitutional debility, complicated by a capricious stomach. "Nervelessness" would better describe my condition at times.

Thanks so much for what you say about the "Witch" poem. I fancy that d——d few are likely to see the qualities in it of which you speak. I've yet to see an intelligent review of my work, and have sworn never to read any of the criticisms of my next book (I saw only about ten of "The Star-Treader", as I don't subscribe to a clipping-bureau) As to fame or "immortality", I "hae my doots." A book of poems, no matter how good, is more likely to go out of print, in these days. If I had a competence, I'd print my work privately, and never dream of offering it to the general public, who don't want my kind of poetry, anyway. Literature and criticism are pretty much demoralized in America, and seem to be getting worse. I prophesy the growing domination of Whitman, especially in poetry, or rather, what passes for poetry at the present day. Democracy and utilitarianism seem to be demanded of poetry, and the "grand manner" grows more and more offensive to the proletariat. I wash my hands of it all—the whole sticky mess of sociology and sentimentalism—

"Oceans of sugar and slush
Seas of molasses and mush",

to quote some of my own doggerels.[1]

Apropos of Baudelaire, I enclose an article by James Huneker, from an old Scribners.[2] It may interest you. I'm sorry, but I've nothing of Baudelaire's in my possession. I read a number of his things in the excellent translation by E. P. Sturm while I was in Carmel several years ago. Sterling has the book. I've forgotten the publisher, and remember only the translator's name. Here are a few lines and stanzas from memory, to give you a taste of the quality:

"The might-have-been, with tooth accurst,
Gnaws at the piteous souls of men:

The deep foundations suffer first,
And all the structure crumbles then,
Beneath the bitter tooth accurst."

"Graveyard odors in the shadow swim,
And my faint footsteps, on the markers' rim,
Bruise the cold snail and crawling toad unseen."

"Goya, a nightmare full of things unknown:
The foetus witches broil on Sabbath night;
Old women at the mirror; children lone
Who tempt old demons with their limb's delight."[3]

And this, on the Flagellants,

"Who mix, in sombre woods, on moonlit nights,
The foam of pleasure with the tears of pain."[4]

These are a fair sample, to use the current phrase. The prose-poems, of which there were a number in the book, probably lost less in translation, and pleased me better for that reason. They are much less ghastly and macabre than the verse, some of which is rather too "rank", even for my taste, tho I greatly admire the courage of a poet who could write such things. Swinburne at his most devilish is mild and pale compared to the passion and intensity of some of Baudelaire's work. I wish I could read it in the original—I've been too indolent to learn any language but my own.

There are a few things that I've written lately—very ill-done, I fear. The lines entitled "The City in the Desert" were remembered out of a dream. They're a bit disordered, but seem to present a sort of picture. The "Orion" is pretty tame, and needs a new ending in place of the rather feeble and perfunctory one which is the best I can do for it at present. You're entitled to copies of everything I write, if you care to claim them. But I'd rather you didn't. I've a large percentage of failures, and don't publish half the work I write.

"The Witch in the Graveyard", of which you ask, was draughted in 1913 and considerably revised and retouched at a more recent date.

Thanks for the interesting Wells letter! Wells must have been a "character," even among poets. The insouciance of his letter-style is remarkable.

Better health and cheer!
Faithfully, your friend,
Clark.

P.S. Please return the Huneker article. It's the only copy I have, and happens to be of considerable interest to me.

Notes

1. Nonextant.

2. James Gibbons Huneker, "The Baudelaire Legend," *Scribner's Magazine* 45, No. 2 (February 1909): 240–49.

3. CAS quotes "The Irreparable" (ll. 36–40, pp. 17–18), "Sunset" (ll. 12–14, p. 57), and "The Beacons" (ll. 25–28, p. 5).

4. "The Accursed" (ll. 19–20, p. 63).

[16]   [ALS]

Cleveland, Ohio.

May 7, 1915.

Mein Lieber Clark,

I hope the enclosed doesn't dismay you. You mentioned Heine in a recent letter and it revived my ambition to translate him—of which you here see the accumulated result.[1] I've been doing one or two a day as the mood takes me. A word in confidence—Heine (of course you know) is literally untranslatable. There is almost as much of my own as there is of Heine's in these. And yet I'm inclined to think that I've retained something even more than the mere spirit. I'm daily expecting a letter—a long 'un—from you.

Your friend,

Sam.

9208 Miles Park Ave., S.E.

Notes

1. Heinrich Heine (1797–1856), German poet, journalist, essayist, and literary critic, best known outside Germany for his early lyric poetry. SL published "Twenty Four Translations from Heine" in *Saturnian* 1, No. 2 (August–September [1920]): 2–13.

[17]   [ALS]

Auburn, Cal.,

May 10th, 1915.

Dear Sam:

This is just a note, to acknowledge your letter, and the stanzas of your "Ode to Apollo." I like the poem, and certainly hope that you'll finish it. *I* don't find it so very suggestive of Keats, except in the stanza-form!

I'm sorry, but the books you ordered have not arrived yet. It's quite possible that they've been lost in the mails. The local post-office people are exceedingly careless, and it will not be the first time that my mail has gone astray.

I, too have been planning a deal of work, but seem to accomplish little. I enclose "The Flight of Azrael", a hasty scribble which is probably not worth preserving, and is rather "too much of a sameness", with many other things that I've written, anyway. A good theme for a painting, tho, don't you think?

I may send you some more work presently. I feel in the mood for writing, and have projected innumerable poems, including several odes. I think I shall give up writing in prose, at least for the present. My prose poems are rather too metrical, I notice. Even third-rate verse, such as mine, is immeasurably superior to bad or indifferent prose.

What you say about Horne's "Orion"[1] interests me, especially as I've never read the poem. However, I don't find myself caring much for my own poem on the same subject. The classical is hardly my forte, anyway. My best vein is probably that of philosophic fantasy, which, to avoid didacticism, I shall in the future work out largely in dramatic form, with a personae of witches, demons, vampires, ghouls, archangels etc, etc. I plan a number of dialogues under such titles as "The Ghoul and the Seraph", "The Lich and the Demon," and "The Confabulation of Gabriel and the Three Vampires."[2] The last is a jewel of a title, but I've no idea for it, yet. I often get my titles first, and write the poems to fit them.

Well, no more of this obtrusive egoism for to-day. I'll probably write you again before long.

> Yours, as ever,
>> Clark.

P.S. I also enclose the fragment of an "Ode to Beauty," written a year or so ago. I've no present prospect of ever finishing it.

Notes

1. Richard Hengist Horne (1802–1884), English poet and critic most famous for his epic poem *Orion* (1843).
2. CAS seems to have written only the first of these.

[18]   [ALS]

> Auburn, California,
>> May 16th, 1915.

Dear Sam:

Your Heine translations are all excellent—indeed, some of them strike me as being better poetry than any others I have seen—the one beginning, "Out of my infinite woe",[1] for instance. I appreciate the difficulty of writing a literal translation of such work—only a paraphrase is possible.

My own work is at a standstill again—a matter of liver, I suppose. My brain feels as if it had been pickled, and I've a sense of accumulated fatigue, both mental and physical. How good it would be to go to sleep some night, and not wake up again for a few aeons! Blessed is the idea of oblivion,—immortality would be worse than a nightmare. Think of that profound legend of the Wandering Jew![2] Also think of some of those True Believers thrust into the heavens of their own imagining! Death will be kinder to them than they conceive.

I presume that George is back in California by this time, tho I've heard nothing from him as yet. He said something about visiting me, on his way to the Yosemite. We never seem to see much of one another . . . Can't we prevail upon *you* to come out this way, sometime? I can't sell anything at all to the magazines—damn the whole piffling lot of them! (the verb to piffle is rather good, don't you think?) However, what can I expect? There's no demand for anything but erotic sentiment, and sociological muck. No one can be popular who refuses to flatter the lusts and vanities of the human species. They want Bergsonian[3] soothing-syrup, rather than truth.

This European war confirms me in my opinion of the modern (so called) civilization. What a tiresome farce it all is! I verily believe that the Japanese are the coming people. And why shouldn't they be? What has this noisy, machine-made civilization done to deserve perpetuity? And why have these bloody, aggrandizing Occidentals any superior right to overrun the planet?

It's raining to-day—a most unusual thing in California at this time of year—I'm told that the cherry-crop will be ruined, thro the cracking of the fruit. I dislike wet weather, and can write at my best only in the warm, clear months,—usually from May to October. Even the mild Californian winter seems to freeze me up.

Some of the subjects you mention for your new poems, strike me as being especially promising—an elegy on Nora May French,[4] for example. I wish I could write commemorative verse—I've thought of Poe and Swinburne as themes—but I fear it's too much out of my usual line.

What do you think of Ahasuerus as a theme for a dramatic monologue? I seem to see possibilities in the old legend. Imagine the accumulated weariness—the disgust for life and humanity, of one compelled to live thro the whole of the Christian era! The theme is really Titanic, and, as far as I know, has not been used in poetry. Ahasuerus is the very antitype of Faust, as someone (I forget whom) has pointed out.

I'll try to enclose a trifle or two of mine with this. The poems that I *want* to write seem to remain unwritten.

> Ever your friend,
> Clark.

Notes

1. No. 8 of SL's "Twenty-four Translations from Heine."
2. A mythical immortal Jew (Ahasuerus), whose legend grew in Europe in the 13th century, had taunted Jesus on the way to his crucifixion and was cursed to walk the earth until the Second Coming. See letter 199.

3. Referring to Henri-Louis Bergson (1859–1941), a major French philosopher who was influential in the first half of the 20th century.

4. Nora May French (1881–1907), poet who committed suicide at GS's home in 1907 at the age of 26. GS, Jack London, Harry Lafler, and Porter Garnett published her *Poems* (1910).

[19]   [ANS postcard][1]

[Postmarked East Auburn, Cal.,
18 May 1915.]
Auburn, Cal.,
May 18th, 1915.

Dear Sam:

I've just received the volumes of Darley and Coleridge,[2] which, I find, have been waiting for me at the local express-office since May 1st! Through some inadvertence, their notification-card failed to reach me.

Ever yours,
Clark.

Notes

1. *Front:* Mt. Tallac, Lake Tahoe, California.

2. Hartley Coleridge (1796–1849), English poet, biographer, essayist, and teacher; eldest son of the poet Samuel Taylor Coleridge. The volume may be *The Complete Poetical Works of Hartley Coleridge* (London: George Routledge; New York: E. P. Dutton, 1908).

[20]   [ALS]

Auburn, Cal.,
May 21st, 1915.

Dear Sam:

The post-office was at fault about the books. They were evidently mailed on time, since the local express-office received them about the first of the month. The express-agent sent me two successive cards informing me of this, (I live beyond the delivery-limits) neither of which was allowed to reach me, through some slight irregularity of the address, and the inconceivable stupidity of the postal officials. I'm sorry there's been so much trouble about the matter, since no one is to blame but the wooden-witted postal-clerks ... Auburn is a ghastly sort of place—a town of the perambulating dead. The Wells Fargo people once "held up" a telegram addressed to me, for two days, before they decided to risk sending a messenger. They didn't know where I lived, and were too lazy to make any immediate effort toward locating me! Incidentally, the telegram was quite valueless by the time I received it.

I like Darley and Coleridge, tho not so well as Beddoes. "Nepenthe" is a most amazing sort of poem. I fail to get much of it as a whole, but find a few lines and passages which please me greatly. Half a page of it, beginning at the lines

"Air
Hung like a hell-blue vapor there"[1]

is really tremendous. "Sylvia" is very charming, and more readable than many better known dramatic poems. Hartley Coleridge has a number of exquisitely beautiful sonnets. He is unquestionably a genius, and a most peculiar one. I can't quite think of a word to describe the quality which I find in his work. Simple and tender beauty, and the truest pathos—these I find in many of his poems.

Many thanks for the loan of "Orion,["] which I'll return in a few days, with the markings and marginal comments with which (at your request) I've defaced some of its pages. The poem is readable, tho not great, except in a few lines and passages, some of which possess the very highest imaginative value. In spite of much that is vague and ineffective, Horne evidently had a fine visual imagination. I wish he had "boiled" his poem down to a few hundred lines, instead of letting it simmer thro as many thousand. On the whole, I share Poe's prejudice against the long poem . . . By the way, don't you think that the "Wine of Wizardry" contains more real poetry, line for line and phrase for phrase, than almost anything else of equal length in the language? I've always thought so, in the bottom of my heart. There's a lot of "lumber" even in the best of the English poets, but none in "The Wine of Wizardry", which contains nearly all the qualities for which I value poetry most. It has everything but "human", dramatic, or philosophic interest, and these, as I'll maintain even at the cost of my last breath, are not the **purest** poetic qualities. People who think otherwise don't really care much for essential poetry. The demand for the (so-called) "human", or "heart" interest narrows itself down to mere egotism—a demand to be soothed or flattered. However, I've nothing against emotional or dramatic poetry in itself—I merely maintain that these are not the most *essential,* or *quintessential* kind, for the very reason that they are not the most abstract or disinterested. . . . I daresay no one will agree with me.

The verses by John Clare[2] are exquisite. I like especially the sonnet, tho the simplicity of the longer poem is of the truest kind—not the false simplicity so current now among poets of a certain school. It's so very, very easy to affect simplicity, and the dangers of prosiness and baldness are great for most poets—especially the inferior kind. There are many poets of the third rank in America at present, and a few of the second.

I agree with you about Masefield.[3] I'd not mind his subject-matter, tho, if he'd make poetry out of it. But I protest that social muck, squalor, and bad English are not necessarily poetry—when they're served up in the rawest and rottenest of doggerel.

Thanks for what you say about my sonnets. I'm glad to have my own inner judgement ratified. I've been thinking of late that it might be well for me to concentrate more upon sonnets. I've a number of ideas that might well be worked out in that form—indeed, almost any conception should gain rather than lose, by being compressed. With me, at least, the form serves rather as a burning-glass for the rays of thought.

> Ever yours,
> Clark

Notes

1. Darley, "Nepenthe," *Poems of George Darley* 42. CAS echoes this image in "The Colossus of Ylourgne": "a thin haze of hell-blue vapor hung upon the battlements." Darley is also the author of *Sylvia; or, The May Queen* (1827).
2. John Clare (1793–1864), English poet, son of a farm laborer, known for his celebrations of the English countryside. His work underwent major re-evaluation in the late 20th century, and he now is regarded as one of the major 19th-century poets.
3. John Masefield (1878–1967), English poet and writer, Poet Laureate of the United Kingdom from 1930 until his death.

[21] [ANS][1]

> [Postmarked Cleveland, Ohio,
> May 25, 1915.]
> 5-24-1915

Dear Clark—

There will probably come to you two more copies of the two books—but don't worry. Give them to some one who you think might find 'em of interest. I'll write you at length in a day or two. By the gods! I live again in this warm weather. Greeting, Brother!

> Yours
> S L

9208 Miles Park Ave., S.E.

[Note on front by SL:] The only artistic statuary in Cleveland!

Notes

1. *Front:* Public Square, Cleveland, Sixth City.

[22]   [ALS]

Auburn, Cal.,

May 28th, 1915.

Dear Sam:

Your bookseller has sent me two more volumes, of Darley and Coleridge! What am I to do with them? In my uncertainty as to your wishes in the
matter, I am holding them at your disposal. Damn all postal clerks, anyway! See
what a lot of trouble they can cause, thro a little carelessness. The more I think
of it, the madder I get. I'm certain that I lose letters, and hardly know how many
enemies I may have gained thro the negligence of the local post-office.

I'll return "Orion" in a day or two, and take damned good care to register
it. The book is too valuable to send thro the Auburn post-office without *some*
security.

I've had another "off" period. Seven or eight poems begun, and no present prospect of finishing them. I'd give them all for one single sonnet or lyric
of whose fineness and perfection I could feel assured. Confound all this interminable groping and fumbling. But I suppose everyone has to do it.

I enclose a lyric and a prose-poem, neither of which I've probably sent
you. The lyric is in trochaic meter,—an unfortunate form for me, since I never really succeed with anything but the iambic, which is the natural meter for
English, anyway.

I'm expecting a letter from you any day, if *my* previous letters have not
miscarried. I never feel secure with the pampered and indolent parasites who
preside over human destiny in the local post-office.

Yours, as ever,

Clark

P.S. I also enclose an old review of my book, by that Bostonian heavy-weight
and intellectual slugger, William Stanley Braithwaite[1] . . . I'd like to present
him with a bouquet of thistles. Don't bother about returning the thing.

Notes

1. William Stanley Braithwaite (1878–1962), American writer, poet, and literary critic,
literary editor of the *Boston Evening Transcript,* and editor of the annual *Anthology of
Magazine Verse* (1913–29). The review was "Our Modern Poets," *Boston Evening
Transcript* (2 April 1913): 24.

[23]   [ALS]

Auburn, Cal.,

June 1st, 1915.

Dear Sam:

I'm sorry to hear that you feel so gloomy, and much fear that I'm likely to prove a poor source of consolation, since I live in a state of almost chronic disgruntlement myself. I'm so constituted that everything but poetry is dust and ashes to me, and the world of art and impossible imaginations the only world in which I feel at home. However, since the dust-flurry of life is over so soon, and the very worlds but the foam of infinite Lethean seas, there's little use or propriety in what the vulgar call "belly-aching." If you could assure me that this particular planet would be chucked into the sun tomorrow or the day after, I'd feel rather enlivened than otherwise.

Oblivion *is* the only possible solution or recompense. The mere will-to-live, as Schopenhauer points out, can never satisfy itself, and therefore cannot lead to happiness. The Buddhists knew this thousands of years ago, which, to my mind, proves the intellectual superiority of the Orientals to the crude and egoistic optimists who are at present overrunning the western hemisphere. What does all this infernal machinery, these cities like nightmares in iron and stone, amount to, anyway? All such things are made of dust, and will crumble back to dust in one swing of the stellar pendulum. In a few aeons, human life and its works will be but a grime in the granite wrinkles of the earth. However, no more of this Jeremiad.

I enclose a rather fantastic sonnet, for which I've no title as yet. I shall probably specialize on sonnets for a time, since most of my conceptions appear suitable for working into that form. Somehow, a good sonnet is always more effective and memorable than a brief lyric. It's the firm symmetry of the structure that gives this effect, I suppose. However, I do think that the Petrarchan octave is a bit too difficult and artificial for the language. As in the enclosed sonnet, I think it best to use two sets of rhymes for the octave, and divide the whole poem into four stanzas, the last two interrhyming. George, however, has great success with the strict octave. His rhymes never seem forced nor do they hamper the expression of the thought, as in so many sonnets that I've read.

I like the one you send me, since the thought is so much in accord with my own. I wish you'd try the form again.

As ever, your friend,

Clark.

P.S. By "water-weeds of Lethe"[1] I mean the water-hemlock, from which the Greeks got their poison. It's a pale-green, pernicious-looking sort of plant, and grows in this neighborhood, along with two or three kinds of nightshade, one of which has violet-coloured, rose-scented flowers, and livid berries—a weird and sinister object.

Notes

1. In "Duality" the line reads "lolling weeds of Lethe."

[24]   [ALS]

Auburn, Cal.,

June 3rd, 1915.

Dear Sam:

Here are a few old sonnets that I've raked up. They're not among my best, and need revision, but may interest you. I also enclose a slightly altered copy of the one I sent you the other day. It still displeases me in many ways, and will have to be done over, I'm afraid; but I'm sick of it for the present, after tinkering at it for several days. I've no facility for composition, and hesitate interminably over phrases and images. My ear seems to be turning on me, and I find it increasingly difficult to please myself in matters of sound-sequence and rhythm. Everything sounds wrong to me—a most distressing affliction, which, I suppose, is part of my general disease of doubt and vacillation.

Speaking of sonnets, have you ever read any of those of Heredia, who is the great French sonnet-writer? Here's a translation of one that I've read somewhere—I forget by whom.[1] The title has also escaped me:

"The temple falls to ruin on the cape,
And utter sleep has mingled with the mould.
    The marble gods and paladins of old—
Locked in the prison whence is no escape—
Sometimes the lowly herdsman drives his kine
To the clear lake, and wakes the ancient pain
    With the sad piping of an old refrain—
Clear-cut against the far horizon-line.

The kindly Earth guards well its old regime,
And each spring, vainly eloquent, doth dow'r
    The fallen pillar with a new-born flow'r;
But man, unheedful of his father's dream,
Fears not to hear each night, unchangingly,
    The vast, eternal sorrow of the sea."

Write to me soon, please, and pardon this "hasty scribble".
    Ever your friend,
        Clark.

Notes

1. John S. Reed, "Forgotten," *Harvard Monthly* 48, No. 3 (May 1909): 106 (under "Three Sonnets of Heredia"); *American Magazine* 73, No. 2 (December 1911): 200. In *Tamburlaine and Other Verses* ([Riverside, CT]: Hillacre, 1917), 37. Smith later translated several poems by the French poet José-Maria de Heredia (1842–1905).

[25]   [nonextant]

[Envelope postmarked Cleveland, Ohio, June 7, 1915.]

[26]   [ALS]

Auburn, Cal.,

June 13th, 1915.

Dear Sam:

First of all, I must thank you for Gosse's book, from which I've gotten a deal of entertainment. The article on Swinburne is especially interesting.[1] I agree with you that he (the author) had no right to present Horne in such a ridiculous aspect. That sort of thing makes my gorge rise.

I like the portion of your ode, and certainly hope that you'll finish it. I await with delight and curiosity the copy of your book which you promise me. Why *don't* you publish another volume of your work? I like the pamphlet idea.

As to the publication of my prose poems, I think of including them for a separate section in my next volume of verse—that is to say, if Robertson is willing. The idea is sufficiently unusual to recommend itself to me, and might even prove a good advertisement. I may call the volume, "Poems in Verse and Prose."[2]

You ask me what I have of Swinburne's. I've two volumes of selections, containing the first and second series of "Poems and Ballads," and all the earlier plays, "Atalanta", etc. However, I've read nearly all of Swinburne's verse—the local public library has his poems complete, for a wonder. I've seen very little of his prose.

Here's another sonnet,[3] a companion for the unnamed one that I sent you. I wonder if such poetic deviltry really offends people, in spite of their loud and disgusting pretence of being shocked. It seems to me that many must find it more entertaining than the ordinary banalities. . . . Apropos of some of the things in the sonnet,[4] did you know that mandragora was at one time in great repute as an aphrodisiac? I don't remember to have seen any poetic reference to the fact. Few will get the full force of the lines in which I've made use of this.

By the way, don't you think it's about time for a revival of Romanticism? It would be a good thing for American poetry, which has always been full of dry-rot. Singular to note how little Poe has affected the poets of his native land. Outside of Sterling, Bierce, and myself, none of them seem to have even read him . . . The New England poets are all so painfully respectable—even those of the present day. One of them, whom I met, seemed to think that Poe was "unhealthy"—a futile and meaningless adjective which seems to be the sole defense of the Philistine against anything original.

Oh! that James Whitcomb Riley! Bierce said of him that his work affected his sensibilities "like the ripple of a rill of buttermilk falling into a pig-trough."[5] What more can one say, after that? All else is unnecessary, and a sinful waste of ink or breath. However, his work is good enough for this welter of mediocrity and vulgarity which stump-orators call the "American people". Most of them neither deserve nor appreciate anything better than literary hog-wash.

What you say about Dermody is very interesting. Your poem on him is a fine thing—one of the best of yours that I've seen.[6]

I've ideas for a number of sonnets, and may try to work some of them out before long. Also, I may write some more prose-poems. I wonder what George is doing with his odes—I've not heard from him since his return. The subject is tremendous—so tremendous that I can't think of anyone else who could do much with it.

As ever, your friend,
Clark.

Notes

1. Edmund Gosse (1849–1928), a leading English critic and editor. The volume in question is probably *Portraits and Sketches* (London: Heinemann, 1912), which has a chapter on Swinburne and also one on Richard Hengist Horne.
2. CAS's next volume was *OS*. The book that followed, *EC*, was subtitled *Poems in Verse and Prose*.
3. Possibly "Love Malevolent."
4. Referring again to "Duality" (l. 2).
5. "The Passing Show," *New York American* (27 December 1903): 32; *San Francisco Examiner* (10 January 1904): 44 (abridged).
6. Thomas Dermody, Irish poet and child prodigy. See SL's "Thomas Dermody 1775–1802."

[27] [ALS]

Auburn, Cal.,
June 19th, 1915

Dear Sam:

Your letter has just come, and I'm answering it immediately, since I've a deal of idle time. Your generosity in sending me so many books, makes me feel rather guilty, since I'm unable to give you anything adequate in return. However, perhaps the truest gratitude consists in the whole-hearted acceptance of an obligation. The Arabs have a proverb to that effect, I believe . . . I'll be very, very glad to have the volume of Blake.

I've just written to George, who is unable to visit me this summer, it seems. He won't miss so very much, since the country is not inviting at this time of year, on account of the dry grass. We've no rain here, usually, between May and September or October.

I've been in a state of hellish temper for the past week—a fit of exasperation springing from a complication of causes—and find myself too feverish, mentally and physically, to concentrate on my work. I've written a brace of bad sonnets, one of which I may send you. The other is too torrid for publication. I may "turn loose" sometime, and scandalize everyone with a volume of erotic verse. It won't be in the least sentimental, but it *will* be honest, even if I run the risk of suppression in this benighted land of Anthony Comstocks.[1] I've not the slightest hope of ever approaching Swinburne, but I might approach something of the intellectual quality of Baudelaire—almost the only poet who ever had the courage to write the truth about things. However, this is only one of my literary ambitions, and I'll probably not do much with it for a number of years.

Have you ever read the "Cynara" of Ernest Dowson? a lyric full of melody and passion.[2] I'll copy it for you, if you haven't.

I've refused several invitations to visit the Fair in San Francisco.[3] I don't care for crowds and advertising-displays. Aside from that, San Francisco is one of my pet abominations, anyway. There are times when I hate Auburn from the blackest bottom of my heart, but San Francisco is worse, because it's so much larger . . . Why, I wonder, was I born in a world and among a people that I'm forced to dislike and disparage? I fear I'm an anarchist at heart, since the whole social system and its conventions and restrictions seem intolerably tyrannous to me, and its morality a sham and an imposition.

    Yours ever,
     Clark.

P.S. The volume of Blake has arrived, and I've had time to run through it hastily. The better known lyrics are familiar to me, but not the longer poems, like the amazing "Marriage of Heaven and Hell", which is full of the most startling conceptions. On the whole, tho, it seems to me that Blake obtained his fullest and clearest expression in those weird and wonderful engravings of his, which are like nothing else in art. Many of the lyrics, tho, are marvellously beautiful and strange, such as "Tiger, tiger, burning bright," an "old favourite" of mine. Ever so many thanks for the book, which will prove a source of great interest and pleasure to me.

Notes

1. Anthony Comstock (1844–1915), American morals crusader and founder of the New York Society for the Suppression of Vice.
2. Ernest Dowson, "Non sum qualis eram bonae sub regno Cynarae" (1896).
3. CAS refers to the Panama-Pacific International Exposition, held in San Francisco from 20 February to 4 December 1915. GS wrote an ode for the opening of the exposition.

[28]   [ALS]

Auburn, Cal.

June 26th, 1915

Dear Sam:

The word "unhealthy" as applied to literature, is rather a compliment, I'm thinking. Nothing is "healthy" to the Philistine unless it's grossly commonplace and blatantly optimistic. I'd rather have written one lyric of Poe's than all the so-called "sane" and "healthy" poetry turned out by Messrs. Longfellow & Co. in a lifetime. Alas! it's not only the public who fall into this vulgar fallacy. Even poets, who should know better, speak of the "morbidity" of Poe's work. And it will take a more enlightened age than this, I fear, to forget the "moral stigma" attached to the dipsomania of which Poe was the victim.

Apropos of Keats' "Ode to Melancholy," which you mention, I must say that I've long had a secret preference for that poem over much of Keats' work that's better known. Indeed, in company with "La Belle Dame Sans Merci," it really pleases me better than anything else of his, with the exception of the "Ode to a Nightingale" . . . To me, "La Belle Dame Sans Merci" is weirder than anything in English poetry outside of Poe, not excepting Coleridge, for whom I've never been able to develop the highest enthusiasm (This is poetic heresy, I suppose.)

I don't know where I ran across that superstition about mandragora. However, I find that the Encyclop[a]edia Britannica, Chambers', and the Century Dictionary all make mention of the supposed aphrodisiacal properties of the plant. It was also used in the composition of love-philtres, and the fruit was believed to be a cure for barrenness. There's some reference to the latter belief in the Bible (Chap. XXX of Genesis)[1] As to the line in "Antony and Cleopatra," I rather think that Shakespeare refers to the narcotic properties of mandragora.[2] It really is a narcotic, but the aphrodisiacal qualities are probably a matter of superstition. All sorts of magical virtues were at one time attributed to the plant on account of the human shape of the root. Phosphorus and cantharides are said to be the only drugs really capable of exciting venereal desire.

I've about given up the idea of writing narrative verse, myself. I doubt if I've any talent for it. However, *you* might do something of that kind—a ballad, for instance, or something in the heroic couplets of "Lamia." I'll do what I can for the cause of Romantic beauty in my lyrics and sonnets. I find a certain Oriental vein of my imagination reviving, and shall use a deal of exotic imagery in my future work. At one time I wrote reams of stories in the manner of the Arabian nights, and a large amount of crude and immature verse on Eastern themes, among them an imitation of the Rubaiyat!

The sonnet you send is very good, and in subject peculiarly resembles one that I wrote a few weeks ago. I'll copy it for you, even tho it's rather faulty as it stands . . . Possibly there's something in thought-transference, after all. At any rate, the coincidence is noteworthy.

Miller,[3] whom you mention, was a good poet, but the mannerisms of his work, and the hasty and careless style, literally set my teeth on edge. I can't read him with any comfort. Stoddard,[4] I think, was a much better poet in his prose than in his verse. The latter, from what I've seen of it, is much too mild for my taste. I fear I've a craving for strong and even acrid flavors, since I prefer Poe and Swinburne to Keats and Milton. I've no real complaint against the latter two, but poetry that's merely bland or luscious rather palls upon me, after a time. This is all personal, of course, and if I were a professional critic I should not dare estimate the relative greatness of these poets by idiosyncrasy of preference . . . I begin to suspect that I'm a true modern and Romantic, with little real sympathy for the Greek or classic spirit.

Pardon the prolixity of this rather conversational letter. I've few correspondents, and there's no one hereabouts to whom I can speak my full mind without danger of being misunderstood.

> Ever yours,
> Clark.

P.S. I copy the sonnet on the next sheet. It's very crude, and obviously wouldn't "do" for any respectable periodical. I shan't publish it, anyway. English is too brutal a language for erotic verse.

Alien Memory

Thy body like to rosy ivory,
　　The fervours of thy beauty warm and bare—
　　I knew them all, I knew not when nor where,
In lands beside an amber-foaming sea.

For once I found thee, lying by a palm,
　　Upon thy terraces of serpentine,—
　　Thy dreamy breast, voluptuous and divine
All given to the winds of myrrh and balm.

We saw the sun, a molten amethyst,
　　Sink in the scented seas of foam and fire,
　　And a slow night with ruby planets rise;

And all the night was curtain for our tryst,
　　With all thine eager breast, thy burning thighs
　　And amorous arms a couch for my desire.

Notes

1. Gen. 30:14–16: "And Reuben went in the days of wheat harvest, and found mandrakes in the field, and brought them unto his mother Leah. Then Rachel said to

Leah, Give me, I pray thee, of thy son's mandrakes. And she said unto her, Is it a small matter that thou hast taken my husband? and wouldest thou take away my son's mandrakes also? And Rachel said, Therefore he shall lie with thee to night for thy son's mandrakes. And Jacob came out of the field in the evening, and Leah went out to meet him, and said, Thou must come in unto me; for surely I have hired thee with my son's mandrakes. And he lay with her that night. And God hearkened unto Leah, and she conceived, and bare Jacob the fifth son." Here the sense is that the plant would make a barren woman fruitful.

2. "Not poppy, nor mandragora, / Nor all the drowsy syrups of the world, / Shall ever medicine thee to that sweet sleep / Which thou owedst yesterday" (*Othello* 3.3.334–37); and "Give me to drink mandragora ... / That I might sleep out this great gap of time/ My Antony is away" (*Antony and Cleopatra* 1.5.3, 5–6). Shakespeare mentions it in different contexts in *Romeo and Juliet* and *2 Henry II.*

3. Cincinnatus Hiner Miller (1837–1913), better known by his pen name Joaquin Miller, American poet and frontiersman known as the "Poet of the Sierras."

4. Charles Warren Stoddard (1843–1909), American author, poet, and editor.

[29]   [SL to CAS, nonextant]

[Envelope postmarked Cleveland, Ohio, June 27, 1915.]

[30]   [ALS]

Auburn, Cal.,
July 5th, 1915.

Dear Sam:

I'm hopelessly in debt to you for all these volumes of poetry that you send. Ever so many thanks for the volume of John Clare, who is a true poet, with a peculiar flavour of his own. I agree with you that he surpasses Wordsworth in certain qualities for which the latter is especially celebrated. I never could endure Wordsworth's kind of simplicity myself—he never seems to know the difference between the fine and the banal; but Clare, in many of his Asylum poems, and a few others scattered thro the book, is thoroughly enjoyable, tho by no means great or perfect. Some of the sonnets are very good, especially in thought.

I've written nothing at all of late, but am sending you a number of lyrics and sonnets, written at earlier dates. I don't think any of them very good, but you may find ideas in some of them. I'd like to know which ones you think worth preserving—I don't entirely trust my own judgement. I enclose a prose-poem, too—one of my few essays in symbolism. You will understand it, I think. You will notice that the conception is developed from that of one of my sonnets—indeed, it's very much the same, except that in the prose-poem the serpents crawl from the tomb itself,—a more explicit, more terrible image. The serpents, of course, are the thoughts or impulses bred from the corruption of a dead hope, or love, or ideal.

I wish to the deuce a new idea, or at least, a new image were possible. I'm sick of all the customary banalities, the "stock" diction, the "stock" emotions, upon which even the best poetry seems largely to rely. I'd sell my soul for something really original. As it is, I think I use fewer "cliches" than most American poets—or English poets, either—at least those of the present day. I've sworn never to use such a phrase as "golden leaves" or "music of the spheres", indeed, any of the "old favourites", unless with some novelty or application. A phrase belongs to anyone who can get a new value out of it, I think. However, we should all strive for more preciosity.

Tho I've done so little of late, I've at least settled more definitely upon what I wish to do—which is a great advantage, and probably a sign of growth. I shall write sonnets, prose-poems, and lyrics in certain of the stricter and more solemn verse-forms. As to themes, I find I've a growing predilection for the "rich and strange," and a desire to seek poetry in places where few have cared, or dared, to seek it. You can readily see that I'm in very little danger of becoming popular.

Do you read the magazines? I hope you don't. Their mediocrity is no less than amazing—it seems to increase without culmination. Apart from Joseph Conrad, I detest the whole crew of present-day fictionists. And the poets!!! . . . I have to read Poe to get the taste out of my mouth.

Ever yours,
Clark.

[31]   [ALS]

Auburn, Cal.,
July 10th, 1915.

Dear Sam:

I'm deucedly sorry to hear that you've been sick—existence is painful enough and tiresome enough without the complications of ill-health. As for myself, I dare say a physician would tell me that I'm not really ill. However, I might as well be, for a little exertion, mental or physical, seems to tire me, and I rise in the morning with a sense of accumulated fatigue. Concentration, enthusiasm, inspiration—these seem impossible to me at present.

I hope that you carry out your plan for an Elegy on Nora May French. Lafler, of whom you speak, is an excellent poet himself.[1]

I've long intended to write an ode in honour of Poe. But, like so many of my literary projects, it seems to have been relegated to the limbo of an indefinite future, along with similar poems on Swinburne and Baudelaire.

Thanks so much for what you say about the sonnet,—even tho I've a darkling fear that your praise is not entirely deserved. I think there's rather a field in erotic verse, since few English poets have written anything of the kind that is noteworthy—Swinburne, Rossetti, Dowson, and possibly Symons being the sole exceptions. I can't think of anything at all by an American poet. Of course, by erotic poetry, I don't mean the usual sugar-and-water of sentiment, which is entirely too common . . . The poem of Rossetti's to which you refer is not included in my edition.[2]

Do you read the Chicago magazine, "Poetry?" I've just received the current issue, containing two poems of mine which were accepted in 1912.[3] The magazine seems to get worse and worse, if such a thing is possible. The best things in the number were quotations from an anthology of poems written by English schoolboys![4]

The poem of Clare's which you enclose, has a simplicity which disarms all criticism. You'll have gotten my letter acknowledging the receipt of the book, by this time. Clare is an exquisite poet, with an eye for natural detail that is all his own—an idiosyncratic faculty of observation.

Thanks for the interesting sketch of yourself. I'll send you one of me, some day—I used to draw, but am frightfully out of practice. I've no extra copies of any of my photographs, but will have some new ones taken the next time I visit San Francisco. The snapshot enclosed is rather good of me, I think.

I've nothing to send you, since I've not written a line in weeks. However, I may have a sonnet or so to enclose with my next letter.

> Ever your friend,
>
> Clark.

Notes

1. Henry "Harry" Anderson Lafler (1873–1935), literary editor, advertising manager, and author of the *Statistical, Industrial and Market Survey of Oakland* (1920).
2. CAS probably refers to "Jenny" by Dante Gabriel Rossetti (1828–1882), English poet, illustrator, painter, and translator, and founder of the Pre-Raphaelite Brotherhood in 1848 with William Holman Hunt and John Everett Millais.
3. "Fire of Snow" and "In the Wind."
4. Edward J. O'Brien, "The Younger Bards," *Poetry* 6, No. 4 (July 1912): 188–91.

[32]   [ALS]

> Auburn, Cal.,
> July 21st, 1915.

Dear Sam:

Many, many thanks for the pamp[h]let of your poems![1] I like "In Pierrot's Garden", the "Ode to Dionysus," and the translations from Heine best, I think, especially nos. 2 of the first, and no. 4 of the latter. The diction and imagery of the ode are very clear and vigorous, and more in the simplicity of the Greek manner than most of the similar odes of Keats, of whom the poem is but slightly suggestive. In all sincerity, I think it would do no discredit to Keats. Certain single lines or verses of yours haunt me persistently, such as the two last (lines) of the "Dionysus," and the line, "The sleep that circles in our wearied eyes," which I treasure beside one of Swinburne's—"Soft as sleep sings in a tired man's ear."[2] Also the fine image at the end of the sonnet—"That spins its fabric on our inverse prayers."

I'll be very, very glad to have the volume of Landor which you promise me. I've read most of his work, but possess no copy . . . Drawing books from a public library is rather unsatisfactory at best, since if a book is worth reading at all, it's worth reading more than once. I **do** like Conrad very much. By all means read his "Heart of Darkness," which you'll doubtless find in your public library. His imagination, and his use of English will be a revelation to you, if I mistake not. No one else writes at all like him.

I've no poems to send, and am wondering if the little drawings I enclose will interest you at all.[3] I really don't know anything about drawing, and these are the first attempts that I've made since my childhood. The one of George (drawn from memory,) looks rather like him, I think.[4] That of myself (copied from a rather shadowy artistic photograph) is probably not so good, except for the brow and eyes. The other drawings are phantasms of my own invention.

I agree with you about the "Vision of Satan."[5] In conception, the sonnet is one of my best, tho scarcely in execution.

> Ever your friend,
> Clark.

P.S. I haven't heard from George for several weeks, but that's nothing unusual. Why do you ask?

Notes

1. This is SL's *Poems* (1911).
2. SL, "A Twenty-Second Birthday" l. 6 (CAS's twenty-second was in January); Swinburne, "Memorial Verses on the Death of Théophile Gauthier," l. 26.
3. The drawings CAS sent to SL are published in *Grotesques and Fantastiques*.
4. *In the Realms of Mystery and Wonder* contains a drawing titled "Father Sterling" (n.p.).
5. I.e., "A Vision of Lucifer." See letter 104.

[33]   [ALS]

> Auburn, Cal.
> July 29th, 1915.

Dear Sam:

Many, many thanks for the little volume of Landor, which arrived several days ago. I should have acknowledged it ere this, and must plead lack of time and fatigue as excuses. I read "Gebir" and several of the "Hellenics" with great pleasure a few years ago, and promise myself a more careful re-

reading now that I have them in my possession. I certainly agree with you as to the refreshing quality of Landor's style—which is comparable to nothing less than a mountain spring—the "true Hippocrene." One can't have too much of it after the cheap champagne and soda-pop of the present-day writers.

The sonnet of Rossetti's that you send is most excellent. Personally, I don't find anything in it that could be considered "objectionable". However, it's very easy to excite the Puritanical imagination.

I had a letter from George yesterday. He's *back* in San Francisco,—a sort of cheap inferno in brick and steel. He'd like me to come down and join him, but I'm in no mood to visit a place that I hate so much, and am too desperately poor to afford the trip, anyway.

I've written nothing, but have amused myself with a few attempts at drawing. A list of the titles may interest you—"The Vampire", "The Ghoul", "The Red Death", "The Mandrake", "The Lich", "The Lamia", etc—a ghastly exhibit, of which "The Ghoul", and "Red Death" are perhaps the ghastliest.

I'll write again in a few days, and will try to send you some sonnets, or perhaps a prose-poem. Have I sent you any of the following titles—"The Black Lake", "A Phantasy", and "The Sun and the Sepulchre?" It occurs to me that perhaps I haven't.

> Ever your friend,
> Clark.

[34]   [ALS]

> Auburn, Cal.,
> Aug. 9th, 1915.

Dear Sam:

Many thanks for your pictures, which, to my mind, indicate a genuine artistic talent. I like best the two girls' heads, which are very lightly and delicately done. Your "Vampire", Sam, is very charming.

Outside of a little drawing, my days have been quite idle of late. I don't feel in the least like writing poetry, and have amused myself by drawing devils, grotesque animals of the nightmare breed, and pretty girls. I'll try to enclose a few of the latter. They're all of a type, as you'll notice, tho "Cynara" and "Berenice" are my favourites. My other drawings include a "Head of Satan", an alchemist, a witch, a ghost, and no end of sea-serpents, demon turnips, doodlebugs, etc. I'll make copies of some of them for you presently. Also, in a few days, I'll send you copies of the prose-poems I promised you. I'm having to wait for a new typewriter-ribbon, since none is obtainable in Auburn.

I agree with you that the "Scroll" would make a good cover-design. But I'm not sure that my publisher would want to use it. It might help to repel a certain class of buyers, you see! I'd certainly use the picture, with a few more that I've drawn, if I were publishing my work at my own expense.

I'm expecting the book of which you speak, with interest. You overwhelm me with your kindness—I only wish I could make some sort of return for it.

I'm sorry to hear of your accident. Sprains are the deuce, as I know, from a week's experience with a turned ankle.

I quite understand the craving of which you speak—the desire for Oriental or pagan life. To me, the average modern existence seems an insupportable bore. I ought to have been a Sicilian shepherd in the time of Theocritus,—granting that I had to be born on this planet at all. I've an almost physical horror of machinery, and of all the multitudinous activities of the social ant-heap. I am unable to see any place for myself in the modern world.

Here are the girls that I promised you, with a little Naiad in pen-and[-]ink that I've just drawn. So I'll say good-night, since it's about my bed-time.

> Ever your friend,
> Clark.

[35]   [ANS postcard]¹

> [Postmarked East Auburn, Cal.,
> 16 August 1915.]
> Auburn, Cal.,
> Aug. 10th, 1915.

Dear Sam:

A letter to-morrow. I'm holding it over till I've time to make copies of some of my pictures for you.

> Ever yours,
> Clark

Notes

1. *Front*: Eruption of Mt. Lassen, California.

[36]   [ALS]

> Cleveland, Ohio.
> Aug. 12, 1915.

Dear Clark,

I sent you a day before yesterday a copy (rather tattered) of Burton's "Kasidah"—hope it comes to you in due time and that you enjoy its contents. I know that Burton's noble and unconciliating pessimism will be to your taste, especially the passages so full of scorn and fire over all the modern creeds and hectic religions. Good cheer, brother!

I've done little but work lately. My father has been (and still is) dangerously sick at a local hospital. This has placed a double burden upon me and I usually round up my day with twelve or fifteen hours of hard labour, mental

& physical. It seems somewhat strange that I, a person least likely to care for the world and the world's way[,] am continually forced to do battle with her—it should have been otherwise. I'm going to try and make the S.W. this winter—more than one informant has confided to me that it is an easy matter to obtain a position as sheep-herder out there—usually ending with the statement apologetic—"but so lonesome." I think I might build up, too—and I could write Poetry. As Simeon Solomon,[1] Swinburne's friend, once said—"the night, the stars, and death—these are the most beautiful things I know of."[2]

Have you written much? I'll send you in my next, probably Sunday, a poem called "Nepenthe." I hope a longer letter, too. Write soon, Clark and believe me with kind and affectionate regards

Your friend
Sam

Notes

1. Simeon Solomon (1840–1905), a English Pre-Raphaelite painter. SL wrote a quatrain titled "Simeon Solomon."
2. Actually, "Night, Sleep, Death and the Stars they are the themes that I love best." as related in *The Bibelot: A Reprint of Poetry and Prose for Book Lovers* ... Vol. 17 (Portland, ME: Thomas B. Mosher, 1911), n.p. Walt Whitman's "A Clear Midnight" ends with the lines "... pondering the themes / thou lovest best, / Night, sleep, death and the stars."

[37]　[ALS]

Auburn, Cal.,
Aug. 20, 1915

Dear Sam:

Many, many thanks for the "Kasidah"—another of the treasures that you seem forever finding. I *do* like Burton's noble and splendid perversions, and find little in the poem with which I disagree. It's curious, but I had never heard of the book till you mentioned it. I wonder how many fine things are hid in obscurity and public disregard. It would interest, and doubtless surprise one to know. You seem to have a great facility for finding such trove.

The necessity of making a living is certainly a curse, especially for an artist ... Damn it all, why weren't we born rich? In spite of all the fool beliefs and superstitions to the contrary, I can see no blessings or compensations in poverty. ... In the name of Abaddon and all his lieutenants, what cosmic purpose can be good or beneficent, that must be served by all this sordid misery of millions? I incline to Heine's view, that life is the dream of a malevolent demon.

I'm sorry, but I've written nothing in months. I feel too restless, too feverish, even to make an attempt of it. When I really get to work again, I may do rather different things than in the past. I seem to have expressed only the purely imaginative and intellectual side of my nature. One seems to change, or, to put it more exactly, different aspects of one's existence gradually reveal themselves. At the centre, perhaps, there is no change, more than in the axle of a wheel.

I've just written to George, who is back in San Francisco. He speaks of having to go to "work",—a most appalling word to a natural-born loafer like me. Damn such an industrious world! Have we no more sense than the emmet and the pismire? Unless my father's property turns out to be a gold-mine, I'll be up against the disagreeable necessity of earning a living, myself—a thing for which I've no preparation of any kind, nor any disposition. May the devil help me!

　　　　　Ever your friend,

　　　　　　　　　　Clark.

[38]　[ALS]

　　　　　　　　　　　　　　　　　　　Auburn, Cal.,

　　　　　　　　　　　　　　　　　　　Sept. 6th, 1915.

Dear Sam:

　　　　Please accept my sincerest apologies for my tardiness in answering your letters. I've had a good deal of work to do of late (enough to keep me in mind of what drudgery is like) and have found myself too tired at the end of the day for correspondence. I promise you (and myself) that I'll not be so remiss in the future.

First of all, to thank you for the excellent little book on Sappho. I've enjoyed reading it, and liked especially the prose translations at the end.[1]

I'm pleased by the drawings you send, and wish you would do more of them. I've daubed a little with a brush of late (I can draw even when I can't do anything else) and have gotten some rather weird results . . . I enclose a purple devil (devils are my specialty, and I do them in all colours, from black to vermilion.)

I like your idea of putting out poems in pamphlet form.[2] Why don't you try it? . . . Robertson thinks he can publish another book for me in about a year's time. I suppose I can scrape together enough material for some sort of volume. I've written nothing at all since early in the Summer, but may do a little work presently. George insists that I should write an elegy on Nora May French, for a book of tributes that her friends plan to publish. I'd like to, but doubt if I've any talent for occasional verse.[3]

I know just how you feel about Cleveland (how we all hate the place to which circumstances confine us!) from my own feeling in regard to Auburn. I do wish we could get together, and have a good talk. Letter-writing is damned unsatisfactory. I hope you carry out your plan for coming west. I can assure you of a hearty welcome, even tho my accom[m]odations are scarcely palatial.

I doubt if the Auburn library has **any** translation of the Arabian Nights, let alone Burton's. They haven't even a complete set of Poe, and nothing at all of Bierce. What can you do? The library Board is made up mostly of Church members.

I'll write you another and longer letter in a few days. I'm not forgetting the prose-poems, but I've no no [*sic*] extra copies ready to send with this. Here are a few more of my bum drawings in lieu of them. You may like the head of Belial.

Ever your friend,
Clark

P.S. I'm sending the pictures under separate cover.

Notes

1. Probably Wharton's ed. of 1877.
2. Instead of a small booklet, SL published his verse in three issues of the *Saturnian* between 1920 and 1922.
3. CAS began an ode to French, completing it in 1920 as "To Nora May French." The book, planned by Harry Lafler, never appeared.

[39]   [ALS]

Auburn, Cal.,
Sept. 16th, 1915.

Dear Sam:

Please accept my thanks (again delayed) for the "Life of John Clare,"[1] which (as you must have known it would) has interested me greatly. The record is one that both saddens and elevates. After reading it, I feel re-impressed with a sense of the irrational in human destiny—"The cruelties the mindless Fates decree."[2] How can anyone believe in the existence of an omniscient, omnipotent God? If I were forced to such a belief, (which the devil forbid!) I would be able to think and speak nothing but blasphemy.

Our Californian autumn is beginning, tho to-day there's not a speck of cloud above the horizon—only an azure haze that has filled the further valleys, and blurred the outlines of the mountains, till they seem half-dissolved in the sky of liquid blue. The hot days are over (I hope) and a spice of coolness in the wind tells me that the spirit of autumn is abroad. The orchards below my hill-top will blaze with gorgeous colour in another month.

Again, I've nothing to send you. These long sterile periods are trying. The worst of it is that I don't half-care whether I write anything or not. The difficulty I find in doing anything to please myself, makes me reluctant even to attempt composition. I dare say you understand the feeling. Every artist or poet must be familiar with it at times. . . . Also, I'm suffering from too much monotony, and a lack of pleasure. Auburn is worse than a desert—for a poet, at least, tho I'm not saying that the real-estate agents don't find it to their taste.

Do my attempts at picture-making interest you at all? I can send you some more, if you care to have them. Many of my new ones are grotesque enough, at any rate—especially the red priestess with green hair and eyes, and the devil-headed bat with vermilion wings. Also, there's a scarlet creature with the beak of a parrot, the face of a demon, and the body of a serpent. I seem to draw mostly in red—an appropriate colour for the conceptions depicted.

I'll write you a longer letter next time. I seem to have little enough to say (and, to-day, at least) not overmuch time in which to say it. I'm hoping for a letter from you soon.

Ever your friend,
Clark.

Notes

1. By Frederick W. Martin.
2. From GS, "Nora May French," l. 6.

[40]   [ALS]

Auburn, Cal.,
Sept. 25th, 1915.

Dear Sam:

The volumes of John Clare arrived yesterday, and I've just had time to run through them hastily. I'm struck by the vastly superior quality of the "Rural Muse" compared with the first volume. Not all poets have kept on improving to the end. I find page after page of pure and delightful poetry in the volume of 1835. Many, many thanks to you for these rare and beautiful books. Where do you find such treasures?

I'm glad you like my pictures. I think I shall keep on with the practice, with the ultimate object of illustrating my own poems. All I need is a little more technique, and **that** I can pick up for myself in time. I care very little for the elaborate realism of Western art, anyway, and shall base my manner more on that of the Japanese. . . . I confess that I care more for the drawings of Beardsley and Dorè [*sic*] than for anything else in Occidental art. Paintings bore me, unless they're very unusual. To me, the strangeness of a conception, whether in art or in literature, is half the charm. Poe, Swinburne, and Shelley, as you might guess, are the poets whom I value the most, and among prose-writers, De Quincey, Bierce, Poe, and Lafcadio Hearn are my favourites, together with their French compeers, Loti and Baudelaire, whom, however, I am able to read only in translation. Dumas, Gautier, Flaubert and De Maupassant delight me also, in a lesser degree, while I care little for any of the Anglo-Saxon novelists or romancers. I'm wondering if you have read "Mademoiselle de Maupin",[1] or the "Aphrodite" of Pierre Luoys, [*sic*] books which have to be sent by express in this land of Anthony Comstocks.

By the way, I hear that Anthony Comstock is dead. I dare say the country will go clean to the devil now, what with the sentimental voluptuousness of certain American novelists.

I may write a memorial poem (probably in the ode-form) in honour of Nora May French. I more than agree with you in regard to her work. No other woman-poet since Sappho (and certainly not the grotesquely overrated Mrs. Browning) is worthy to stand beside her. Nearly every line that she wrote was pure poetry. And of how many poets (irrespective of sex) can you say that? Also, she's the only one of her sex in whose writing I can find no trace of feminine hysteria. Don't think that I've anything against the ladies (most of my letters of appreciation are from women, and my best friends are mostly women) but as a rule I'm unable to conceive any very high opinion of their literary output. It seems rather strange to me that they've not done more in literature, especially poetry, in spite of the intellectual bondage to which men have subjected them in the past.

I may have something to send you in my next. I think my long rest is doing me good. People say that I look better than I did a year or two ago, and I certainly feel better. I don't feel nearly so old and worn-out as I did when my book appeared.

As ever, your friend,
Clark.

Notes

1. By Théophile Gautier.

[41]   [ALS]

Auburn, Cal.,
Oct. 6th, 1915.

Dear Sam:

Many thanks for "The Life and Remains of John Clare,"[1] which I should have acknowledged ere this. The book is less detailed and more dispassionate than Martin's. The "Remains," many of which are very beautiful, interest me greatly. Even lunacy may have compensations, it would seem.

I've never read "The Temptation of Saint Anthony."[2] I'm sure it would interest me immensely; but I feel guilty at receiving so much from you, when I've nothing to give in return.

I've just read George's "Yosemite" ode, in the San Francisco Call. The poem is worthy of him, and is better than I thought *anyone* could write on such a subject. He tells me the ode is to be published in book-form later in the month, together with the Exposition ode.

I'll send you a new batch of drawings in a few days, when I've time of [*sic*] make copies of them. You'll probably like some of them—they're far more fiendish and monstrous than anything I've sent you before.

I may do a little writing, now that the hot weather is over—probably something in prose. I think of a volume of fables and fairy tales to follow my next book of poetry.

Pardon this hasty note, and the abominable pen with which I'm writing it. I'll write you more at length when I send the pictures.

Ever your friend,
Clark

Notes

1. By John Law Cherry.
2. By Gustave Flaubert.

[42]   [ALS]

Auburn, Cal.,
Oct. 19th, 1915.

Dear Sam:

Please accept my delayed thanks for "The Werewolf." The tale is beautifully written, and gives me more pleasure than anything of the kind I have read recently. If I am not mistaken, it is worthy of a place in any list of the shorter master-pieces of fiction. Certainly, the tale is superior in artistic workmanship to many that are far more famous. The author's name is new to me. Is he related to Laurence Housman, the poet?[1]

I've sent you a number of my pictures under separate cover, and am wondering if you will care for them. I may be mistaken in thinking that I've any artistic talent. Hardly anyone seems very enthusiastic over my drawings. However, I'm inclined to think that some of my conceptions are at least original, however faulty the workmanship. Originality, as you know, counts against one with most people, since the human mind is naturally fearful and suspicious of the new and the strange.

I think of sonnets, odes, prose-poems and stories ad infinitum; but nothing seems to materialize as yet. Everything conspires to keep me in a sterile and destructive mood. I dare say you know how it is. The malice of circumstance is nothing less than fiendish . . . Perhaps I am too deeply convinced of the evanescence of all things, and the vanity and futility of effort, to work at anything with a firm hand. There are days when life impresses me as a bad joke; nothing seems worth hoping for, and all the possibilities of action or experience fail to tempt me. Everything that one can do or think seems futile and puerile. This all [*sic*] morbid, I suppose; but I can't help the feeling.

We've had no rain this autumn, and scarcely a cloud. I like these clear October days—days of mellow light and tempered warmth, when the mountains swim in a mist of luminous purple. I feel soothed by such weather, especially to-day, when everything is touched by the pale blue haze. All impressions are softened, and become vague and tender as a dream or a memory. The world and its rumours are muffled and remote, while sense and spirit seem to gang on the verge of Nirvana.

I'm hoping for a letter from you ere long. I positively *swear* that I'll have something to send you next time. I've several prose-poems outlined in my note-book, but my poor head feels like a dill-pickle when it comes to actual concentration.

Ever your friend,

Clark

Notes

1. Clemence Housman (1861–1955) was the sister of Laurence and A. E. Housman. H. P. Lovecraft briefly mentioned the novelette in "Supernatural Horror in Literature."

[43]   [ALS]

Auburn, Cal.,

Nov. 2nd, 1915.

Dear Sam:

It's very strange that you didn't receive my last letter. I'm willing to swear that I wrote to you—also that I sent the batch of pictures promised. "Something is rotten" in the postal service.

However, I've received **your** letter, and the two books by George Moore. I owe you many thanks for the pleasure and amusement they have given me. I like the "Impressions and Opinions" best, however—it contains less of the disconcerting egotism and coxcombery of which you speak. The article on Verlaine is interesting,[1] tho Verlaine's poetry itself rather baffles me. I very much prefer Baudelaire—he, at least, is usually intelligible.

I'll send you some more pictures presently. There's one you will probably like—"The Idol with Diamond Eyes"—a detail for Poe's "City in the Sea." . . . I'm ashamed to confess that I've written nothing since early in the Summer. Discouragement, self-distrust, nervous ill-health and depression—these have conspired to inhibit the poetic impulse in me. I seem to have no "divine certitude" of my own talent, and can feel but little pride or pleasure in anything that I have done. The prospect of publishing another book dismays me—I would rather wait until I have done something to win my own approbation. . . . There's too much of the Oriental in my temperament, perhaps—will and desire in me are paralyzed by the sense of fatality and evanescence—an inherent conviction of the vanity and worthlessness of life. Fame is the most empty of all illusions, but it may serve as well as any other. As Baudelaire said, "The one thing necessary is to be drunken"—whether with wine, love, fame, ambition, or what you will. "Be drunken; otherwise you become the slave of Time."[2] As for myself, I sometimes fear that Lethe alone can drown my perception of the emptiness and horror of existence.

This is all morbid, I suppose, and I shouldn't inflict it upon you. But I've nothing to write about except my thoughts; and the tissue of my mental life seems made up largely of such dismal reflections as these.

Write to me soon. I shall be very glad to see the poems of which you speak, and will try to send you something of my own before long.

       Ever your friend,
          Clark.

Notes

1. George Augustus Moore (1852–1933), Irish novelist. CAS refers to the essay "A Great Poet" (pp. 98–110). The book also contains "Two Unknown Poets," about Verlaine and Rimbaud (pp. 111–22).
2. From the prose poem "Enivrez-vous" [Get Drunk]. Symons's translation reads thus: "Be always drunken. Nothing else matters; that is the only question. If you would not feel the horrible burden of Time weighing on your shoulders and crushing you to the earth, be drunken continually" (p. 58).

[44]   [ALS]

                       Auburn, Cal.,
                          Dec. 6th, 1915.

Dear Sam:

       Both your letters, and the two books, are "safely at hand". I've delayed answering, so that I might have time to read "Wuthering Heights", and give you the opinion upon its merits which you request. I dare say my literary judgement is more than usually capricious and independable when it comes to the novel, a form that I seldom read of late years; but the intellectual power and grasp of the tale, and the simple effectiveness of its style, held me for several hours beyond my customary bed-time. I think it great and remarkable—immeasurably superior to the melodramatic "Jane Eyre" of Charlotte Bronte. Many thanks for the book, and for "Marius the Epicurean", which I've not yet had time to read thoroughly. My eyes have bothered me a bit of late, so that I dare not read as much or as constantly as I used to. I like the passages (of "Marius") into which I have dipped at random. George Moore improves on acquaintance, and I often return to certain essays in "Impressions and Opinions." The one on Verlaine is especially interesting.

I've seen only a few of Rupert Brooke's[1] poems, quoted in various periodicals, and found some of them very much to my taste. It seems odd that you shouldn't like his work. But perhaps the quotations I saw were his best and not representative of the volume as a whole. The sale of the book seems astounding, for poetry of that character.

I'm glad you liked George's "Yosemite". I'll send you his "Exposition

Ode" as soon as I can get a copy of it for you. The book is too high-priced to sell very well, I'm afraid. Personally, I dont [*sic*] see the sense of putting out new books in a de luxe edition. I wouldn't mind publishing my work in pamphlet form, if it's to be offered to the public at all.

I was in San Francisco a few weeks ago, and saw the much-advertised Exposition. Some of the architecture is excellent, some of it very bad, and the colour-effect as a whole, very beautiful and surprising, especially at night, when the scene is that of a city of Oriental enchantment. The statuary, and the pictures in the Palace of Fine Arts, displayed the same extremes of merit and demerit as the architecture. It was, I dare say, inevitable that most of the buildings should be given over partially or wholly to commercial and horticultural displays. A Fair wouldn't be a Fair without that.

Have you written anything of late? I'm ashamed to say that I haven't. My health is to blame, as usual. I was ill and run-down when I went to San Francisco, and I came back from a week of sight-seeing with a sense of accumulated fatigue and general demoralization from which I've hardly yet recovered. It's a constitutional lack of vitality, I'm afraid.

I'll send you the pictures in a few days. Write soon, and believe me,

> Your affectionate friend,
> > Clark.

Notes

1. Rupert Brooke (1887–1915), English poet known for his idealistic war sonnets written during World War I. The book referred to is presumably *1914 & Other Poems*.

[45]   [ALS]

> Auburn, Cal.,
> > Dec. 28th, 1915.

Dear Sam:

Many, many thanks for the volumes of Arthur Symons.[1] I like many of the poems, especially "The Dance of the Daughters of Herodias," the translations from Verlaine and Mallarmè [*sic*], no. XI of "Mundi Victima," and some of the shorter lyrics—"To a Photograph", "Autumn Twilight", "Nerves", "Bianca", "Moonrise", "Haschich", "The Opium-Smoker," and several others, whose titles I cannot recall at present. Symons, I think, has a fine and notable talent, tho his range is remarkably limited. No one poem of his reaches the lyric intensity of Dowson's "Cynara", but the general level seems better than that of Dowson—at least to my taste.

"Marius the Epicurean" gives me a better idea of Pater than I had formerly entertained. I thought the manner too elaborate and ceremonial; but the grave and stately beauty of the cadences, the choice of chryselephantine words, the sad serenity and loneliness of thought—all these grow upon me with the reading. I am in your debt for a new favourite to place among the prose-writers whom I value most.

I am sorry indeed to hear that your father is so dangerously ill. So far, I have had no griefs myself, (unless the chagrin of an unsuccessful love-affair can be counted as such) but my own heart tells me what it would be like to lose one for whom I cared greatly. Truly, I sympathize with you . . . Partings, estrangements, the indignities of time and change, the death of those whom I love—my heart is prescient of all these, and the sense of them haunts me like a shadow at times.

My own health is much better of late—everyone notices the improvement. My spirits are much improved, too—which, perhaps, is what makes the difference. I shudder to think of all the energy that I've wasted in worrying over the irremediable. Egotism, and a tendency to overmuch self-preoccupation, are my worst faults. To some extent, they have been forced upon me by my method of life, which gives me too much time for introspection. I have been too much alone, and for long intervals have had no one at hand in whom I could really confide. There is one such at present (a woman) so I'm not nearly so unhappy and depressed as I have been . . . Indeed, I'm not unhappy at all. You'll gather from all this, I suppose, that I'm not nearly so inhuman as some of my poetry would indicate!

It's very kind of you to think of writing an article on my work. That would be quite a resurrection for me—to find my name in print once more. Truly, I am grateful for the more than generous appreciation of my work which you have expressed. The receipt of your letters has lightened many a black mood, many a gray hour. I only wish we could meet, and get to know each other better than is possible by correspondence. I never can say half what I want to say, in a letter.

Don't worry about the expense of the books I send you. I have them charged against my royalties,—a good method of indemnification, since I never get any royalties!

I'll write again in a few days, and will send you a new prose-poem or two. I'll try to work more, this coming year. I've enough projected to keep me busy for several years.

   Affectionately, your friend,
    Clark.

Notes

1. The poems listed are in Symons's *Poems* (1919; 2 vols.).

[46]　[ALS]

Auburn, Cal.,

Jan. 7th, 1916.

Dear Sam:

Your letter came yesterday, and I hasten to reply, inasmuch as I've been intending to write for the last week or more. Somehow, I've not gotten around to it. Constitutional procrastination is my besetting sin, I'm afraid.

I am very sorry to hear of your father's death.[1] Even tho we haven't met, our correspondence seems to have drawn me very close, and my heart goes out to you with the sympathy that I would feel for a brother, if I had ever had one. . . . Perhaps I've never told you that I'm an only child. Most of my relatives are aunts, and uncles, and cousins.

I'm enclosing a new prose-poem, "The Memnons of the Night." George thinks very highly of it, but I dunno. The thing is original, at any rate. I'm struck by the fact that people, as a rule, overpraise the other qualities of my work, but tend to underrate its originality.

George tells me that one of his friends has really received a letter from Bierce, who, it seems, was in some small English town at the time of writing. It's good to know that the old man is still alive: Everyone seemed to have given him up long ago, and the "Bookman" actually published an obituary article.[2] I'd like to hear Bierce's comment on the obituary! also on the obituarist!

We've had beastly weather ever since Christmas—rain, fog, anchor-ice, and even a day or two of snow and slush. I'm the only person in the county who hasn't caught a cold. I get my feet wet every day, and sit in all kinds of temperatures with perfect impunity. But I hate this weather,—it afflicts me with a sort of spiritual asthma, a sense of oppression from which I recover only in the warm blue days of spring, and summer and early autumn.

I'll be very glad to have the poems of Lionel Johnson. I'm very much interested in the English (so-called) decadents, Dowson, Wilde, Symons, Beardsley, and Johnson. I've read hardly anything of Johnson's . . . By the way, do you know the imaginative prose of Lord Dunsany, or the poems of Lord de Tabley?[3] I've seen a little of both, (there's a poem or two of de Tabley's in Stedman's Victorian Anthology.) and find them very fascinating.

I suppose you're familiar with Oscar Wilde's "The Sphinx"—a poem that I've just been reading for the sixth or seventh time. On the whole, I enjoy it more than anything else of Wilde's, tho some of his lyrics are very beautiful, and there's no denying the greatness of "The Ballad of Reading Jail." I am fondest of the strange, the weird, the exotic in poetry, and "The Sphinx" has all these qualities in the highest degree, along with the novel and luxurious music of the verse-form.

It seems rather strange that you should be so lonely in a big city like Cleveland. But I suppose one can be lonelier in a city than anywhere else—especially in the crass commercial atmosphere of the middle states. I imagine you'd like

San Francisco better—you'd find as much bohemianism there as anywhere in America. Even **that** doesn't interest me very much—the attempts of city-dwellers at amusing themselves, all impress me as being desperate and pitiful. I care very little for theatres, moving-picture shows, and the like, and I never enjoy eating in public; so you can readily see that cities have few temptations for me, inasmuch as my nervous malady causes me to shrink from crowds. I am, I believe, peculiarly psychic in all my perceptions, with an uncomfortable amount of intuition; and I suffer from the telepathies of all the diseased or troubled lives that one touches in a city. Nothing depresses me more than being in a crowd.

Well, no more for today. Write me when you can, please, and give me some good news of yourself.

As ever,

Your affectionate friend, Clark.

P.S. "The Garden of Dreams" is an old poem, written in 1911. It's rather peculiar, and may interest you.

Notes

1. Marcus Loveman (b. 1860) died on 27 December 1915.
2. CAS appears to be referring to Bailey Millard's article "Personal Memories of Ambrose Bierce," *Bookman* (New York) 40, No. 6 (February 1915): 653–58.
3. Edward John Moreton Drax Plunkett, 18th Baron Dunsany (1878–1957), Anglo-Irish writer of fantasy tales. John Byrne Leicester Warren, 3rd Baron de Tabley (1835–1895), an authority on ancient Greek coinage but also the author of such poetry volumes as *Poems Dramatic and Lyrical* (1893) and *Orpheus in Thrace and Other Poems* (1901).

[47]   [ALS]

Auburn, Cal.,

Feb. 1st, 1916.

Dear Sam:

Many, many thanks for the beautifully bound volume of Oscar Wilde's prose. I have never happened to read any of the stories before, and find them wonderfully interesting—marvellous in every way. "The Picture of Dorian Gray" is the first novel that I've read through at a sitting in many months; and there are few books in which I have marked as many paragraphs or sentences. Some of the epigrams are tremendous—"A grand passion is the privilege of people who have nothing to do"—for example, tho there are even greater ones than that. I like even the most paradoxical ones—a paradox often presents an unfamiliar aspect of truth. The fairy tales and prose-poems are very beautiful and subtle. "The Young King,['] "The Nightingale and the Rose,['] "The Doer of Good" and "The House of Judgement," are my favourites so far. I agree with you perfectly in regard to the artistic qualities of the fairy tales. I like also the Biblical simplicity of style in the prose-poems, contrasting so curiously and so effectively with the subtle thought. The book has given and will continue to give me, more pleasure than anything else that I have read for a long time. I am more taken with Wilde's prose than with most of his poetry (always excepting "The Sphinx"). It seems richer, subtler, and more original than the verse.

Thanks for what you say about "The Memnons of the Night." I'm not sure that it's the best of my prose-poems, tho. I **do** think that some of them are among the best work that I have done so far—certainly among the most original.

I like your "Triumph of Anarchy," tho there are parts of it that I fail to "get." Some of the lines and images are very beautiful. I am eager to see what you will write on Nora May. I've promised to do something in memory of her, myself, if I can. I am still idle, partly on account of the abominable weather we have had all thro January. I've never seen so much snow before in my lifetime. I suffer from the unusual cold—it takes all my vitality and energy to keep warm. Real estate agents speak of Placer Co. as being part of the "citrus belt," but the oranges are all frozen on the trees his year. The climate seems to be changing—it gets colder and wetter every season, I believe.

If you can come out to Colorado in the Spring, why can't you come the rest of the way, and pay me a visit? My accom[m]odations are anything but sumptuous, but I would try to make up for that with hospitality. You could see George too, since it isn't so very much further to S. F.

Please write to me soon and send whatever you have written. I'll try to rake up something for you before long.

Faithfully,

Clark.

[48]   [ALS]

Auburn, Cal.,

Feb. 18th, 1916.

Dear Sam:

Your letter and your card are both "at hand," as business people say. I, too, have been under the weather (in a literal sense, since the warm days we had during February, seem to have given me a touch of Spring fever[]). The sudden changes of temperature are the worst feature of this climate.

I *do* hope that you manage to reach California this year. Your visit would be a godsend to me, in the way of a little companionship. My opportunities for friendship are strictly limited, in a place like Auburn ... The mere fact that one writes poetry, exposes one to suspicion, and hostility, and misunderstanding, especially in a small community. I seem to have found rather more than my share of these things.

If my publisher is willing, I shall put out another volume before the end of the year—a smaller and more select one than my first. I doubt if it will be very "popular". There is little or no demand in America for the sort of poetry that I write. I can't sell anything to the magazines.

I'll be very glad to have the plays of Oscar Wilde. I *have* the complete edition of Dowson, with the preface by Arthur Symons. What a tragic life, and how similar, in a way, to that of Keats! . . . All self-respecting poets seem to die of consumption and unrequited love . . . People think, sometimes, that *I* have a consumptive tendency, on account of my thinness. I am 5 ft. 11 as I stand, and my weight is seldom more than 125 lbs. However, I am small-boned, and scarcely need to carry the average weight. On the whole, my health is distinctly better than it was at this time a year ago, so I scarcely anticipate a premature demise.

Please write me soon. *I* shall write again in a few days.

Faithfully,

Clark.

[49]   [ALS]

Auburn, Cal.

March 3rd, 1916.

Dear Sam:

Just a note to acknowledge the plays of Oscar Wilde. The book came two or three days ago, but no letter. You spoke of writing, in the card that I received nearly a week ago, so I'm wondering if your letter hasn't gone astray. I lose mail occasionally, thro the carelessness of the local post-office.

Many, many thanks for the book. I've read "Salome", and two of the comedies, but haven't had time to finish the volume as yet. "Salome" is certainly great, and the comedies fairly sparkle with cleverness. I know I shall enjoy the book immensely.

I've had a relapse lately, into my old state of nervous depression. Nothing is more tiresome than this perpetual slipping-back, when one is trying to get well, and seems almost at the point of recovery.

Had a letter from George the other day. He says that his new book[1] will be out in April. So there's *something* to look forward to, at any rate. I don't know when I shall publish mine, or whether to publish one at all. All my poems need revision, and revision, to me, is the most heart-breaking of tasks. I feel indifferent to everything at present, and yet I am restless and miserable. Nothing would please me, excepting, perhaps, a ticket to Aldebaran or Betelgeuse, *via* the Milky Way.

Ever your friend,

Clark.

Notes

1. *The Caged Eagle and Other Poems.*

[50]   [ALS]

Auburn, Cal.,

March 20th, 1916.

Dear Sam:

I'm ashamed of not having answered your letter before. I seem to have let everything slide, these last few weeks. I am feverish, upset, and altogether disorganized, physically, mentally, and spiritually, and don't even sleep well, half the time. In addition to my nervous trouble, I've drifted into a bad, hopeless, impossible sort of love-affair—an affair that makes me both happy and miserable. Perhaps I can tell you about it some time, if we are ever together.

I'll be very glad to have the books of which you speak. I'm fond of the old dramatists, and would certainly take a great interest in anything that pertains to my favourite, Lafcadio Hearn. I've just been reading an essay on his work in a new book by James Huneker—"Ivory, Apes, and Peacocks."[1] Get the book, if you haven't seen it—I'm sure it would interest you greatly. Huneker's criticism is always brilliant—and literary criticism is usually anything but *that*.

The binding of the Oscar Wilde volumes is wonderful. But you ought to see some of the neckties that I wear—I've a barbaric fondness for bright and gorgeous colours! Purple is my favourite, tho I incline also to ruby-red and jade-green. . . . I've more than the usual poetic antipathy to modern costume, and would love to wear something Oriental or mediaeval. One would be arrested or mobbed, I dare say, for wearing anything sensible or beautiful, in this age when even Art seems to be growing ugly—not to mention the costumes. However, such sartorial monstrosities are sufficiently expressive of the spirit of modern life, and are appropriate to the hell of machinery, utilitarianism, commercialism, etc, etc. into which the world is turning. I don't think there is any hope for western civilization. This monstrous European war is perhaps the beginning of the end. America, too, is ready for the reign of the Abomination of Desolation. I seem more and more to despize [*sic*] the world, with all its madnesses, fatuities, and stupidities. Think of living in such a world, as many do, with no intellectual outlook! My philosophy is all that saves me from utter and abject despair.

Thanks for your sonnets. I like "Understanding" best of the two—it's more clearly expressed than the other. The conception is indeed beautiful and splendid.

I'm sorry that I've nothing to send in return. I've written a lyric or two lately, but they're hardly in a fit shape to send. It's hard for me to write, or care about writing, in my present state of mind. There are times when even Art seems the vanity of vanities to me.

Write soon, if you can; I'm always eager for your letters. And don't forget to send me anything that you have done. I'm immensely interested in the Scene for King Lear, of which you speak.

As ever, your affectionate friend,

Clark.

P.S. I shall publish my book in the Autumn, if possible. Some of the contents *will* "raise a howl," I suppose. I shan't read any of the reviews, if I can help it. I care less and less about fame, literary reputation, and the opinions of critics and the public. What does it all signify?

Notes

1. The essay is "The Cult of Nuance: Lafcadio Hearn" (*Ivory, Apes and Peacocks* 240–48).

[51]   [ALS]

Cleveland, Ohio.

[late March 1916]

Dear Clark,

I've missed your letters of late and was doubly glad to receive your last one. I'm distressed to hear of your continued poor health. I believe that if you had someone with tastes or characteristics in common with your own near you that much of your discomfort would disappear. As it is, even Nature is a poor anodyne when one is actually out of sorts. Ever read George Borrow, Clark? I have great pleasure in quoting you my favourite passage from "Lavengro":

"What is your opinion of death, Mr Petulengro [a gypsy]?" said I as I sat down beside him.

"My opinion of death, brother, is much the same as that in the old song of Pharaoh, which I have heard my grandam sing. When a man dies, he is cast into the earth, and his wife and child sorrow over him. If he has neither wife nor child, then his father and mother, I suppose; and if he is quite alone in the world, why then, he is cast into the earth and there's an end of the matter."

"And do you think that it is the end of man?"

"There's an end of him, brother, and more's the pity."

"Why do you say so?"

"Life is sweet, brother."

"Do you think so?"

"Think so!—there's night and day, brother, both sweet things; sun, moon, and stars, brother, all sweet things; there's likewise a wind on the heath, Life is very sweet, brother; who would wish to die?"

"I wish to die—"

"You talk like a gorgio—which is the same as talking like a fool—were you a Romany Chal, you would talk wiser. Wish to die, indeed!—a Romany Chal would wish to live forever!"

"In sickness, Jasper?"

"There's the sun & stars, brother!"

"In blindness, Jasper?"

"There's the wind on the heath, brother; if I would only feel that, I would live forever. Dosta, we'll now go to the tents & put on the gloves; and I'll try to make you feel what a sweet thing it is to be alive, brother!"[1]

I believe I told you that my father's business was recently disposed of—and of course I had to find work, which I proceeded to do. I had my first fling at it today. I wonder if you know what it is to scribble away at a desk for some ten hours every day. By the grace of the devil I hope to end my drudgery before winter. I shall roam where it listeth me and if I choose to go to the dogs none of my relatives need be the wiser.

I haven't mailed you the two vol's of Hearn but will do so Sat. of this week. I can't get down to the post-office before that time.

I'm enclosing what I've done of the scene of "Lear" and will await your criticism with unusual eagerness.

This is only a note—I'm dreadfully tired. Until Sat.—with kind and affectionate regards

Faithfully

Sam

P.S. My favorite colour is blue!

Notes

1. From *Lavengro* (ch. 25; pp. 162–63 of the 1902 ed. [revised slightly]).

[52]   [ALS]

Auburn, Cal.,

April 3rd, 1916.

Dear Sam:

I'm sorry that I've not written you oftener of late. It's more the lack of subject-matter, I think, than anything else, that makes me put off my correspondence from day to day. I haven't answered George's last letter yet, and it's been lying on my desk for several weeks. Remiss as you must think me, you fare better than any other of my correspondents.

I like what you send of the Scene for "King Lear", and certainly hope that you'll finish it. There are lines, touches, cadences that come very close to Shakespeare. I'm eager for the rest, so that I can judge it as a whole.

Yes, I've read some of George Borrow. The passage you quote is very good. Personally, I find it hard to agree with the philosophy, even in the midst of a Californian spring. Flowers and scenery aren't everything, especially when one is half sick . . . I've had a number of disagreeable symptoms lately, some of them suggestive of malaria, which is rather prevalent in these inland valleys. I'd rather have anything else, pretty nearly, from what I've observed of its effects.

I don't know anything about office-work, but I can imagine what it's like. Out-door work, of which I have to do a certain amount, is bad enough, especially when one isn't very strong. I wish I were rich—I've all the tastes of an idler, with none of the facilities. My poverty is pinching me more tightly than ever—indeed, all my troubles seem to be closing in upon me. The loneliness and monotony of my life are hurting me more and more, too. I wish I could see some way out, but there's none visible at present.

I enclose a lyric or two—nothing at all good. I may try some short-story-writing, tho I hate the drudgery of it. I used to write stories, years and years ago, and even sold a few of them to magazines!

I await the Letters of Lafcadio Hearn with eagerness.[1] Hearn, as I've probably told you, is one of my favourite prose-writers.

I've just been reading the poems of Rupert Brooke. Many of them, I think, are splendid, especially some of the sonnets (not the war-sonnets, tho those are very good in their way) and certain others. "Dining-Room Tea," "The Great Lover," "Blue Evening," etc. I draw the line, tho, at "Jealousy", and the sonnet on sea-sickness! Outside of Baudelaire, I've never seen anything quite like the former. There are suggestions of Baudelaire, and also of John Donne, in many of the poems. I don't understand your aversion to Brooke—is it because of his popularity?

Write me soon, please, and send the rest of the Scene for Lear, if you've finished it. I'll write again soon as the books arrive.

> Faithfully,
>> Clark.

Notes

1. See Bibliography under Elizabeth Bisland.

[53]   [ALS]

> Auburn, Cal.,
>> April 26th, 1916.

Dear Sam:

Please pardon my delay in acknowledging the Letters of Lafcadio Hearn. I've been a little more under the weather than usual, and have had little heart or energy for correspondence. I'm very much ashamed that your letter and the new chapter of "Philip Heather", have found the volumes still unacknowledged.

The books came safely, and without a scratch, tho the wrapping was broken in one or two places. Many, many thanks to you for the hours of entertainment they have given me. Hearn's personality, and his life, seem no less remarkable than his extraordinary writings.

I like "Philip Heather," and certainly hope that you finish it, even tho prose, as an art, is far inferior to verse. Good fiction is well worth writing; and I'm not praising you so *very* much when I say that yours is far out of the current ruck.

I enclose the few verses that I've written lately—nothing that seems at all good or satisfactory to me. "The Crucifixion of Eros" is a good enough conception, but the phraseology seems flat, and the versification intolerably monotonous. The other poems are full of my usual faults—harshness and obscurity. I enclose also a few epigrams—the result of reading Oscar Wilde.

I just don't feel in the mood for ode-writing. The sonnet and the brief lyric seem better fitted for the class of conceptions in which I deal at present. I'm coming to share Poe's prejudice against length in a poem, anyway. You'll note that I'm trying to train myself more to the expression of sentiment—a thing that's very difficult for me. So far, the effect upon my form is that of new wine on old bottles.

I shall expect the new volumes of Oscar Wilde with eagerness. I *do* wish I could give you something in return! You overwhelm me with kindness.

> Affectionately,
>
> Clark.

[54]   SL to CAS [nonextant]

[Envelope postmarked Cleveland, Ohio, May 4, 1916.]

[55]   [ALS]

> Auburn, Cal.,
>
> May 8th, 1916.

Dear Sam:

Your note, and the last of the three prose-poems came yesterday. I've been intending to acknowledge the others for several days past, but somehow, I've kept putting it off. I'm sorry that I'm such a wretched correspondent.

I like all of the three prose-poems, tho "The Flagellant" is my favourite. Personally, I don't see why the writing of prose should injure one's faculty for poetic composition. It's rare, tho, to find a writer who combines the two talents in equal degree. Most of us have to specialize in art, for the highest success.

I've written little of anything, myself, other than the beginning of a poem on Nora May French, which I enclose. Do you think the fragment worth finishing? I wish I had more heart [to]* work. My personal life is barren and un-happy to a degree that almost kills the literary impulse in me. It's the irony of my life that the things which **could** make me happiest are always the things which seem destined to make me suffer most.

I don't know when my next book will be published. The price of paper has gone up on account of the war, so the issue will have to be delayed. The war seems to affect everything.

I'll try to write you again very soon. This note seems all that I'm capable of to-day.

> Affectionately,
> Clark.

[56]   [ALS]

> Auburn, Cal.,
> May 23rd, 1916.

Dear Sam:

Your last letter has been lying on my desk for several days, but, as usual, I've put off answering it. I'd like to write you oftener—truly, I always intend to—but it's hard to spin a letter out of nothing, especially when one is tired and half-sick most of the time . . . I, too, have few regular correspond-ents—you and George are almost the only ones.

I *have* the Everyman edition of Beaumont and Fletcher, which you speak of sending. I'd be very glad, too, to have the Johnson [*sic*], since there's noth-ing of Johnson's in my library. My collection (some two hundred odd vol-umes) is of a very miscellaneous nature. The bulk of it is poetry, and the philosophy is mostly contained in a volume of selections from Schopenhauer. I've read very little fiction lately, outside of Poe and de Maupassant, and have read Symons and Dowson more than any other poets. Dowson, in particular, fascinates me, and his life interests me as much as the poems.

I've re-read your prose-poems, and find myself liking them more and more. The conceptions are all splendid and original. I think I told you that I liked "The Flagellant" best. Your worst fault is an occasional vagueness or obscurity of phrase, but flaws of that sort are not fatal, if the main conception is clear.

The magazines are "impossible," when it comes to poetry. I can't sell *any-thing* at all, and have practically given up trying. Postage stamps are too expen-sive! I can understand, tho, why they don't want my work. Peculiarity of diction and subject-matter are enough to damn an unknown writer, in this day when the banal and the commonplace seem to have been exalted into a sort of reli-gion. Democracy, and Walt Whitman, are demoralizing modern literature.

I hope I'll have something to send you when I write again. The worst of it is that I've gotten to the point where I don't half care whether I work or

---

*[word obscured by inkblot]

not. My life here exposes me to what De Quincey calls "the formidable curse of taedium vitae,"[1] and, apart from that, I am never in good health. It isn't easy to go on, under the circumstances.

I'm writing this after a long walk in the river-canyon nearby. I wish you might have been with me—you would have enjoyed it so much more than I did. Even the beauties of nature get to be a bore, when one doesn't see anything else. I collected a dozen different kinds of wild flowers during the walk, including the blossoms of the wild syringa, which is very much like the garden variety. One ravine that I passed was full of the fragrance of wild grape-flowers.

I enclose something that George sent me. It may amuse you a little. The comments are by John Neihardt, the Nebraska poet.[2]

> Affectionately,
> Clark

Notes

1. From a note appended in 1856 to the original preface (1822) to *Confessions of an Opium Eater*. In *The Collected Writings of Thomas De Quincey* (London: A & C. Black, 1897), 3.214.
2. John Gneisenau Neihardt (1881–1973), American writer and poet, amateur historian, ethnographer, and correspondent of GS.

[57]   [ALS]

> Auburn, Cal.,
> May 26th, 1916.

Dear Sam:

The volumes of B. J.[1] and your letter, are both "at hand," as they say in commercial parlance. The books came the same day that I mailed my last letter. I've only had time to glance through them as yet, but foresee a lot of solid enjoyment in many of the plays. I am already familiar with "The Alchemist," and one or two others. On the whole, I much prefer Webster and Marlowe (I have the latter complete) to Johnson. "The Duchess of Malfi" is my favourite among Elizabethan plays, outside of Shakespeare. Many, many thanks to you for the volumes—if thanks could only repay you!

I fear you'll get d——d little satisfaction out of such people as Braithwaite. When it comes to critics, I'd much prefer a stuffed owl, myself. He possesses an almost unerring instinct for piffle, and no instinct whatever for anything else.

I'm eager to see the new prose-poems of which you speak. I don't know when I'll finish the poem on Nora May. I feel so indifferent toward work, so distracted with desire for everything my life (better say, existence) denies me, that it's difficult for me to do anything. Art is only the shadow of life, after all. I'd rather *live* one poem than merely *write* a thousand. I know (as surely as I know anything) that literary fame or achievement, by themselves, can mean little or nothing to me in the way of happiness.

I'm glad you like "The Crucifixion of Eros." A thousand such poems, tho, aren't worth the price that one pays for the inspiration.

I've heard nothing from my publisher for a long time, so I've really no idea as to when he'll be ready to put out my next book. George told me that he thought the going up of paper would necessitate some delay.

> As ever, Affectionately,
> Clark.

Notes

1. Ben Jonson (1572–1647), English playwright, poet, actor, and literary critic.

[58]   [ALS]

> Auburn, Cal.,
> June 9th, 1916.

Dear Sam:

The exquisite little volume of "Studies in Sentiment,"[1] came Wednesday. I think the stories very beautiful, very precious, and delicately done—much in the spirit of the poems. The binding and the paper are a delight to the hand and the eye. I love small volumes—don't you?—something that one can carry in one's pocket. This one is just the right size. Many thanks to you, and again, many thanks!

I've not heard from George for some time—for a very good reason, since I've not yet answered his last letter. As far as I know, he is still in San Francisco; he returned from his tour in Southern California several weeks ago.

As usual, I've little or no news. I've written two or three poems, of which I'll send you copies presently. **All** the things that I write, cry out for a revision that I am powerless to give them.

I am eager to see your new prose-poem. I've projected a number of prose-poems, myself, but, for the present, I seem to have more of a talent for titles than for anything else. I've a whole note-book full of titles and conceptions.[2]

This is only a note. I've had a sleepless night, and feel too stupid for anything more. I'm looking for a letter from you, but will write you again very soon, in any case.

> Affectionately,
> Clark.

Notes

1. By Ernest Dowson.
2. Published as *The Black Book of Clark Ashton Smith*.

[59]   [ALS]

Auburn, Cal.,
June 24th, 1916.

Dear Sam:

The prose-poems and your letter are both at hand. In some respects, I think "The Faun" is the best and most beautiful of your prose-pieces. The conception is extremely original, and very finely wrought, with much imaginative detail. I'm very glad to have it, and am eager to see the new one of which you speak. I'd like to see *all* your prose-poems published in book-form.

The book of which you speak will interest me very much. To what unfortunate and tragic ends they all came,—the poets of the 90's!

I'm writing this after a night of the most infernal torture. I've had a toothache, a head-ache, and a wicked attack of chills, fever, and sweating, all at the same time! I'll have to have a tooth pulled to-day, possibly. The dentist has been trying to kill the nerve, but I don't think he succeeded very well. The drugs that he used, nearly poisoned me.

I don't seem to have anything worth sending you. I've not tried to write much lately. George wants me to try some of my new poems on the magazines. But, oh, hell, what's the use!

I'm expecting George's new book, almost any day. *That's* something to look forward to, at any rate. Robertson won't be able to do anything with my next volume till 1917; I've been trying to find a collection title for it (since I'll not care to use a title-poem) and have almost decided upon "Poppy and Cypress", tho I'm not any too fond of floral titles. I thought also of "Bronze, Ebony, and Silver." "The Flowers of Night" would be a better one, if it weren't too suggestive of "The Flowers of Evil." Can you think of anything yourself?

As ever,
Clark.

[60]   [ALS]

Cleveland, Ohio.
[29 June 1916?]

Dear Clark,

I'm awfully glad that you like "The Faun"—I wrote the last part of it one Sunday on the bank of a ruined canal near our locality—waist-deep in buttercups & high grasses. I love those lonely places. Nature, for once, seems to forget the wounds & the torture of mankind & becomes herself again.

I'm going to apologise about the "1890's".[1] Our servant has either mislaid or lost it along with two or three others, so that if you will accept my apology & take it philosophically I shall try to procure you another one. It is already out of print in America but I believe that I can procure one in England. I keep most of my book upstairs in my room but I took your copy below—hence! Oh, it exasperates me to think of it! I came home one evening &

found my "Nuremburg Chronicle"—A.D. 1493, exceedingly damp.[2] Further inquiry revealed the fact that the Kitchen Mechanic had given the covers a cleansing (thoroughly, she assured me) with soap & water. I believe I sum[?].

By the way, Clark, have you Plato? I am going to mail you at the end of the week a copy of the cat of Swinburne's library which went up for auction in London this month. I bid on one item, a Beaumont & Fletcher in folio.

I rather regret that your bookseller can't print your book this year. It seems to be high-tide with everything and columns are devoted critically to people who couldn't tie your latchets. I like the title "Poppy & Cypress"— still, there may be something even better that will turn up. I still think of that marvellous poem "Satan Unrepentant"—and that, as I once had occasion to tell you, will make a hellofa good title.

I sent a copy of the Mosher[3] collection of Dowson's stories to Victor Plarr who wrote the recent life of him. He had never read them!—having been (he confesses) in the Jap. camp at the time but he is writing an article on the book & will send it to me. (Of course, I want you to see it too). He tells me that he has discovered a bunch of new Dowson letters. Some day next month I'll send you a copy of Plarr's book[4] with another volume of short stories that Dowson published in his lifetime—"Dilemmas"—beautifully graven things.

I'm distressed over George's non-reply to my letter and I catechise[5] myself & wonder if I offended him. Of course, I shall write him to find out. I'm awaiting his book with much eagerness. His position in English literature seems so assured that it is marvellous to wonder at the stupes who still persist in classing him with the "contemporary poets!"—ah, "contemporary"—in a certain sense of the word.

I'll write you Sunday, Clark. Write soon—

Affectionately
Sam

P.S. I copy the Beardsley letter for you.

[P.P.S.?]
You delighted me so with your appreciation of the "Faun" that I'm going to write a companion to it, the "Sphinx." It's going to be frankly Decadent, however, and full of roccocco [*sic*]. (or some such thing.) Arthur Symons once said that prose should be played upon as a master does a violin—it most assuredly has wonderful melodic possibilities.

You mention the fate of most of the "Yellow Book" clique. I heard the following at second-hand but my authority is safe. A woman (from Ohio) visited Stephen Phillips shortly before he died. She came back and to an inquiry concerning the poet merely answered—"Simply rotten!"—which leaves room enow for one's imagination. Arthur Symons (so I heard) is a hopeless paralytic. He will never write again. Most of the stuff of his that one sees published

nowadays was written years ago. Did you read his fine one-act drama on Cleopatra in last month's "Forum?"[6]

Well, Clark, I believe I've bored you to the limit. I'm just getting over an
attack of the blues and as a consequence rather talkative. I'm not much of a
talker, as it is. There are whole days when I keep my mouth complacently
closed—— And so.

Aff.

S L.

[Envelope postmarked Cleveland, Ohio, June 29, 1916.] [envelope placed
here conjecturally]

Notes

1. See Bibliography under Holbrook Jackson.
2. See Bibliography under Hartmann Schedel.
3. Thomas Bird Mosher (1852–1923), American publisher in Portland, Maine; notable
member of the private press movement in the United States, and major exponent of
the English Pre-Raphaelites and other English Victorians.
4. Victor Gustave Plarr (1863–1929), English poet. The book in question is *Ernest
Dowson 1888–1897* (1914).
5. SL meant to write "chastise."
6. *Cleopatra in Judea, Forum* 55 (June 1916): 643–60.

[61]   [ALS]

Auburn, Cal.,

July 10th, 1916.

Dear Sam:

Please pardon my long delay in answering your letters. Even letter-
writing has been too much for me of late, and I already owe four or five others, besides this.

I like your last prose-poem—"He Who Found Pity." I've mislaid it for
the present, so I can't speak of it in detail. Your prose-pieces will make a fine
volume some day. The new subject you mention sounds good to me.

I've just received George's new book. I like "Conspiracy" best, tho there
are many good things in the volume. Some of the war-sonnets ought to put a
flea in the ear of any German sympathizer.[1]

I'll certainly be glad to have the books of which you speak. Anything on
Dowson would interest me. The books you send me are among the treasures
of my library.

That's news to me about Symons. Baudelaire (as I believe) died of paralysis, too. There are many other things that I would prefer to die of, myself—
even consumption would be better than *that*. . . . I hardly ever see the Forum,

so I've not read the play of which you speak.

I enclose a few verses. I've sent out a number of my things to the magazines lately, tho I've little hope of selling anything. I wish I could, tho—I need the money so much. Poverty seems to make everything impossible.

Please excuse this wretched scrawl, and repay good for ill by writing me before long. I'll write again in a few days.

Affectionately,

Clark.

Notes

1. *The Caged Eagle* contains a section titled "On the Great War" with many poems on the subject. These were later gathered, with additional poems, in *The Binding of the Beast and Other War Verse* (1917).

[62]   [ALS]

Auburn, Cal.,

Aug. 1st, 1916

Dear Sam:

You seem to have missed my last letter, since I'm fairly sure that I wrote you not so long ago. However, both of *your* letters are safely at hand, maugre the carelessness and incompetence of the Auburn post-office.

I'm awfully sorry to hear that you are so unwell. I'm much better, myself, for the time being, as far as my physical condition goes . . . Defective circulation can play some queer tricks. Mine is very poor at times, and has given me some of the most alarming symptoms. I even though that I had arthritis, a few years ago.

I've written nothing at all during the last month, beyond a few entries in my note-book. I think of writing a number of fables and prose-fantasies, and already have titles and ideas—or the germs of ideas—for eight or ten. Here's one, copied from my note-book. I hardly know what I'll make of it as yet: "A man in royal robes, mounted on a chimera, comes riding into the city of Nuth from the desert at the world's end, proclaiming himself the king of No-Man's-Land."[1] Everything in these prose-pieces must be as wild, and weird, and strange, and utterly monstrous, as I can make it. Nothing will do but nightmares, Hippogriphs, hashish, dragons'-blood, black angels, poisonous perfumes, mountains of emerald, black flowers, animated mummies, prophesying peacocks, moons of ebony, and deserts of opal-dust.

The summer has been phenomenally cool, here in California, except for a few days now and then. The weather to-day is remarkably like autumn weather—there's the same feeling in the air, the same softness and tempered warmth. Autumn, by the way, is my favourite season, tho I rarely write much at that time.

I don't seem to have anything to send you this time. If I do anything with any of the prose-fantasies, I shall, of course, send you a copy. I feel anything but industrious, when it comes to the point of actual composition.

I fear I'm an execrable sort of correspondent. I owe George a letter, besides the two or three that I owe to you. I've a fatal tendency to let everything slide,—a tendency that extends even to my letter-writing.

Good luck to you! Write soon, and tell me that things are better. I'm hoping that your health will improve,—as it certainly should, if you give yourself a chance, and if the reasons are only physical ones. Nervous ill-health with a mental or emotional basis is the most difficult to cure.

As ever,

Clark.

Notes

1. *The Black Book* 72.

[63]   [ANS][1]

[Postmarked Cleveland, Ohio,
Aug. 15, 1916.]

Dear Clark—

A letter soon. I ask your pardon for my neglect. My mother[2] has been dangerously sick.

Faithfully

Sam

Notes

1. *Front:* Blank.
2. Rosa (Goodman) Loveman (1857–1942).

[64]   [ALS]

Auburn, Cal.,
Sept. 18th, 1916.

Dear Sam:

I've been intending to write you, all these many days (or is it months) but, somehow, I haven't—partly, perhaps, because I was looking for a letter from you all the time, and partly because of a state of mental, or rather, emotional depression which has left me in no mood even for correspondence. Even letter-writing has to wait upon inspiration, with me.

I like the melodious poem that you enclose. I wish I could send you something in return. But I've done nothing at all, since the last sonnet that I sent you. I've recently sold one of my sonnets ("Love Malevolent,") to a magazine called "Snappy Stories." They paid me the princely sum of $3.00!

The editor refused some of my other sonnets as being "too hectic."

My mother[1] has been laid up with a bruised leg for the last month or more, and my father has had sciatica. Consequently, everything has devolved upon me. I've worked part of the time, to earn a little money. It's hell to do that, when one is unhappy. I, too, would go to the devil, if I were free. Life seems to hold nothing but torture for me, and apparently, I lack the power to make myself or anyone else happy. So far, I've succeeded only in hurting myself (and worse still) in hurting someone for whom I care.

I wish I could be a good Christian (since I lack the opportunities for being anything but a bad pagan.) If I could believe in Christianity, I would make a good woman very happy—happier, perhaps, than I could make her in any other way. But alas, anything of the sort would be absolutely impossible. I could no more believe in revealed religion than I could believe in fetichism. Yet, in a way, I can see the advantages of such belief.

This isn't much of a letter. I'll try to write again before long.

> Affectionately,
> Clark.

Notes

1. Mary Frances (Gaylord) Smith (1850–1935).

[65]   [ALS]

[c. 6 October 1916]

Dear Clark,

I want to ask your pardon for not writing oftener. I've been sick for nearly 2 weeks & was even home from work for a few days. I believe I told you of the trouble I had with my hand. It originated from nervous trouble. The 1st doctor I went to scared me into seven fits by telling me that it might mean paralysis. This was the M.D. who "saw" my Father "off." At that time he told someone in the family that I "didn't look good." So I went to another one and *he* told me that it was poor circulation. Of course, there's no smoke without fire & I'll have to stop burning the candle at both ends. Anyhow, things aren't exactly as they should be with me.

I received George's book but I was only able to give him a perfunctory acknowledgement at the time. It contains noble & inspired poetry and the war-sonnets will raise a holocaust of argument.

I'm awaiting a letter from you most any day. Forgive this scribble.

> Yours as ever,
> Sam

P. S. I'm having Burrows procure the Dowson books. I've a lot of new Clare material coming from abroad. Five Clare letters to his publisher (Taylor &

Hessey) who were Keats' friends, a humorous letter to the London Magazine, etc. I'll make a transcription for you if I find them as interesting as my agent says they are.

SL

[Envelope postmarked Cleveland, Ohio, Oct. 6, 1916.]

[66]   [ALS]

Auburn, Cal.

Oct. 7th, 1916.

Dear Sam:

Will you ever pardon my delay in acknowledging the book on Oscar Wilde,[1] and the facsimile of the Keats MS.? I've been worried (and harried) to death for weeks, and this letter to you is the first that I've written in many days. I'm treating you shabbily, I know, but, even at that, you fare better than any other of my correspondents.

For the book, many thanks! I like much of the criticism, particularly the part about "The Sphinx,"—the only adequate appreciation of the poem that I remember to have seen. The Keats Ms. is very interesting—but what an awful handwriting—almost as bad as mine!

I enclose three poems, two of which were written recently, the other ("Coldness") sometime in June. For safety's sake, I've been trying to throw myself into my work by main force—and these poems are the result. "The Kingdom of Madness" is symbolical of a spiritual (or emotional) state.

I enclose also a letter from the Atlantic Monthly. The poems rejected were "Inheritance," "Orion," and "The Orchid of Beauty."

That's a d——d good idea, about publishing your Clare material. You should certainly be able to write a good introduction.

I, too, have given away some of my work. "Coldness" appeared recently in a San Francisco weekly called "Bohemia," and I've given "The Refuge of Beauty" to "Town Talk." Nary a copper bean have I raised for either of them.

My mother and father are both improving. They celebrated their silver wedding yesterday. My best friend here is very ill, so my worries aren't over, by any means. Her disease (consumption) seems to have reached an acute stage. I can't bear to think what her death would mean to me.[2]

Do you ever see a magazine called "Vanity Fair?" There's an article on Poe in the last number, written by Arthur Symons.[3]

I may have some more poems to send you, when I write again. Don't think that you've seen my worst, when you read the ones enclosed. I've written and destroyed several that were rottener than these!

Affectionately, as ever,

Clark.

Notes

1. Probably *Oscar Wilde: A Critical Study* by Arthur Ransome.
2. CAS refers to Mamie Lowe Miller, who died in November 1917. He dedicated "Requiescat in Pace" to her (as M. L. M.).
3. "On a Certain Misconception of Poe," *Vanity Fair* 7, No. 2 (October 1916): 57.

[67]   [ALS, JHL]

Auburn, Cal.

Oct. 24th, 1916.

Dear Sam:

Your card, and the volume of Flecker's poems[1] are both at hand, but no letter, as yet. I've delayed writing because I expected one from day to day, but I'm ashamed to put it off any longer.

I enjoyed the volume of poems greatly—many of Flecker's things are very much to my taste, tho some are perhaps too colloquial, and others somewhat obscure. I particularly like "Felo de Se," "Mary Magdalen," "Mignon," "Tenebris Interlucentem," "Gravis Dulcis Immutabilis," and the translations from Baudelaire—also certain parts of the "Town Without a Market," the poems on Helen of Troy and the fascinating (tho not perfectly intelligible) sonnets of Bathrolaire. My sincerest thanks to you for the volume. By the way, there's an interesting article on Flecker in a late (I think the October) number of the Bookman.[2] This article quotes from a later volume, entitled "The Golden Journey to Samarkand, and other Poems." Some of the quotations are very fine.

I've written nothing new since the last poems I sent you. Everything seems to hang fire with me. I've not sold anything lately—my one recent sale seems to have been pure accident—"the exception that proves the rule." I hope things are better with you.

Have just been reading the Journal of Marie Bashkirtseff[3] for the first time. Are you familiar with the book? It saddens, fascinates me, stirs my sympathy, tho certain portions are tedious or trivial, as they could hardly help being, in a transcript from life.

Good luck to you! I'll try to send you something in the way of poetry, or at least prose, before long.

Affectionately,

Clark

Notes

1. Probably *Forty-two Poems* (1911), which includes all the poems mentioned in the next paragraph. Flecker (1884–1915) was an English poet and playwright.

2. Milton Bronner, "James Elroy Flecker: English Parnassian," *Bookman* (New York) 43 (August 1916): 631–36.

3. Bashkirtseff, a diarist, painter, and sculptor who died at the age of twenty-five, kept a diary since the age of thirteen that offers a near-novelistic account of the late nineteenth century European bourgeoisie.

[68]   SL to CAS [nonextant]

[Envelope postmarked Cleveland, Ohio, Nov. 6, 1916.]

[69]   [ALS]

Auburn, Cal.,

Nov. 20th, 1916.

Dear Sam:

Will you pardon my delay in acknowledging the "Contemporary Portraits?" I've been about half-sick lately, between my teeth and my stomach, and your letter has overtaken me in the midst of my good, but, as usual, unexecuted intentions.

Yes, I like Harris'[1] book (not all of it, by any means—many things that he says impress me as being too prejudiced or too impertinent). I enjoyed the articles on Wilde, Davidson, and Meredith in particular. I am in your debt once more for much pleasure, as well as for a valuable addition to my library.

Harris' life of Wilde must be tremendously interesting, and I should certainly like to read it, if ever I have the opportunity . . . I've seen extracts from the newly-published portion of "De Profundis."[2]

I enclose a few trifles, mostly in prose. I seem to have written less this year than ever before. At present, I hardly feel up to anything. My weight is down to 109 lbs.—a falling-off of 8 lbs in the last three weeks. My stomach has troubled me a great deal, and I've had any number of toothaches, together with a total loss of appetite.

Mrs. Miller, the friend whom I mentioned, is better. Yes, she writes poetry—she has even sold some of her things to the "Sunset Magazine," which is more than I've succeeded in doing. I'll hunt up copies of them for you, sometime.

You pay my "Satan Unrepentant" a tremendous compliment. I only wish that my work deserved half the praise that my friends have accorded it. Did I tell you that I had decided on "The Flowers of Night" as the title of my new book? It seems more appropriate, and more memorable than any other.

I'll hunt up my copy of "The Faun" and send it to George next time I write. I think that one is my favourite among your prose-poems. Certainly it's a thing that one doesn't forget—its beauties impressed themselves upon me at the first reading, and I retain a most definite memory of the piece, tho I've not come across it for many months.

Write soon! I shall, whenever possible, and I'll try not to delay so much in the future, unless I'm really too ill to write.

Affectionately, as ever,

Clark.

Notes

1. Frank Harris (1855–1931), Irish editor, novelist, short story writer, journalist, and publisher.
2. Wilde's *De Profundis,* a letter he wrote in Reading Gaol in 1897, was first published as a book in 1905, edited by Robert Ross. In 1915 Ross issued an expanded edition (London: Methuen), but even that edition contained only about half of Wilde's text.

[70]   [ALS]

Auburn, Cal.

Dec. 23rd, 1916.

Dear Sam:

Please excuse any delay in answering your last letter. I've been in San Francisco since the first of the week, and only returned last night, so this is really the first opportunity that I've had for letter-writing.

I'm sorry to hear that you've had the grippe. There's nothing that lays one out more, with the possible exception of malaria. I feel better, myself, than I have for some time past, tho I've been coughing a good deal all morning. The doctor tells me that my right lung is affected, and I'm under orders to keep quiet, live in the open air, and eat all the eggs and milk that I can get.

I saw George while I was in the city; also my publisher, who tells me that the edition of my book (2000 copies) is nearly all sold. He doesn't want to put out another, tho, till the price of paper comes down.

I, too, was shocked to learn of London's death.[1] While I was in the city, I attended a memorial service held by the San Francisco Socialists. George was one of the speakers, and his talk on London was all that saved the occasion. The Socialists (mainly Russian Jews) seemed to think of nothing but passing the hat. They asked for contributions at the end of every speech, and kicked afterwards because the audience wasn't liberal enough! Socialism is all right in the abstract, but the socialists themselves are a mangy lot.

Yes, I've read Watts-Dunton's essay in the Britannica[2]—the best thing on the subject that I know, with the exception of Shelley's essay,[3] and one or two by Poe.[4]

Write me soon. I'll send you some new prose-poems, as soon as I have time to make copies of them. I want to send you some new drawings that I've made, too, since you liked the others so well.

Affectionately,

Clark.

Notes

1. When the American writer Jack London (b. 1876) died on 22 November, he had been suffering from dysentery, late-stage alcoholism, and uremia. He was a close friend of GS. GS believed that London committed suicide, but most scholars now affirm that London died of uremia, as stated on his death certificate.

2. Theodore Watts-Dunton (1832–1914), English critic and poet, wrote the essay "Poetry" in *Encyclopædia Britannica* (9th ed.), discussing the first principles of poetry.

3. Percy Bysshe Shelley, "A Defence of Poetry" (1821), published posthumously in *Essays, Letters from Abroad, Translations and Fragments* (1840).

4. "The Poetic Principle" (1850) and "The Philosophy of Composition" (1846).

[71]   [ALS]

Auburn, Cal.,
Dec. 28th, 1916.

Dear Sam:

I dare say you will have received my last letter by this time. Yours came rather belatedly, having been missent to some town in Southern California!

I feel hellishly sorry, and guilty, because I've procrastinated so much in writing to you. I *could* have sent you a card; but I hate postcards, and am so little in the habit of using them, that it never occurred to me. I meant to write, and reproached myself at the end of each day because I had not done so. But the weariness, weakness and languor from which I suffer, overcame me, and I simply let things drift. I fear that some of my correspondents are hopelessly offended, and will never forgive my silence during these last months.

I told you, did I not, that I had been to see the doctor? I've simply *had* to obey his orders during the last week. The day after my return from San Francisco, I caught the worst cold in all my experience, and have done nothing but cough ever since. I've been kept awake by it every alternate night. The weather is perfectly abominable—rain, frost, anchor-ice, fog, drizzle, and a little snow. And yet the real-estate agents call this country the "citrus belt." I'd hate to be an orange-tree in Auburn on a December night. The fruit on those that grow here develops a skin half an inch thick, to protect itself against the cold.

My friend is better again, after her last acute illness. Her powers of recuperation are marvellous. She always makes me think of the Lady Ligeia, in Poe's story. It is marvellous, too, how little she shows the effect of her disease. People find it hard to believe that she has consumption, because her appearance is so healthy and without the characteristic emaciation.

The Chatterton autographic material of which you speak, must be very interesting and valuable. When do you find all those things?—You seem to have a wonderful collection of them.

Thanks for your kind wishes, Sam. Here are mine for all the health and happiness that the coming years can bring you!

    Affectionately,

                Clark.

[72] [ALS]

                             Auburn, Cal.

                           Jan. 4th, 1917.

Dear Sam:

    The books came on New Year's Day, and I've read both of them through. I like the "Vision of Love"[1] very much—it is beautiful, melodious, imaginative, and full of infinite vague suggestions. The "Pilgrimage of Pleasure" gives me a heightened opinion of Swinburne's critical sanity and acumen. I like the articles on Solomon and Charles Wells, the review of Baudelaire, and the appreciation of Dickens. I was a little surprised by the last. Please accept my most cordial thanks for the two volumes. I wish I could send you something in return; but I'd hardly dare send a book, since I suppose you have nearly everything.

    The last two days have been clear, with a little frost in the mornings. Everything points to an early spring this year,—the leaves of the cyclamen are out, and the acacia-trees are already beginning to bud. I'm happy that the back of the winter is broken—but still, one never can tell, in California.

    I've recently sold two of my poems to a magazine called "Live Stories," the same that published my sonnet, "Love Malevolent." They paid me eight dollars for two![2]

    The 13th of this present month will be my 24th birthday. The thought of it makes me feel ancient and venerable. However, I still have a chance to die at the same age as Keats![3]

    I'm looking for a letter from you almost any day. Please write whenever you can. For my part, I shall try to be a better correspondent in the future. I've treated you shamefully at times in the past; but I shan't any more, unless it happens that I'm seriously ill.

    Affectionately, your friend,

                Clark.

Notes

1. By Simeon Solomon.

2. So far as is known, only one poem aside from "Love Malevolent" appeared in *Live Stories:* "Give Me Your Lips."

3. John Keats (1795–1821) died at the age of 25.

[73]   [ALS]

Auburn, Cal.,

Jan. 16th, 1917.

Dear Sam:

My wits are nearly frozen (not to mention my fingers) from the
north-east wind that's been blowing off the Sierras for the last two days. The
cold is almost without precedent for this section; certainly I've never suffered
so much from it before as I have this year. The weather is clear, tho, except
for an occasional fog that drifts in from the coast.

I've not succeeded in writing anything lately. The poems I enclose were
written in October, but I don't remember having sent them to you before.
Both of them have been published (one in "Live Stories," the other in "Snappy Stories," two very cheap magazines that seem to make a specialty of the
erotic.)[1] I seem to be breaking into print more of late—my "Memnons of the
Night" is due to appear in a San Francisco publication called "Bohemia."

I'll send you the pictures presently; but I simply haven't had the energy to do
anything with them so far. I'm tired and languid half the time, and nearly crazy
with nervous irritation the other half. As to my chest condition, I hardly know—
t. b. is so insidious and uncertain, and the symptoms differ so in individuals. I
cough a good deal at times, and suffer from occasional pain or discomfort in
the chest; but for the present, I don't seem to be losing in weight or strength.

George was well as ever when I saw him in the city. His hair is turning
grey—the only thing about him that betrays his age. However, that's nothing—I have a few grey hairs myself.

I'm still in the dark as to the publication of my next book. Robertson
seems inclined to wait till the price of paper drops—but the devil knows
when *that* will be. I wish I could afford to do my own printing—these delays
are getting on my nerves.

I should be very glad indeed to have anything else that Johnson has written. The "Vision of Love" is pure poetry, both in substance and form.

Write soon, if you can. I'll try to send you the drawings before long.

Affectionately,

Clark.

Notes

1. The poem that appeared in *Snappy Stories* at this time was "A Prayer."

[74]   [ALS]

Auburn, Cal.,

Jan. 22nd, 1917.

Dear Sam:

This is only a note, to acknowledge your last letter, and accompany the package. You may like to have the copy of my book that I'm sending, for the friend of whom you speak, who was unable to obtain one. I have practically the entire remainder of the edition (25 copies or so) and I don't think there were more than half a dozen on sale in S. F. at the time of my visit. I suppose they're all gone by this time. Nora May French's book is out of print, too—I obtained one of the last ten copies from a friend while I was in the city, and I hear that none are obtainable now.

I'm sending a few of my new pictures along with the book. If you care for them, I'll be glad to make you copies of some others that I have. Drawing is one of my chief amusements.

Pardon the brevity of this. I'm tired this morning (I took a long walk yesterday, in express disobedience of my doctor's orders) and I have several other unanswered letters on my conscience. I'll write you more at length in a few days.

> Affectionately, your friend,
> Clark.

[75]   [ALS]

> Auburn, Cal.,
> Feb. 11th, 1917.

Dear Sam:

Many, many thanks for the beautiful volume of Simeon Solomon.[1] The half-tone reproductions are exquisite, and as for the pictures themselves, I must say that I like them better than those of Watts, or any other Pre-Raphaelite except Rossetti. Of course, I am unable to criticize them from a technical standpoint—I speak merely of the imaginative impression that they make upon me. Certainly they are remarkable; there is a quality of weirdness and strangeness in most of them that appeals peculiarly to me—a weirdness that even Rossetti doesn't always achieve. Some of the faces are such as one might see in the mist and twilight of No-Man's-Land—faces that have looked upon the Abomination of Desolation, till they themselves are turned to ashes and shadow, retaining but the mask of human form.

Pardon my delay in writing. I've had precious little news, even less than usual, and it hardly seemed worth while to write. My health is about the same, or perhaps a little better—at any rate, nothing to be alarmed about, since I've been really nearer to a breakdown at several times in the past. I'm beginning to think that my doctor was a false prophet—he told me that I had a pretty good chance of dying in a few years, if I wasn't careful.

I've written nothing, but have read a good deal lately, mostly in the way of fiction. I go on a periodical debauch of novel-reading, and sometimes average one a day, for weeks or months at a time.

Glad you liked the drawings so well. I'll make you some more presently,—I get in the mood for drawing every once in a while.

I'm still hesitating over the title of my next book. I want something to indicate the mixed nature of the collection—something like "Ebony and Cinnabar," tho there ought to be a still better one than that. "Flowers of Night" is hardly appropriate for some of the poems. . . . "Ebony and Silver" would have been a good title for my first book, since most of the poems are in black-and-white.

Ever yours, Affectionately,

Clark.

Notes

1. Possibly Julia Ellsworth Ford, *Simeon Solomon: An Appreciation* (New York: Frederick Fairchild Sherman, 1908), which contains 23 half-tone reproductions of Solomon's paintings.

[76]　[ALS]

Auburn, Cal.,

April 3rd, 1917.

Dear Sam:

Did you get my last letter? I've not heard from you for so long, that I begin to think that either my letter, or yours, must have miscarried. So I'll write you another.

As usual, I've a dearth of news. I seem to keep in uncommonly good health (physically, at least) due, perhaps, to the fact that I've done little or no work for a long time, and have had comparatively little to worry about. I've not written anything, but have read a great deal, including a number of Balzac's novels, several books by Lafcadio Hearn, Wilde's De Profundis, and a lot of miscellaneous fiction and poetry.

The wild flowers are beautiful now, and the weather perfect, except for a cold north wind that's been blowing all morning. I can't endure a north wind—it always makes me feel cross and mean, and seems to bring all my worst devils with it. I wish you could see the flowers—I've just brought in a great bunch of them—poppies, wild hyacinth, wild iris, Indian paint-brush, cyclamen and a few sprays of the purple night-shade.

Won't you write to me soon, and send me some good word of yourself? Have you written anything lately? I'm sorry I've nothing to send you, but I hope to have, before long. I've idled long enough, and must get myself down to work—which isn't easy, considering my constitutional laziness.

I plan a walking-tour this summer—my father and I think of going to Lake Tahoe. I wish you were here to go with us—you'd love the Sierran scenery.

Affectionately,

Clark.

[77]   [TLS]

[April 1917]

Dear Clark,

   This is the letter I wanted to write last Sunday—but didn't. Our weather has been so cold (12 degrees below zero) and our heating supply of gas so inadequate that I daresay you would have found a communication of mine uncomfortable. For a space of four days we slept in our overcoats. Now that it's all over everybody votes it to have been glorious weather and entirely stimulating.

   I rejoice more than I can tell you to hear of your improvement. Are you gaining in weight under your new treatment? Also, are your Father and Mother both recovered from their illness of last year? Now having catechised you, so to speak, I proceed.

   I was glad to hear of your liking for the Solomon pictures. I wish that one might have an opportunity to view their originals. I want to send you some day this week another Dowson volume which I don't believe you have. It is the "Dilemmas." These are written in the same delicate, unshadowed prose as the "Studies in Sentiment." By the way, Frank Harris, who now edits "Pearson's" has a write-up of Dowson in the current number, entitled "The Swan-song of Youth"—it's awful.[1] He has openly cribbed about half of it from Symon[s]'s essay and the rest of it contains a Zolaesque delineation of Dowson—drunk . . . and poverty-stricken. Victor Plarr has written to me that Dowson never was really hard-up and that he could easily have had a sufficient amount of money to tide him over any difficulty.

   I recently purchased from across [the ocean?], the very rare little 1633 edition of Marston's[2] collected plays—got it for a few shillings on account of defective leaves. At the end are seven pages of the wickedest kind of lampooning epigrams which I am convinced are by Marston himself and more than likely in his handwriting. There is quite frequent mention of w....s and tobacco which are unusually characteristic of Marston in his comedies and beside a little unevenness in the elision that one finds in his blank verse. Here's a clean one—I shouldn't dare to copy any of the others:

   "Katherine, that hid those candles out of sight,
    Might well conceive they'll come at length to light."

I recently wrote to Dr Wallace of Kansas[3] concerning my Shakspere signature but the good Doctor, who himself discovered a new signature of Master Willy in the London office of the archives, hasn't deigned an answer. I wish I could show you the thing. Fraud or forgery it isn't, I could swear, owing to the utter unassuming position of the writing, and besides, much of it has been trimmed in the rebinding of the book. Still, so many people have played dupe to such things that I don't blame their incredibility,[4] but to deny that Shakspere had a library or to deny that he ever appended his name to a volume, as some do, is rank, heretic nonsense. "The Two Noble Kinsmen"—Shakspere's share of it, is bodily taken from Chaucer. N.B. I believe mine is the Chaucer.

Does all this bore you, Clark? Write when you can. With kind and affectionate regards,

S. L.

1537 East 93 St. Suite 2.

P.S. Your last letter was missent (by the postal authorities, of course!) to Oakland! Can you beat it?

Have you read anything of Alan Seeger's, the young American who was killed in France?[5]

Notes

1. Frank Harris, "The Swan-Song of Youth: Ernest Dowson," *Pearson's Magazine* 37 (March 1917): 218–23.
2. John Marston (1575?–1634), English poet, playwright and satirist during the late Elizabethan and Jacobean periods.
3. Charles William Wallace (1865–1932), scholar on English Renaissance drama. He taught not in Kansas but at the University of Nebraska. He and his wife, Olive McEwen Wallace, discovered Shakespeare's 1612 deposition in a lawsuit and other documents by or relating to Shakespeare.
4. SL is said to have pasted Hart Crane's bookplates, obtained after Crane's death, into random books in his own stock and forging Crane's signature on them.
5. Alan Seeger (1888–1916), American poet who died in World War I during the Battle of the Somme, serving in the French Foreign Legion; uncle of American folk singer Pete Seeger.

[78]   [ALS]

Auburn, Cal.,
April 24th, 1917.

Dear Sam:

I am so glad to hear from you again, so sorry to know that you are unwell. Defective circulation (I suffer from it myself) can give rise to all sorts of queer and uncomfortable symptoms; but they're just as painful and bothersome as if the cause were something really serious.

Thanks, hearty thanks for the collection of "Dilemmas". I read them all at a sitting, last night, and, of course, found them very much to my taste. Dowson's talent for story-writing was certainly of a most delicate and distinctive sort. I've placed the book (along with the "Studies in Sentiment") in one of the shelves that I treasure most.

I happen to have nearly all of Oscar Wilde—everything, I believe, but the "Essays." The two that you sent me were the "Novels and Fairy Tales", and the "Plays."

I, too, have read a great deal lately—Hearn's "Stray Leaves from Strange Literature," the plays of Webster and Tourneur,[1] "The Temptation of Saint Anthony" (in a most abominable translation)[2] "The Journal of an Author" by Dostoevsky, Wilde's "Intentions," and "The Philosophy of Disenchantment," by Edgar Saltus, among others.[3] The last-named is a fascinating and finely-written exposition of the history and theory of pessimism.

Personally, I think very highly of Symons (whom you mention). Many of his poems are very much to my taste, and his prose, from what I have seen of it, is uniformly brilliant, or at least excellent. There's an article of his on Swinburne in the last issue of "Vanity Fair" (or "Harper's Bazaar", I forget which)[4] Some of the anecdotes are extremely entertaining.

I seem to keep in pretty fair health, and find myself able to gain weight rather too easily—doubtless because I have been so inactive for months, and have put myself under so little strain, either mental or physical. Loss of weight, however, isn't always a characteristic of t. b.—at least in the early stages. I cough considerably at times, and suffer from occasional pains in the chest and shoulders—otherwise, there's no indication that anything is wrong. In many ways, my health seems improved—I'm not nearly so nervous as I used to be, and my fits of depression are comparatively infrequent.

My trip to Tahoe is all in the air, as yet. I may not go, after all; but if I do, I shall be glad to keep a descriptive diary for you.

The letter of Hartley Coleridge's that you enclose is strange and interesting. The tender and pathetic beauty of many of his sonnets persists in my memory.

Write to me whenever you can. I shall write again before long.

Affectionately,
Clark.

P.S. I enclose a bad sonnet. I've tried to work a little lately, but I'm horribly out of practice, and the hinges in the metrical machinery of my brain are all rusty. However, the poem may interest you.

Notes

1. Cyril Tourneur (1575?–1626), English soldier, diplomat and dramatist.

2. By Gustave Flaubert. CAS probably refers to G. F. Monkshood's translation (1910).

3. Edgar Evertson Saltus (1855–1921), American writer known for his highly refined prose style. SL wrote the "Foreword" to his *Poppies and Mandragora: Poems* (1926).

4. Arthur Symons, "Algernon Charles Swinburne: Memories and Appreciations," *Vanity Fair* 8, No. 2 (April 1917): 61, 136, 138.

[79]   [ALS]

April 30th, 1917.

Dear Sam:

Thanks, hearty thanks for the volume on Dowson. I *do* appreciate Plarr's attitude. The book is tremendously interesting to me, and I am moved and touched by many, many things in it, especially certain passages of the letters.

No, I don't happen to possess Colvin's "Life of Keats."[1] The book is one that I've been wanting to obtain for a long time; but it never seems to have come in my way. Anything pertaining to Keats or Dowson always has a peculiar and surpassing interest for me, since I love both of them so much, and, in certain ways, feel myself akin to both—if it is not too presumptuous for me to say so. The kinship, perhaps, is more in my misfortunes than in my poetry.

I've done very little of late, except a few drawings, which I'll send you presently. For the most part, I've sat around and read, with a pillow behind my shoulders, which ache abominably most of the time. I've not slept well for several nights because of the pain. Apart from that, I don't seem particularly unwell—only tired and nervous, and perhaps a bit feverish at time. I dare say it's partly due to this uncertain weather, and the wild, ferocious north wind; this time of year is always a very trying one for me.

Pardon the brevity, personality, and stupidity of this note. I owe half-a-dozen letters, and my poor head feels as if it had been boiled, steamed, and fried, and afterwards pickled in a solution of vinegar, vermouth, and cod-liver oil.

Affectionately,

Clark.

Notes

1. CAS refers to Colvin's *Keats* (1887). About this time Colvin published another biography, *John Keats: His Life and Poetry, His Friends, Critics, and Afterfame* (1917). See letter 90.

[80]   SL to CAS

[Enclosure only?—Bookmark with untitled poem ("In Florence, under morning skies, . . ."),[1] with note at bottom: "Dedicated by Samuel Loveman to all those whose love of books brings them now and then to the shop of Richard Laukhuff[2] at 40 Taylor Arcade Cleveland 3." Envelope postmarked Cleveland, Ohio, May 6, 1917.]

Notes

1. One of "Two Poems for Book Marks."
2. Richard Laukhuff (1876–1957), an immigrant from Germany, who opened his famous bookstore in 1916. See Gladys Haddad, *Laukhuff's Book Store of Cleveland: An Epilogue* (Akron, OH: Northern Ohio Bibliophilic Society, 1997).

[81]   [ALS]

Auburn, Cal.,

May 10th, 1917.

Dear Sam:

The "Temptation" came the day before yesterday, and I've spent most of the time since in reading and re-reading it. The drama is tremendous, amazing, and I agree with you fully as to the merit of the well-nigh flawless translation—one of the few translations that are great literature in themselves.[1] Thanks, a thousand thanks for the book. Parts of it have stirred me more than almost anything I've read in years, particularly the vision of space, and the dialogue between the sphinx and the Chimera. I hardly realized the import of the book in Monkhood's unspeakably crude translation—indeed, it is not easy to grasp at once, thro the immense, phantasmagoric pageantries of strange and stupendous detail.

I'm sending you, under separate cover, a collection of drawings, selected rather at random from the hundreds that I've made at odd times during the last three years. I've given titles to a few of them, such as the "Terminus of No-Man's-Land," but most of them are manifestly innominable. I enclose also a few "squiggles" or word-blots, some of which are very curious, and, I think, rather remarkable . . . By the way, some of my drawings might not do badly for certain of Flaubert's queer monsters!

I took a six-mile walk the other day without getting particularly tired. It would seem that the microbes are finding me a rather tough mouthful. Probably it's my being in the open air so much that saves me. At any rate, the t. b. isn't making any visible progress,—which, with my suicidal and naturally destructive tendencies, I find rather discouraging. I am so unhappy at heart, and hate life for so many reasons, that almost any way of dying, even the slowest and most painful, seems preferable to an indefinite term of existence. . . . I laughed in the doctor's face, when, after making his diagnosis, he told me not to be scared.

I'm eager to see "The Sphinx". Send it along as soon as possible. Sorry I've nothing of my own to send; but my mood lately has been essentially destructive rather than creative; so I've taken to drawing again. I enclose my latest with this letter. Do you see any technical improvement over my earlier ones?

Affectionately,

Clark.

Notes

1. Probably Lafcadio Hearn's translation (first published posthumously in 1910).

[82]   [TLS, mutilated]

[13 May 1917?]

Dear Clark,

   This is Sunday—my one day of "rest" (funny word!)—and gorgeous out of doors. This afternoon I propose to take a walk with the possibility of ending up at the Cleveland Museum of Art where a very fine exhibition of paintings from the Luxembourg is to be seen. There are Manets, Degases, most of the Barbizon school, and I believe an Ingres. I wish that I had Mr George Moore by me to point out some of their specious [*sic*] excellences. I am singularly obtuse to some of the things that he professes admiration for.

  Hardly a day passes by without my thinking—not once but any number of times—how you feel. If one could only follow a postage-stamp. If one could only make an overnight-journey as Ariel did on a bat in an enchanting sunset. If one could only do many things!

  I have just finished two [books?] by Hearn both of which I suppose you know but which were new to me, "Stray Leaves from Strange Literature" and "Two Years in the West Indies." Wonderful! and each written before he became afflicted with the mania for the Japanese.[1] These books about the tropics afflict me with such acute nostalgia that I find life simply unbearable here—"The sky, a cupola of blinding blue, shading and paling into spectral green at the rim of the world—and all fleckless, save at evening. Then, with sunset, comes a light gold-rift of feathery cloudlets into the west—stip[p]ling it as with a snow of fire."[2] And again, wonderful!

  I'll send you something in my next—sure! Also, and as soon as I can get to town, some reading matter. Prof. Martin who published the ode will probably print something else of mine, may-be the completed "Ode on the departure of Youth" and his brother-in-law, young Sargent, "Thomas Dermody." Did I send you the "Sprite" containing my contributions?[3]

  I stand a very good chance of being drafted in the forthcoming conscription business. I did think of enlisting as a hospital aide, having no particular desire to assist in reckless and indiscriminate onslaught on humanity, but the time will be too short and I have several teeth that need tending to. There is very little individual hope of com[ing] out alive in the holocaust in France. My eye-sight is too poor for admittance in the navy. Write when you can. With kind regards,

   Affectionately,

    [no signature]

1537 East 93 St., Suite 2.

P.S. My first typewriter-ribbon in two years!

[Envelope postmarked Cleveland, Ohio, May 13, 1917.] [envelope placed here conjecturally]

Notes

1. Lafcadio Hearn (1850–1904) was born in Greece, raised in Ireland, then moved to the U.S. where he became a journalist, first in Cincinnati, then primarily in New Orleans. He was sent as a correspondent, first to the French West Indies, where he stayed for two years, and then in 1890 to Japan, where he assimilated Japanese culture and remained the rest of his life.

2. *Two Years in the West Indies* 420.

3. The January 1917 *Sprite* contained "Ode to Apollo" and "John Clare in a Madhouse." It was published by Henry E. Martin, a professor of English in Mt. Union College, Alliance, OH. "Thomas Dermody" appeared in the *Adelphian,* edited by Howard A. Sargent (Scio, OH).

[83]   [ALS]

Auburn, Cal.,

May 20th, 1917.

Dear Sam:

I have finally summoned up sufficient courage to type my latest verses for you—the vain and desperate diversion of idle days. Worthless as they are, they serve at least two purposes—the writing of them kills time, and consumes energy.

I've not been up to much, the last few days. Even reading, at least of any systematic or protracted order, seems too strenuous for me. The weather has been warm, too, which accounts in part for my laziness. The long semi-tropical summer of these mountain-sheltered valleys, is nearly upon us—indeed the grass is turning brown already, and all but the more deeply-rooted flowers are beginning to fade and fall. Oh! for a cool, delicious iceberg, the colour of creme de menthe, in a sea of clear and bottomless green!

The European war is worse than the hashish-dream of a maniacal demon.[1] I almost wish I were eligible for service—which, for a number of reasons, I would hardly be—I'm too much underweight, for one thing, even if my tubercular condition escaped the military doctors. How I would hate to be a German—I'd cut my throat with a dull butcher-knife, if I were.

Yes, I've read "Stray Leaves", and parts of the "West Indies" papers, which appeared in Harper's many years ago. Have you ever read "Chita"? I have it, saved from an old magazine, and can lend it to you, if you like. Hearn's prose, I think, is unsurpassed in English for colour and perfume.

Yes, I received the copy of the "Sprite" containing your two splendid poems. Pardon me for not acknowledging it, and thanking you before—I had most certainly intended to.

Balzac, whom you mention in one of your letters, is an old favourite of mine. I've read more than a dozen of his books, including two or three of the

Lucien de Rubempré series. "The Wild Ass's Skin", ["]Beatrice", "The Lily of the Valley," "The Passion in the Desert," and the "Provincial in Paris," are my favourites. I've read "Snapshots," over which George Moore enthuses so much, but found it rather in the nature of a Swedenborgian tract.[2]

To-day, I've been browsing through several of the books that you've recently sent me—Dowson's life, the poems of Flecker and Swinburne's "Pilgrimage of Pleasure," especially the articles on Johnson and Baudelaire. Can you re-construct my mood from that?

Here's hoping that all is well with you, and that you'll write me soon. Did you receive the drawings?

Affectionately, your friend,

Clark.

Notes

1. CAS was writing a month after President Woodrow Wilson declared war on Germany and joined the Allies, and two days after the Selective Service Act, which resulted in the drafting of 2.8 million Americans in the war effort, was enacted.
2. Moore had written favorably about Edmund Gosse (1849–1928), *Critical Kit-Kats* (1896).

[84]   SL to CAS [nonextant]

[Envelope postmarked Cleveland, Ohio, May 27, 1917.]

[85]   [ALS]

Auburn, Cal.,

June 6th, 1917.

Dear Sam:

Your two letters, and the book of Gautier's *contes*,[1] are all at hand, as they say in the world of bills and dollars. Thanks, and again thanks, for the beautiful translation—the book is one that I had been intending to buy for a long time past. "Clarimonde," on the whole, is my favourite among the stories, tho the title-story is marvellous enough in itself. Reading such things is as good (or perhaps better) than a dose of hashish.

I enclose a few more drawings—nearly all that I've made these latter days. I'm glad they amuse you; I've gotten considerable diversion from drawing them.

My poem "Strangeness" (which I gave away) has just appeared in the San Francisco publication, "Bohemia." They gave it the place of honour—the entire front page, opposite a photograph of the latest "movie" actress!

I went several miles down country yesterday, to register at my voting-precinct. I had to wait while four Indians were being registered, and while I was there, four Japanese entered. Does that give you an idea of the rural population hereabouts?

My health is about as usual—that is to say, pretty well in the physical sense. I can't certify, tho, as to my mental condition; I dare say that almost any alienist would consider me a likely candidate for Bedlam, if he knew my real thoughts and emotions. Personally, I'm inclined to think that my madness is rather of the Hamlet variety—I am still able to distinguish a hawk from a handsaw,[2] on occasion.

>Affectionately,
>Clark.

Notes

1. Possibly Lafcadio Hearn's translation of *One of Cleopatra's Nights and Other Fantastic Romances* (1882), which includes the pioneering vampire tale "Clarimonde."
2. "When the wind is southerly, I know a hawk from a handsaw." Shakespeare, *Hamlet* 2.2.395.

[86]   [ALS]

>Auburn, Cal.
>July 14th, 1917.

Mon cher Sam:

It's good to hear from you again, and I'm ashamed of not having answered before. But the hot weather (the mercury has been playing hide-and-seek around the hundred-mark for the past fortnight or so) has nearly laid me out, and my mental energy is at the vanishing-point.

I've had to give up my projected walking-tour, partly because my father is hardly well enough to accompany me, and partly because of the expense. I bid fair to swelter and curse and cough and sulk in this pestilential hell-hole for the remainder of the summer.

I've just received some new books—Flecker's "Collected Poems," and a volume of "Fifty-One Tales," by Lord Dunsany. Flecker, as you know, is very much to my taste, and I find many things to admire in Dunsany. Some of his fantastic fables are simply splendid,—fine and perfect, both in style and imagination.

I've recently sold two of my poems ("Autumnal" and "Arabesque") to a magazine called the "Art World."[1] They paid me $10 for the two.

I'll try to send you some prose-poems in my next. I've written (and cared to write) damned little. Wilde has something about "a broken heart running to many editions,"[2] but the effect is hardly that with me. I feel paralyzed—frozen at the source. Even thought is a painful fatigue.

Please pardon this grouchy and egotistical letter, and write me again before long.

>Ever yours, affectionately,
>Clark.

Notes

1. Neither poem appeared there.
2. "Nowadays a broken heart will run to many editions." From *The Picture of Dorian Gray* (1891), ch. 1.

[87]   [ALS]

Auburn, Cal.

Aug. 8th, 1917.

Dear Sam:

This is merely a note, to accompany a few little prose-jottings that I've typed for you. You may find ideas in some of them—in "Remoteness" and "Gray Sorrow," at least.

I've been anything but well for the past month, and have done absolutely nothing in the way of work. What's the use, when one doesn't care? This morning, I feel worn, and tired, and faint, as with the accumulated fatigue of many lives and many cycles. I wish only for a thousand aeons or so of sleep. What particular anodyne or nepenthe do you recommend? I've thought of everything lately, from laudanum to strychnine and powdered glass.

I, too, am on the draft, tho I won't be called up for examination before the middle of the month, at least. My case won't take more than a minute or two, I imagine. I must weigh less than a hundred lbs, stripped, since I'm down to 103 or 4, clothing included. Apart from that, my teeth and my feet would doubtless disqualify me.

I'll be very glad, indeed, to have the life of Keats. A thousand thanks to you in advance!

I'll send you a Ms. of "Satan Unrepentant" in my next. If there's anything else you care to have in Ms., don't hesitate to ask for it. I'd be very glad, indeed, to give you anything I have. I only wish it were something better.

No, I've not heard from George lately. He's a slow-coach, like myself, when it comes to letter-writing.

Faithfully,

Clark.

[88]   SL to CAS [nonextant]

[Envelope postmarked Cleveland, Ohio, Aug. 12, 1917.]

[89]   [ALS]

Auburn, Cal.,

Aug. 14th, 1917.

Dear Sam:

The "Life of Keats" came Sunday, and I've read and re-read it during the two days past. Few biographies are both so just and so sympathetic, it seems to me. I treasure the book, and thank you a hundred times.

I appeared yesterday before the local draft board for examination, but was rejected on at least two counts—underweight and t. b. I had to wait two hours for my turn, and was thoroughly disgusted by the whole proceeding—the system of examination seemed brutal, slipshod, and inefficient.

To-day, after a long period of heat, the temperature has dropped 15 or 20 degrees, and there's an autumnal poignance in the air. I love such days, tho they drive me wild with unhappiness and longing. I am more sensitive to the approach of autumn, and its influence, than to that of any other season, and it arouses far deeper emotions in me.

Have just been reading Hearn's "Japanese Miscellany". Do you know it? Japanese folk-lore fascinates me tremendously—many of the stories are so weird and monstrous, with so strange and novel devices of horror. "Kwaidan", I think, contains some of the best that Hearn has transcribed—certain of them are almost unimaginable.

I must try to work a little—my long idleness preys upon me. I *should* be able to write—my head is clear and active, in spite of the bodily weakness and languor that I so often feel. My sterility springs in part from a profound discouragement, and this *can* and *must* be overcome. I positively swear to send you something in my "next."

Affectionately,

Clark.

[90]   [TLS]

[August 1917?]

Dear Clark,

You are right—Colvin's "Keats" is a gem of biography—no rant, no sentimentalism but a dispassionate and sympathetic outline of his life. No other book has superseded it as yet. I have one or two other things that I'll send you in the course of a week—bear up with my foible, please—which is to make you like the books I do.

The enclosed are "snaps" of our new art museum, a wonder of Grecian architecture. It does an infinite good to the artistic folk altho' to confess the truth it is patronized mostly by foreigners.

The news you write me of your determination to write again fills me with joy. Too much self-brooding isn't good and writing is always an outlet for such a mood.

I half-wish I had been drafted—my home-life isn't particularly happy. It is so easy to procure work anywhere now that I've nourished a half-hearted idea of breaking away to another city this autumn—and live my own life in my own way.

Write me a good, long letter—I hear from few people nowadays. With best wishes to you and yours,

Affectionately,
S. L.

1537 East 93 St., Suite 2.

[91]   [ALS]

Auburn, Cal.,
Aug. 27th, 1917.

Dear Sam:

Your letter, the copy of "The Sprite", and the translation of Verlaine, are all "at hand," as they say in the world of bills and dollars. As I must have told you before, I admire the finely imaginative conception, and the rich Shakesperian [*sic*] language of your "Scene for Lear." It reads even better in print, as one's work usually does (psychologically, I suppose, it's because of the subconscious impression and assurance of publicity and permanence that comes from the printed page, as opposed to the written or even the type-written.)

Have you done anything more with "The Sphinx?" You have mentioned it several times, and always in a way that intrigues my curiosity.

Many thanks for the Verlaine, which *is* of interest and value to me, tho poor stuff, on the whole, as poetry. The book achieves the customary badness of almost all translations, except in a few poems, where the diction and versification are tolerable. Compare Symons' translation of the first stanza of "Mandoline," with Wingate's, for the absolute difference between poetic worth and unworth:[1]

Symons
"The singer[s] of serenades
Whisper their fated vows
Unto fair listening maids
Under the singing boughs."

Wingate
"The swains that give the serenade,
And the fair listeners too,
Exchange some ponderous conceits
Beneath the sonorous bough."

However, I dare say (judging from its curious banality of diction) that Wingate's is the more literal rendering. French verse, as a rule, seems frightfully banal in a word-for-word translation . . . The "Baudelaire" in this series, which I have read, (Sterling has the book in his library at Carmel) is infinitely better stuff, and I have long been trying to obtain it. Baudelaire, because of his far greater solidity and intellectuality of matter and manner, loses much less in translation than Verlaine, who is said to depend so much upon musical subtleties—fugitive and volatile effects of meter and assonance.

There's no news in especial since my last writing. I've not heard from George in over a month; and most of my other correspondents preserve a similarly enigmatic silence. However, I don't blame them—I'm getting to be something between an owl and an eremite, myself; or, precisely speaking, rather *more* of these, even, than I used to be. I feel better, tho, what with the first oncoming and premonitory coolness of autumn, and may be able to work a little presently.

I enclose a few scenic snapshots, all taken within half a mile of my house. They may interest you.

> Affectionately,
>
> Clark.

Notes

1. "From Paul Verlaine: Fêtes Galantes—I. Mandoline," in Symons's *Poems* 211; Ashmore Wingate, *Paul Verlaine* (London: Walter Scott Publishing Co., 1904), 61.

[92]   [ALS]

> Auburn, Cal.
>
> Sept. 20th, 1917.

Dear Sam:

I'm dreadfully ashamed of having allowed your poem and the copies of the Cornhill Booklet[1] to lie unacknowledged so long. The weather has been enervating, and I have not felt very well at any time,—certainly I have lacked the strength and resolution of mind for letter-writing. This is the first letter I have written in weeks—probably the first since my last one to you.

For your Ode, and the Booklets, many thanks. I like the poem—your thought is fine and beautiful, and the unusual verse-form is handled in a masterly and melodious way, with many delicacies of cadence. The booklets are very interesting. I was particularly struck by the selections from Crackanthorpe,[2] of whose work I have seen very little. The admirable sharpness of detail, the steel-cut clarity of phrase, the whole effect as of silhouettes on a clear, pale sky—these are very much to my taste. Even a very, very little of such writing is worth countless tons and carloads of the usual slop. It stands out like a Damascus dagger in a pile of broken barrel-hoops and rail-road spikes.

I have read Allan Seeger (of whom you speak) and like many of his things. He was a true poet, tho by no means the peer of Brooke.

Have you heard from G. S. lately? I have not heard for months and months, it seems to me. George is getting to be a worse correspondent than I am.

Affectionately, as ever,

Clark.

Notes

1. *The Cornhill Booklet* (1900–14) was one of many little magazines that appeared throughout the U.S. at the turn of the twentieth century.

2. Hubert Montague Crackanthorpe (1870–1896), Victorian English writer who primarily wrote essays, short stories, and novellas. The supplement to the November 1914 number of the *Cornhill Booklet* (4, No. 2) contained his "Vignettes" (40–42).

[93]   [SL to CAS, nonextant]

[Envelope postmarked Cleveland, Ohio, Sep. 20, 1917.]

[94]   [ALS]

Auburn, Cal.,

Oct. 9th, 1917.

Dear Sam:

Will you pardon my delay in acknowledging the books: I went to San Francisco last week, to see the doctor (and incidentally the dentist) and this is the first day since that I've had time or strength for letter-writing.

"Tristan and Iseult"[1] is full of excellent workmanship, but seems to me to lack the originality of inspiration that alone would justify the re-working of a theme so often and so ably handled by others. Young Sorley[2] I like very well. There is true power, both of thought and expression, and true poetic inspiration in his verses. Also, they are extraordinarily free from outside influence, and possess a surprising distinction and personality of style.

Thanks for what you say about my drawings. I'll send you another batch presently. I seldom, if ever, make copies, so the pictures I send you are all originals.

Have you read anything of Verhaeren's? I have a number of his things in a little volume, "Contemporary Belgian Poetry," published in the Canterbury series.[3] Some of them are gross and lascivious to an almost superhuman or demoniacal degree. One of the longest and most characteristic is a detailed and extraordinarily graphic (or pornographic!) description of a brothel.

The doctor tells me that my t. b. is much improved. I had to have some teeth pulled tho (three of them, all molars) and went under the gas—a terrific experience, like falling through space for an aeon or so, and then lying buried under the wrack and rubble of the universe for another aeon—all in the few seconds while one is "going off." That was a strenuous day for me—I went to the doctor in the morning, and found a whole conclave of M. D.s waiting for me (he had called them in to see a demonstration of his methods of diagnosis). So, with the aid of electropodes, and batteries, etc, they tapped and thumped and thudded me for hours. In the afternoon, I went to the dentist, and then, with Sterling and some other friends, motored out to the Cliff House. In the evening, I "took in" most of the Bohemian restaurants, and accumulated about 15 drinks, of a miscellaneous and cosmopolitan nature—everything from vermouth to rum and arrack. The last is delightful,—far more potent and also more palatable than any sort of gin or brandy.

Write soon.

Ever, your affectionate friend,

Clark.

Notes

1. By Arthur Symons.
2. Charles Sorley (1895–1915), a Scottish poet of World War I.
3. See Bibliography under Jethro Bithell. CAS refers specifically to Emile Verhaeren (1855–1916), a Belgian poet who wrote in the French language.

[95] [ALS]

Auburn, Cal.

Jan. 27th, 1918.

My dear Sam:

How is it with you? It's so long since I've heard, tho I wrote you in October, and again in December. Is it possible that both my letters miscarried, or that yours has miscarried? At any rate, here goes for another. I feel ashamed of having delayed so long; but things have gone so badly with me for the past months that I have been in no state for correspondence. Physically, I am far from well; and I hold too many sessions with Messrs. Grief, Regret, and Co., to retain any degree of mental health or peace. The road to Lethe is long, and leads thro what interminable deserts, and among what numberless mirages! But enough of this; one should be patient, and not complain. There is, there must be, slumber and repose at the end: else the universe were too hideous, too monstrous for a demon's nightmare.

I have written absolutely nothing; my Muse, like Memnon, seems turned into stone and silence; and I know not when the morning shall come to awaken her. In my present mood, it hardly seems to matter.

The Book Club of San Francisco is shortly to publish a few of my poems ("Nero," the "Abyss," "To the Darkness", and ten sonnets, mostly unprinted heretofore) in de luxe binding and paper.[1] I'll try to obtain you a copy.

I celebrated (?) my 25th birthday on the 13th of the month. I am already beginning to find grey hairs in my brush—no uncommon thing, tho, in people with incipient consumption. Shelley's hair was touched with grey.

Write me soon, if you can. It worries me a bit, not to hear from you. Please assure me that things are well with you.

> Affectionately, as ever,
> Clark.

Notes

1. *OS* reprinted some poems from *ST* and contained unpublished poems later reprinted in *EC.*

[96] [TLS]

Cleveland, Ohio.
Feb. 4, 1918.

Dear Clark,

Was I glad to get your letter—you bet! For weeks and weeks I've been fighting first, an obstinate case of hand, then finger-infection, all on my right hand. Within the past ten days this has healed almost as by a miracle and I find myself in the enviable position of being able to write a letter without squirming in pain. I did not receive your letter of December, Clark. Be sure I should have answered you, even if by dictation. It grieves me poignantly to hear that you don't feel at your best. I've wished many things in the past but none more than that your health should return to you. I know how you feel about Life, Clark—surely it owes you an apology. I've often found myself wondering what a privilege it would be to spend a few days with you if I ever peregrinated out your way.

By all means I want a copy of your book but if procuring one involves any difficulty I'd consider it a privilege to subscribe—if subscription be allowable. Have I these unpublished sonnets? I hope it includes that magnificently glorified one to Satan—one of the greatest sonnets ever written and in its proportion as tremendous a work as "Paradise Lost." Is there any outlook for your publication with Robertson? Hang the man! what does he mean by his diffidence? There never were as many books printed as there are nowadays!

I am sending you under special cover a book that I ordered for you some time ago but which the N.Y. people seem to be out of temporarily, so I send you my own copy. Unless I am mistaken the combination of James Thomson and Leopardi will be of unusual interest to you. In many ways Leopardi is more genuinely the writer and artist than Schopenhauer. I tried to procure for you at an auction recently a book entitled "The Amazing Heliogabalus",[1] which I have not read but which Robert Sherard says is the most remarkable of books[2]—but wasn't successful. I thought that the subject might entertain you, knowing your predilection for any thing savoring of the Neronic. Didn't Verlaine write a poem on Heliogabalus—or was it Baudelaire?[3] I also want to send you Burke's very remarkable book of short stories, "Limehouse Nights."

I like the little grotesque you enclose. I want to send you in my next the three folio pages I have written of the "Sphinx." This may never see print, if it should ever find completion, altho' Vincent Starrett who is to edit "The Flame" (a name adopted at my suggestion) would be foolhardy to print it simply for the sake of exasperating the public.[4] Anyhow, this is what I suggest—if you find one or two things in the context worthy of illustration will you do so? Some day, I should like to scrape a few dollars together and print it privately.

Starrett, the editor of the aforesaid "Flame" offered me the assoc. editorship which, after inconsiderable pro and con, I turned down. It carries with it no financial remuneration, the contributors are not paid, etc. As far as the honour is concerned one feels capable of evoking only the sublimely adhesive commonplace of Miss Tanguay—"I don't care."[5] The editor of the "Dial" who is a friend of Starret[t]'s recently wrote me asking for a contribution of poetry or essays—I sent him "Understanding."

Write soon, Clark. I promise you a letter once a week after this. And here's hoping that Spring simply makes you find your health again. With best wishes to yourself and yours,

Affectionately,

Sam

1537 East 93 St. Suite 2.

Notes

1. See Bibliography under John Stuart Hay.
2. SL refers to Robert Harborough Sherard's *The Real Oscar Wilde* (Philadelphia: David McKay, 1916), where Sherard refers to Hay's book as "masterly" (221) and quotes extensively from it, believing that aspects of Heliogabalus' life parallel those of Wilde.
3. Verlaine, "Résignation."
4. Vincent Starrett (1886–1974), American writer and journalist. No such periodical titled the *Flame* ever appeared. Starrett did edit a magazine called the *Wave* (Chicago: Hinrichsen & Lunoe, 1922–24).
5. Eva Tanguay (1878–1947), Canadian singer and entertainer who billed herself as "the girl who made vaudeville famous." She was known as the "I Don't Care Girl," after her most famous song, "I Don't Care" (1905; words by Jean Lenox, music by Harry O. Sutton).

[97]   [ALS]

Auburn, Cal.

Feb. 12th, 1918.

Dear Sam:

Thanks—a thousand thanks—for the translation of Leopardi—a book that I have been wanting for years past. How did you know that it was on my list of prospective purchases? Leopardi is all that I had expected him to be—perhaps, tho, a little *more* like Schopenhauer than I had thought. The main difference between the Italian and the German lies in the fact that the former was a poet, and the latter wasn't. I wish I knew Italian—if only for the sake of reading Leopardi's poems.

I'm hellishly sorry to hear of the trouble you have had with your hand, and happy to know that you are better. I have been laid up for a week or more with a stiffness and swelling in my lower limbs—a puffiness of the ankles, and, at times, of the knees and calves, that has an uncomfortable resemblance to dropsy. It's practically all gone at present, and I'm sincerely hoping that it won't return. The doctor said that it might come from poor circulation.

I'll be very glad to see what you have written of the "Sphinx," and happy to illustrate it to the best of my ability. I've spent most of my time lately in drawing, or attempting to draw, and will send you some of the results as soon as I can make copies. I've attempted four illustrations for Poe, two for "The Temptation of St. Anthony," one for the "Wine of Wizardry," a book-plate for myself, and several miscellaneous grotesques.

The Book Club volume will be privately printed, I believe, and for the members only. But I understand that I will have a few copies given me for my own use, and, of course, you will receive one of them. There aren't many people to whom I would care to give away copies of my work . . . I think you have seen all the sonnets in the collection—two of the passional ones are included ("Exotique" and "The Crucifixion of Eros") and several pessimistic ones ("The Medusa of Despair," "The Harlot of the World," "The Refuge of Beauty,") but not the Satan sonnet, which I want to revise before it's printed. . . . The revisions, of course, will be technical only.

I've heard of "The Amazing Heliogabalus". It must be a wonderful and most excellent book—a terrific roast of it appeared in the same issue of the London "Academy" in which my sonnet, "A Dream of Beauty," was published several years ago.[1]

No, there's not the least likelihood of Robertson's doing anything with my second volume—at least till the war is over . . . Why in hell don't the German people revolt?—but perhaps they will, in the end. As Balzac says, "Nothing is more horrible than the rebellion of a sheep";[2] so there's hope that the Kaiser and his Junkers may receive something of what is due them, even yet. Apart from its inconceivable horrors, the war is getting to be a d—md bore, anyway—which isn't altogether the least of its horrors. I'd rather go [to] the front, and get shot, than endure another year or two of war talk, and war books, and war bread.

Thanks for the neat little bookmark you enclose, with its charming verses. I hope that the box of manzanita blossoms I'm sending you will arrive in good condition. They keep better than most wild flowers, so I thought it worth trying.

Write soon.
    Affectionately,
           Clark

P.S. I enclose a few of the drawings mentioned. Will send the others under separate cover.

Notes

1. [Unsigned], "An Imperial Voluptuary," *Academy* 81 (12 August 1911): 206.
2. "Lost by a Laugh," in *Balzac's Shorter Stories* (Philadelphia: Henry Altemus, 1895), 162 (revised slightly here).

[98]   [TLS]

                              Cleveland, Ohio.
                              Feb. 17, 1918.

Dear Clark,

    You couldn't have sent me anything that pleased me more than these beautiful blossoms, the most wonderful part being that they arrived here in a howling snow-storm and that when I came home from work and found them on the table there was a marvelous array of guesses as to their identity which ranged everywhere from lilacs to arbutus. Thanks, Clark, your gift has surely taken me poignantly.

    I seem to have a second-sight perception about your likes but hasn't it been a most remarkable fact that in most cases your choice of books has been mainly my own? I've never forgotten that you once called John Clare "an exquisite poet"—an appreciation that I wouldn't change for all the gold of a mythical Midas. I believe that there has been a translation of Leopardi's poetry published in the Camelot classics but if it is as ill-done as the Verlaine, heaven help it. But a translation of the prose and with such introductions by a poet like James Thomson would provisionally be pure gold. I've known this little volume for some time.

    I sent you under separate cover Symon[s]'s translation of the immortal Baudelaire and—I am selfish enough to hope that this is your first reading. Mosher's preface reveals some curious information concerning Symons and I wonder just how far true it is. By the way have you or have you ever heard of a book on Baudelaire by Guy Thorne?[1] It's quite a large book, contains a fine portrait, one of this pen-drawings and several engravings with a note on the influences of Baudelaire in English art and poetry. Mr. Laukhuff (the artist savior of this gr-r-eat city) has an edition in French of the "Fleurs de [*sic*] Mal"—will you let me know Clark, if you could get enough out of the French to make possession worth while? My own knowledge is confided to a few scattered words or phrases. This book, complete and without the hoof-marks of Comstock, is in the usual yellow paper covers, and I have more than once been on the point of procuring it for you—so I thought I'd ask first. Please let me know.

Thanks again for the new set of pictures. That one illustration of Poe's "An Eidolon named Night",[2] is superb, not only in the isolation of its artistic note but in the same quality that makes your poetry different from anything else. I shall await the others.

I've been drafted into Class 1-A, of this second draft and expect to come up for physical exam. this week. I hope it ends the uncertainty as I'm pretty well weary of all this indecision. I understand that they are much less strict in their eye-sight exemptions and I suppose that by summer I'll be in it. One of my cousins, a first lieutenant, is stationed at San Diego, another is an ensign somewhere's across (the last card I got was from the Azores) and a third is training at an Ohio camp. My two brothers are both in Class 1, so that it's pretty certain some one will be representing the family.

I want to send you the "Sphinx" by my next letter, in a few days. I've started a scene for "Macbeth", the death of Lady M., which promises well. Also, I started a prose one-act play entitled "The Death of Helen", depicting the miserable end of that golden dame with her swilling husband, the classic Menelaus, at her side. Isn't all this industry promising?—Apparently so, but most of my spare time is spent in a sort of aimless, noncommittal loafing and equally aimless reading. I've been wanting to do every sort of an ambitious thing but it dwindles down into the ghost of a phantasm, or the proverbial dead-sea apples.[3]

Have you read much of John Addington Symonds, a writer for whom I have a great admiration? I've just been reading his biography (it should be auto-biography) by his executor, Horatio Brown, a book that stirs me profoundly. Symonds and Pater and Arthur Symons—these three, I don't know or can't conceive what my indebtedness to them means. After that, Wilde and Sir Thomas Browne.

It pleases me to hear that the volume includes the "Crucification [*sic*] of Eros", another one of my favorites. You bet, I am going to await the book with impatience. News has reached me here of a new volume of George's, "The Binding of the Beast", in the shape of a clipping from a review in the [*sic*] "The Transcript" which states that the sonnets were previously printed in his last two books.[4] I've ordered it for the sake of possession. These sonnets must eventually take their place as the finest [w]ar-literature of the past four years.

I hope that things are coming along better with you, Clark. In "that swete seasoun Spring," many things take place for the better. That swel[l]ing you mention is just such another phase of the curious attack which deprived me temporarily of the use of two fingers a year ago. I know—hang it!—I know, and the cursed M.D. bade me keep perfect quiet in anticipation of an attack of paralysis. More anon. Regards to you and yours.

1537   Affectionately
                                           [Sam]

[Envelope postmarked Cleveland, Ohio, Feb. 18, 1918.]

Notes

1. This is in fact Thorne's translation of Gautier's biography of Baudelaire.
2. Poe, "Dream-Land," l. 3.
3. A fruit, supposed to disintegrate into smoke or ashes when plucked.
4. The poems in *The Binding of the Beast* were mostly taken from *The Caged Eagle*, but some had appeared in *Beyond the Breakers* (1914). Braithwaite reviewed the volume in the *Boston Evening Transcript* 89, No. 134 (9 February 1918): Part III, p. 4.

[99]   [ALS]
                                                    Auburn, Cal.,
                                                    Feb. 27, 1918.
Dear Sam:
        I'm so glad that the flowers arrived in good time, and that they gave you pleasure. The manzanita blossoms keep better than most of our wild flowers, many of which are extremely delicate . . . the season is phenomenally early this year—I've been finding buttercups and shooting-stars for a week past, and to-day my father brought in a yellow violet, or wild pansy, as the flower is commonly called.
        Thanks for the exquisite little volume of Baudelaire! Symons is the ideal translator, and he certainly seems to have done justice to the prose-poems selected. I have several of them in the volume, "Pastels in Prose," an anthology of French prose-poems translated by Stuart Merrill,[1] and have been comparing the two translations. Merrill's rendering is so excellent, that, in many respects, I find it difficult to choose between the two . . . "The Eyes of the Poor",[2] is new to me. It certainly is a wonder, and I thoroughly understand Dowson's enthusiasm over it.
        I know so little French that I fear I would get practically nothing, or worse than nothing, from B. in the original. French verse seems frightfully banal in a word-for-word rendering, anyway, so one would have to comprehend not only the letter, but the spirit of the language, to appreciate it.
        No, I've never read Guy Thorne's book, tho I've seen it mentioned somewhere. It certainly ought to be interesting. Guy Thorne, I believe, is the author of a one-time best-seller, "When It Was Dark".
        Thanks for what you say about my drawings. I fear, tho, that they would be a sad waste of time, if time were of any value. Bad as they are, I can't always do them—I have to be in a certain mood even for drawing—else the result is likely to prove a total botch.
        Did I tell you that George was to write a preface for my Book Club vol-

ume? I'll certainly be proud of that volume.

I wrote a prose-poem yesterday, under the title of "Ennui". I fear the title is perhaps the only stroke of good workmanship it possesses. I may send it along, however, in my next, if it stands revision.

> Affectionately,
> Clark.

Notes

1. Stuart Merrill (1863–1911), American poet of the Symbolist school, wrote mostly in French. CAS translated his "Celle qui prie" ["A Woman at Prayer"].
2. The prose poem by Baudelaire ("Les Yeux des pauvres") is in Symons's translation, pp. 21–25.

[100] [ALS]

> Auburn, Cal.,
> March 11th, 1918.

Dear Sam:

I'm glad you like the pictures, and feel proud of what you say about them. I begin to take my drawing more seriously than I did at first, and latterly have given more care and attention to its technical side. Of course, my work may be valueless; but at least I get a lot of fun out of it.

I've just received the galley proofs of my "Odes and Sonnets," the Book Club volume. "Satan Unrepentant," you will be glad to know, is included, besides "Nero,["] "The Abyss,"[1] "To the Darkness," and eight unpublished sonnets, including "Exotique,["] "Ave atque Vale,["] "The Medusa of Despair", "Crucifixion of Eros," "Belated Love," etc; also the poem "Alexandrines," which you may remember. I suppose the edition will be about 300 copies. I found some atrocious misprints in the proofs; also, some changes of punctuation by a professional proof reader that simply made hash of my meaning.

I'm sorry to hear that you have been drafted—not that I don't envy you, in a way, the chance of getting killed—certainly a clean and honorable death. But the whole d——d business is so detestable, so senseless, and monstrous. Satan in a hashish-dream could conceive of nothing worse. However, you shouldn't talk so fatalistically about not returning; everybody doesn't get killed in action; and you've as good a chance of coming back as anyone.

That's a queer yarn about Bierce—possibly the name your acquaintance saw belonged to some relative of the old man's. It's likely enough that one of them might be named after him.

I'll write again very soon, and send you my prose-poem, "Ennui." My type-writer ribbon is worn out, and I've not yet secured a new one.

Have just received a small consignment of books—"The Shaving of Shagpat", by George Meredith, the "Travels of Marco Polo,["] "The Way of

All Flesh" by Samuel Butler, and a collection of stories by de Maupassant including "Boule de Suif", and "The Horla".² The latter, I think, is one of the weirdest and most terrible conceptions in literature. It belongs with "The Red Death",³ and one or two of Bierce's—"The Damned Thing", and "The Death of Halpin Fraser." [*sic*]

I'm looking for a letter from you any day, and expecting the Scene for "Macbeth." I liked your one for "Lear" very much, as I must have told you.

Au revoir (if the phrase can be used in an epistolary sense).

> Affectionately,
> > Clark.

Notes

1. I.e., "Ode to the Abyss."
2. Probably *Mademoiselle Fifi and Twelve Other Stories* (1917).
3. I.e., Poe's "The Masque of the Red Death."

[101] [ALS]

> Auburn, Cal.
> March 13th, 1918

Dear Sam:

Just a note to acknowledge, and thank you for the volumes of Pater and the notebook, all of which arrived yesterday. I've read very little of Pater, apart from "Marius" (which you sent me) and certainly promise myself a feast.

I enclose the prose-piece "Ennui," also a couple of poems written during the autumn, which I don't remember having sent you.

I like the picture of your mother—a most beautiful and striking effect of light and shade to have secured with a snapshot.

I'll write again very soon (this isn't a letter) and send you some more drawings. I enclose one—a sort of octopodal orchid, probably from the equatorial forests of Saturn.

> Affectionately,
> > Clark.

[102] [TLS]

> Cleveland, Ohio.
> March 17, 1918.

Dear Clark,

The big thing in your letter is the news that "Satan Unrepentant" is actually to appear in your book. I had been hoping all along that it would, but hardly expected it. If that poem doesn't cause comment and an instant valuation of its high qualities, then "Prometheus Unbound" is minor poetry and "Hyperion" a failure.[1] I measure it with these. Clark, if you ever find a[n] hour's leisure, don't forget me on that mss. proposition of "Satan Unrepentant." I should dearly like to have it for insertion in your book. Indeed, I remember "Alexandrines." It is the most haunting lyric of its kind since Dowson's "Cynara." I like immensely your choice of a title for the volume. It is dignified and has a classic quality and makes a good companion to that chosen for the first volume.

Your list of new books interested me. I'm rather puzzled over the prevailing popularity of Butler's book. Frankly, it was simply dry-rot to me and I couldn't get beyond the first few chapters. Maupassant is sure-enough a great writer. I once read his seventeen volumes of short stories and novels through from beginning to end[2] and if there had been seventeen more I should have continued. That's the test for any writer of fiction.

I enclose as much as I have revised of the scene for "Macbeth." Do you think it drags? I find it much more difficult, maybe on account of the subtle psychology that is to be found in the original play. Some of Lady Macbeth's inferences there, read almost like Ibsen.

I'm awaiting "Ennui". Do you find the paper in that yaller note-book a good working-medium?

I've read very little lately. Spring is coming here but in its own peculiar way. Our temperature registered 70 degrees at noon the other day. By night it had begun to show and at midnight we had twenty above zero. People simply suffer here from colds all the winter long. There were 125 souls sick in one day with an epidemic of grippe at the office I work in. How are you, Clark?

> Affectionately,
> Sam

1537 East 93 St., Suite 2.

Notes

1. By Shelley and Keats, respectively.
2. *The Complete Writings of Guy de Maupassant: Stories of the Tragedy and Comedy of Life* (Akron, OH: St. Dunstan Society; Boston: Desmond Publishing, 1903).

[103] [ALS]

> Auburn, Cal.,
> March 20th, 1918.

Dear Sam:

I want to thank you again, and yet again, for the volumes of Pater. The reading of these, especially the "Renaissance," has been a great treat for me. I like best the article on Leonardo; in "Imaginary Portraits," the one of Watteau[1] interests me most. The curious and recondite charm, the involuted rhythms of this elaborate but graceful style, are things that grow upon one. If Pater's genius had been exercised more upon artistic creation, less upon criticism, I should doubtless place him among my prime favourites.

Have you read the "Shaving of Shagpat?" a most outrageous romance, in the manner of the Arabian Nights. I like the book very much more than anything else of Meredith's I have seen, with the exception of "Love in the Valley."[2]

I've done little but read for the past week or so. My fit of drawing has worked itself off, and my old languor and indifference have returned, incapacitating me for any serious effort. However, I'm much stronger than I was during the autumn, and have gained considerably in weight.

The weather is clear—supernally clear, after a week of storm. The mountains, ceremented in snow to their foothills, are visible today. The sight of them evokes my old desire to wander—to wander for a whole summer among their pines and lakes, and glaciers and canyons. This year I swear that nothing shall hold me back.

Adios.

Affectionately,
Clark.

Notes

1. Jean-Antoine Watteau (1684–1721), French painter.
2. *Love in the Valley* is a long poem first published in 1851 and revised in 1878.

[104] [ALS]

Auburn, Cal.,
March 24th, 1918.

Dear Sam:

I mailed you a few drawings the other day, one of which was made on the tablet paper that you sent me. The paper is more suitable for work in black than for color-drawing, on account of the yellow background, unless one wanted a yellow field.

I'll send you a transcription of "Satan Unrepent[ant]" in a few days. Please forgive my remissness in the matter—I have to force myself when it comes to making copies of anything. Every flaw in my work causes me acute torture whenever I return to it—a torture that I seek to avoid by referring to the work as little as possible.

I like what you have done of the "Scene for Macbeth"—there are many Shakespe[a]rean accents about it. No, I don't think that it "drags"—the whole atmosphere, of course, is one of psychological suspense.

I enclose a new sonnet—probably a bad one; also, a little prose-poem. I think of "doing" a whole volume of prose-fantasies and fables with which to assail the Eastern book publishers—a vain enough project, I dare say.

I managed to read the Butler book through, but agree with you as to its qualities, on the whole. The blind, slavish, unimaginative realism so much in vogue nowadays, interests me very little. "The Way of All Flesh" is a peculiar and salient example of such—it reads like Zola de-odorized. "Dry rot", as you so aptly call it, doesn't gain much by merely being deprived of the stench.

I feel restless and tired at the same time, these days—a s[uit]able sort of combination. People tell me that I look well—but it seems to be all on the surface. My nervousness is like a nightmare at times; also, I've a certain amount of pleurisy and dysponoeia. I don't anticipate (or desire) a protracted span of years; if my lungs are really affected the disease will "get" me in time, as it nearly always does. I only wish it would hurry up a bit.

The latest news from Europe is positively sickening. If Germany wins the war, it will be time for a new Deluge—without any Noah's-ark.

> Affectionately,
> Clark.

P.S. I've spent part of this Sunday afternoon in making a transcription of "Satan" for you. I fear it will prove horribly illegible—my hand is so nervous today that it's hard for me to write at all. On reviewing the poem, I find some good lines in it; but on the whole I prefer the sonnet "A Vision of Lucifer," the conception of which seems more original to me. However, I dare say a poet is often the worst judge of his own work.

[105] [ALS]

> Auburn, Cal.,
> April 6th, 1918.

Dear Sam:

It's good to hear that my new poems and pictures have given you pleasure. I wish I had something really good to send you; but when one works (as I do) with little heart for the effort, and less ambition, I scarcely see how the result *can* be very good.

I am curious to see the "Sphinx". Thanks for your suggestion in regard to the "Dial." I shall certainly try them, tho I have almost given up submitting anything of mine to the magazines.

There seems to be some delay in the publication of my book. They are waiting for the decorations, I believe; these are being done by a New York artist.[1]

Here are a few more verses—also a little prose-poem, which is probably the best of the lot. My late sonnets are all more or less personal; the one enclosed is a companion for "Sepulture."

I am very much alone these days, and rarely see anyone, or venture into the town. I don't mind the solitude, tho I dare say it's unhealthy, and poisonous. My one intimate friend (the lady of whom I once told you) died in November; and since then, Auburn has been more of a desert to me than ever.

I am very tired to-day, and have gotten into a peculiarly suicidal mood. I torture myself endlessly, since nothing else gives me any pleasure. You've no idea what an excellent Yogi or monk I would make. I'd probably kill myself with fastings and vigils, if I were left to my own devices. It's a natural reaction—I go to the other extreme at times.

> Affectionately,
>
> Clark.

Notes

1. The decorations were done by Florence Lundborg (1871–1949), who began her artistic career in San Francisco but later moved to New York. She also illustrated *The Rubaiyat* and *Yosemite Legends.*

[106] [ALS]

> Auburn, Cal.,
>
> April 27th, 1918.

Dear Sam:

Your good letter (most welcome, as always) came last night. This morning, I am idle as a blackbird with a sore throat, and feel totally disenabled and disinclined for the writing of either verse or prose-poetry. Therefore, I am trying to clean up at least a portion of my correspondence. Your letter, of course, comes first.

Thanks for the tremendous compliment you pay my prose-poems! Personally, I am afraid that most of what I have written in that form is too metrical and monotonous—lacks the large and varied movement of good prose. I am glad you like "Winter Moonlight." Of its kind, the thing is nearer perfection than most of my verse.

George has written his preface for my book (the draft of which I enclose for your perusal) and I understand that the volume is due to appear in another month. Book-publishers, as a class, are slower than Lethe in winter, or a dead toad at the bottom of a dry mud-puddle.

Stoddard's verse, of which you speak, is pretty tame, on the whole. His prose, the "South-Sea Idylls," is infinitely superior, as I remember it (I've not seen the book for years) and I advise you to read it, by all means. The "Idylls" are full of charm and romantic beauty.

I enclose all that I have written since the last verses I sent you. God knows why I write at all—surely everything I do or think is aimless, or also mischievous to my own welfare, and I am unhappy at heart . . . "Requiescat in Pace" is for my dead friend. Yes, her poetic tastes were congenial to mine. We agreed on all things but religion (she was a devout Christian) and I fear that she was made unhappy because I could not share her faith. To-day, strangely enough, is her birthday; and when I go out into the fields, after finishing this letter and certain others, all the flowers that she loved will torture and reproach me. The snow-drops and larkspurs I carried to her a year ago, will ask for her; and I shall have no answer.

Pardon all this, if you will. I have not spoken of it to any one else; and my heart is sick with its hidden memories.

I like very, very much the little snap-shot of yourself. Wish I had a picture to send you; but I've not faced a photographer (even an amateur) for years. Devil knows what I look like—nothing very impressive or engaging, I dare say.

Write soon. I'm always looking for your letters, and worrying a bit if they are long delayed.

> Affectionately,
>
> > Clark.

[107] [ALS]

> > Auburn, Cal.,
> >
> > > May 8th, 1918.

Dear Sam:

The books came yesterday, your letter to-day, and I hasten to acknowledge them. I had been intending to drop you a line for days, or weeks past; but somehow my constitutional indolence (to put it euphemistically) prevailed upon me.

Thanks, a hundred thanks for the books. I ran through both of them last night, reading parts of the translations from "De Rerum Naturae", which are splendid,—strongly and majestically worded, and altogether very much to my taste. The sublime and irrefutable philosophy of Lucretius is far more worthily rendered by Mallock than I have seen it elsewhere. I like very much the pathetic little volume on Wilde—it gives many glimpses that touch and interest me.

I have revised the page-proofs of my book, and expect that it may be out by the 20th or 25th (d—m this pen!) of the present month. I am to have ten copies for my own use, one of which I will forward you as soon as I receive them. The decorations (grey peacocks, rubricated letters, etc) are really quite beautiful, and better than I had hoped, or expected.

I enclose two sonnets in Alexandrines[1]—the tail-end of my April output. I've written nothing at all this month—having demoralized myself too much with a variety of follies, such as under-eating, overdrinking, and over-exercise in the form of long walks. By a combination of these, I attain to some sort of oblivion. Fatigue is a good enough anodyne, as such things go.

I enclose also a little poem by my friend. Some of her things (she wrote many short lyrics) were even better, and I am sorry that I have no copies of them at hand.

The Keats collection you saw must have been tremendously interesting! And imagine a relative of his, with the same name, living in Missouri! Truly,

America is a land of wonders—the real-estate advertisements and railroad folders have not exaggerated!

Write soon.

> Affectionately,
>> Clark.

[Enclosure: printed text of "A San Francisco Fog" by Mamie Lowe Miller.][2]

Notes

1. "Ennui" and probably "Inferno."
2. *Sunset* 35 (October 1915): 721.

[108] [ALS]

> Auburn, Cal.,
>> May 22nd, 1918.

Dear Sam:

I should have written before this, but have been too unwell to get my wits together for correspondence. I've had fever half the time lately, and have slept badly, with dreams that made me think I was about ripe for the jim-jams—corpses flying through the air in a flash of phosphorescent light, and dappled serpents dancing in a ring! My mother, too, is ill with a nervous breakdown, and my father anything but well. "Life is a hospital," certainly, as Baudelaire says somewhere.[1]

I'm glad you like my friend's poem. I'll try to find you some more of her things presently; but all my papers, mss. and clippings are in hopeless confusion, and I hardly know where to lay hands on them now. I wish something might be done toward collecting her best work into a volume. But, alas! you know how it is.

It delights me to know that you have decided to collect and print your own work. I like the idea of the journal form, but certainly think you should confine it to your own poems and prose-poems. The pamphlets would be most unique.

My own book may be out any time now—I look for it each day. It is so kind of you to think of writing an appreciation, and I would value your review more than any other.

No, I have not drawn lately, but think of doing some more work in that line. If so, I should certainly make a number for you.

Pardon the brevity of this letter. I'll try to write again very soon, and hope to have a copy of my book for you by that time.

> As ever, Affectionately,
>> Clark.

P.S. Here are some old drawings that I've raked up. They're hardly my best, but some of them may interest or amuse you.

Notes

1. "Life is a hospital, in which every patient is possessed by the desire of changing his bed." "'Anywhere out of the World,'" in *Baudelaire: His Prose and Poetry* 52.

[109] [ALS]

Auburn, Cal.,

June 4th, 1918.

Dear Sam:

I should have answered your last letter immediately (or anticipated it) had I not been waiting for the appearance of my book. But to-day finds me still waiting, with nary a word or sign of life from the publishers. I can't imagine what's causing the delay, and feel horribly vexed. I wanted so much to have the book reach you before you were called up.

My mother is better, though none too well, and I feel a bit more cheerful myself. But I'm in no mood or condition for creative work of any kind at present. Numerous duties devolve upon me, since my father is not well or strong; and I spend most of my leisure time reading. I've gotten through a tremendous number of books lately—Hearn's "Youma," and "Japan: An Interpretation"; "The Gods of Pegana", by Lord Dunsany; books from the Russian by Korolenko and Chekhof; and no end of fiction. I even tackled a book by Arnold Bennet[t]; but it was all about misers, and middle-class love, and bread-and-cheese, and she–Sunday school superintendents;[1] so I had to give it up, and flee to Anthony Hope and Jack London for relief. James Huneker's "Egoists" which includes his essay on the Baudelaire legend, together with one on Flaubert, has given me more pleasure than any other serious volume I have read for a long time. "Ennui" has been accepted by "Smart Set" (on George Sterling's recommendation) and the editors offer me five dollars for it. They ought to be d——d well ashamed of themselves. Still, five dollars is five dollars more than nothing, and is sufficient to cover the price of two quarts of good Kentucky Bourbon, or a whole bathtub-ful of the common red wine that I usually drink.

Glad you like the drawing. I'll try to send you some more presently. I've not made any for months.

I'm not familiar with the writings of Symonds, whom you mention. But he must be worth knowing, if he's anything like Wilde and Pater.

Do you know "The Centaur?"[2] I'm enclosing a translation of it from an antique issue of Scribners, on the chance that you haven't. I fancy it will be very much to your taste.

Affectionately,

Clark.

Notes

1. *Anna of the Five Towns: A Novel.*
2. Annie Adams (Mrs. James T.) Fields (1834–1915), "Guerin's Centaur," *Scribner's Magazine* 12, No. 2 (August 1892): 224–32; a translation of "Le Centaure," a prose poem by Maurice de Guérin (1810–1839).

[110] [ANS][1]

[Postmarked Cleveland, Ohio,
6 June 1918.]
6-5-1918

Dear friend Clark,
      I leave a day after tomorrow for the south and will write you when settled. At least I want to hear from you once a week. I anticipate lots of enjoyment over the out-of-doors work—believe me, I need it. Write Clark. A letter to the old address will still reach me.
      Sam

1537 E. 93rd St., Suite 2.

Notes

1. *Front:* Blank.

[111] [ALS]

June 11th, 1918

Dear Sam:
      I've been wanting and intending to drop you a line; but the weather has been hotter than a Fourth of July in Hell, and I feel absolutely wilted and frazzled. Then, too, I've had little to write: my book won't be out till the end of next week, having been delayed for a slight alteration in the design of the title page. At any rate, the alteration will doubtless be an improvement—one small consolation for the delay. I'm hellishly sorry that the book couldn't have come out before you left for training-camp; but you should have it as soon as possible.
      I think I told you in my last that "Smart Set" had taken "Ennui." They have also accepted one of my best sonnets ("Sepulture") and seem very well disposed toward me, tho their preference, of course, is for prose. I may be able to "land" some more of my prose-poems with them. Apropos of editors and magazines, I must quote you the "Atlantic's" last letter of rejection: "We are unable to make an appropriate selection from among these poems." How is that for a specimen of the fine art of "hedging"?
      None of us have been very well lately—my mother's condition, though

slightly improved, is not good. I feel tired and worn-out, myself, and it's an effort for me to do anything. I've not even the energy to get thoroughly drunk!

Will write again very soon—this is a mere note.

Affectionately,

Clark

[112] [ALS]

Auburn, Cal.,

June 21st, 1918.

Dear Sam:

I'm mailing you to-day the first copy of my book that has been struck off and bound. It was numbered 300, so that I should be sure to get it in advance. [Page mutilated] so many of the _____ would be putting in bids for the first numbers.

I'm just back from three days of dissipation in the city, and feel completely done up. I slept fourteen hours last night, but am still so worn-out that I can write no more than this note. Will answer your letter in a day or two.

Affectionately,

Clark.

[113] [ALS]

Auburn, Cal.,

June 24th, 1918.

Dear Sam:

I had just mailed you a copy of my "Odes and Sonnets," addressed to you at Camp Gordon, when I received your last letter. The book ought to be forwarded, since it was insured, and went as first-class mail. If it isn't, I'll not forgive Uncle Sam very quickly.

I'm awfully sorry that you feel so depressed, but understand perfectly. I don't think I could stand a training-camp, myself—the monotony of the discipline would drive me mad.

I saw George while I was in San Francisco. We dined together every evening of my visit, in a Bohemian restaurant down in the Latin quarter. George was on the wagon; but I had so many drinks one evening that the wall-paintings began to look like a movie! I had a pretty severe case of Katzenjammer[1] by the time I left the city; but on the whole, I feel better for my visit—the change and excitement, and the cool salt air of the coast, rather helped to set me up. Also, my doctor gave me a very good report—said that my t. b. had practically cleared up. I brought back a few books with me—Bierce's "Shadow on the Dial," the "Poems and Songs" of Richard Middleton, Gertrude Hall's rendering of Verlaine (the best translation I have seen, on the whole) Edwin Arnold's translation of the Gulistan,[2] and "Some Chinese Ghosts," by Lafcadio Hearn. The list may interest you, since it is quite representative of my tastes. I like Middleton very much—the paganism and the singing music please me greatly. Have you read Gertrude Hall's Verlaine: I quote a stanza or two, for specimens of its quality, in case you haven't; this, for instance, from "Clair de Lune:"

> "The melancholy moonlight, sweet and lone,
> That makes to dream the birds upon the tree,
> And in their polished basins of white stone
> The fountains tall to sob with ecstasy."

Also, the whole of the poem entitled "Bruxelles."

> "Hills and fences hurry by
> Blent in greenish-rosy flight,
> And the yellow carriage-light
> Blurs unto the half-shut eye.
>
> Slowly turns the gold to red
> O'er the humble darkening vales;
> Little trees that flatly spread
> When some feeble birdling wails.
>
> Scarcely sad, so mild and fair
> This unfolding autumn seems;
> All my moody languor dreams,
> Cradled by the gentle air."[3]

Let me hear from you soon. I promise faithfully to write you at least once a week—oftener, if I am able.

> Affectionately,
> Clark.

Notes

1. *Katzenjammer,* a German word meaning "cat's wail" (caterwaul); it was used at this time to denote a hangover.
2. By the Persian poet Sa'di.
3. "Clair de Lune," p. 3; "Bruxelles," p. 35.

[114] [ALS]

> Auburn, Cal.,
> July 6th, 1918.

Dear Sam:

I had meant to write before, but have felt rather under the weather most of the time. The heat has been pretty severe—106 one day; but it's much cooler this morning, with a breeze from the coast, and even a wisp or two of fog in the valleys below.

I hope you've received the "Odes and Sonnets" by this time. I'll never forgive the U. S. postal service if it goes astray.

I'm enclosing a little account of the Book Club and its activities, clipped from the San Francisco Chronicle. It may interest you.

Sorry, but I've written nothing lately. I devote most of my spare time to reading and have developed or re-developed an interest in books of travel, of which I have read comparatively few since boyhood, when I used to literally devour everything of the sort. The West Indies, the Orient, northern Africa, and, in fact, all the countries that border on the Mediterranean—these have come to fascinate me strangely, and draw my thoughts and longings. I believe that a year or two of travel would be the one thing that might save me—I am killing myself as it is.

Yes, I saw George when I was in the city. He spoke of wanting to write you; but his correspondence has become enormous of late years—an accumulative avalanche of letters, scores of which must perforce remain unanswered from lack of time.

Have you ever seen Remy de Gourmont's "A Night in the Luxembourg", translated by Arthur Ransome? I have come into possession of a copy, and find it most interesting. The book is a dialogue, in which a Parisian journalist, three complaisant nymphs or goddesses, and Christ in the guise of an Epicurean philosopher, discourse the most daring and revolutionary theories on life, matter, morals, etc.

Write soon. I shall, in a few days.

    Affectionately,
        Clark.

[115] [ALS]

                Auburn, Cal.,
                July 15th, 1918.

Dear Sam:

I'm hellishly sorry that you haven't received the book. However, I can send you another copy if it doesn't turn up—and I'm afraid it won't. The registration no. was 2346.

I've meant to write for days past, but have felt out of sorts, and didn't care to inflict my ill-humours upon you ... I understand, and sympathize with how you feel about the life in the training-camp. Indeed, it must be dreary and depressing. I wish I could say or do something that would help to cheer you up.

As usual, I do little but read—old friends and favourites of late, for the most part. The books that you have sent me are often in my hand—Pater,

Leopardi, Wilde, George Moore, and how many others that I esteem or love! What friend is more faithful than an old book?

Certainly, keep the poems that I sent you. The Dowson prose-poem *is* good.

Have you ever heard of Stuart Merrill? I enclose an interesting article on his work, clipped from an English publication, "The New Age."[1] "Pastels in Prose," an anthology of French prose-poems very beautifully translated by Merrill, is one of the books to which I oftenest refer. Baudelaire, Huysmans, Banville, Ephraim Mikhael, Regnier, and many others, are represented.

Another letter in a few days. Write whenever you can.

Affectionately,

Clark.

Notes

1. Richard Buxton, "Stuart Merrill," *New Age* 10, No. 1 (2 November 1911): 17–18.

[116] [ALS]

Auburn, Cal.,

July 22nd, 1918.

Dear Sam:

I'm so glad to know that the book arrived safely, after the long delay, and that it gave you so much pleasure. Indeed, it is a beautiful production from the standpoint of bookmaking; and I believe that the Book Club, and the printers, consider it the best piece of work they have done.

I don't think there will be many reviews of the book, on account of the limited edition. I enclose one from "Town Talk,"[1] and will try to keep you posted on others. Please return this one when you have finished with it.

I've not felt well of late, though our weather is phenomenally cool and pleasant for the time of year. Possibly I've a touch of malaria, to judge by the languor and debility from which I suffer.

Wish I had something to send you; but the literary impulse seems exhausted in me, for the time being. In lieu of anything of my own, I enclose a clipping or two that may interest you. I rummage through a vast number of periodicals, old and new; and occasionally find good stuff in odd corners.

This is a mere note, but I don't feel capable of more, just at present. I'll try to write you a real letter, in a few days.

Affectionately,

Clark.

[Enclosure? Clipping re: Benjamin De Casseres.]

Notes

1. [Theodore Bonnet], "The Spectator," *Town Talk* No. 1352 (20 July 1918): 10.

[117] [ALS]

Auburn, Cal.,
Aug. 2nd, 1918.

Dear Sam:

  I should have written you before, but have been quite unwell for some time past, and scarcely in a condition for correspondence. However, I'm better this morning, and will try to collect my wandering wits to the extent of an epistle.

  There's no news, in particular. You ask as to the reception of my book; but the only reviews I have seen are the two I sent you.[1] I don't imagine that many copies have been given out for review, in so expensive and limited an edition. If any other notices come into my hands, I shall certainly send them on.

  I feel utterly incapable of any literary work at present, and my ambition (such as it was,) has fallen dead. I wish I could revive it—it is not well to live thus, if one is to live at all. Alas! I am forever at war with myself; and without internal concord and concertion, [*sic*] little is possible in the way of happiness or achievement. My several personalities maintain amongst them a sort of Kentucky feud.

  I read a great deal—fiction and books of travel, for the most part. The local public library is pretty well stocked in these two departments. A book on Kashmir by Colonel Younghusband, illustrated with reproductions of almost impossibly beautiful paintings, affects me with something akin to nostalgia—a homesickness of the unseen and the unknown.

  I've not heard from George since I was in the city; but was told that he had gone, or intended to go, to New York. I imagine the trip may be in connection with some prospect of producing his drama, "Lilith," which he has recently finished. I've read the manuscript, and think it very beautiful, and "daring" enough to create a sensation, the only possible way, of course, in which it could succeed as a stage production.

  I fervently hope and pray for an early ending of the war ... D—n it! I want you to come out to California and visit me before Phleget[h]on becomes a glacier! . . . It does seem now that there is some prospect of a termination in reasonable time.

  Write when you can, and pardon the foregoing—a jerky, sketchy sort of epistle, but all I am capable of writing in my present condition.

  Au revoir,

Affectionately,
Clark.

Notes

1. The second is unidentified but probably "Clark Ashton Smith of Auburn Lauded for His Latest Book of Poems," *Auburn Daily Journal* (1 July 1918): 1 or "Auburn Poet Greater Than Chatterton," *Auburn Daily Journal* (19 September 1918): 4 (both unsigned).

[118] [ALS]

Auburn, Cal.,

Aug. 14th, 1918.

Dear Sam:

Only another note, since I don't feel up to a regular letter, and, indeed, haven't the materials for one. Life in the vicinity of a dead mining-town like Auburn is not wildly exciting or eventful. My existence here seems an eternal preparation for nothingness, a novitiate of oblivion.

Sterling's divorced wife committed suicide—a terrible and heart-rending thing, which, I fear, will cause him great grief.[1] I don't think he has been happy since their separation in 1912. I enclose a clipping from the S. F. Chronicle, giving an account of the suicide.

I feel better of late, and may do a little writing or drawing presently. The weather is delightful, with all the spicy coolness and calm blue air of mid-autumn—a thing without precedent for August among these inland hills. The jays and woodpeckers are already beginning to gather their store of acorns, snatching them half-ripened from the trees!—a sure sign of an early winter, according to the Indians.

My recent reading includes two books by George Borrow—"Lavengro["] and the "Bible in Spain," both of which are fine and fascinating, with all the strangeness, the unexpectedness, and the triviality, irrelevance, and baffling import of life itself. Also, I have read Loti's "Romance of a Spahi," which might have been called "A Romance of Miscegenation"; and a new book of exquisite and delicate poems by Alice Meynell.[2] Yesterday, I took up Kingsley's "Westward Ho," which I have not read for many years, and straightway became absorbed in it. The book is a fine, straightforward romance; but somehow, I never cared for "Hypatia"—it seems childishly crude and clumsy beside such mighty reconstructions of the antique world as "Salaambo," [*sic*] "Thais," and the "Aphrodite" of Pierre Luoys [*sic*].[3]

Write when you can.

Affectionately,

Clark.

Notes

1. Carrie Sterling (b. 1880) had married GS in 1896; they divorced in 1913. She com-

mitted suicide on 7 August.

2. Alice Meynell (1847–1922), English poet and feminist. CAS was in touch with her and said she offered to help him by recommending him. The book in question is probably *A Father of Women and Other Poems* (London: Burns & Oates, 1917).

3. Kingsley's *Hypatia* (1853) is a novel set in ancient Greece and features the female philosopher Hypatia. Flaubert's *Salammbô* (1862) is set in Carthage, Anatole France's *Thaïs* (1890) in Egypt in the 4th century C.E., and Pierre Louÿs's *Aphrodite* (1896) in ancient Alexandria.

[119]　[ALS]

Auburn, Cal.

Aug. 26th, 1918.

Dear Sam:

　　　　I'm a bit behind with this letter, chiefly because of the infernally hot weather we've had during the last few days. It takes all one's energy to keep alive, when the California sun really gets "het up."

　　　George is back in California, and writes me that he never wants to visit the East again. He speaks of New York as a "stone inferno."

　　　It rejoices me to know that there's such a revival of interest in Bierce; but I can well imagine the ferociously sardonic smile with which the old man would greet it, were he here. Boni and Liveright's "Modern Library" is certainly a praiseworthy institution. I have a number of their publications, and have ordered others. I have just been going over the "Art of Aubrey Beardsley," with its startling reproductions. No one, it seems to me, has ever delineated so much evil, so much horror, so much deformity, in a single line or quirk of the pen, as Beardsley. His drawings are crowded with connotations of inexpressible and almost unimaginable depravities.

　　　I've also been reading a volume of translations—"Contemporary French Poets"—in the Canterbury series[1] and two volumes of literary essays by John Cowper Powys[2]—a brilliant writer and a sound and original critic, with many illuminating things to say. The "Contemporary French Poets" are very much ala [*sic*] Baudelaire—the "Flowers of Evil" run wild, and gone to seed.

　　　I enclose a poem of George's which you've probably not seen. Also a few arabesques and grotesques.

　　　　Affectionately,

　　　　　Clark.

Notes

1. CAS means *Contemporary French Poetry,* ed. Jethro Bithell. See letter 208n1.

2. John Cowper Powys (1872–1963), English poet, novelist, lecturer, and literary critic. CAS may refer to *Visions and Revisions: A Book of Literary Devotions* (1915) and *One Hundred Best Books, with Commentary and an Essay on Books and Reading* (1916).

[120] [ALS]

Auburn, Cal.
Sept. 9th, 1918.

Dear Sam:

This letter is a bit overdue, but try to pardon me. I've not been at all well of late, and even letter-writing is an effort to which I have to nerve and drive myself.

There isn't much news, except that I've actually sold a poem ("The Desert Garden") to Ainslee's, of all magazines. Did I ever send you the poem? It's not a very good one.

I've been reading the collected works of Francis Thompson, and am greatly struck by the resemblance of much of his prose to that of De Quincey. Everard Meynell's Life of Thompson, which I am also reading at present, is tremendously interesting. The points of parallel with De Quincey (in his personal life) are certainly curious and striking.

I actually wrote a sonnet the other day, under the influence of a pint of sherry! It may interest you, as a curiosity. I doubt if good work is ever done under the direct influence of drugs or drink. . . . Also, I enclose a few little drawings—all that I have made lately.

I'll try to write you a real letter, in a few days. This is merely a note.

Affectionately,
Clark.

[121] [ALS]

Auburn, Cal.,
Sept. 16th, 1918.

Dear Sam:

Another note, to let you know that I'm still alive, and able, at least, to curse the climate. I've not felt at all well, lately—my chest is bothersome, and I seem to reach the exhaustion-point very easily.

Had a letter from George the other day. He asked me for your address, and has promised to write you. Macmillan's are to publish his "Lilith,"[1] the ms. of which I read when I was in S. F. last June. It is very, very beautiful, and full of splendid lines. The "write-up" I enclose (from "Town Talk") quotes fine passages, but I remember some even finer ones.[2]

I've received another consignment of books, among them two more of Boni and Liveright's publications—"Best Russian Short Stories,"[3] and "A Miracle of St. Antony, with Five Other Plays," by Maeterlinck. Some of the Russian stories are tremendous—"Lazarus," by Andreyev, is weird and awful beyond conception—an epitome of all the terror of night, and the horror of infinite emptiness. . . . I rather fancy Maeterlinck, in his earlier vein; but I can't abide the optimistic platitudes of his later books. The volume I have includes his best plays—"Pelleas and Melisande,['] "Interior," "The Intruder," etc.

Write soon.

Affectionately,

Clark.

Notes

1. First published by A. M. Robertson (1919), then by the Book Club of California (1920). Macmillan did not publish an edition until April 1926.
2. The Spectator [Theodore Bonnett], "George Sterling's 'Lilith,'" *Town Talk* 33, No. 1360 (14 September 1918): 6–7.
3. Ed. Thomas Seltzer.

[122] [ALS]

Auburn, Cal.,

Sept. 27th, 1918.

Dear Sam:

I'm glad you liked the poem and the drawings. I wish to hell I had something better to send you, but I've written hardly anything, of late. I enclose the "Desert Garden," however. Also a poem of George's, which you will appreciate, I know.

I'm sorry you continue to feel depressed. Can't I contrive to make you cheer up, somehow? I wish you had some of the port and sherry I've been drinking lately—I've located a small winery not so many miles from Auburn, that makes some superexcellent stuff. D—n these Prohibitionists, tho—this bill they've put through is the most horrible outrage committed on human liberty since the days of Puritanism, or the Catholic Inquisition.[1]

I envy you the acquisition of that volume of Solomon, with the original drawing. Solomon, I think, had more genius than any other of the Preraphaelites, excepting Rossetti. Watts and Burne-Jones are thin and tame compared to him.[2]

I intend to make some more drawings presently. Our rainy season is settling in early this year, so I'll have to spend a lot of time indoors. Drawing is more of an amusement to me than anything else I can do, outside of my reading. I'll see that you get some of the pictures.

I'm sending you, under separate cover, a drawing of myself, made in 1915 by a Miss Bremer, of San Francisco.[3] It's not very good of me, however—idealized in some ways, and incomplete in others.

Write soon.

Affectionately, as ever,

Clark.

Clark Ashton Smith (1915). Drawing by A. M. Bremer.
Made during the Pan-Pacific Exposition in San Francisco.

Notes

1. A resolution calling for a constitutional amendment to enforce nationwide prohibition of alcoholic beverages was introduced in the U.S. Congress in December 1917. By January 1919 it had been ratified by 36 states (three-fourths of the 48 states); California ratified it on 13 January 1919. Prohibition went into effect on 17 January 1920.

2. For Rossetti, see 31n2. George Frederic Watts (1817–1904), popular English Victorian painter and sculptor associated with the Symbolist movement. Sir Edward Coley Burne-Jones, 1st Baronet, ARA (1833–1898), English artist and designer associated with the later phase of the Pre-Raphaelite movement. For Solomon, see letter 36n1.

3. Anne Bremer (1868–1923), a California painter, influenced by post-Impressionism, called "the most 'advanced' artist in San Francisco" in 1912. Her drawing is published in *Grotesques and Fantastiques,* inside front cover. CAS inscribed it for presentation to SL.

[123] [ALS]

Auburn, Cal.,

Oct. 2nd, 1918.

Dear Sam:

I knew you would appreciate the extracts from "Lilith," which is probably the best poetic drama ever written in America. I shall certainly see that you receive a copy when it comes out—if possible, an autographed copy . . . I am giving George your address, so you will doubtless hear from him in due course. He tells me that his correspondence is becoming a deluge—the inevitable penalty of fame.

There's no drawing under the title "Felaise," in the list at the end of the volume I have. However, the list is only a partial one.

Our weather has been showery of late, with more than one thunderstorm. I'm not fond of rain, and feel anything but enthusiastic at the imminence of a sodden autumn, and a long, diluvial winter. I wish to hell I were in Spain, or Peru, or Egypt, or Borneo, or any other place sufficiently remote from the so-called temperate zone.

Another letter in a few days. I've nothing to send you this time, and nothing to write, it would seem, with the exception of complaints. I don't feel particularly well, and am tired and nervous most of the time.

Affectionately,

Clark.

[124] SL to CAS [nonextant]

[Envelope postmarked Atlanta, Ga., Oct. 4, 1918.]

[125] [ALS]

Auburn, Cal.,

Oct. 10th, 1918.

Dear Sam:

I've finally managed to mail you a copy of Miss Bremer's drawing of myself—the ones I had were mislaid, somehow, and I couldn't find them till yesterday. The picture isn't much, anyway—I had been "doing" all the galleries, buildings, streets, etc, of the Panama-Pacific Exposition at the time it was made, and felt half-dead from fatigue.

I should have written before, but, as usual, have not been very well. I went for a long walk the other day, and overdid, with the consequence that I've felt weak, exhausted, and feverish ever since. I don't seem to recuperate as quickly as I did at one time. Each day seems to find me with less energy, less enthusiasm, than the day before. I seem to have lost all interest in my writing, and even reading is more or less of an effort. If I could only travel, it seems to me that I might escape from this rut of ill-health, discouragement, and semi-dissipation. I dream impossible dreams of Spain, Egypt, the West and East Indies, Peru, Japan, and a thousand other places—of lands beyond the last and bluest horizon.

How is it with you, brother? Write soon.

Affectionately,
Clark.

[126] [ALS]

Auburn, Cal.,
Oct. 22nd, 1918.

Dear Sam:

I trust you will have received the drawing by this time—I mailed it a week or so ago. The picture of yourself came to hand in due time. I like it very, very much, and imagine that it must be an excellent photograph.

There's absolutely no news. I've written nothing, drawn nothing, have read only old books, and thought only old thoughts. I seldom see anyone, and seem to have a monopoly of the solitude which you praise. However, I've no complaint to make on that score—I prefer my own company, poor and irksome as it is, to that of the multitude.

I'm sorry you have a cold—I know what they're like, though my outdoor life, and abstemious diet have kept me singularly free from them of late years. You're right about the remedy—a hot toddy and a good old-fashioned "bake-out," is the only thing.

My own trouble seems more a case of nervous or cerebral exhaustion, than anything else. Weariness, indifference, ennui,—these possess me, body and soul, till nothing seems worth doing or worth having. "The formidable curse of taedium vitae," as De Quincey called it, and praised opium as a palliative. But, alas, I have no opium; and alcohol, the only available substitute, is perhaps the least satisfactory of narcotics.

Affectionately,
Clark.

[127] [ALS]

East Auburn, Cal.,
Oct. 30th, 1918.

Dear Sam:

A note to acknowledge your letter and the accompanying poem. I'll write at length in a few days; but I have been quite unwell (sick in bed for part of one day) and am still indisposed.

I like the lyric you send. I'm sorry you feel so ill and despondent—physical malaise is bad enough without a mental or emotional accompaniment.

Your friend, Vincent Starrett, wrote asking me for a copy of "The Star-Treader," and I've mailed him one, with compliments. Anyone who is a friend of yours, is welcome to as much.

Certainly, keep everything I send you, unless I ask you to return it. I'm glad you like the picture of myself; but I fear it's very much idealized, not to say etherealized.

By the way, please address me at East Auburn, after this—I'm having my mail changed because of the carelessness and frequent errors of the Auburn office.

Affectionately,
Clark.

[128] [ALS]

East Auburn, Cal.,
Nov. 7th, 1918.

Dear Sam:

It's good to know that you are feeling better—even an ordinary cold is a sufficiently severe affliction. This "flu" that's sweeping the country is equal to the plague,[1] almost. I've escaped it, so far, but have felt unwell most of the time. A little overexertion, such as a long walk, fatigues me greatly, and I take days to recover.

I'm not familiar with the David Gray whom you mention;[2] but what you tell me is certainly very interesting. Your mention of "Timon" reminds me that I should re-read a number of Shakespeare's plays—I've hardly looked into him for a year past, or more. Most of my reading now will have to be in the form of **re-reading,** since I can't afford new books. The prices have gone up astoundingly. . . . I spent yesterday afternoon with Omar and Leopardi (the latter the volume you sent me) and found them better company than ever.

I hope you do something with the prose-poems of which you speak— you know how well I think of your essays in that form. The little poem you enclose is charming. I wish I had something to send you in return; but my poor brain is dead these days; and the onset of our cold weather (I found frost this morning) is scarcely liable to revive it.

Contrary to my expectations, we have had a dry autumn, so far; and grapes are still on the vine. I've obtained a few basketfuls from a neighboring vineyard (owned by a Prohibitionist!) and am allowing the juice to ferment. I expect to have three or four gallons of excellent Muscatel against the impending "dry" period!

As ever, affectionately,

Clark.

Notes

1. The 1918 flu pandemic (January 1918–December 1920) was an unusually deadly influenza pandemic. It infected 500 million people across the world and resulted in the deaths of 50 to 100 million (three to five percent of the world's population).
2. David Gray (1838–1861), a Scottish poet.

[129] [ALS]

East Auburn, Cal.,

Nov. 11th, 1918.

Dear Sam:

The news to-day[1]—that the Germans have accepted Foch's terms—seems too good to be true, almost. I'm thinking that you'll not have to go across, after all. I'm sorry you continue to feel so depressed; but I understand and sympathize perfectly.

I've not much to report, excepting the sale of two of my sonnets, "The Mummy," and "In Saturn," to a magazine called "The Sonnet," which is given over entirely, I believe, to poems in that form. Have you ever seen it? I received seven dollars for the two . . . The editor, Mahlon Leonard Fisher, has written some creditable sonnets himself.[2]

Starrett's address is in care of "The Austinite," 5611 South Blvd., Austin—Chicago. I had a nice letter from him the other day, thanking me for my book.

I've done nothing lately, except potter around with some job-lots of fermenting grape-juice. What sort of booze the stuff will make, I can't say; but it's fascinating to experiment.

I'll try to enclose a drawing or two with this—it pleases me to know that you liked the others so well. I'll make you some more presently.

Affectionately, Clark.

Notes

1. Celebrated hereafter as Armistice Day, the end of World War I.
2. Mahlon Leonard Fisher (1874–1974?), poet and editor of the *Sonnet,* author of *Sonnets: A First Series* (1917).

[130] [ALS]

East Auburn, Cal.,
Nov. 17th, 1918.

Dear Sam:

Here are a few drawings, made at different times, that I've raked up for you. Also, two or three poems, written during the present autumn, that I've probably not sent you before. Also, three sonnets of George's, and a book-review from an S. F. paper that speaks of me.[1] Note the slurring reference to Bierce in the same . . . Yellow curs and spotted hyenas—none of them can open their fetid mouths to mention Bierce, without snapping and snarling.

No news at all. I keep closely to my hill-top, not because I'm afraid of the "flu," but because the wearing of a gauze mask is a more than Chinese torture to me. But life is not without compensations—I've laid in a dozen gallons of assorted vino, and a gallon of brandy. Also, I've five or six gallons of grape-juice in process of fermentation, and when it's "gone" far enough I'll fortify it with some of the brandy and keg it up to age a little. Boulder Ridge won't "go dry," if I can help it.

I've heard nothing more about the publication of "Lilith," but will ask George when I write him again. Has he written you? He promised me that he would.

Affectionately,
Clark.

Notes

1. Apparently Helen Dare, "Book Club Garners Treasures Right Here from Home Field," *San Francisco Chronicle* (30 June 1918): 10. Dare writes that the Book Club of California "has set up in the libraries of its members, where obeisance is made . . . to native genius . . . [including] that youngest and amazingest of the starry group, Clark Ashton Smith."

[131] [TLS]

[19 November 1918?]

Dear Clark,

Thankee for the letter and your drawings. I am holding on to all I have here and will place them in with the others when I return home—and unless the unforeseen happen, I hope to be there before the close of the winter. It surely is going to be a fine thing to get back into civilian life again—and the end seems now not far in sight. I have read very little here although I did try to do so—but the demands are many upon a person here and most of them amount to little. I started to read a very fine little play by Dana Burnet in a recent "Post" entitled "Christus", which seems very fine.1 I look forward to finishing it this evening. Vincent Starrett has a very interesting memorandum relative to my Keats' discovery2 in an introduction to a catalogue of autographs for sale by Walter Hill, the bookseller of Chicago.3 Starrett is decidedly a person of talent and I believe you will find him an interesting letter-writer. Discipline seems to have relaxed very much here since the cessation of hostilities—and everybody seems easier and happier. I get to Atlanta oftener than before although there is very little to see in Atlanta. They have a Carnegie Library there which has an interesting stock of books. I found in the shelves a book of poems—fairy-poems by one Walter Ramal, who is no other than Walter De La Mare—a pseudonym for this writer away back in 1902. They are quite charming. I wonder if most of the modern collectors have heard of the volume. I would like to get to Chattanooga for Thanksgiving but can't just now afford to pay the full fare. This is only a note. Write soon.

                    Aff.
          Sam

Corp Sam Loveman
Headquarters Detachment,
4th Repl Reg't, Camp Gordon, Ga.

Notes

1. Dana Burnet (1888–1962), *The Christus, Saturday Evening Post* 191, No. 21 (23 November 1918): 8–9, 89.
2. "A Keats Discovery."
3. Walter M. Hill (1868–1952), a prominent bookdealer in Chicago. He published Vincent Starrett's bibliography of Ambrose Bierce (1920), *Rhymes for Collectors* (1921), *Banners in the Dawn* (1922), and numerous privately printed editions of Christmas mementos.

[132] [ALS]

                    East Auburn, Cal.,
                         Nov. 21st, 1918.

Dear Sam:

          I've not yet celebrated the announcement of peace, and shan't till the Kaiser, the Crown Prince, and the balance of German Junkerdom are taken captive and hung up with hooks through their ears. Then I shall fire off both barrels of my shotgun (which has brought down the makings of many a rabbit-stew or dove pot-pie) and mix myself a double drink of port, sherry, and whisky.

          I hope (and trust) you won't have to "go across." It would certainly be rotten luck, now that the war is really over.

          I want to tell you how much I like the little poem you enclose—a lyric as beautiful and poignant as anything you have translated from Heine. The thing has haunted me ever since it came, and there is no surer test of poetic quality than that—a prolonged reverberation in the memory, and a calling-forth of echoes unknown or forgotten. Your poem has taken me so.

The autumn leaves are late in turning, this year, and the orchard below me is just beginning to put on its saffron and scarlet and purple. The trees are like hierophants, celebrating in robes of splendour, before the vast blue misty altar of the vales and hills, the solemn ceremonial of the passing of Beauty.

I enclose an attempt at sketching myself, which, at least, is no worse than some of my photographs. But even at that, I might escape future incrimination, if represented by it in the Rogue's Gallery.

As ever, Affectionately,
Clark.

[133] [TLS]

[23 November 1918?]

Dear Clark,

Things are so quiet here that I thought I would write—not so much to give vent to my boredom, but just because it seems like the old days to be writing to you. I've been dragging myself around for two weeks with a bad cold that the physician defined as acute bronchitis but they don't give one admittance to the infirmary here unless there are signs of fever, so I am trying my damndest to rid myself of it—but by the living god that made me,[1] it sticks to me more pertinaciously than the brick-red Georgia mud. Aspirin and quinine are the main remedies, both worthless in my case. They don't seem to have any effect upon me. One tumbler of hot—but what's the use?

I've done no writing in spite of my threat to break into it again. The only inspiration I've had since I left home was up on Signal and Lookout Mountains when I visited Chattanooga a short time ago—it wasn't creative but more in the shape of peace from the fret and fever about me. I wonder if a few years would not have made Keats re-consider his "Nature is fine but human nature is finer"[2]—and I wonder if Prospero[3] didn't see the pathetic fallacy of returning to flesh and blood from the loneliness of his miraculous island. I see nothing to marvel at in human nature—much to wonder at. When I return home, Clark, be sure that I shall return to my loneliness again for I know where I have hidden my wand, and if I have never been Prospero I can at least be Pierrot. Somehow, with all the strangeness about me, I cling the closer to Beauty. For I know, as only they know who have read and understood her litany, that everything else is but the figment of a vision and that her ways alone are the ways of peace. Pray forgive this incursion into poetics—it affords me all sorts of relief.

I'm sorry that your portrait never reached me. If you had it insured please give me the number so that I can make some effort to trace it up—altho I suppose it will be futile effort.

Tell me about any interesting book you have recently read. We have a little Jewish lad in our company who danced with the Granville Barker ballet[4]—he's pretty stagey and like most of his ilk vaunts the sublimated ego, but withal interesting. He has read a great deal, although I shouldn't imagine much for the sake of literature—and knows his bohemia in Washington Square well.

I've had two letters from Morris Miller,[5] both full of philosophy and containing some quiet allusions to the beautiful old world towns and the fields lined with popular trees and covered with poppies, of northern France.

Write soon and forgive this sort of a letter.

Affectionately,

Sam

Corporal Sam Loveman,
Company H,
4th Inf. Repl. Reg't,
Camp Gordon, Georgia.

[Envelope postmarked Atlanta, Ga., Nov. 23, 19[18].] [envelope placed here conjecturally]

Notes

1. Rudyard Kipling, "Gunga Din" (1890) l. 83, as "By the livin' Gawd that made you."
2. "Scenery is fine, but human nature is finer." John Keats, letter to Benjamin Bailey (13 March 1818).
3. The protagonist of Shakespeare's *The Tempest.*
4. Harley Granville Barker (1877–1946), leading English playwright and theatre manager.
5. Morris Longstreet Miller (1891–1918), a cartoonist with the *Cincinnati Post,* to whom SL dedicated his story "The Faun." He is also mentioned in "Winter." Miller died of "heart failure" on 1 October serving in France, but SL stated in an interview that Miller died of an epileptic fit. In "Memoralia," SL describes him as having a "Keats-like radiant face" (l. 10).

[134] [TLS]

[28 November 1918]

Dear Clark,

This is Thanksgiving Day afternoon, and I'm on duty at the office. This evening I shall probably go to Atlanta and take in a picture show—they say that Theda Bara in "Salome" there is exotic enough to suit the most moral tastes[1]—and about midnight betake myself back to Gordon again. They predict the demob[i]lization of the Replacements by Christmas and every indication seems to point that way. I hope they don't retain me on the outgoing examinations on account of any physical disability, but anything is likely to happen. So wish me good luck in getting home early.

Thanks for the picture of yourself which seems amazingly Balzatian. And for the appreciation of the little lyric contained in your letter. I've an elegiac poem in mind for Morris Miller—but not here, not in this place. I can just imagine Miller's words at the announcement—"Really, it's gratifying to feel myself entitled to it." All this with a smile and a certain hesitancy in proceeding. I've never ascertained how Miller fell—I shall do so from his friend (and mine) Murphy, when I arrive home, but his dying must have been entirely in consistency with his living, a sort of quiet heroism, sans the flamboyant heroics of war-time stress and tragedy.

Have I ever sent you this lyric?—I forget whether I ever named it but you can call it a "Song"—

> In the Spring of the year, in the silver rain,
>   When petal by petal the blossoms fall;
> The robins begin to mate again—
>   But the heart forgets not all.
>
> For within the budding flowers and leaves,
>   A spirit of joy awakens and stays;
> But the soul of grief remembers and grieves,
>   All her lonely and alien days.

I see that Edward Marsh, Rupert Brooke's executor, has published a memoir of the poet, and I've made a note of it as one of the books I want to read. It's next to impossible to procure the latest books here—but in Cleveland—praise the Gods, there is still Laukhuff.

Vincent Starrett (did I tell you) has an interesting mention of my Keats-discovery in an introduction to a catalogue of autographs pub. by a Chicago bookseller. He starts out thuswise—"I know a youth, etc."[2]

Today is like a spring day here but they tell me that it is growing quite cold in Cleveland. The heavens here seem always to be starred. Some of the nebulae which are fairly indistinct or misty in Cleveland shine with piercing brilliancy in this accursed state of Georgia. The evening skies are either of a deep blue or a marvellous violet and a full moon that I saw a week ago seemed like a description from the miraculous word-painting of Coleridge's "Ancient Mariner." And there is always the long, long road that leads into the heart of the darkness (excuse the Conradism) with the automatons chatting and walking up and down the long stretch of light and their disappearance into what might seem chaos, or a final nullity.

I read an interesting appreciation on Degas this morning which I found in an old number of "Vanity Fair" at the barracks.[3] By Arthur Symons, I forgot to mention. The more I read of Symons, the more I realize that of all the great prose writers, he alone, gives us the profundity of the spiritual qualities of literature. Pater[,] even, seems wordy by comparison. And nothing that

Symons has ever written is uninteresting. Write when you can and believe me with best wishes to yourself and your folk,

Affectionately,

Sam

Headquarters Detachment,
4th Infantry Replacement Regiment,
Camp Gordon, Georgia.

Notes

1. *Salome* (Fox Film Corp., 1918), directed by J. Gordon Edwards; starring Theda Bara, G. Raymond Nye, and Alan Roscoe.
2. SL at the time was 31.
3. Arthur Symons, "On the Genius of Degas," *Vanity Fair* 10, No. 3 (May 1918): 60, 90–94.

[135] [ALS]

East Auburn, Cal.,

Nov. 30th, 1918.

Dear Sam:

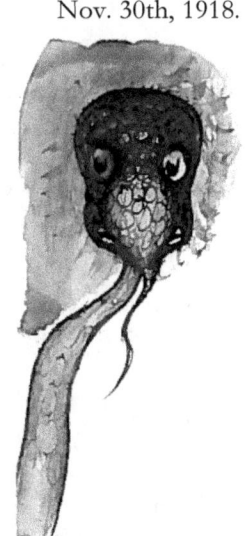

It's good to hear that you liked the pictures and verses. Keep George's sonnets, if you like—never return anything I send unless I particularly request you to. I'll try to obtain you a copy of "The Binding of the Beast" as soon as possible. Robertson had plenty of them last June, when I was in S. F.

I've heard of Norman Gale but don't remember reading any of his work. Is it like that of the rest of the Yellow Book crowd?[1]

I like your idea of writing a book on Clare—you are certainly fitted to deal with the subject, both by reason of sympathy and knowledge. Your book should be the ideal biography of that strange and unfortunate being.

I've nothing to send this time, and nothing much to say, it would seem. I feel better of late, but am horribly lazy. I ought to work, but I'm too indifferent, too indolent even to play; and I don't seem to give a tinker's-damn whether I *ever* write or do or draw anything again. The Muse that would arouse me, must needs be a termagant. And the goddesses are not given to nagging.

Affectionately,

Clark.

Notes

1. Norman Rowland Gale (1862–1942), English poet and reviewer.

[136] [TLS]

[30 November 1918?]

Dear Clark,

I am still here but just wanted to ask you to address all your letters to me for the time being to the old address—1537 East 93 St., Suite 2,* Cleveland, Ohio. I expect to be shifted to a development Battalion—all class c men are to be sent there, pending discharge or transference, and I shall feel myself safer in receiving your letters. This is a hell of a life—but one must take it come what may.

I read a very fine appreciation of D'Annunzio in the current Vanity Fair by Arthur Symons.[1] There is nothing more beautiful in the world than these jewelled essays of his.

And how are you?

Affectionately,
Sam

Headquarters Detachment,
4th Regiment Casuals (White)
Camp Gordon, Ga.

I go to Chattanooga over Sunday tomorrow.

Notes

1. "Gabriele d'Annunzio," *Land and Water* 70 (30 August 1917): 14–17; *Vanity Fair* 11, No. 4 (December 1918): 47, 74.

[137] [ALS]

East Auburn, Cal.,
Dec. 9th, 1918.

Dear Sam:

Your copy of "The Binding of the Beast" has come, and I'm mailing it to you forthwith.[1] The book is mainly a reprint of the war-sonnets in "The Caged Eagle"—by far the best things of their kind ever written. I know that you agree with me.

Have you seen the poems by George that I enclose? I like both of them, especially the one on Bierce.[2]

---

*[Note in pen:]—dropping the corporalship!

I like the lyric that you send in your letter. "Song" as a title describes it well—all your work has the "singing" quality.

I certainly hope that you obtain an early release—it would be the most senseless and abominable of hard luck to have to spend the winter in that training-camp.

I heartily agree with you about Symons—I think more and more of him, both as a poet and a prose-writer. His "Studies in Seven Arts" is in the local library, and I intend to draw and re-read it before long.

My reading has been desultory of late—snatches of Marco Polo, some of Hearn's Japanese fantasies and essays, and a re-reading on successive nights of "Thais" and the "Tale of Two Cities.["] Last night I read Swinburne's "Pilgrimage of Pleasure" and Edgar Saltus' "Philosophy of Disenchantment" by turns. I've not read anything new for some time.

Affectionately,

Clark.

Notes

1. CAS's presentation copy of the book, dated 7 December 1918 and sent to SL at Camp Gordon, Georgia, is held at Columbia University.

2. "The Passing of Bierce," *Reedy's Mirror* 25, No. 30 (28 July 1916): 491; *Bohemia* 1, No. 2 (15 August 1916): 37; *Town Talk* No. 1307 (8 September 1917): 9. In *Sails and Mirage and Other Poems*.

[138] [TLS]

[c. 12 December 1918]

Dear Clark,

Got the book, your letter and George's poems. I don't like the idea of your spending money on my luxurious desires, Clark—so will you please tell me just what the book comes to and I shall gladly remit? The volume contains new poems, does it not? Some of them are distinctly unfamiliar. It is by far the most dignified, the most inspirational exposition in poetry of the terrible business that I have ever read—and its motive is Aeschylean. One of the sonnets—has it struck you as being the same?—"The Little Farm"— reminds me with all its horror, all its cumulative effect of pathos—of a story by Bierce.[1] I want to thank you for the two mss. poems of Sterling's. Both are new to me, and the one on Bierce is powerful in its magnificence and solemnity. I sometimes wonder at Bierce's fate. During my visit to Chattanooga I was told that there was another theory afloat—I forget just what it was. They urged me to give that last letter of mine that I had from him for print—but what's the use?—and I know that Bierce hated all such triviality and such truckling to the ironic concessions that are made for the average public. I would like to get out a book of criticism on his work—but it seems that I had better forgo any literary plans I have made as I am pretty assuredly salted here for some months to come. I always wonder whether a certain thing that Elbert Hubbard said "about Bierce's ascending Mt Horeb like Moses of old and forgetting to come down"[2] had anything to do with his disappearance—he must have had it in mind as he once annotated a publisher's announcement of his work with the comments of well-known writers, with some caustic remarks.

I can picture your leisurely sort of an existence, Clark—that sort of thing seems to me like the paradisal state of Andrew Marvell's Garden. I long for the time when I can simply isolate myself and "forget in being forgotten." Here this faculty is almost an impossibility. Your inmost thoughts are pried at and pestered with—and one is never alone. There is always the conversational bore who demands an audience—and the slightest tendency toward being alone, "queers" one.

Write soon, and believe me with kind and sincere regards,

Affectionately,

Sam

Sgt. Sam. Loveman
4th Reg't Casuals (White),
Camp Gordon, Ga.

Notes

1. The poem is in *The Caged Eagle*. It tells of a farm that is besieged in warfare. SL may have been thinking of Bierce's Civil War story "Chickamauga."
2. Source unknown, but quoted (without attribution) in Vincent Starrett, *Buried Caesars: Essays on Literary Appreciation* (Chicago: Covici-McGee, 1923), 32.

[139]   [ALS]

East Auburn, Cal.,

Dec. 15th, 1918.

Dear Sam:

I owe you a long, fat letter after my lapse of silence, and the receipt of four or five letters from you. I wish I had more to write—but nothing ever happens here—the nearest approach to excitement is the "flu", still prevalent hereabouts, though in a milder form than at first. There have been yarns to the effect that the "flu" was really the Black Plague, and many people, especially the country people, are horribly scared!

Thanks for the poems you send, all of which I like. The lyric by Miss (or is it Mrs. Aldrich?)[1] that you quote, is a fine thing.

I've done little but read, and have accomplished a pretty fair amount of perusing and browsing in the last fortnight. My table is covered with a litter of borrowed books—"The Rubaiyat of Hafiz,"[2] "Thus Spake Zharathrustra," [*sic*] "A Feast of Lanterns," and others . . . Do you know this rendering of Ha-fiz, by L. Cranmer-Byng? Much of it is excellent (d——d if I can see much difference between Hafiz and Omar, in regard to thought and feeling) and one stanza haunts me:

> "That night we wrought Love's miracle again;
> For one brief gloom one soul was born of twain:
> Now Death shall weary at the springs of Youth,
> By singing waters that he sealed in vain."[3]

"The [*sic*] Feast of Lanterns" is an anthology of lyrics from the Chinese, also translated by Cranmer-Byng, who seems an expert in the Oriental tongues, as well as a writer of admirable English verse. Many of them are very beauti-ful—poems delicate and fragile as porcelean, [*sic*] and full of the fragrance of wine and roses. Listen to this, by Han Yu, who lived in the 8th century A. D.

["]*Disappointment*

> Still moonlight floods the inner gallery,
> Where the japonica sets fluttering
> Her silvered petals. Languidly
> I rise, and let my absent glance
> Fall where the shadows of the swing
> Over the door-step dance.
>
> I am possessed
> By Spring's rough humid winds that penetrate
> The silken curtains of my lonely state,
> And cannot rest,
> For all my sorrow.
> During the night I hear the heavy rain
> Crash on the lotus pools afar.
> To-morrow! ah to-morrow!
> The little boat lies swamped that I would fain
> Have steered in search of the golden nenuphar."[4]

I do hope you will be released before long—the training-camp life must be a hell of tedium.

I enclose a page of peace-poems from the S. F. Chronicle, which lately held a competition. Here are the winners. Talk of the horrors of war—how about the horrors of peace—of which the "poems" are surely not the least!

Affectionately,

Clark.

Notes

1. Possibly a poem by Anne Reeve Aldrich (1866–1892), American poet and novelist; author of *Rose of Flame and Other Poems of Love* (1889), *Songs about Life, Love and Death* (1892), and *Nadine and Other Poems* (1893).
2. By Syed Abdul Majid.
3. *The Rubáiyat of Háfiz* 53.
4. *A Feast of Lanterns* 63–64.

`[140] SL to CAS [nonextant]

[Envelope postmarked Atlanta, Ga., Dec. 17, 1918.]

[141]   [ALS]

East Auburn, Cal.,
Dec. 20th, 1918.

Dear Sam:

It's a good day for the writing of a Christmas letter—dull, dark, cold, and foggy. We've had an uncommon quantity of fog this year, alternating with severe frost—a most unpleasant combination.

Thanks for the excellent poem on Wilde. Oddly enough, I had been reading the little volume "Recollections of Wilde," by Andre Gide, Ernest Jones, etc (which you sent me) the day the poem came.[1]

I sat up last night, reading "Thus Spake Zharathrustra," which gives me a new and better opinion of Nietzsche. There are hundreds, nay, thousands of splendid apothegms, of magnificent passages. The copy I have is in the Modern Library, the best edition of cheap reprints that I know. It contains dozens of books that are almost unobtainable otherwise. I have just ordered three of the latest additions—de Maupassant's "Un[e] Vie," the poems of Villon (Payne's translation) and D'Annunzio's "Flame of Life." Think of such stuff being offered broadcast in America at 70¢ per volume! The prospects of literature are improving, it seems to me.

My brain seems dead, these days, or benumbed with winter, and the tedium of an isolated, nay, insulated, existence. At any rate, I don't suffer much, feeling always, as I do, the unreality and immateriality of things. Even neurasthenia has its compensations, and this feeling of unreality is one of them. Sensation is curiously muffled, and even the vibrations of pain seem to come from a distance in time and space. To-day, my memories are a drift of dead leaves, and the more precious of them but petals laid away to wither between the pages of a book.

I enclose two issues of "The Sonnet," which, as I told you, lately accepted some of my work. Don't return them. Also, a snapshot of George, who was duck-hunting at the time it was taken!

Here's wishing you the best of Christmas dinners, and a speedy release!
Affectionately,

Clark.

Notes

1. CAS meant to refer, not to Ernest Jones (1879–1958), the Welsh neurologist and col-
league of Sigmund Freud, but to La Jeunesse, a French author. See Bibliography under
La Jeunesse.

[142] [ALS]

East Auburn, Cal.,
Dec. 26th, 1918.

Dear Sam:

I'm glad you liked "The Binding of the Beast." Some of the poems
are new, I think. Certainly, I have seen nothing else in the way of war-verse
that seems at all comparable with the best of them. You mustn't talk of paying me for the book, since it really didn't cost me a cent. I had it charged to
my "account" at Robertson's—an account I never expect to pay.

I'm hellishly sorry to hear that you are stuck in that training-camp. It seems
so entirely senseless that you should be, now that the war is over. I wish you were
here to share my solitude,—of which I've had rather too much, lately.

My father and I spent Christmas eve in a good, old-fashioned English way,
with walnuts and port wine—tawny, eighteen-year-old port. We'll hardly do that
next year, with this damnable Prohibition bill impending. We had a quiet
Christmas, with a bountiful dinner, of which I ate little. I've not felt at all well
for some time, and last night was a bad night, with chills, fever, and pleurisy. I
feel abominably weak to-day, as I write, and my ears are ringing with the fever.

I'll try to write again, very soon. Pardon the brevity of this. I have several
other letters to write, and am almost too ill for the task.

Affectionately,

Clark.

[143] [TLS, mutilated]

[31 December 1918?]

Dear Clark,

As usual mighty glad to hear from you. That page of competitive
poetry is pretty poor, I agree with you—all such competitions are. Where you
have men of genius like Brooke or Sorley or Seeger (who isn't a major) you
have the mob who imagine that genius is a matter of business not inspiration.

I recently drew from the Atlanta Library here a book of translations by
Stuart Merrill called "Pastels in Prose", and most strangely published by

Harpers Brothers with an introduction by (of all people) William Dean How-
ells. There are translations of prose-poems by Mallarme, Huysmans, Catulle
Mendez, Judith Gautier, Baudelaire, and I forget how many more—beautiful,
delicate things, so evanescent that one wonders at the artistry with which they
are constructed. I've felt a great desire to do something in that line. I note
that Judith Gautier's translations of Chinese Lyrics may now be procured in
an English version and I have made note of this book as one of the things I
wish to own when I get back to life again. I also read Huneker's "Apes, Ivory
and Peacocks", and I liked it.

Clark, there are many things I aim to do when I get home, but one of the
first things will be to get all the stuff I've written together and see if I can't
get them under cover. You see, I haven't even got a single professional publication of anything of mine to my credit. It may be that the "Dial" and other
magazines will find some of my literary poetry of interest—altho I concede
that it will never become as popular as the stuff being turned out by the
Teasdales, the Untermeyer's [*sic*],[1] and the Robert Frosts—the latter of whom
is especially my abomination.

Our weather is still surprisingly mild. We expect to be liberated—that's the
word—some time in January, so please address me care my home address in the
future. If I stay I can easily advise you. Everybody is anxious to return home as
you can well imagine—I pretty well lost my taste for things here after Miller's
death. I can't imagine him dead—it seems scarcely credible that a person who
took life as cheerfully as he did could have succumbed so easily. But it happened—and I've never taken the trouble to ascertain why. More in a few days.

                         Affectionately,

                                     Sam

Sergeant Sam Loveman,
4th Reg't Casuals (White)
Headquarters Detachment,
Camp Gordon, Ga.

Notes

1. Sara Teasdale (1884–1933), American lyric poet; Louis Untermeyer (1885–1977), an
American poet, anthologist, editor, and critic.

[144] [ALS]

                                     East Auburn, Cal.,
                                       Jan. 3rd, 1919.

Dear Sam:

          Glad you got the mistletoe. It's very common here, and even kills
some of the oaks on which it flourishes as a parasite. I've seen them thicker

with mistletoe than they ever were with their own foliage. I admit a fondness for the stuff, with its old Druidic associations.

Here's "The Ghoul and the Seraph." It's horribly rough and prosy in parts, and I'm not sure that the songs add anything to it. I may try some more dialogues, either in blank verse or prose. I have titles enough in my note-book, such as "The Lich and the Demon," "The Girl from Venus," "The Ape and the Crocodile," "Amaimon, Ashtaroth, and the Monk," ["]Asmode-us and the Gargoyles," etc, etc. The last title has its possibilities, I think. Imagine Asmodeus pausing to chat with the gargoyles of Notre Dame!

I've seen the book of Hindu myths you mention.[1] The illustrations were magnificent, but I didn't have time to read much of the text.

Have been reading Loti's "Lands of Exile," with its odoriferous and col-oured evocations of the many-peopled East. California seems abominably drab, after reading a book of that sort.

Here's my attempt at John Webster and Marlowe. I've never seen a pic-ture of either.

> Affectionately,
> Clark.

Notes

1. By Sister Nivedita and Ananda K. Coomaraswamy.

[145] [ALS]

> [East Auburn, Cal.,
> __ January 1919.]*

Dear Sam:

Yours of the 31st. came this morning, and I've two more of your letters lying unanswered. Please pardon my seeming neglect—I've felt half-dead most of the time, and have had catarrh and a sore throat.

I'm horribly sorry to hear that you are ill again. "Myo-carditis" has a terrible sound, tho I've only the vaguest of ideas as to what the word really means.

I envy you your visit to the lady who knew Chivers—that strange and fascinating personality, who, in some respects, was almost a psychic double of Poe—at least of the emotional side of Poe.

I have the "Pastels in Prose" which you mention reading, and consider it one of the treasures of my library. Stuart Merrill, the translator, an American by birth (as perhaps you know,) has a high reputation as a writer of French verse.

Pardon this hurried scrawl, which I'm mailing to your Cleveland address, in the hope that you may have been released by the time it arrives. I'll write again, at greater length, in a few days.

---

*[corner folded over—error in microfilm?]

Affectionately,
Clark.

[146] [ALS]

East Auburn, Cal.
Jan. 12th, 1919.

Dear Sam:

How is it with you? Forgive my week or more of silence—I had deferred writing in the expectation of hearing from you any day, and in the uncertainty as to your address. Also, I have been far from well.

To-morrow, the thirteenth, is my 26th birth-day. Damme, but I begin to feel ancient! The fourteenth is your birthday, is it not? I seem to remember that it is.

I received a new consignment of books yesterday—"Gil Blas,"[1] "The Egoist," by George Meredith, Victor Hugo's "History of a Crime," Kipling's "The Day's Work," and "The Little Book of Modern Verse," compiled by Miss Rittenhouse.[2] The last is a representative selection of contemporary American verse, and not a bad one, were it not for the excess of little emotional lyrics by women. Some of these are good enough—but there are too many of them. Three of George's poems are included, and one ("The Outer Gate") by Nora May French. Also, three by Le Gallienne, and several by William Vaughn Moody, who, it seems to me, was a great poet.

I re-read Symons' "Studies in Seven Arts" the other day, and found it excellent, though most of the subjects are not of immediate interest to me. The essay on Rodin is splendid, and I particularly enjoyed the one about Whistler.

I expect some new volumes of the Modern Library before long—John Payne's rendering of Villon, Maupassant's novel, "A Parisian Life,"[3] and D'Annunzio's "The Flame of Life." All of them (some of which I have read) should be very much to my taste.

I've written a sonnet this morning. I may send it to you in my next, if it prove at all viable. In the meanwhile, I enclose a drawing or two, anticipatory, as usual, of the D. T.'s.

Affectionately,
Clark.

Notes

1. CAS refers to *Histoire de Gil Blas de Santillane* (1715–35), a picaresque novel by Alain-René Le Sage (1668–1747). CAS must be referring to an English translation, but it is not clear which one he obtained.
2. The book contained GS's "The Black Vulture," "The Dust Dethroned," and "The Ashes in the Sea: N. M. F."
3. CAS probably means *Une Vie*.

[147] [ALS]

East Auburn, Cal.,
Jan. 20th, 1919.

Dear Sam:

Your letter came yesterday, (the 19th) the birthday of Edgar Poe, as you may remember. Yes, the thirteenth was my birthday. A young friend of mine, whose anniversary is the sixteenth, and who writes verse and is in all ways a true Saturnian, came to dinner and helped me celebrate (!) How I wish that you could have been of the party!

I was certainly glad to hear from you, since I had worried a little over your silence, fearing that my letters might have missed you, or that you were too ill to write. I hope this finds you in condition to travel homeward.

There's no news, unless my wanderings in book land be accounted such. I've sauntered through four or five hundred pages of "Gil Blas," which is entertaining enough in places, and doesn't lack for change or variety of scene and situation. Also, I've read de Maupassant's "Un Vie," which is a masterpiece of its kind, creating (or re-creating) like all of de Maupassant, the illusion of reality. But the books which interest me most are John Payne's rendering of Villon, and "The Flame of Life" by D'Annunzio. The poems are etched as with a dagger-point on tablets of stone or lead. And the novel (my first reading of D'Annunzio) astounds one with its fertility of strange and subtle thought, and the versicolored splendour of its pyrotechnic images . . . I am ordering several more of these Modern Library volumes—Voltaire's "Candide," Dunsany's "Book of Wonder," and "The Art of Aubrey Beardsley," which latter contains 64 reproductions of drawings together with the essay by Symons.

I remember your poem on Wilde—a fine thing, and worthy of the subject. The criticism you quote is disgusting. Tolstoi happens to be one of my favourite abominations—I like him the least, or, rather, detest him the most, of any of the Russian literary Bolsheviki.[1]

I enclose a dim and misty sort of sonnet. However, the vagueness is not inappropriate to the theme.

As ever, affectionately,
Clark.

Notes

1. In *What Is Art?* (1904), Leo Tolstoi wrote: "The Decadents and aesthetes of the type at one time represented by Oscar Wilde select as a theme for their productions the denial of morality and the laudation of vice" (ch. 17).

[148] [ALS]

East Auburn, Cal.,

Feb. 3rd, 1919.

Dear Sam:

My last letter, addressed to you at the hospital, has just been returned, with "Dis." written on the envelope. So I'm sending it to your Cleveland address, in the hope that you have reached home by now.

Don't consider this as a letter. I'll write again, shortly, at length. I feel rather "done up" to-day, after a real, old-fashioned tooth-ache that lasted thirty-
six hours,—a versatile and acrobatic tooth-ache, that performed everything in
the way of gymnastics and fancy dancing, from the goose-step to the highland
fling and the turkey-trot.

Affectionately,

Clark.

[149] [ALS]

East Auburn, Cal.,

Feb. 23rd, 1919.

Dear Sam:

I've not heard from you for so long, that I begin to fear that either
you are too unwell for letter-writing, or that my last letter (or yours) has miscarried. My letter was returned from the hospital in January, with "dis-
charged" written on the envelope, and I re-mailed it to your Cleveland
address. Did you receive it?

There's nothing very sensational in the way of news, unless the fact that
I'm still alive, and have continued to side-step the influenza, be considered
such. February has been unusually wet, cold, and disagreeable, so we've already received (it seems to me) nearly our seasonal quota of rain, and should
have an early spring by way of compensation.

The current issue of "The Sonnet" (a copy of which I enclose) contains
"In Saturn," juxtaposed with a lunar sonnet of George's.[1] George tells me
that Boni and Liveright are to publish "Lilith" next autumn. Robertson thinks
of getting out a new volume for him before the end of the year.

Did I send you a copy of "Forgetfulness?" Fisher, the editor of "The
Sonnet," has just accepted it. Why don't **you** tackle the magazine? You have
some unpublished sonnets (if I remember rightly).

What little work I have done lately has been in the sonnet-form. Nothing
at all good, I'm afraid. But I'll try to enclose a specimen or two. There's not
much incentive toward work. Everything is so unsettled, and I fear that conditions will be much worse next year, with Bolshevism and Prohibition. I believe Bierce was right—America is doomed to end in absolute anarchy.
Nothing else seems possible, the way things are heading. I feel like hoofing it
for Mexico—that country is free from Prohibitionists, at any rate.

Write me soon, if you can. I shall not feel easy till I hear from you.
 Affectionately,
                                        Clark.

Notes

1. "Outward," *Sonnet* 2, No. 2 (January–February 1919): 3.

[150] [ALS]
                                        East Auburn, Cal.,
                                        Feb. 27th, 1919.
Dear Sam:
        Your welcome letter came to-day, and I was overjoyed to hear
from you. It's good to know that you are safely home; but I'm sorry that
things are not all for the best. Work is hell—at least when one's health is below par, or if the work happens to be uncongenial.
        No, I've never read Vance Thompson's "French Portraits," but have
seen the book mentioned—I forget by whom—someone who referred to it
as "amusing but misleading." I've read two little books by Thompson,[1] entitled "Eat and Grow Thin," and "Drink and be Sober." The first of these is instructive, and the second is at least diverting. He has written verse, too—I seem
to remember something by him in Stedman's "American Anthology"—a Pre-
raphaelitish sort of poem in which "her" and "stir" were rimed with "wa*ter*."[2]
        The young friend of whom I spoke is Andrew Dewing.[3] He has written
sonnets and prose-poems that you would like—most of them unpublished.
I'll get copies of some of them for you, when I see him again.
        By the way (apropos of "The Rural Muse") when are you going to write
your life of Clare? I should like to see you do something with the subject, for
I believe you could handle it better than anyone else of whom I know.
        My reading has been desultory and rather patchy. Voltaire's "Candide,["]
and Dunsany's "Book of Wonder" are the latest additions to my library. "The
Book of Wonder" strikes me as being more uneven than "The Dreamer's Tales," though it contains some splendid things.
        I enclose a grotesque or two in pencil. I want to make you some draw-
ings in coloured ink before long, on the yellow paper that you sent me last
year. I feel in the mood to draw, and shall delineate for you certain of the flo-
ra and fauna that exist in the equatorial jungles of Saturn.
        I await the new poems of which you speak, with interest. Write me
whenever you can. I promise to be a better and more faithful correspondent
in the future.
                 Affectionately,
                         Clark.

P.S. I find that I have a copy of Andrew Dewing's sonnet "Memory," and enclose it for your perusal. Please return it, and return also "The Generous Gambler,"[4] of which I have no other copy, and of which, indeed, I have seen no other translation.

Notes

1. Vance Thompson (1863–1925), American literary critic, novelist, poet, and diet food writer.
2. The anthology contains Thompson's "Symbols" and "Linen Bands," but neither contains the rhymes CAS mentions.
3. Andrew Dewing (1897–1977), friend of CAS from Auburn.
4. A prose poem by Baudelaire.

[151] [ALS]

East Auburn, Cal.,
March 14th, 1919.

Dear Sam:

I should have written you before this, but have felt "under the weather" for the past week—horribly tired and nervous, with spells of indigestion and insomnia.

I am awaiting Thompson's book with eagerness, and feel sure that I will enjoy it greatly. Your tastes and mine seem to coincide almost invariably. I'm glad to hear that you're at work on "The Sphinx." The hints concerning its composition, that you give in your letter, intrigue my deepest interest. You know the high opinion that I have of your prose-poems.

I enclose "Forgetfulness"; also a new sonnet, "Laus Mortis." I'll send you a number of drawings next week. At present, I feel too tired and "done-up" even for drawing.

I enclose the prospectus of a new magazine, "The Thrill Book." The editor actually wrote, asking me to contribute! I must be getting famous! I sent in a number of poems, and may submit some of my prose-poems. You'll notice that they accept "fillers" of 500 words or less. Why don't you try them with some of your prose? I hope to hell the magazine succeeds—the project is certainly a fine and brave one.

Another letter, in a few days . . . I'll get you something more of Dewing's when I see him again—he has prose-poems that you would like.

Affectionately,
Clark.

P.S. I like your "Memoralia." Please don't deprecate your poems—even the slightest ones have quality.

[152] [ALS]

East Auburn, Cal.,

March 18th, 1919.

Dear Sam:

Thanks, many, many thanks, for the "French Portraits," which I've enjoyed immensely. The illustrations *are* more remarkable, and more satisfying than the text, which is rather sketchy—necessarily so, of course, in a book representative of an entire school, or several schools. Samain[1] and Verhaeren interest me most, of the latter-day crowd. Giraud and Gilkin,[2] both Belgians, interest me also. What I have seen of their work is supra-Baudelaireian. I notice that Laforgue, one of George Moore's enthusiasms, is not mentioned in Thomson's [*sic*] book.

I've just finished reading "Karma," which is now published by B. & L. in the Penguin Series. I care as little for it as for anything of Hearn's that I've yet seen, though the book is worth having for the article on "Belial," the great muezzin, and several other things. "Chinese Ghosts" is marvellous, tho not more so than "Stray Leaves from Strange Literature," and many of the Japanese books. Have you read "In Ghostly Japan," which contains that enormous fantasy, "The Mountain of Skulls?" Some of the legends in "Kwaidan" are unimaginably monstrous. "Chita" is full of tropic splendour and colour, tho I don't care so greatly for the story itself. "Youma" I have read, but cared less for it than for Chita. Hearn, it seems to me, is entitled to full rank with Poe, De Quincey, Wilde, and Bierce among the masters of English prose. His periods are chryselephantine, or like painted sculpture.

The quotation from "The Sphinx" is fine, and certainly whets my eagerness to see it. I'll probably do some prose, myself, before long; I feel as if my verse were worked out, for the time; but I have a number of conceptions that should "go" well in prose-form.

I'm enclosing a script of the Satan sonnet, and am sending you, under separate cover, nearly all of the new drawings that I've made. I hope they amuse you. You'll notice that I've given titles to many. The unnamed ones are all Saturnian—sea-scapes, and friezes of tall blind flowers in vague fields beneath grey and hoary skies. Do you think anything could be done with them, in a commercial way? Some of my acquaintances here seem to think they might be used for decorative purposes—screens, wall-paper, etc.

Affectionately,

Clark.

P.S. Read Charles Warren Stoddard's "South Sea Idylls"—the best and most poetic impression of that sort of life I have come across. You'll find it far, far better than Stoddard's verse. Herman Melville's books, "Omoo" and "Typee," especially the former, are well worth reading, if you don't know them already. Indeed, I understand the allurement you feel—if I were free, and had a little money or a little health, I'd hike for the tropics and eventually, the Orient, to-morrow. And the South Sea Islands would be one of my first stopping-places. Some day—ah, some day, you must come out, and join me, and we'll go a-vagabonding together towards Cathay, and beyond Cipangu,[3] and far, far beyond the great thousand-mile Wall!

P.P.S. Dewing, of whom I told you, is also a true Romany Rye, and would go with us. I spent yesterday afternoon with him, and we drank sherry out of claret-glasses, criticized English poetry and Russian fiction, and planned a dozen little excursions in Ultima Thule, Cockaigne, Egypt, and China. D. has a predilection for China.

Notes

1. Albert Victor Samain (1858–1900), French poet and writer of the Symbolist school. CAS translated his "Myrtil et Palémone" and another untitled poem.
2. Albert Giraud (1860–1929), Belgian poet who wrote in French; Iwan Gilkin (1858–1924), Belgian poet associated with the Symbolist school in Belgium.
3. Cipangu was the name Marco Polo applied to Japan, deriving it from Mandarin Chinese.

[153] [TLS]

[March 1919?]

Dear Clark,

I am mailing you today Charles Sorley's "Marlborough and other Poems". He accomplished so little. But the few things he did were done well and he died in only his twentieth year. I am hoping that you will set your seal of approval on the book.

I received your letter yesterday with the three pictures. The one in mauve is particularly beautiful and you seem to be gaining a decorative effect in your grotesques that is at once terrible and an added perfection to their exoticism. Thanks—heartily. I showed some of them (I am religiously holding them all!) to an acquaintance of mine, Ernest Nelson,[1] whose criticism on poetry as well as art is unusually significant and his reply was instant—they showed genius.

I appreciate your praise of my poem—I get little enough of it, heaven knows. Barring yourself and Eric Levison[2] of Birmingham Alabama, my work seems to be as unpenetrated as the Egyptian Book of the Dead. By the way, I want to send you one of Eric's short stories in my next. At twenty-two he is landing stuff in "Everybody's". He admits that some of it is pot-boiler work but this short-story that I speak of "The Man who was Mad", is exceptional. He agrees with me in my opinion of your work.

I've been unable to locate that Baudelaire for you—I am damned sorry, too. Alack! I would that I could find some of Crackanthorpe's books. I only know him thro' these little prose poems and "Sentimental Studies."[3] Vincent Starrett of Chicago has a complete short-story of Crackanthorpe's in his own handwriting, as yet unpublished—it was presented to him by Crackanthorpe's mother who is still alive.

I want to write to George this week. I owe him a letter. With best wishes to yourself and yours,

Affectionately,

Sam.

1537 East 93 St., Suite 2.

P.S. I'm reading the Shakesperian translation of Plutarch and have made a little discovery—not much, but a little—of which more anon.[4]

Notes

1. Ernest Nelson (d. 1921), Norwegian immigrant, poet and artist, a member of the Hart Crane circle (Crane was a pallbearer at his funeral) and a co-worker with William Sommer at Otis Lithography in Cleveland. SL published a brief memorial notice in *Saturnian* No. 3.
2. Eric Levison (1894–?), prolific magazine writer.
3. SL eventually read his works. See "Hubert Crackanthorpe: A Realist of the Nineties."
4. SL presumably refers to the translation of the late Greek biographer Plutarch translated by Sir Thomas North (1579); it significantly influenced Shakespeare in the writing of some of his historical plays. A volume entitled *Shakespeare's Plutarch*, edited by Walter W. Skeat, appeared in 1875.

[154] [TLS]

[March 1919]

Dear Clark,

Sent away to you last Saturday a bundle of Conrad books—a pretty good representation, I hope—I'm trusting that a few of them will be new to you.

Thankee for the two sonnets—"Forgetfulness" and "Laus Mortis" both of which are exquisitely beautiful and antiphonal—the former with its bitter evocation to the deity strikes a responsive chord—I believe you remember Clark, from "The Triumph" that I am a liberal on such things and as far as religion goes, have none whatever. I don't believe in a personal god and if there be a power it is just possible that it may be one of malignity. Funny, Milton's Satan has always stirred within me a passion of pity—pity for the supreme soul that dared to revolt. The rest is literature.

I hope that you find acceptance in the new magazine. I'll not try. Just at present my stock of faith in my work is pretty low. I burnt and destroyed nearly all the prose poems I've written, leaving only the "Faun" and "The Departed", not to mention stories and poems, leaving a very little to remain. "The Sphinx" (what I have written of it) I still have—but that too has a tale. Nelson, who is pretty fair otherwise, deprecated its exceeding paganism and inferred that it would never be published. Vale. It will probably go the way of the rest.

I've recently acquired a complete Rossetti containing the Italian translations and the prose criticisms and fragments, all very fine. I'm so sorry to hear that you are unwell, depressed and nervous. I still think, mon ami Clark, that your lack of companionship makes to a good bit of this condition—not entirely perhaps, but somewhat—and I don't mean any sort of a haphazard acquaintanceship either, but the kind that understands your dreaming and your reticent suffering. But I've never found that sort in a city of near a million souls.

I await the drawings. You know of old how I appreciate them. I've a book here that I intend to send you in the near future—a book of travels in Palestine by George Sandys the poet written in 1600 or thereabouts and printed in 1611—the copy that I shall send you is the first edition folio with the original plates—and the original information.[1] The information therein is much in the nature of what booksellers call "curious." Better health to you, Clark.

Affectionately
Sam

Notes

1. George Sandys (1578–1644), English traveler, colonist, poet, and translator. The earliest extant version of his *A Relation of a Journey begun An. Dom. 1610 . . .* dates to 1615.

[155] [ALS]

East Auburn, Cal.,
March 22nd, 1919.

Dear Sam:

A thousand thanks for the set of Conrad![1] When I opened that immense package, my pleasure equalled my surprise—I have wanted that particular set for years past. I have always thought Conrad the greatest of living storytellers, with the possible exception of Kipling. He combines some of Kipling's best qualities with much of Flaubert, and the tang of something utterly strange and individual, a tang like the savour and perfume of tropic seas, or the taste of some dark-coloured, and deeply scented fruit of the jungles . . . Many of the books are new to me, and I foresee days and weeks of pleasure and oblivion in their pages—those pages where the shadows and mists, and terrors and glories of the sea mingle with the balms and burning colours of many an alien Paradise.

Apropos of the sea, have you read Masefield? He, too, is one of those who know the manifold secrets, and the "beauty and mystery of the sea." Parts of "Dauber" are magnificent, and all his (Masefield's) narrative poems are surprisingly readable—far more than one can say for most narrative poems. I like many of the lyrics, too, and the sonnets, all of which latter are in Shakesperean form. Masefield is probably the best English (not English-writing) poet of the day, since Arthur Symons is hardly a contemporary poet.

How are you coming on with the "Sphinx?" Are you plotting new riddles, for her to propound, or have you found the old ones sufficiently insoluble? I have done nothing myself, except read, and potter a little with coloured inks and pencils. I lag and lie around like a lazy Jacob, while the Angel hardens his thews against me on the hill-top[2] . . . However, spring is coming—a languid spring with pale foliage, and reluctant flowers, overcast with occasional mists from the sea.

"The Thrill Book" (of which I told you) has accepted my sonnet, "Dissonance." They pay at what seems to be the usual magazine-rate for sonnets—25¢ a line—little enough to purchase fodder for Pegasus nowadays. Poets with a lust for monetary profit are not likely to select the form of Petrarch and Milton—which isn't the least of its recommendations!

Affectionately,
Clark.

Notes

1. There was no collected edition of Joseph Conrad published at this time. Most of Conrad's major works were being published in the UK by J. M. Dent (London) and in the US by Doubleday, Page (Garden City, NY). SL may simply have sent CAS a batch of these editions.

2. CAS alludes to Gen. 32:22–32 (also Hosea 12:4), in which Jacob wrestles with an angel.

[156] [ALS, JHL]

East Auburn, Cal.,
April 1st, 1919.

Dear Sam:

Our weather has turned warm and fair, all of a sudden, as it usually does. Lady April promises to be a buxom sort of lass. I've more than a touch of "spring fever," and have found nothing better or more pleasurable than to lie around and read the consignment of Conrad books that you sent me. With the exception of "Youth" and "Falk," all of these are new to me. I like the "Tales of Unrest" in especial. "Karain" is worthy of Flaubert, and at least one other story in the volume ("The Idiots") has all the best qualities of De Maupassant. "Romance" is well-named, and I wish I had read it in the days when I first read "Treasure Island," and other books of the same ilk. In all ways, it is far superior to Stevenson.

I've made a few purchases lately—Hearn's "Japanese Fairy Tales" in the Penguin series of B. & L., "The Private Papers of Henry Ryecroft," by George Gissing, and Hearn's translation of "The Crime of Sylvestre Bonnard."[1] The fairy tales are charming, but only four of them are by Hearn; the rest are by Basil Hall Chamberlain and others. I've not found time to read the other books as yet. I notice that Boni and Liveright announce a translation of "The Flowers of Evil" among the next additions to the Modern Library, and I shall certainly obtain it; also, a new selection, "Love and Other Stories," from de Maupassant. Things begin to look more hopeful, when such books are published in a "popular" edition.

Why in Hades are you destroying any of your work? I like nearly all of your prose-poems, and am haunted recurrently by several of the unpublished lyrics you have sent me. I earnestly advise you against destroying *any* of your work. Moods of depression are not to be trusted,—I know them too well, since I have been tempted several times a month, at least, to make a holocaust of my own writings.

The editor of "The Thrill Book" is a "good sport"—he "raised the ante," to use his own phrase, and paid me seven dollars for "Dissonance"—double the price I expected. I'm investing the boodle in books, though, with the Great National Drouth impending, I was sorely tempted to add a few more demijohns to my hoard of liquid treasure. The G. N. D. is no joke—things are bad enough now, with the prohibitive taxes on wine and brandy. Harry Leon Wilson, in an article in the Saturday Evening Post, predicts that coffee and tobacco will also be prohibited in a few years.[2] I don't care about tobacco personally, since my smoking is confined to an annual, or semi-annual cigarette, but, damme, if coffee is banned, I'll stow away on the first hooker[3] that leaves for Java!

Dewing (the young rip!) has gone to San Francisco for a few weeks. I wish I were with him—the vie de Boheme has its allurements even for me. Bohemia will be a dull and tawdry sort of place when the light of wine is faded from its walls and tables. It's hard to imagine S. F. "on the wagon." I'll contrive to visit the old burgh, for a day or two at least, before June 30th, if I have to go hog-stealing to raise the funds!

Here's hoping that you are in a brighter mood by now. I feel better myself, apart from the languor due to the changing weather. Much of my nervousness is due to indigestion, I believe, though, of course, the lack of companionship you mention is an aggravating factor. I should go mad with loneliness were it not for my books—those tongueless but eloquent friends— friends who never accuse or betray!

Well, an end to this long-winded letter—a rigmarole of trivialities.

You must pardon me, for there's nothing else. Life seems an endless chain of banalities—even pain becomes banal with repetition. And all roads lead to the hell of boredom—that 10th circle which Dante never penetrated, and, apparently, never suspected. Lucky Dante, for whom the inferno was only flame, and slime, and ice!

As ever, your affectionate friend,

Clark

Notes

1. By Anatole France.
2. Harry Leon Wilson, "Here's How!" *Saturday Evening Post* 191, No. 40 (5 April 1919): 8–9, 103, 107. Wilson (1867–1939) was a widely published novelist.
3. An old worn-out or clumsy ship.

[157] [ALS]

East Auburn, Cal.
April 11th, 1919.

Dear Sam:

I should have written you ere this, but didn't feel up to it, and preferred to spare you my dulness and depression. I'm not at all well, and find it hard to drag myself around. My legs are weak, my chest and back are sore and twingy, and I have the most infernal ringing in my ears.

The drawings you mention *are* probably the best that I have done. I have a little story to go with "The Flower-Devil," and will try to write it out for you some day. The flowers *are* more or less symbolic. I call them "Flowers of Ennui." Burbank,[1] if he were the reincarnation of Baudelaire, might breed or invent such blossoms!

Got a letter from George yesterday. He seems to have written scarcely anything since last year. I enclose a sonnet that he sends me, together with one of my own that you've probably not seen. By the way, can you rake up the copies of my prose-poems, "Ennui," and "The Princess Almeena," which I must have sent you about a year ago? I've lost the only fair copies that I possessed, and can't remember just how some of the final revisions went. Will you make copies of them for me, if you can find the mss.? Or lend them to me, and I will make the copies myself.

I remember Huneker's article on John Martin,[2] none of whose drawings I have ever seen. Certainly, I shall be delighted to see the Milton illustrations you mention. Space, and night, and the terror of space, are the most difficult things to express or convey in painting or drawing. With the exception of Doré, [*sic*] I find it hard to recall any artist who has succeeded even partially in the attempt.

Frank Harris' criticisms of your poem on Wilde are interesting, but altogether too meticulous. I can't see the objection to "black" nenuphars. Blue roses, and even green carnations have been heard of. Why not black water-lilies?

Here's a catalogue of my recent reading: Turgenev's "Virgin Soil," a mildly interesting but not madly exhilarating, sort of novel (I like Turgenev best in his prose-poems and shorter tales) that charming book, "The Crime of Sylvestre Bonnard," Pater's "Appreciations" (a re-reading and re-appreciation) and "Shandygaff," by Christopher Morley, a good, sound, Rabelaisian sort of

book, touching on everything from boiled potatoes to poetry and on everyone, almost, from Conrad to Kirke White.[3] Also, I've read Joyce Kilmer's poems, but am unable to work myself into a condition of delirious, or even
hilarious, enthusiasm over them. Kilmer was the sort of poet for whom the
editorial check-book sheds its leaves, together with a rain of literary merit-
stars from the hand of Mr. W. S. Braithwaite. However, the gods must have
loved, or at least, pitied him. "He died young!"[4]

Have you gone on with the "Sphinx?" Don't leave the riddle un-
propounded, even though it be one of those that must remain unsolved.

Affectionately,
Clark.

P.S. Keep all the enclosures, if you like.

Notes

1. Luther Burbank (1849–1926), American horticulturist and pioneer in agricultural science.
2. "John Martin, Mezzotinter," *Promenades of an Impressionist* 182–94.
3. Henry Kirke White (1785–1806), English poet who died at a young age.
4. Joyce Kilmer (1886–1918), American writer, journalist, literary critic, lecturer, editor
and poet, mainly remembered for his short poem, "Trees" (1913). Critics disparage
his work as being too simple and overly sentimental.

[158] [ALS]

East Auburn, Cal.,
April 20th, 1919.

Dear Sam:

To-day is Easter Sunday—a day that I mustn't permit to pass
without easing my conscience of this delayed letter. I have been vaguely unwell most of the month—listless, languid, dull, indefinitely depressed—a
semi-neurasthenia, a chronic ennui that threatens at whiles to become acute,
with complications of a general malaise, to use the terminology of doctors
and hypochondriacs. I wish to hell that I **could** break away, and leave for the
Orient, or, at least, the American tropics. Would you come with me? It's out
of the question, though, on account of my parents, who would be altogether
alone, without me.

I've never heard of the book of letters by Hearn that you mention.[1] I've
just begun to read "Out of the East," one of his (Hearn's) earlier Japanese
books. There are splendid things in it, in exposition of Buddhism and of Japanese art and thought.

I read the Mosher reprint of "Hand and Soul"[2] (Dewing has the book)
last night, and liked parts of it. I agree with you that it lacks the artistry, and
even the poetic integration of so vague an allegory as the "Vision of of [*sic*]

Love.["] Certainly, it hasn't a tithe of Solomon's glorious imagery, and regalities of ceremonial music.

Have you seen the March number of Pearson's? Frank Harris has a rather interesting article on James Thomson in it.[3] There's not nearly so much of Harris' usual mixture of tears, filth, and slobber in the article . . . Harris makes me sick, with his exploitation of dead men, and of himself as the Fides Achates of dead men[4] . . . A weeping hyena, proffering ribs, and hair, and toe-nails, and knuckle-bones for sale in the market-place!

Conder's name is altogether new to me[5]—I don't believe I've ever heard him mentioned. Was he a painter? I infer that he was, because of the comparison to Watteau that you quote.

Dewing has returned from S. F. He met Sterling and Ina Coolbrith[6] during his visit. He describes Miss Coolbrith as being bright and sprightly in defiance of her seventy (or is it eighty?) odd years. He even takes an interest in her free verse, and has her opinion on everything from Bolshevism to Amy Lowell!

Another letter before long.

Affectionately,
Clark.

Notes

1. See letter 159 (in which CAS refers erroneously to Hearn's *Letters from the Raven*).
2. By Dante Gabriel Rossetti.
3. "James Thomson: An Unknown Immortal," *Pearson's Magazine* 40, No. 5 (March 1919): 218–22.
4. Latin, literally "faithful Achates," referring to the faithful companion of Aeneas in the *Aeneid*. Thus any faithful friend or companion.
5. Charles Edward Conder (1868–1909), British-born painter, lithographer, and designer who emigrated to Australia.
6. Ina Coolbrith (1841–1928; née Josephine D. Smith, niece of the Mormon prophet), early editor of the *Overland Monthly*, librarian in Oakland, and the first poet laureate named in the U.S. (1915–28).

[159] [ALS]

East Auburn, Cal.,
May 12th, 1919.

Dear Sam:

I, too, have suffered from the same trouble that you mention—listlessness, and a total lack of energy and ambition. Otherwise, I should have written before now. Life, as I am forced to live it, is too regular, too monotonic, too much like the turning of a Buddhist prayer-wheel. Also, as you know, I am alone too much, and the consciousness of the encompassing void is ever with me. Ether is a somewhat irrespirable medium.

Yes, I liked your Chinese poems, as I told you in my last letter, which you've doubtless received by now. I'd like to see you write more poems of the same sort. Orientalism hasn't been so exhaustively overworked as most other fields of poetic ideation.

By the way, I've sold two of my own experiments in the cultivation of the exotic—"Palms" and "Flamingoes." "Asia," a sumptuously printed and illustrated magazine published by the American Geographical Society, has accepted them at five dollars apiece! At that rate, I'll soon begin to break even in paper, postage, pens, ink, type-ribbons, and machine-oil!

The Sandys' volume is a rare and precious addition to my shelves. I've refused to lend the book—and I'm not churlish, as a rule, about loaning. Half-a-dozen of my books are scattered about the neighborhood at present; but I feel like keeping this one under lock and key. The contents are "quaint and curious"[1] to the last degree—the second line of "The Raven" comes to mind every time that I take the volume down.

I shall be glad indeed to have the "Letters from a [*sic*] Raven". The title sounds good. I've heard of the "Fantastics," but understood that it was out of print. "Leaves from an Impressionist" is an unfamiliar title to me. The amount of work that Hearn managed to accomplish is no less amazing than the quality. All of it is good, and at least half is super-excellent.

Do you know Edgar Saltus? I begin to think him one of the best American prose-writers, after reading his "Imperial Purple," which deals with the pomps, perversities, and poisons of Nero, Tiberius, Heliogabalus, etc., in a rich, embroidered style impeccable as that of Poe and Bierce.

I enclose a little prose-poem by Andrew Dewing. The symbolism is based on the Catholic ritual, referring, I believe, to the robes worn in celebration of the funeral mass—black without, as an emblem of grief and death, and green within, for hope and resurrection.

> Affectionately,
> Clark.

Notes

1. Poe, "The Raven": "Once upon a midnight dreary, while I pondered, weak and weary, / Over many a quaint and curious volume of forgotten lore . . ."

[160] [ALS]

> East Auburn, Cal.,
> June 4th, 1919.

Dear Sam:

It was *I* who should apologize for delayed letters, if apologies be necessary between us. . . . It vexes me, however, to learn that one of my letters went astray, even though the letter can scarcely have contained anything of importance. I am beginning to nurse a homicidal grudge against the American post-al service and all its officials and employees, from the arch-tyrant, Burleson,[1] to the pro-German with a mental hump, who mishandles the mail in the local office . . . By the way, have you received a poem of mine entitled "Quest?" [*sic*] Perhaps it was in the letter that went astray. I seem to remember sending you a copy.

Selling poetry to the magazines is probably the most uncertain, the most hazardous of all the games of chance. My luck has apparently played itself out with the two sales of which I told you—I sent out a ream of stuff on the strength of them, but have not succeeded in placing a single poem.

Certainly—keep Andrew's prose-poem. He made the copy for you, when I told him of your interest in his work. I'm glad you like it—I consider it a fine thing, myself.

I've tried to work a little, the last few day, but with small success. I en-close a sonnet—"The Absence of the Muse." It's well-named, at any rate. I've draughted a prose-poem—"The Traveller," which will take an endless amount of revision before it's presentable. The conception is good, though.

Physically, I've grown much stronger and heavier since the first of the year. I weigh close to 130—as much as I've weighed at any time in my life.

I enclose a satire that George sent me in his last letter.[2] Some of the stan-zas are very clever, and I know you will enjoy it.

Affectionately,

Clark.

Notes

1. Albert Sidney Burleson (1863–1937), U.S. postmaster general (1913–21) who gained infamy for his crackdown on purportedly "seditious" materials sent through the mail.
2. I.e., "The Modern Muse."

[161] [TLS]

[c. June 1919]

Dear Clark,

And I too, hope to be more prompt. I can't tell you what came over me lately—my hope seems as dead as my ambition—but I hope to mend—apace, apace, as one of the Falstaffian characters says. Thanks for your poignant song on the silence of the Muse and for George's brilliant po-em. "Jesus Yeats"[1] is a stroke of inspiration as surely certain as anything else therein, and the thing has and still is furnishing me with much amusement. I treasure the privilege of reading it, no doubt it will never be publicly printed on account of the not entirely "Grecian chorus" which would furnish the rounding of a bit of Aristophanic comedy.

I am sending you Saturday the books I promised you some time ago. The two-volume Martin Milton—and I hope the illustrations please you. Pardon the delay as I get very little opportunity to have Laukhuff wrap my bundles up—he being the dependable person—you probably remember the absurd bundles I've already sent you.

I recently picked up two of the most remarkable Jap (Chinese or Hindoo, I am not certain) antiques I have ever seen. One is an ape, a half foot in height, and clustered on and about her are her three young ones. This is carved from a piece of very hard flinty gray and black stone. The pathos of the thing is astounding. The second piece is simply marvelous. It is a foot in length, over a half foot in height, and is carved out of a piece of pale green, vermillion, and brown steatite (I think) wonderfully lustrous—and it represents an antlered deer who has come to a water vessel, whilst above it is perched a gesticulating monkey with one arm warding off the deer and the other grasping at a piece of bread-fruit on the foliage. And the expression on the face of the deer! I paid ten dollars for the two and I believe them to be worth two or three hundred.

I did not receive "The Quest". Will you send it to me? I shall surely copy your prose poems for the next.

There's a very fine book called "170 Chinese Poems"[2] out that I have read with great interest. The Chinese were a great artistic race and I believe superior to the Japs.

Write soon and often—and don't forget me. I'm isolated.

Affectionately

S. L.

1537 East 93 St. Suite 2.

[Envelope postmarked Cleveland, Ohio, June __, 1919.]

Notes

1. The phrase is not in the final poem.
2. Translated by Arthur Waley.

[162] [ALS]

East Auburn, Cal.,
June 17th, 1919.

Dear Sam:

I had not intended to wait for *your* letter before writing you again—it overtakes me in the sloughish ways of my habitual procrastination. I'm mighty glad to hear from you; and your letter comes to break an epistolary void of unusual protraction. I've received nothing else, with the exception of rejected mss., and one acceptance, for weeks past. The acceptance (for an eight-line lyric entitled "Crepuscule") was from "The Thrill Book."[1]

I await the illustrated Milton with uncommon interest. By the way, didn't Doré illustrate "Paradise Lost?" I seem to remember that he did.

Yes, I suppose the satire in "The Modern Muse" is a little too strong, too poignant, in places, to be entirely suitable for publication. How Bierce would have enjoyed it! . . . I enclose two sonnets of George's, written several years ago, and as far as I know, still unpublished. The second one is magnificent, but, I suppose, too frankly and gloriously sensual for a reading-public fresh from the literary lupanars of R. W. Chambers and Co. Keep the sonnets, if you like,—also the rest of my enclosures.[2]

I envy you those Oriental antiques. I've not seen anything of the sort since my last visit to the Museum in Golden Gate Park, nearly two years ago. One doesn't find such things in a place like Auburn—I don't know anyone who owns a valuable or noteworthy object of art.

Yes, the Chinese are a far greater people, artistically, than the Japs. The latter owe to the Chinese the same debts of derivation and spiritual fecundation, that the Romans owed to the Greeks. Chinese poetry is wonderful, in its feeling for the beauty, and sadness, (and even, at times, the terror) of nature and human life. By all means, obtain, if you can, the two Chinese anthologies, "A Feast of Lanterns," and "The Lute of Jade," translated by A. Cranmer-Byng, and published, if I remember rightly, by E. P. Dutton & Co. Cranmer-Byng is one translator in ten thousand—no less than a genius, to render, as he has done, a hundred or more of Chinese lyrics into noble and plangent English verse. Consider, for instance, the following stanza, which I quote from memory:

> "Here, Kings of Wu were crowned and overthrown,
>   Where peaceful grass along the ruin wins;
>   Here—was it yesterday?—the royal Tsins
>   Called down the dreams of sunset into stone."[3]

Can one conceive a finer, a more haunting and portentous image, than the image expressed in the two last lines?

I went for a long walk with my father yesterday—six or seven miles up the canyon to an old wooden bridge, built and roofed over with tremendous timbers, and abandoned for years. A deliciously cool and quiet place, miles from any sound or movement of life, other than the monotonously rippling and susurrous river. We ate our lunch in the bridge, and shared a big flask of home-made wine—leaving the empty flask for the horrification of any stray Prohibitionist who might happen along.

Write whenever you can.

Affectionately,

Clark.

Notes

1. The magazine folded before the poem could appear.
2. "The Golden Past," consisting of two sonnets. They are explicit in their depiction of sexuality and torture. They were first published in T. R. Smith, ed., *Poetica Erotica* (New York: Boni & Liveright, 1921–22, 1927), 2.317.
3. "To the City of Nan-King," *The Lute of Jade* 59 (ll. 5–8).

[163] [ALS]

East Auburn, Cal.
June 21st, 1919.

Dear Sam:

I've just received the magnificent two-volume edition of "Paradise Lost," with the illustrations by John Martin. The drawings almost exceed my anticipation, though I was prepared for something strange and marvellous by your description, and the praise of Baudelaire and Huneker. Many of the pictures create a "new thrill"—or a "new shudder,"—especially some of those in the first volume—the erection of Pandemonium, Satan enthroned, and the encounter with Death and Sin. It's hard to particularize, however, for all of the pictures are successful in their conveying of depth, and darkness, and terror, or of light, and altitude, and sublimity. The panoramas of the Garden of Eden are full of a strange, supernal beauty—the rhythmical massings of intricate light and shade, the combination of delicate lines with incommensurable slope in the rendering, the endless, vague horizons, the weird waters, and the supernatural trees, all have the effect of some vast, Beethoven-like harmony, or the measured runes and incantations of a lost, primeval magic. It's hard to compare Martin with anyone else; Dorè is doubtless the nearest analogue, but there is a weird, sinister, even monstrous beauty in Martin, apart from all the technical differences, that I find lacking in Dore's work. Martin might really have *seen* the things he drew—his visions are so convincing that they shake my nerves; and I'm not easily affected in that way, since I can read or used to read "Clarimonde," "The Horla," and "The Black Cat" at midnight without scarcely a tremor. I'm tremendously indebted to you for these books—I'd be proud to own them, even without the pictures, for the beauty of binding and the fine print, which make them a luxury and a solace to the eye.

Are you writing anything? I'll send you a prose-poem, "The Traveller," in my next. I wonder, at times, that I've even the strength to attempt writing, since I feel so bewildered, so benumbed, and overpowered, by the emptiness and nullity of my existence. There are moments when life assumes all the hideous unreality of a nightmare, or the meaningless but unendurable perplexities of delirium. Doubtless there's nothing wrong with me, though, apart from boredom, which always makes me feel creepy. Boredom is a thousand times worse than positive pain. In my present mood, I feel ripe for almost any folly—if the folly were available. I might even fall in love; but, alas, there is no one to "fall for."

> Affectionately,
>> Clark.

[164] [ALS]

> East Auburn, Cal.,
> July 21st, 1919.

Dear Sam:

How is it with you? I have been expecting a letter from you for weeks and weeks; otherwise I should have written long before this. Are you "under the weather" again? Perhaps you *have* written me, and your letter has gone astray, in the fearful and wonderful intricacies of our postal service.

The thermometer has dropped to an endurable temperature, after a fortnight of Phleget[h]onian heat. I've not been able to write, and have read nothing but the lightest fiction. Judge my intellectual prostration, when I tell you that I've been reading E. Phillips Oppenheim[1] and "The Thrill Book!" I feel anything but well, with this infernal weather, and a fierce attack of intestinal indigestion that seems to have become chronic. My brain feels as if it were full of inspissated mead—or mush that's been boiled too long.

I saw Andrew Dewing the other day. He has made a rendering in English verse (from a literal prose translation by a friend) of Verlaine's "Colloque Sentimentale." I'll get you a copy of it before long—it's immensely superior to any other rendering that I've seen . . . Dowson's translation, which I've been comparing, is very poor stuff.

Hoping that all's well with you, I am,

> As ever, your affectionate friend,
>> Clark.

Notes

1. E[dward] Phillips Oppenheim (1866–1946), enormously popular English novelist. He wrote more than 100 novels of mystery, adventure, and espionage between 1887 and 1943.

[165] [ALS]

> East Auburn, Cal.,
> Aug. 6th, 1919.

Dear Sam:

Glad you liked the sonnets on Heliogabalus. I shall dedicate them to you, if they are ever published—and providing you are not afraid of the dedication! Without your suggestion, I should scarcely have thought of writing them. I know little enough about the gentleman, apart from the reference in "Imperial Purple," and a long, minutely excoriating review of the Stuart Hay book you mention. The review, I believe, was in the London "Academy," but I am unable to lay hands upon it at present. The reviewer, after the manner of his kind, gloated with a fearful rapture over the details that he decried.

Andrew's version of "Colloque Sentimentale" is certainly a fine thing. Have you compared it with Dowson's? The latter seems pretty weak and lame beside it—but then, as Plarr justly observes, Dowson's renderings from Verlaine are the poorest things he ever did.

I enclose a poem of Richey's (the Frenchman I mentioned), from an old issue of "Bohemia," a San Francisco publication long since (and happily) "defunct." I rather like the thing—it shows novel possibilities in *vers libre*.[1]

Will you please return the extra copy of the "Traveller" that I sent you? My type-writer is old, and begins to develop the maladies of age—arthritis, and even paresis! I hate using it more than is absolutely necessary.

I've just received a copy of the Brentano edition of Baudelaire, which turns out to be a reprint of the translation by E. P. Sturm, published long ago, together with the Wingate version of Verlaine, in the Canterbury Classics. But the translator's name is not given in the reprint, nor the preface written by him, which, as I remember, was excellent stuff . . . I wonder why . . . There is, (or was to be) a "complete" translation of Baudelaire in the Modern Library. Have you seen it, or heard anything concerning it?

Yes, I received your "Five Poems." Didn't I mention them? I liked "Shadow-Love" and the "Burden" in particular.

Here's a new poem of George's—also, my latest sonnet.

> Affectionately,
> Clark.

P.S. Keep all the enclosures.

Notes

1. See further letter 167n1.

[166] [ALS]

> Auburn, Cal.,
> Aug. 12th, 1919.

Dear Sam:

My heartiest thanks for that consignment of Stevenson's Letters, and the little volume of Chinese Lyrics! I've always had a fondness for Stevenson—a fondness, I dare say, not altogether justifiable on grounds of literary greatness. But then—there are *great* writers whom I can't read, and never intend to read; and Stevenson, whatever else he may be, is readable in almost everything he wrote; and the letters are no exception. D——d few professional literary men have put so much of themselves into their correspondence.

The Chinese Lyrics are charming. I am much taken with the gaillardise[1] of the one beginning, "I am going to gather the wheat, In the fields of Mei."[2] Also, I am struck by the antiquity of the poems in this volume. Those in the Cranmer-Byng translation, as I remember, belong mostly to the mediaeval eras. But in this, dates like 1121 B. C., occur as casually as the date on a business letter!

No, I don't possess the Cranmer-Byng volumes. Dewing has them, however—which is next door to it, since we borrow each other's books with the least permissible ceremony. D's library is "small but select"—it contains enough philosophical dynamite and intellectual t.n.t., in the shape of Niet[z]sche, Max Sterner, Dostoievsky, Gorki, etc, etc., to wreck and shatter the brains of half the local population—if they could understand it.

It desolates me to hear that you have been unwell. There's d——d little in life, beyond the brief Epicurean category of Omar's stanza, "A book of verses underneath the bough, etc." Even art is a kind of Barmecides[3]-feast, when one is sick, or indisposed. As for the rest—the "wine" and "bread" are worse than mockery to a sick and queasy stomach. And love—love is the shadow of a dead, forgotten dream,—or a ravenous, writhing, serpent-shapen flame from the cauldron-fires of Malebolge.

Don't send me "Imperial Purple"—I have the book. I agree with you about Heliogabalus—a stunning subject for a poem. In fact, I've already scribbled a brace of sonnets dealing with him. I'll send them along,—if they survive the ordeal of revision.

I'm sending you a copy of "The Star-Treader"—I have a number of them left. But I absolutely forbid you to dream of paying for it—that is impossible! I'm not so poor as all that!

I enclose a prose-poem, "The Traveller." The idea is good, even if not strictly original. I wish the rendering were better. But I've little energy, and less patience—and good art is impossible without both.

Write me very soon, if you can. My solitude would be well-nigh complete, were it not for your letters. My other correspondents are few and desultory, with the exception of Sterling, with whom I exchange letters once every month or so. And a month is one hell of a long time, in Auburn.

Affectionately,

Your friend,

Clark.

Notes

1. Boastful gaiety.
2. Helen Waddell, *Lyrics from the Chinese* 19.

3. The Barmecides, an influential Persian family from Balkh, were remarkable for their majesty, splendor and hospitality, are mentioned in some stories of the *Arabian Nights.*

[167] [ALS]

East Auburn, Cal.,

Aug. 23rd, 1919.

Dear Sam:

Thanks, many, many thanks for the copies of "Ennui" and "The Princess Almeena." My original mss. were harder to unscribble than a Babylonian palimpsest . . . I'm horribly sorry that you missed my letter—I certainly wrote to thank you for the Stevenson Letters and the Chinese Lyrics. Also, I sent you a new prose-poem, "The Traveller." There wasn't so much in the letter, apart from my appreciation of the Stevenson Letters, which I am glad to repeat—I think there is better stuff in some of them than in much of Stevenson's professional work. And I don't mean to disparage the latter—I've a great and ineradicable fondness for "Treasure Island," "Kidnapped," "Travels with a Donkey," ["]Virginibus Puerisque" and many others.

I like the Chinese Lyrics, and am greatly impressed by their antiquity. 1123 B. C.! etc, etc! It makes me feel like an infant of yester-week, to read those headings.

There isn't much news. Some of the early grapes are ripe, and I'm trying to infuse the season with a modicum of Theocritean romance by the manufacture of a few gallons of wine. Also, I'm making cider, and perry (the liquor of pears). The greatest of the arts shall not become a lost art, if I can help it— in spite of all the Purityrannical fanatics between Los Angeles and Cape Cod.

I enclose Andrew Dewing's rendering of "Colloque Sentimentale" by Verlaine, versified from a word-for-word prose-translation by Roubaix de La Brie Richey.[1] "Robo," as he is familiarly called, is a poet of no mean talent himself, and, according to Andrew, who knows him well, is a perfect type of the decadent in all respects. Andrew's verses are much more literal than any other rendering.

Your suggestion about Heliogabalus, prompted me to the scribbling of a brace of sonnets. To punish you for the suggestion, I enclose the sonnets. Also, a copy of the lost "Traveller.["]

I'm glad to hear that some of your work is to be printed. "The Faun" was great stuff—not to mention some of the lyrics. The favour and protection of Thoth be with you!

I'll write again in a few days.

Affectionately,

Clark.

P.S. Don't dream of paying for "The Star-Treader." I'd never forgive you if you did!

Notes

1. Roubaix "Robo" de l'Abrie Richey (1890–1922). Originally a farm boy from Oregon named Ruby Ritchie, the artist and poet assumed the more bohemian name Roubaix. Author of *The Book of Robo, Being a Collection of Verses and Prose Writings by Roubaix de L'Abrie Richey* (1923). The poem mentioned in letter 171 is unknown.

[168] [ALS]

East Auburn, Cal.,
Aug. 29th, 1919.

Dear Sam:

Thanks for the printed poems you send me—several of these I've never seen before. "Shadow[-]Love" is doubtless the best, with its poignant echo of Heine. I like the musical "Burden," also. The "futuristic" sketch of yourself is very interesting—the aspect that it brings out is unmistakably pagan, and oriental. I can readily imagine you in Alexandria or Lesbos, or, in a later incarnation, wandering through the Baghdad of Haroun or Almansour, after the journey of the Persian wastes. . . . Alas, for Omar, and Saadi, and Shiraz with its golden wine and golden roses! I wish we were there in Shiraz or Baghdad or Ispahan, with "Time's purple" a thousand years deep between us and this nightmare of the modern world!

Yes, I've seen something of Upson's before. The poem you quote is very fine. I showed it to Dewing, who also liked it very much . . . But what an abominable death[1]—poets ought to display a little originality in the choice of their taking-off. When I get ready to "croak," I shall hie me to the upas valley of Java, or the fatal caves about Lake Avernus, or take a flying leap from El Capitan, or the battlements of the Grand Canyon. Or else I shall wander out in the track of the simoom, or start in a rowboat for Samoa. Even death has become so damnably trite and banal, that any self-respecting poet owes it to himself to give the art an original inflection, a fresh *nuance* . . . By this, you musn't [*sic*] think me insensible to the pitiable tragedy of such an end as Upson's—the sordidness makes it the more terrible, after all. Death is robbed of its horror, if it can be made romantic or sublime.

Forgive these horrible pothooks—my ordinary scrawl, plus the contrariety and all-round cussedness of which only a bad pen is capable!

Affectionately,
Clark.

Notes

1. Arthur Wheelock Upson (1877–1908), American poet who died by drowning, pre-sumably a suicide.

[169] SL to CAS [nonextant]

> [Envelope postmarked Cleveland, Ohio,
> Sept. 12, 1919.]

[170] [ALS]

> East Auburn, Cal.
> Sept. 14th, 1919.

Dear Sam:

This isn't a letter—merely a note in acknowledgement of *your* letter, and the books. Many, many thanks. I've not found time to read either of them thoroughly, but my hasty perusal shows me that both are full of fine things. Was there ever such a combination of the artist and the scientist as Leonardo?

I'll write again in a few days.

Hastily,

Clark.

[Envelope postmarked East Auburn, Cal., Sep. 14, 1919.]

[171] [ALS]

> East Auburn, Cal.
> Sept. 15th, 1919.

Dear Sam:

I've just finished "The Art of Thomas Hardy,"[1] and like it very much in parts. I've read so little of Hardy that I'm scarcely able to agree or disagree with Johnson's dictums. But I can enjoy the sc[h]olarly and illuminative criticism, the rapier-like play of wit and penetration. It's odd to note the Catholic bias in Johnson, when he comes to Hardy's philosophy. Johnson seems to have been the most thorough-going of the 1890 crowd, in his conversion.

There are hundreds of subtle and splendid things in Leonardo's "Note-books." I've not read them through as yet, but have found many passages to mark. I'm certainly indebted to you for these books.

Thanks for the suggestion about Solomon. I may "do" a sonnet, some-time, in praise of him. I've thought vaguely of a series of sonnets on such men as Baudelaire, Swinburne, Gautier, Poe, Wilde, James Thomson, Hearne, [*sic*] etc. Solomon is worthy of addition to the list.

"The Moon and Sixpence"[2] is certainly a striking title. I'll look it up on my next visit to Auburn's literary museum. The article that mentions Gauguin is in "Ivory, Apes, and Peacocks," which also contains a paper on Hearn.[3]

The current "North American Review" contains an article by Arthur Symons, entitled "Baudelaire and his Letters."[4] It's very interesting. One of its most striking paragraphs is "lifted" (perhaps unconsciously) from Poe's "Marginalia."

I enclose another of Roubaix de La Brie Richey's poems, together with a picture of him. You'll doubtless agree with me that the picture is even more interesting than the poem.

There's little or no news, hereabouts, except that the grapes are ripening fast. I'm making wine from many varieties—a little of each kind. I shall have red wine and yellow wine, and wine of purple and chrysoprase—wine that is pale as the moonstone, and wine the colour of myrtle-flowers. 'Twill be hard luck if *some* of it doesn't turn out well.

> Affectionately, as ever,
> Clark.

Notes

1. By Lionel Johnson.
2. A novel by W. Somerset Maugham that features a character (Charles Strickland) loosely based on the painter Paul Gauguin.
3. I.e., "Kubin, Munch, and Gauguin: Masters of Hallucination" (222–39) and "The Cult of the Nuance: Lafcadio Hearn" (240–48).
4. Arthur Symons, "Baudelaire and His Letters," *North American Review* 210 (September 1919): 379–87. Not to be confused with an article entitled "Baudelaire in His Letters," *Saturday Review* (London) 103 (26 January 1907): 107–8.

[172] [ALS]

> East Auburn, Cal.,
> Sept. 22nd, 1919.

Dear Sam:

I'd have written before, had it not been for the spell of phenomenal heat (phenomenal for September) which has sucked me dry of what little energy I normally possess.

I like your conception of "The Death of Helen." I'm eager to see what you'll make of it—there should be novel possibilities in the prose-medium you describe, in dealing with such a theme. And don't forget to finish "The Sphinx"—you can't possibly "overdo" the paganism for me.

I'm glad you've located the book on Heliogabalus, and shall be very grateful for a chance to read it. The price mentioned is pretty "tall."

I didn't buy the Baudelaire—it was a present from a rich friend. I can't afford to buy books at present. But, my dear Sam, you mustn't beggar yourself by sending me *all* the literary treasures you come across. I feel the pangs of a guilty conscience when I look at all the books you've given me. There's enough of them to fill a separate case—a case that would be about the choicest one in my whole library!

No, I've not read "The Story without a Name"[1]—is it as good as the title? Huneker speaks of the "honey and tiger's-blood of D'Annunzio's prose"[2]—which is as fine a recommendation as one could desire. Huneker ought to know.

Here are a few pencil sketches. Perhaps they'll amuse you. Have you ever seen a picture of Heliogabalus? I never have. But here's my conception of him—one conception, at least.[3]

> Affectionately,
>
> Clark.

Notes

1. By Jules Barbey d'Aurevilly.
2. CAS appears to be mistaken. Huneker wrote of the "'honey and tiger's blood'" of Barbey d'Aurevilly in his introductory preface (xxiv) to *The Poems and Prose Poems of Charles Baudelaire*.
3. CAS's rendering of the emperor depicts him with mustache and beard, and rather middle aged (he lived only to be eighteen). The bust of Elagabalus at the Capitoline Museum represents him with a mustache and sideburns, but no beard.

[173] [TLS]

[late September 1919?]

Dear Clark,

Glad the books came safely—the postal service is a very funny thing nowadays. I am going to have Laukhuff mail you a copy of the "170" this week—and please pardon the delay.

I've one or two things that may interest you—recently "got". What do you say to a Borrow mss. seven quarto pages of a scene translated from a Swedish play and done during the "veiled period", i.e. 1830?[1] Some day I want to make a copy of it for you—it's a really fine piece of work. Also there came to me today, the 1632 edition of the Florio translation of Montaigne, a rare book, but my copy isn't in a very good condition.

I've been despondent recently. Believe I'll take to writing again.

Nelson here, who recently underwent a dangerous operation, after being run down by a machine, tells me that he is writing a book on Flaxman.[2] He's a keen artist, is Nelson.

Please excuse this note. How does Dewing? My best wishes to yourself and yours.

                              Affectionately,
                              Sam

1537 East 93 St., Suite 2.

P.S. Here's a question I wanted to ask for a long time—have you entirely given up your drawing?

Notes

1. SL wrote a preface (dated 24 September 1922) to a scene, translated by George Borrow, from *Hakon Jarl,* by Adam Gottlob Oehlenschläger (1779–1850), a Danish poet and playwright, which George Kirk intended to print.
2. John Flaxman (1755–1826), English sculptor and draughtsman, a leading figure in English and European Neoclassicism.

[174] [ALS]

                              East Auburn, Cal.,
                                  Oct. 7th, 1919.

Dear Sam:

          Pardon this delayed letter—I've felt so damnably dull, so accursedly inert, for the past week or more, that even letter-writing seemed an impossible task. I hardly know what's the matter—perhaps a complication of causes (damn this dribbling pen!) with the everlasting infernal monotony of my life as the chief one. There may be physical reasons, too—the symptoms might indicate anything, almost, from hardening of the liver to softening of the brain!

          I'm awaiting the Chinese anthology with unusual eagerness—it must be a veritable blue moon of a translation, if it's superior to the Cranmer-Byng volumes.

          Your quotation from Herodian is very beautiful, in its "quaint and curious" way—filled with the fresh and simple felicities of a language undeflowered by time and use.

          I have the Florio Montaigne, in the Temple edition, which reprints the old-time spelling. Montaigne is a sovereign remedy for mental dyspepsia, a specific for many spiritual ills. I should read him more than I do.

          I've not seen Huneker's essay on Martin. It should be a fine thing—it's hard to think of a critic who would do better justice to Martin. There's a reference in the paper on Baudelaire, where he speaks of a certain stanza, "which might serve as a text for one of John Martin's vast sinister mezzotints."[1] Your description of the Bible illustrations, interests me immensely. Aside from Blake, Martin should be the most capable illustrator of the Old Testament.

I've just received some new volumes from Boni and Liveright—Pater's "Sketches and Reviews," "Renee Mauperin," by the Goncourt brothers, and a new selection from de Maupassant, translated by Michael Monahan. The Pater volume, like so many others in the Penguin series, is a bit of a "sell." There's not much in it, of literary importance, after the essay on "Esthetic Poetry". Of course, the reviews are all very good, but they're scarcely worth the price of the book to a poor man—especially a book that's bound in the vilest lemon-yellow conceivable to the human eye.

Dewing is back, from the dissipations of Bohemia. The dry law, to quote G. S., "isn't hurting S. F. very much as yet." They sell liquor openly, in the Latin restaurants, or, at least, with the thinnest pretense of a subterfudge [*sic*]—the waiter sets the bottle *under* the table when he serves it. But the glasses are on top!

George has withdrawn "Lilith" from Boni and Liveright (he seems to think the firm is likely to go under) and is having it brought out in California. He's engaged in the proofs at present. I'll see that you receive a copy when the book appears.

I enclose a new poem of George's. I'm sure you'll agree with me that it's a very fine thing. The effect of the repetitions, as Dewing pointed out, is curiously suggestive of "La Belle Dame Sans Merci," though there's no other resemblance.

Affectionately,
Clark.

Notes

1. *Egoists: A Book of Supermen* 74.

[175]   [TLS]

[October 1919]

Dear Clark,

Sent the "170" away two days ago and I hope it comes to you safely. I believe you will agree with me that it is a fine thing, altho probably none of the writers (or poets) represented are quite as lyrical as those contained in the "Lute of Jade" and the "Feast of Lanterns." How do you like the one entitled the "Red Cockatoo?"[1]

I invested in a Poe set of 1858 (4 vols.) yesterday. It contains the rarely reprinted "Eureka" and the Griswold execration. Strangely enough the poems do not include the "To Helen."

One of the boys here has made me a gift of four more of the little carved pieces, all apes and two of them containing tropical birds. I can't understand it. There are two or three more in town. A local pawnbroker (!) has them—they are anemones carved from vermillion and green stone—possibly wind-flowers—but so delicately done that a wind seems to be passing that bends the petals ever tremulously. The Jewish gentleman behind the counter told me a mysterious story of his having purchased them from a sailor who said they came from India. I believe the "India" part of it as they seem a little too sophisticated for anything savouring of Chinese. Anyhow they are well worth having.

I've been offered a reporter's position with a local newspaper, $30 per week to start, but shall probably refuse. I don't mind selling a certain mechanical ability that I've developed in the line of office work, but the brain—that's another story.

Life seems so arid and monotonous here—I can't exactly explain why but people are bores and fools and perfection is farther off than ever. Write soon—write often.

Affectionately,
S L.

1537 East 93 St., Suite 2.

[Enclosure: Clipping of newspaper review of poetry by Siegfried Sassoon.]

Notes

1. A poem by Po Chü-i (772–846 C.E.), p. 215.

[176] [ALS]

East Auburn, Cal.
Oct. 13th, 1919.

Dear Sam:

First of all, to thank you for the books, which I've been reading alternately—a section of Chinese verse sandwiched with a few pages of the Greek Anthology.[1] The Chinese translation certainly gives the impression of literalness, and doubtless has more of the flavour of the original. But I don't see how you can compare it with the splendid lyrical versions of Cranmer-Byng—the two have scarcely anything in common, beyond their source and subject-matter. It's like comparing Fitzgerald's "Omar" with a word-for-word rendering by some good Persian scholar. "The Red Cockatoo," which you mention, is certainly a fine thing—the brief but poignant expression of an inevitable truth. I'm glad to own the book—and glad, also, to have the Greek Anthology—the very opening of whose pages brings a waft of incense and attar, and the sweetness of crushed flowers from the younger world—the sweetness of crushed flowers where Jove and the nymphs had lain, in gardens of gold and crimson that were soon to fade. Alas! there is neither youth, nor passion, nor splendour nor perfume now, unless it be in some exotic garden, or gorgeous isle of eastern or western seas, where time has fallen asleep among the poppies!

Thanks for the poems—I like the renderings of Heine, and especially the song from Chamisso.[2] Your elegy on Chivers is a fine thing. Alas! poor Chivers! Few poets are so completely forgotten as he. But, after all, what does it matter—another swing of the eternal pendulum, and Homer and Dante will be part and parcel of the same oblivion—names that fade on mouldering pages in ruined libraries, amid the barbarism of a senile planet—the "second childhood" of the world.

Pardon these platitudes—the reading of the Chinese and Greek Anthologies, has filled me with the sense of time and change, of evanescence and mortality.

I'm going out to gather a few more grapes this afternoon. The wine I've made is coming on famously, so I purpose to make a little more, before the end of the vintage-time . . . I wish you were with me—you'd enjoy the California autumn.

As ever, affectionately,
Clark.

Notes

1. It is unclear which edition of the *Greek Anthology* (a compendium of poems from the classical and Byzantine periods) CAS read. There have been many English translations since the early 19th century.
2. Adelbert von Chamisso (1781–1838), German poet, botanist, and author of *Peter Schlemihl,* a story about a man who sold his shadow. SL published a translation of one of his "Hochzeitslieder" (wedding poems).

[177] [ALS]

East Auburn, Cal.,
Oct. 22nd, 1919.

Dear Sam:

I've wanted to write before this, but have had a severe cold—something between the grippe and a common catarrh. Also, I've expected to hear from you, any day. Did you get my last letter, with Sterling's new poem?

Life drags on, as usual, like a snake with a broken back—or an elegy in Alexandrines. Were it not for the leaves that kindle here and there, in the orchards below, and the sharpness of the morning air, I should scarcely know that it was autumn. I think of Swinburne's line: "The years with soundless feet and sounding wings."[1] But the wings are soundless, too, in the piny hills and vineyard-laden vales of this borderland of Lethe.

I've re-read the Chinese volume with increased pleasure. The simplicity and naiveteé [*sic*] of the translation, certainly has all the earmarks of verisimilitude. It's the way that one would expect the Chinese to write . . . Cranmer-

Byng is a fine and accomplished poet; but on comparing his translation of a certain poem with Waley's, I feel that the former might better be classed as an original achievement—it hardly seems a *translation*.

I've just ordered a new edition of the "Decameron," advertised as "complete." I hope to hell it's unexpurgated—if so, I suppose the publishers were afraid to use the word "unexpurgated," lest they attract the attention of the police! Shades of Torquemada and Cotton Mather! What a country it's getting to be—a paradise for moral persecutors, and a premature sort of hell for the rest of us. Do you know that there's a law (soon to take effect) forbidding the publication or dissemination of any recipe or formula for the manufacture of alcoholic liquor? Another session of that gang of cowards and dinwiddies, the U.S. Congress, and they'll be putting the thumb-screws on anyone who is suspected or accused of knowing how to make wine!

Good cheer to you! Write me soon, won't you?

Affectionately,

Clark.

Notes

1. "To Victor Hugo," l. 12.

[178] [ALS]

East Auburn, Cal.,

Oct. 26th, 1919.

Dear Sam:

Glad you liked the assortment of grotesques—I should hardly make them were it not for you. No one else seems to care much for them. I sent you another batch in my last letter—a Chinese pirate, a priest from Atlantis, a Mandingo,[1] and some others.

It's good to hear that you are at work again—I wish I could say the same for myself, but I seem unfit for any serious mental effort. Doubtless, as you suggest, "that beast the stomach" is to blame. Indigestion is the most fiendish of maladies, when it becomes chronic. No nervous or mental symptom is too weird and atrocious to have its cause in dyspepsia.

No, I don't think I could endure life in a city—the change would be too radical, after a life-time of solitude. The faun to his wood, the anchorite to his cave—Rome, and Tyre, and Babylon are not for these. I have a horror of crowds and machinery—of street-cars and elevators, in especial. The monstrous and brainless energy by which they are operated, seems almost demoniacal to me.

Yes, I heartily agree with you about the prose-poems of Poe, such as "Silence" and "Eleonora," and "Shadow." The "Gold Bug" and other detective tales are enormously clever, but when all is said, they remain prose,—essential, untransmutable prose,—while the others are poetry, in every sense.

I'm awaiting the "Fantastics" with tremendous interest. Hearn, to my mind, never surpassed his early work, such as "Chinese Ghosts." Sometimes I wish he had never gone to Japan. So much of the stuff in his Japanese books (not that I wish to decry their value) is not literature in the finest sense,—but is mere scientific, historic, or ethnological research, which others, lacking Hearn's literary genius, could have done as well.

I don't know much about Havelock Ellis.[2] He sounds rather formidable to me. I'm inclined to fight shy of medical literature—I read too much of it at one time, and the surfeit brought on an attack of mental nausea from which I've never entirely recovered.

Yes, I've heard the yarn about Wilde,—a most unlikely tale, considering the evidence of all his best friends. The sonnet by Chivers is interesting—he certainly anticipated the "Celtic revival." Chivers was a strange being; he undoubtedly had access to the same poetic fountain as Poe; or, to vary the image a little, they were streams with a common source. The waters ran clear in one, and turbid in the other.

I shall cherish that promise of yours. I'll put aside some of the best of my vintage, and the seal shall remain unbroken till you come.

>Affectionately,
>Clark.

Notes

1. A member of a subgroup of Mande-speaking peoples, including the Malinke and Bambara, of Sierra Leone.
2. Henry Havelock Ellis (1859–1939), English physician, writer, and social reformer and a pioneer in the study of human sexuality.

[179] [ALS]

>East Auburn, Cal.,
>Nov. 9th, 1919.

Dear Sam:

I've just returned from my usual morning walk, among the brown leaves and pale dead grass covered with a fretwork of frost that was already beginning to blur and disappear. Our autumn is in full flame now—I've seldom seen such marvellous colour. The plum-orchard at the foot of my hill[1] has put on a deep and purplish red, and behind it the peach-trees are like innumerable golden fires beginning to darken. The poplars at the verge are like masses of chrysoprase—filled with the pale green and yellow of shoaling water.

Are you writing anything? I've written a sonnet, which I may send you in my next. It needs a lot of tinkering.

My "Decameron," printed on India paper, and apparently "unexpurgated," came the other day. Also, I've picked up fifteen volumes of Balzac at second-hand, including the magnificent "Harlot's Progress" (which I had never read before) with the rest of the Lucien de Rubempre series.

Have you seen the Baudelaire in the "Modern Library?" I'd order the book, if I felt sure that it wasn't the same translation as the Brentano edition.

I look forward to the new Chinese volume. The "170" certainly give an authentic impression of every-day life in Cathay. The charm of it "grows" upon me, like the charm of Whistler's etchings.

Symons has an illuminating article on Verlaine in the September "Vanity Fair."[2] Have you seen it? "Vanity Fair" is very nearly my favourite, among the periodicals of our literary soviets. I find entertainment in a few others, such as "Life," and (occasionally) the "Smart Set." But the bureaucratic "Century," "Harpers," ["]Atlantic," etc, and the proletarian "Post," "American," "Everybodys," and the rest, give me a sort of intellectual appendicitis.

I quote the last letter I received from the "Atlantic," verbatim: "These lines are full of light and colour, and we have enjoyed reading them. Yours faithfully, the Editors." Wouldn't that beat the Chinese for a polite refusal? Dewing suggests that I might return the poems with a note to this effect: "Glad you enjoyed reading my poems. You may print them, too, if you like!"

Another letter in a few days.

> Affectionately,
>
> > Clark.

Notes

1. See CAS's haiku "Abandoned Plum-Orchard."
2. "Paul Verlaine," *Vanity Fair* 13 (September 1919): 43, 106.

[180] [ALS]

> East Auburn, Cal.
>
> Nov. 21st, 1919.

Dear Sam:

"Promenades of an Impressionist" came yesterday, but no letter. Did you write? I've been expecting a letter for the past week or more.

Hearty thanks for the book. I devoured the major portion of it last evening, and found it surpassingly good, like all of Huneker's stuff. Huneker may be wrong at times, but he is never dull. I particularly liked the papers on Watteau, Rodin, and Rops, though I've seen scarcely anything of the latter's work. The bit on John Martin is good also. Odd—I had just finished re-reading "Ivory, Apes, and Peacocks" when the book came. That phrase appears to be a favourite with Huneker—he uses it twice in this volume, in describing the works of certain artists. Huneker is by all odds our best living critic—at least when it comes to continental literature and art, on which he seems to specialize. John Cowper Powys is his only rival—and Powys is at his best in dealing with the English poets and novelists.

Have you read anything of Christopher Morley's? I recommend "Shandygaff," if you haven't—a book that the Prohibitionists ought to suppress on account of its title,[1] and the quality of the contents. I've just started "The Haunted Bookshop," by the same author—delightful stuff, as far as I've got.

I hear the weather has been stormy in the middle and eastern states. But there's no sign of it here—the skies maintain a merciless azure, an implacable serenity. I wish it would rain—the little spring on our hill top is nearly exhausted. The autumns have been growing dryer and colder each year for six or eight seasons past, and when the rain comes, it will come like a deluge in January, February, and March.

Have I sent you a copy of "Quest" before? It was written last spring, but I find no mention if it in your letters, so I'm sending you a copy to make sure.

Do you remember a drawing of mine called "The Flower-Devil?" I've written a little fantasy to go with it, which I'll send you before long.

> Affectionately,
>
> Clark.

Notes

1. The term, chiefly British, refers to a mixed drink of beer and ginger beer.

[181] [ALS]

> East Auburn, Cal.
>
> Nov. 23rd, 1919.

Dear Sam:

Received your letter after mailing mine, last Friday. The programme you enclose is certainly interesting. I've heard fine things about Claudel, but have never seen any of his work.[1] "Salome," which you mention, is a magnificent thing, in spite of all the prudes in Prohibition-dom. In my opinion, it's one of the three best things Wilde ever wrote (the other two being "The Sphinx" and "The Picture of Dorian Gray.") Sterling, if I remember rightly, considered it Wilde's master-piece. Huneker, though, mentions it somewhere with rather "scant courtesy."

I hope you let me see that new poem of yours. The dramatis personae you mention is "some crowd," as they say in the American argot.

The "Night in the Luxembourg" is one of my favourites—I keep it in the same shelf with "Mademoiselle de Maupin,["] "One of Cleopatra's Nights," "The Temptation," "Studies in Pessimism,"[2] the poems of Arthur Symons, and a complete set of Poe.

I like the idea of having some of our work printed in brochures. But I'd like to pay my share of the expense. I've no arrangement with Robertson as to the publication of my next book—devil knows when he'll get around to it:—Utopia will be established, and the Huns and Bolsheviks will all be in hell by that time, I dare say.

"Smart Set" has accepted "The Princess Almeena." They don't pay much,—but they're the only market I've found, so far, for prose-poetry.

Yes, I remember Swinburne's mention of "Stories after Nature."[3] I've had a curiosity about the book, ever since reading "Joseph and His Brethren," with the magnificent Potiphar scene, which would add lustre to any of the Elizabethans after Shakespeare.

I think of investing in a few books. Saltus' "Anatomy of Negation," "The Garden of Epicurus," by Anatole France, Symonds' "Life of Shelley," and the "English Poems" of Richard le Gallienne, comprise the list—which will leave my purse in the condition of a pricked bladder. Do you know Le Gallienne? I think very highly of him. He and Bliss Carman[4] and John Masefield are the most important of living poets, after Sterling. Dewing would add Yeats to the list—but Yeats is too exiguous, too will-o-the wispy, for my taste, except in a few early things.

> Affectionately,
> Clark.

Notes

1. Paul Claudel (1868–1955), French poet and dramatist.

2. By Arthur Schopenhauer.

3. By Charles Wells.

4. Richard le Gallienne (1866–1947), English author and poet. Bliss Carman (1861–1929), Canadian poet who lived most of his life in the U.S., where he achieved international fame; acclaimed as Canada's poet laureate during his later years.

[182] [ALS]

> East Auburn, Cal.
> Dec. 3rd, 1919.

Dear Sam:

It's raining to-day—a slow, continuous downpour, without wind or tempest—a rainfall that resembles the minor monotones of Oriental music. I've been turning the pages of the Chinese translations, and thinking of what you say in your last letter anent the poet-philosophers of "long ago and far away." Certainly, they knew all that can be known about life, and the sense of its brevity and futility pervades or underlies their slightest poems. One even finds them doubting the benefits of civilization—a doubt that we are wont to think of as peculiar to modernity. Truly, there is no progress, in any proper sense of the word—time is a circle,—or a wheel that forever returns upon itself.

Have you read Balzac's "Droll Stories?" It's quite unlike anything else of Balzac's—more in the manner of Rabelais than any other writer, tho happily lacking in the gratuitous filth of the great Touranian. Even at that, it makes the Decameron look like a Sunday-school reader! It presents mediaeval, or post-mediaeval, life with astounding verisimilitude and realism.

No, I've not ordered the Modern Library Baudelaire—I'm stone-broke for the present. Certainly, I should like to have it, since I've never seen the Shipley and Robertson translations.[1]

I've made a few drawings, some of which I'll send you presently. I'll have to suspend work for awhile, though, on account of my eyes, which are troubling me more than in many years. I've been reading too much, I suppose. Alas! Reading is almost my only refuge from an all-devouring boredom. Books are my chief society, and without them, I should be face to face with the Abomination of Desolation.

By the way, I've a bit of news for you—I've been "discovered" in Canada—a group of scholars and literary men in Toronto are considerably exercised over my work. I enclose a letter from one of them, which I must ask you to return. It's the only direct communication that I've received,—and my publisher apparently held it for about a month before forwarding it to me. I heard the rest through an English cousin. Other letters have been written to me from Toronto, it seems—but I've not received them. It's a curious sort of affair. I feel like a corpse who hears that someone is planning to resurrect him. Faith! I had thought myself decently and comfortably dead!

Do you know anything about my correspondent, Frank Pollock?[2] The sonnets he encloses are quite good, especially for the thoughts and images.

The theatre program you enclose looks good to me—that arrangement of coloured lights, thrown on a white stage with actors in white costumes, should be tremendously effective.

I await the new Chinese volume with eagerness. What magic is in these bare and childishly simple arrangements of words, that they should awake in one the very sentiment, the very sensation of life in ancient Cathay?

      Affectionately,

            Clark.

Notes

1. *Baudelaire: His Prose and Poetry* contained translations of some prose poems by Joseph T. Shipley and some poems in *Les Fleurs du mal* by W. J. Robertson.
2. Possibly Frank Lillie Pollock (1876–1957), Canadian writer of adventure stories, mostly for juveniles.

[183] [ALS]

East Auburn, Cal.,
Dec. 11th, 1919.

Dear Sam:

Don't send the "Shelley," if you've not already mailed it. I ordered a copy days before your letter came. You must be mistaken about "The Garden of Epicurus"—the Chicago firm (The Book Supply Co.) with which I deal, quoted it at $2.25 when I asked them for the price, so it can't be out of print. Certain other books on which I asked quotations were unobtainable, however, such as the poems of Francis S. Saltus, the first real American "decadent" (do you know him?) who, (among other things) wrote a series of sonnets on various liquors, ranging from arrack to vermouth.[1] Some of his best sonnets (I remember one on the Sphinx in particular) are given in Stedman's American Anthology.[2]

The bit from Chivers is certainly "choice," though the false rhyme troubles my ears not a little. One is irresistibly inclined to pronounce it "Yuby," in the "down-east" manner. The title of the book you mention, "The Sons of Usna,"[3] reminds me of one of Yeats' best lyrics (the one about Helen) in which "Usna's children" are introduced.

I like your "Chinese" poem.[4] Have you read Hearn's "Kwaidan," which includes a magnificent rendering of the legend of Urashima, the Japanese Rip Van Winkle? Your lyric brings it to mind. I didn't know that the Chinese possessed a similar legend.

I'm sorry you've been ill—the stomach is an unruly and malignant beast. My own seldom attempts an open rebellion, but prefers a furtive, underground state of general disaffection and sedition. . . . Some novelist (I think it's S. Weir Mitchell) makes a character in one of his books remark "that no-one dies a triumphant death from any disease below the diaphragm."[5] Verily, I am prepared to believe it.

Here are a few drawings, mostly of poets—four celebrated soaks, and one who drank only water . . . Also, a pessimistic sonnet, and a decadent lyric.

Affectionately,
Clark.

[Envelope postmarked East Auburn, Cal., Dec. 11, 1919.]

Notes

1. "Flasks and Flagons," in *The Bayadere and Other Sonnets* 93–123. Francis Saltus Saltus (1849–1889), American poet and elder half-brother of Edgar Saltus.

2. "The Sphinx Speaks," p. 522.

3. Perhaps Fiona Macleod, *Diedrê and the Sons of Usna*.

4. I.e., "A Chinese Pavilion."

5. "A learned divine said a thing of extraordinary wisdom when he announced that no

man, however secure he may be in mind as to his future life, ever dies a triumphant death with disease below the diaphragm." Mitchell, *Characteristics* 12.

[184] [TLS]

[c. 13 December 1919]

Dear Clark,

I'm mailing you with this letter the second book of Chinese translations. Good cheer with it! I succumbed to another handmade-paper copy. I think it equally as good as the first and call your attention to the prose-translation of the Autumn poem, a beautiful piece of writing. Cranmer-Byng translated it into metre but it seems oddly affected in comparison with this of Whaley's.[*sic*] I specially like the poem on page 13.[1]

I want to keep Mr Pollock's letter until my next. I hope you answer him—such a fine appreciation deserves an answer. But what he says I knew five, six—nay seven years ago, and I've never altered my opinion one jot or tittle. I wonder what he would say to your later work, to the poetry of the "Odes and Sonnets" and to the mss collection that I have—to all the things you have written since "The Star-Treader." One thing should be done—Robertson should be either made to realize that poetry is not a bad investment nowadays, or you ought to have another publisher. I understand that the Seven Seas Company does a great deal of poetry publishing, and I suppose there are others that I don't know of that do too. You know my opinion of your work—it would be piling Pelion on Ossa to comment on Pollock's splendid words. And to think that you put the cockney Masefield ahead of yourself. Perish the thought! You have no living equal.

I'll await the drawings with great interest. Will send you the Baudelaire volume in a few days. When I read this second book of Chinese translations, a shiver came over me as I read the dates. For the men that wrote and sang these things were dead, had been dead for a thousand, for eleven hundred years. And I knew then that I should never see them but that the few things here translated in an alien tongue were mine to the end of my life.

I enclose a self portrait of myself, drawn from a mirror. It looks like—somewhat—and as you can see I am more robust than I was. Also I'm very dark and ruddy, which the pencil sketch doesn't show. The enclosed cards are from pieces by Paul Manship[2] in the Art Museum here. He has a Salome which hasn't been photographed but is equally fine. More in a few days—

Affectionately,

Sam

Notes

1. "The Great Summons" by Ch'ü Yüan (now spelled Qu Yuan) covers pp. 13–19 in Arthur Waley's *More Translations from the Chinese.*

2. Paul Howard Manship (1885–1966), American sculptor.

[185] [ALS]

East Auburn, Cal.
Dec. 15th, 1919.

Dear Sam:

Got your letter and the new Chinese volume Saturday. I like "The Great Summons," and the prose-translation of "Autumn" better than anything in the previous volume.[1] The former is magnificent, in its pictorial catalogue of the good things of Cathayan life. In a way, it suggests comparison with Rupert Brooke's "The Great Lover." The delight in sensuous impressions and sensations is not dissimilar. "Autumn" is splendid—rhythmic prose of a fine and sculpturesque, even metallic, outline. The vigour and clarity of its images is unforgettable. Still, Cranmer-Byng's version has its merits. I contend that it's a fine **English** poem, even though it may not be a **Chinese** poem. Most English poetry sounds "affected," anyway, after one has been reading these literal versions from the Chinese. We are all so d——d professional, and take ourselves in such dull and deadly earnest, as poets. To return to the book: I enjoyed the things from Li Po in especial, and wish Waley had devoted more space to him, and less to Po Chu-i, interesting and representative as the latter is. I hope Waley continues his translations— Chinese poetry must be inexhaustible, to any one, or any dozen, translators: No other Oriental literature can compare with it, with the possible exception of the Persian. What interests me most in these Chinese poems, is the clarity and calmness of comprehension, with which they view the immemorial vanities and futilities, and their unrebellious and undespairing sense of the hopeless mystery of things. Theirs is the most reasonable, the most dignified of attitudes. And with it all, what quiet and grateful acceptance of the beauty of the hour, of chance aspects of light and shade, of leaf and blossom, of the flight of birds, or the nodding of autumnal grasses! But enough of this—I seem to be falling into the furious and windy accents of a professional book-reviewer!

I like the drawing of yourself tremendously—it seems to bring you nearer to me. I, too, have grown much stouter of late. I've not been on the scales for a long time, but would guess myself at 135—more than I've ever weighed before. I wish my ability to work were commensurate with my increase in weight. My chances of dying young begin to look more and more exiguous. I'll be 27 in January. I think of taking up some system of physical exercise, including long walks, running, and a session of several hours daily with the axe or bucksaw. I believe it would be very beneficial, though my muscles are fairly hard now, from what work I have done. One can't be really healthy without thorough elimination of all digestive poisons and effete matter; and for this elimination, strenuous exercise is well-nigh essential.

Yes, I wrote to Pollock, and sent him a copy of "The Star-Treader." His enthusiasm certainly deserved it. I enclose his answer, which will interest you. I've a mind to accept his advice, and submit a collection of my unpublished work to some of the big firms—John Lane as first choice. When you come to think of it, Lane has printed far more good poetry than any other one publisher, during the past 20 or 30 years. Dowson, Davidson, Symons, Le Gallienne, Laurence Houseman, [*sic*] Stephen Phillips (who at least has good lines) Francis Thompson, and Rupert Brooke make a formidable list. I shan't bother about trying Scribners, though. Anyhow, what have they published in the way of poetry? Henry Van Dyke![2] . . . The Seven Seas Co. is a thundering good name. I don't know anything about their publications. Brentano's, Houghton Mifflin, and Mitchell Kennerly, [*sic*] are all better prospects than Scribner's or Harper's—the chief guardians and protagonists of literary provincialism in the east. My chances would be better in England, it seems to me. America is hopelessly divided into sections, and California, as Bierce observed, is looked upon by the others as a sort of literary Nazareth.

Thanks for the post-cards from the pieces by Paul Manship. I like their Orientalism, and the remarkable grace and fluency of line—a sheer fluidity uncommon and difficult of attainment in sculpture.

Have you ever seen "Literary California," an anthology compiled by Ella Sterling Mighels? I'm told that 1500 writers are represented, including myself.[3] Imagine it! Everyone that ever wrote, in this Paradise of "suckers," mosquitoes, piss-ants, and real-estate agents.

Good night! and pardon this letter: I've prosed along at a most unconscionable length.

> Affectionately,
>
> Clark.

Notes

1. "The Great Summons" by Ch'ü Yüan (13–20) and "Autumn" by Ou-Yang Hsiu (141–43).
2. Henry Van Dyke (1852–1933), American author and clergyman.
3. The book contains CAS's "Finis" and "The Price."

[186]   [ALS]

> East Auburn, Cal.,
> Dec. 23rd, 1919.

Dear Sam:

I return the story by Lovecraft.[1] It's a weird and shuddersome sort of thing, and opens up vistas of unfathomable speculation. I admit the resemblance to Poe—Poe would have rioted in such a conception, and made it the source of a "new shudder" or a new thrill—he who created so many such

. . . Undoubtedly, the resources and potentialities of the subconscious mind (or soul—call it what you will) are incalculable—that subconsciousness which knows and sees everything, because it is Life itself, possessing the memory, experience, power, and foreknowledge of all Life. From this infinite sea of being, what faint and broken echoes ascend in the cave we call the conscious mind! A few pebbles, and shells, and fragments of coral, and sprays of sea-weed, are all the treasure we take from that illimitable main . . . As to dreams, I, too have had strange dreams—dreams too strange to remember, or, if re-membered, strange beyond expression; and other dreams, of which words may afford a partial and distorted semblance—dreams that were filled with the confusion and commutation of the senses, with forms and colour dissolved in sound, and sound re-integrate in forms and colour—dreams in which the im-pressions of touch were transferred to ineffable harmonies, and discords like a torture of the Inquisition—kisses that became the music of Paradise, embraces that were visions of supernal light, and iris of empyrean suns; and contacts of abominable sightless things whose merest touch was the bottomless filth of Malebolge, and the slime of the pits of Python. But enough of this.

George's "Lilith" is just out, and I've been re-reading it for the tenth time, finding something new to marvel at with each perusal. I'll send you a copy as soon as I can obtain one for you. I think it will "take you off your feet," as they say. Passion, splendour, terror, beauty, tragedy—all are here, and in a Titan's measure—no scant and parsimonious dole, such as that of Stephen Phillips . . . Here are jewels, too,—and I love jewels:

> "Twin emeralds that were the eyes of Baal,
> And orbs for which Semiramis made war."[2]

And what do you say to such passages as this,—a Wizard's speech:

> "Milk o' the Devil's mare,
> Bubbles on poison! Laughest thou at me,
> Thou shalt not laugh when at thy ribs the yew
> Lets many tickling roots."[3]

And this, a speech of Lilith herself:

> "I have dreamed
> Of evening and a couch of ecstasies,
> Whereon Love moans, like Music on the rack."[4]

I hope you do come west—you know where to stop off, don't you? In-deed, I understand the nostalgia you mention—that thirst for the new and the unknown. But, alas, the only thirst assuagable is the thirst for Lethe—and who knows, they who forget, and find the black sleep of the grave, may hunger for remembrance, even as the dust itself may hunger to be fire and spirit, and the stone to become the white flesh of Beauty, vibrant with all the pains and raptures of all the senses.

> Affectionately,
> Clark.

Notes

1. CAS's first encounter with the work of H. P. Lovecraft (1890–1937), who corresponded with him from 1922 to 1937. The story, in manuscript, was "Beyond the Wall of Sleep."
2. *Lilith* 1.2.52–53.
3. *Lilith* 2.1.48–51.
4. *Lilith* 3.4.88–90.

[187] [ALS]

> East Auburn, Cal.,
> Dec. 31st, 1919.

Dear Sam:

　　　I'm glad you liked the portraits and verses. I thought of making the portraits for which you ask, at the time I drew the others. But I've not felt in the mood lately—for one reason, I've been putting most of my creative energy into verse. I'll make the drawings as soon as I can . . . By the way, did I tell you that a friend of mine who is in New York, had shown a number of my drawings to Oliver Herford?[1] Herford (who writes and illustrates books on animal crackers, and composite beasts!) thought them altogether "too uncanny and decadent." He said they might have amused Paris for ten days, but not longer than ten days! Someone else—a Dr. Guthrie—(Dr. of Divinity, by all the demons of the odd and grotesque!) is greatly interested in my drawings.[2] My friend,—an ex-professor of English, and ex-aviator in the U.S. Corps,—is hell-bent on placing my drawings.

　　When I mentioned Francis Saltus, I didn't mean it as a hint for you to buy a complete edition of the man! Much of his work will disappoint you, I'm afraid. Still one can never tell—he may have better things than any I have seen. Someone—I think Viereck, the notorious Kaiserite,—spoke of "the vast and uncouth visions of Babylonian splendours" in his work.[3] That sounds interesting.

　　"Imperial Purple" is a marvellous tapestry. I agree with you that it would be difficult to excel. As to Edgar's novels—I suppose the man has to live. No fictionist can be popular in this d——d mobocracy, unless he *does* write drivel.

　　I'll be glad to have the address of the Seven Seas Co. I'll try them, if John Lane proves inhospitable. "Ebony and Crystal" isn't a bad title, but one could find others. What do you say to "Incantations" for the verse,[4] and "Fables and Fantasies" for the prose-poems? Doubtless it would be better to publish them separately.

I enclose a few verses. I've completed two longer poems, which I'll send you in my next. One is an ode to Omar Khayam, the other a fantastic dialogue entitled "The Ghoul and the Seraph." The last is an unusual mixture of horror and sublimity.

I hope your copy of "Lilith" comes before long. I asked George to send me one for you.

      Affectionately,

           Clark.

P.S. Did you receive the box of mistletoe and California holly that I sent you? It was mailed a week or ten days before Christmas.

Notes

1. Oliver Herford (1863–1935), American writer, artist, and illustrator known as "The American Oscar Wilde."
2. Probably William Norman Guthrie (1868–1944), Episcopalian clergyman and rector of St. Mark's Church in the Bouwerie, New York (1911–37). When he became rector, he strove to attract people to the church by conducting unusual services and liturgies incorporating the various religious traditions, arts, and literature.
3. Unsigned, "The Ethical Dominant in American Poetry," *Current Literature* 51, No. 3 (September 1911): 325: "Mr. Viereck . . . goes on to speak of the younger American poets with whom he is in more sympathy. Francis Saltus, whose poems are no longer procurable, he calls the 'first American decadent'; his imagination was peopled by Babylonian figures, by uncouth and occult visions." George Sylvester Viereck (1884–1962) was a German-American poet, author, and pro-German propagandist.
4. CAS long envisioned a book of his poetry to be titled *Incantations,* but it was not until the late 1930s that he began to settle on content for it. R. H. Barlow planned to publish the book through his Dragon-Fly Press in Cassia, FL, then the Futile Press of the Beck brothers in Lakeport, CA, who published CAS's *Nero and Other Poems,* but the book was never published. There is, however, a section in *SP* titled "Incantations," that contains most of the poems earmarked for the book.

[188] [ALS]

          East Auburn, Cal.,

          Jan. 14th, 1920.

Dear Sam:

      Did you get my last letters, written somewhere about the first of the year? I've not heard from you since that time, and am wondering if you are unwell, or if some of our correspondence has gone astray. The last is quite possible—the officials at the local mail-office are becoming more careless and inefficient all the time. Hardly a day passes without someone else's mail being put into our box! The people in charge are Democrats, and doubtless anticipate that their tenure will not be renewed. Everyone is complaining about them.

I hope you got the poems I sent. My type-writer ribbon is nearly worn out, and I'm finding it difficult to obtain a new one. My Remington is an old model, and ribbons of the proper size to fit it are in small demand now-a-days.

I've blocked out fifty lines of a new poem in blank verse, entitled "The Hashish-Eater." It's to be a tour-de-force of monstrous imagery—"Continents of serpent-shaped trees, With slimy trunks that lengthen league on league" is a fair sample. I'm putting all the delirium into it that I can; but it's damned hard writing. Some of the images will remind you of the "Wine of Wizardry"—"forgotten glyphs By sinful gods in torrid rubies writ For ending of a brazen book—";[1] but it's darker in colour, and more cosmic in scope, than George's poem.

Your copy of "Lilith" hasn't come yet. I'll send to Robertson (whose imprint is on the book, though it is published in Ukiah) if it doesn't turn up pretty soon.[2]

To-day is your birth-day, is it not? I celebrated (?) mine yesterday with sponge cake and elder-berry-wine. I begin to feel quite ancient: I've outlived Keats by two years.

By the way, Edwin Markham has been passing me a compliment which will interest you. He wrote to a friend of mine, referring to me as a "distinguished poet," and went on to say, "There is something terrific in Smith, as there was in John Martin, Milton's illustrator." That's rather surprising, don't you think, from a conservative like Markham?

Write me soon, will you not? I've missed your letters horribly, the last two weeks.

> Affectionately,
> Clark.

Notes

1. Ll. 14–15; 30–32.
2. Anna M[orrison] Reed (1849–1921), poet and editor of the *Northern Crown* (Ukiah, CA: Excelsior Press), printed *Lilith* for A. M. Robertson.

[189] [ALS]

> East Auburn, Cal.
> Jan. 20th, 1920.

Dear Sam:

I was so glad to hear from you again—I had feared you were ill, from your weeks of silence. I knew there must be some good reason for it. I'm sorry you have to work such ungodly hours—no man should be compelled to work beyond the hours of the solar day.

Thanks for the bit from Chamisso (which I've seen before) and the clipping about Harris' lecture—both of which I've enjoyed. The song has a most "engaging" lilt . . . Harris is undubitably a very brilliant man, though I disagree with him on many things. I heartily second him in his stand against Burleson—a pettyfogging [*sic*] tyrant of the of the [*sic*] kind that is turning America into a Methodist paradise . . . Amaimon take them all, say I—I wish they were put in solitary confinement with nothing to drink but stale beer—beer that [has] been standing with the cork out for at least a week!

I'm glad you liked the poems. All of them were written in December, "The Ghoul and the Seraph" between Christmas and New Year's Day. I'm enclosing my "Omar" ode, written about the same time. People seem to like the thing—Harry Lafler saw George's copy of it, and wrote me a laudatory letter on the "spur of the moment," as they say. I'm regaining the habit of industry, at any rate—no easy thing to do after one has been for years in a state of physical incapacity for any prolonged or systematic effort.

I've blocked out nearly two hundred lines of "The Hashish-Eater," which I mentioned in my last letter. The thing seems to run on—I'm only mid-way as yet. The cosmic delirium of the ground-plan gives me illimitable scope. I'm planning a Wagnerian crescendo of horrors for the finale—the point when the hashish-eater is utterly mastered by his visions, and menaced with insurgencies of terror from all the worlds over which he has claimed lordship in his delirium . . . Some of the imagery I've used would go with my drawings—

> "The sacred flow'r with lips of purple flesh,
>   And silver-lashed, vermilion-lidded eyes
>   Of torpid azure."[1]

By the way, "Ebony and Vermilion" would be a better title for my book than "Ebony and Crystal"—there's rather more vermilion than crystal in it. What do you say to "Poems in Verse and Prose" for a one-volume collection of my work in both mediums? I'm getting a bit leary [*sic*] of mineral and floral titles.

Have you ever read Percival Pollard's book, "Their Day in Court?" Pollard was a great admirer of Bierce—one of the few critics who have dared to give Bierce his due. Also, he praised Wilde at the nadir of Wilde's reputation, and gave short commons to many of the big toads in the puddle of popularity. The book fairly "coruscates" with wit, cleverness, perspicuity, and satire. I've been re-reading it lately for the second or third time.

I don't know much about Noguchi,[2] except that he was at one time a protegee [*sic*] of Joaquin Miller's. What I've seen of his verse is not prepossing. [*sic*] I've never seen *any* poetry by a Jap that I cared for—not even in Hearn's translations. But they're certainly wizards when it comes to pictorial art.

Well, I'll have to say good night. It's late, and I've a slight head-ache from being indoors most of the day. Write me when you can.

Affectionately,

Clark.

P.S. I've added a few lines to the second speech of the "Seraph" (it seemed to require amplifying) and append them herewith:

> "Paradise, where grow
> The gardens of the manna-laden myrrh,
> And lotos never known to Ulysses,
> Whose fruit provides our long and sateless banquet?
> Where boundless fields, unfurrowed and unsown,
> Supply for God's own appanage their foison
> Of amber-scented corn, and sesame
> Sweeter than nard the Persian air compounds
> With frankincense from isles of India—
> Whose flame-like forests infinitely teem
> With palms of tremulous opal"—

Also some lines for the last speech of the Ghoul—

> "For all is change—
> Change, that hath wrought the chancre and the rose,
> And wrought the star, and wrought the sapphire-stone,
> And lit great altars, and the eyes of lions—"[3]

Notes

1. Ll. 67–69.
2. Yonejirō (Yone) Noguchi (1875–1947), influential Japanese writer of poetry, fiction, essays, and literary criticism in both English and Japanese.
3. Ll. 49–59, 85–89 in its final form, though slightly revised.

[190] [ALS]

East Auburn, Cal.,
Jan. 26th, 1920.

Dear Sam:

I enclose "The Hashish-Eater," as far as I've gotten with it. I feel horribly discouraged about the thing—it seems altogether too long and incoherent—and find it impossible to go on at present.

Don't forget me with the Heine translations—your renderings from him are the most satisfactory that I have ever seen. Good luck with the prose-poem drama! I remember your mentioning it, and also the poem you feared to commit to the mails.

I'm horribly sorry about "Lilith"—it was out of print by the time George got around to my request. He was, (as he points out) "pretty thoroughly alcoholized" at the time, and forgot all about the matter till too late. I'm sending you my own copy to read. He'll doubtless issue another edition before the end of the year.

I enclose a review from the "Oakland Inquirer"—a very good one, by Edward O'Day. Also a column in which O'Day quotes some things that *I* said about "Lilith"—to all of which I firmly adhere.[1]

I've got the "blues" to-day (regular Prussian blues—at that) and can't write a decent letter. The damned "Hashish" thing has taken it out of me—I feel as if I'd been engaged in a Babylonian debauch.

The books you sent will doubtless come to-day—so I'll thank you in advance. I'll certainly be tickled to have the Baudelaire. Peacock I don't know much about—I trust his prose is better than his work in verse—the latter is horribly dull, from the specimens in Stedman's anthology.[2]

Affectionately,

Clark.

Notes

1. CAS, letter to Edward F. O'Day, under "Men and Women in the Mirror," *Oakland Enquirer* (10 January 1920): 8.
2. Thomas Love Peacock (1785–1866), English novelist, poet, and official of the East India Company. CAS refers to Stedman's anthology of Victorian poetry.

[191] [ALS]

East Auburn, Cal.,

Jan. 31st, 1920.

Dear Sam:

I like your translations from Heine, and don't see why you should call them "hack work." They're better than anyone else has done, at least to my knowledge. I'm hoping that you'll make a volume of them, some day.

I sent you all I had completed of "The Hashish-Eater" in my last. It certainly "goes" with the drawing I made for "The Spirit of Hashish." I don't feel able to go on with the thing, at present,—after two weeks of continuous labour, I lapsed into a "deplorable" state of indifference, exhaustion, ennui, disgust, etc. I haven't recovered from it yet. However, I'll doubtless get back to work in February. Work is my only escape from ennui. I'm thinking seriously of some more odes. The "Omar" was at least melodious, if nothing else. I'd like to celebrate Poe and Swinburne, and, (for the delectation of our friends the Prohibitionists) Dionysus. I'm not forgetting *your* beautiful, serene, classic ode to *D.*—one of the most perfect things you have written. Mine, if it is anything, will be wild, irregular, dithyrambic—with the reel of intoxication in its very metres. I think of mixing iambics, trochaics, and the other metres at will, and of leaving many lines unrhymed. Such irregularities might be used to great effect. I want to write some more lyrics, too, and will try for greater variety of form. I see possibilities in the use of internal or concealed rhymes. Do you remember the form of "Requiescat in Pace?"

Thanks for the clippings you send. Amy Lowell's dissertation on Li Po is more to my liking than most of her stuff. Torrence's[1] poem is odd—I've seen things by him that I liked better, however. The poem on Crackanthorpe is fine, but I seem to remember reading it before. I know almost nothing about Crackanthorpe—it's news to me that he committed suicide. I like what little I've seen of his work.

More in a few days—
Affectionately,
Clark.

Notes

1. Frederic Ridgely Torrence (1874–1950), American poet and editor. The poem is unidentified.

[192] [ANS][1]

[Postmarked Cleveland, Ohio,
2 February 1920.]

Dear Clark
"H. E." is the greatest poem you have ever written—far greater than the "Wine of Wiz." More in a day or two. My best beloved Uncle is dying here.

S L

Notes

1. *Front:* Blank.

[193] SL to CAS [nonextant]

[Envelope postmarked Cleveland, Ohio, Feb. 2, 1920.]

[194] [ALS]

East Auburn, Cal.,

Feb. 3rd, 1920

Dear Sam:

A note to acknowledge Peacock's novels, the Baudelaire, and your poem, "Memoralia." I hope you've received "Lilith" and "The Hashish-Eater" by this time. Keep "Lilith" as long as you like.

I've dipped into Peacock, but don't find him very entertaining—I'll have to read him some day, when I'm feeling more leisurely, and tolerant, and good-humoured. Some of the translations by Robertson in the Baudelaire are very fine; but, on the whole, it seems to me that Sturm is the most successful of the translators. Many of the new prose-poems in the volume were disappointing to me—Sturm, Symons, and Stuart Merrill seem to have translated all the best ones.

I've been tinkering at some blank verse (uncommonly blank!) on Nora May French and the Carmel scenery. I tried to make the stuff into an ode; but the ode developed a plethora of mixed and overwrought metaphors, and I gave it up.

You sent me a ms. of "Memoralia" from Atlanta—I remember the poem well. It is beautiful and pathetic, as I must have told you before. The third stanza is particularly effective.

I've been reading an excellent book, "Convention and Revolution in Poetry" by John Livingstone Lowes, of Harvard University. He points out some of the fallacies of the free-verse crowd, and quotes amazing passages from Amy Lowell and some of the others. Did you ever see that little piece of Amy's, about "nicking off the fringes of the passers-by," with a brain like a Damascus sabre?[1] One ought to be very careful, with a brain of that sort! Think what might happen if it were handled recklessly! . . .

I've invested in a complete Browning—twelve hundred pages of small print in double columns—and intend to read a lot of him this year. I need him for my dyspepsy—one can't swallow the stuff without chewing it thoroughly. . . . Good sound meat, and no lollipops.

I'm hoping for a letter from you, almost any day.

Affectionately,

Clark.

Notes

1. "Miscast I": "I have whetted my brain until it is like a Damascus blade, / So keen that it nicks off the floating fringes of passers-by" (ll. 1–2). In *Sword Blades and Poppy Seed.*

[195] [TLS]

Cleveland, Ohio.

[February 1920?]

Dear Clark,

I hope the two books I sent you (in separate parcels) arrived safely. You are probably familiar with most of the contents of the Baudelaire, but there are jottings from his note-books which are worth their weight in gold. One of the references on Madame Sand is excruciatingly funny—she was a much-over-rated writer—and Baudelaire seems to have gotten "hep" to her as they say in every-day life.[1]

Our weather has been near the zero mark all day—the house is infernally cold—so cold that I've hauled my typewriter into the kitchen and am trying to warm up to it. I've taken "The Sphinx" in hand again with a view to completion. I'll copy what I have for you as soon as I can get to it. Only—pray be lenient—I'm a bit afraid that in my attempt to uncover the rather bawdy mantle of preciocity—I may have become asinine.

I'm darn glad to hear that your health has improved so much—and your writing bears witness to it. The gods be good to you. I consider it one of the big and fortunate things in this somewhat miserable life of mine that I came in contact with you. Outside of poetry and friendship—what is there, pray?—love, which is a disease—and Life which (as the Buddhists say) is evil.

Congratulate me, Clark. I seem to have reached the limit so far as acquiring books goes. I this day picked up in the original board bindings the three-volume first edition of Trelawney's "Adventure of a Younger Son" published anonymously in 1831. I've never seen it catalogued and have sought it for years. Now I want to procure for you a copy of the reprint published in the nineties, so that you can read it. I don't dare trust this that I have to the mails. Just a note. I expect a letter from you.

Affectionately,

Sam

1537 East 93 St., Suite 2.

Notes

1. "She is stupid, she is heavy, she is a chatterbox. She has, in moral matters, the same depth of judgment and the same delicacy of feeling as innkeepers and kept women." *Baudelaire: His Prose and Poetry* 231–32. The quotation is from an essay entitled "My Heart Laid Bare."

[196] [ALS]

East Auburn, Cal.

Feb. 14th, 1920

Dear Sam:

I'm tremendously grateful for what you say about "The Hashish-Eater," and also a bit overwhelmed. I knew you would like some of the imagery, but I never expected such superlative praise. I'll finish the poem somehow or other. I've gone on with it a little, and wrote 20 lines this afternoon. I'm working out some images that would throw the Editor of the "Atlantic['"] into a blue and green fit.

"Beasts

Wherein the sloth and vampire-bat are coupled,
Pendulous by their toes of tarnished bronze,
Usurp the shadowy interval of cressets
Along the ebon vaultage."[1]

Yes, you were the first to read the poem. I've not shown it to anyone else, so far.

Please send me your revision of "Dionysus." I don't "see" my own poem on the theme as yet. I've been revising some of my own earlier work lately, the prose-poem "From the Crypts of Memory" in particular. The alterations are a gain in definitude, I think. "Over us, like invisible sluggish vampires born of mausoleums, rose and brooded the black hours, with wings that distilled a malefic languor made from all the shadowy woe and despair of perished cycles," is a sample of the alterations. The original sentence ran: "Over us, like invisible vampires, brooded the innumerous hours on their sable and unmoving pinions." Revision is hell, though—I feel as if I had been on the rack.

I like the lines on Dionysus that you quote. What news of the "Sphinx?"—you spoke of sending me what you had done of it.

That's certainly an amusing yarn about Hearn—I've not heard anything so good for a long time. I'll be eternally grateful for "Fantastics"—it's one of the books on which I've set my heart.

Baudelaire's diary[2] is "great stuff"—there are dozens of bits in it that are worth whole libraries. I heartily agree with what he says about George Sand; I've manfully attempted two of her novels and never got beyond the first hundred pages in either . . . The prose-poems translated by Shipley improve on a closer acquaintance. The one about the dog and the vial of perfume is a crackerjack.[3]

Some college-professor in Canada has been giving me a great "send-off." As a result, I've received a letter from another Canadian poet, enclosing a complimentary poem. I'll send it on in a few days—it will interest and amuse you . . . Here's to Our Lady of the Snows, even if she is a prohibitionist.[4]

I'm so sorry to hear about your uncle. I love to think of what Socrates said about death—I forget the exact words, but doubtless you know them: If death is utter sleep, such will be an incomparable felicity; and if not, if the dead have a life of their own, why, who would not die for the sake of rejoining the departed ones he has loved, and the opportunity of meeting all the great men of old, the poets and sages?[5]

Yes, friendship and love (and art) are all that Life can offer worth the having. Friendship is far rarer than it should be, in our land and age. It is only the Chinese (and, perhaps, merely the poets among them) who properly understand and value friendship.

Here's a quatrain that I wrote some time ago, an inscription

"For a Wine-Jar:

"When cup by cup the wine-bearer shall pour
For Omar and his guest my golden store,
Till only slow, black, sullen dregs remain—
Make haste, and fill me to the brim once more."

My poem on Nora May French seems to have fallen through—lines in it are good, but, as a whole it's altogether too rocky. I'll have to lay it aside for awhile.

Yes, "Lilith" was abominably printed. I hope the second edition will be better done. It **ought** to be written on vellum with rubrics and Gothic letters, and bound in ebony fretted with mother-of-pearl.

More in a few days.

Affectionately,

Clark.

Notes

1. Ll. 359–63, though somewhat revised now.
2. "Intimate Papers from the Unpublished Works of Baudelaire," in *Baudelaire: His Prose and Poetry*.
3. "The Dog and the Vial," pp. 63–64.
4. The Canadian professor was William Allison of the University of Manitoba, who wrote an article on or review of *ST* (unlocated) around this time. The assertion that the virgin Mary was a Prohibitionist was made in *Report of the Seventh Convention of the World's Woman's Christian Temperance Union* (Boston: Tremont Temple, 1906), 41: "'We have faith to believe that "Our Lady of the Snows" is going to pluck from the heavens of purity and plant on her own fair brow the bright star of Prohibition.'"
5. Plato, *Apology*, tr. Benjamin Jowett (New York: Charles Scribner's Sons, 1871): "For either death is a long sleep, the best of sleeps, or a journey to another world in which the souls of the dead are gathered together, and in which there may be a hope of seeing the heroes of old—in which, too, there are just judges; and as all are immortal, there can be no fear of any one suffering death for his opinions" (327).

[197] [ALS]

East Auburn, Cal.,
Feb. 20th, 1920

Dear Sam:

Here goes for a letter, though I've little enough to write. We've had visitors lately—a cousin (by marriage) from New Zealand, and his friend, so I've not found much time for writing, up to the last day or two.

I finished the rough draught of "The Hashish-Eater" this morning. I'll send it on as soon as I can; but I want to tinker it up a bit first—it's altogether too rotten in many spots. The thing runs to more than 500 lines.[1] It contains a wonderful menagerie, toward the end—partly "lifted" from Flaubert, "The Faery Queene," and Sir John Maundeville,[2] and partly of my own invention. I wonder what the editor of the "Atlantic" would say to it. White-hot devil-fish, and marble apes with eyes that turn to living coals, would hardly appeal to him, I dare say. Neither would he care for some of the others—

"Things unseen
Whose charnel breath informs the tideless air
With spreading pools of fetor."[3]

"Lilith" came o. k. You needn't have been in such a hurry to return it.

I believe I'll "do" some more drawings. I'm sick of writing, for the time—worn-out with the everlasting problems and insuperable difficulties of verbal expression. . . . Vachel Lindsay, (who wrote "General Booth Enters Heaven!") saw some of my drawings in New York, and liked them very much.[4]

Here's the letter I mentioned in my last, and the accompanying poem. It's rather startling to find one's self put in the same category with Christ and Homer! I've met some weird comparisons before, but this one "caps the climax."

Write when you can—

Affectionately,

Clark.

Notes

1. The final version of the poem (as in *CP*) has 581 lines.
2. Flaubert, *The Temptation of St. Anthony;* Edmund Spenser (1552/53–1599), *The Faerie Queene* (1590); *The Travels of Sir John Mandeville,* a travel memoir first circulated c. 1357–71; the earliest surviving text is in French. The work was extraordinarily popular. Despite its fantastical nature and extreme unreliability, it was used as a work of reference.
3. Ll. 484–86.
4. In his book *The Art of the Moving Picture* (Macmillan, 1915), in a discussion of California poets, the American poet Vachel Lindsay (1879–1931) made brief mention of "Clark Ashton Smith, the young star treader" (223). The two corresponded briefly.

202 ❀ Born under Saturn

[198] [ALS]

East Auburn, Cal.,

Feb. 25th, 1920

Dear Sam:

I enclose the remainder of "The Hashish-Eater," rough and unrevised as it is. The poem seems a failure, as a whole—I feel horribly depressed and discouraged about it. It contains imagery enough for half-a-dozen masterpieces, but in all other respects (particularly in technique,) it seems immeasurably inferior to the poems with which you compare it.

Thanks for the renderings from Heine, which I like very much. I hope you'll make a book of these translations some day. I've never seen any others (from Heine) that compare with them.

Our weather is phenomenally dry. We've had only a shower or two since the first of the year—a serious situation for an agricultural country like this. As a rule, January and February are two of our wettest months. This drought is almost without precedent—at least, there's been nothing of the sort since the early days, before fruit-growing and truck-farming were introduced on a large scale.

I'm sending you a little box of manzanita blossoms. The shrubs are very common here—they form great thickets in places, and are one of the "characteristics" of the landscape. They're in full blossom at present. The wild bees are fond of them, and were inclined to dispute my pilferings.

George's mother has just died—the notice appeared in to-day's paper. She was quite old (74) and her illness was brief. . . . Before seeing the paper, I had mailed a box of the manzanita-blossoms to George. They will reach him with a significance of which I had not dreamt.

Have you read Witter Bynner's book, "The Beloved Stranger?" It contains the best "free verse" I have seen—at least, by an American. It's immeasurably superior to such stuff as Amy Lowell's (Amy, I think, is the most monumental "bluff" in America, at the present day) Some of them were written by way of burlesque on the Imagists, too, such as the following (a complete "poem")

"I Evade"

"The look in your eyes was as soft as the underside of soap in a soap-dish.
"And I left before you could love me."

Of course, it's not poetry, but it's damned clever, all the same.

"Asia" has just returned my "Omar" ode. They seemed to like the poem, but, I dare say, thought its publication in their pages not "advisable." It might "get them in bad" with many of their readers. The hedonism (not to mention the pessimism) of the poem would be anathema to a lot of people in this Puritan paradise. It's incredible, but such is the fact . . . Even in San Francisco, people are being fined or imprisoned for carrying pocket-flasks! The old Blue Laws were nothing to some of these new statutes. I dare say they'll want to stop the publication of such books as "The Rubaiyat." Why not, when it's against the law to publish or disseminate recipes for the manufacture of wine or beer, or even to use the word "beer,[']" "whiskey," etc in an advertisement or label, or on a bill-board!

I wish Bierce were here—he'd find some tremendous material for satire, now-a-days. No other satirist that ever lived (with the exception of Swift) would be adequate to the times.

I've been reading "Mademoiselle de Maupin" this afternoon, for consolation. Before I go to bed, I'll take a dip in La Fontaine's "Tales and Fables", or "The Heptameron."[1] One can't have too many prophylactics against morality, in this puritanical atmosphere.

> Affectionately,
> Clark.

Notes

1. A collection of 72 short stories written in French by Marguerite of Navarre (1492–1549), published posthumously in 1558, inspired by *The Decameron* of Giovanni Boccaccio. Arthur Machen translated it in 1886.

[199] [ALS]

> East Auburn, Cal.,
> March 4th, 1920.

Dear Sam:

I dare say you'll have received the mangled remains of "The Hashish-Eater" before now. What do you make of the thing as a whole? Does it possess any semblance of coherence or scheme? I'm too tired to even look at it.

I'll certainly be glad to see your new poems. Maybe I can "illustrate" them for you. So far, I've not felt equal to any drawings. Good luck with the Ode to Satan![1] I used to dream of writing a "Litany to Satan," long before I read, or even heard of, Baudelaire's poems. But nothing ever came of it. B's poem is excellent, to judge from Flecker's rendering, but there is a *h-ll* of a lot that he leaves unsaid. I dream vaguely of doing a number of odes and litanies—odes to Hecate and Ashtaroth, and Dionysus, the Sierra Nevada Mountains, and at least one of the constellations. Brave intentions—but, alas! Did I ever tell you of the monologue I had planned for the Wandering Jew? It ought to be my "masterpiece"—think of the superhuman pessimism and thirst for oblivion that Ahasuerus would have accumulated, by this time!

Have you ever heard of Edward Moore Gresham, among the English "decadents" of the nineties? There's an interesting article about him in Vanity Fair for February.[2] The quotations from his poetry are pretty fair stuff. He killed himself with hashish, it seems. . . . By the way, I believe "The Hashish-Eater" would make a "real hit" if I were to give out that the spirit of a defunct hashish-fiend had dictated it to me! These "spirit" communications and dictations are quite the style nowadays. There's a novelist (Basil King)[3] and some female poet (I forget her name)[4] who profess to receive their entire output from the "other side."

You seem to "have it in" for our eastern "songbirds"—especially the ladies. Personally, I could forgive them, if they'd refrain from writing prefaces, and proclamations, and fratricidal reviews. However, let 'em go it: "They do not strike a brother, striking me."[5]

That letter of Verlaine's must be interesting. I was reading the wretched Canterbury translation of his poems last night. Wingate's preface is not bad; but some of the verse would set a saw-filer's teeth on edge.

Thanks for the picture of that beautiful group of statuary. Yes, you sent me one of the girl with the fawns—a lovely thing.

I enclose something you may like to have—an "art-photo" of George, taken many years ago on the coast near Carmel. Also, a ms. of his,—a poem that appeared in "Beyond the Breakers." Also, my poem on Nora May French . . . The comparison with Sappho was obvious, but no one else seems to have made it.

> Affectionately,
> Clark.

P.S. Nietzsche was a great philosopher, and a great poet. I know him best through that marvellous rhapsody, "Zarathustra," and have never read the "Antichrist." He was one of the most original thinkers of the last century and I believe, or at least, hope, that his influence will increase. His hatred of Christianity and the mob is enough to endear him to me, even without the rhapsodic splendours. However, I don't think that his philosophy supersedes that of Schopenhauer, who, as Huneker points out, was a far more *solid* thinker. But Schopenhauer was not a poet.

Here's a little drawing for one of my favourites among the prose-poems of Baudelaire.

[Enclosures: Printed drawing of "Heine, from a sketch made in 1851"; printed painting: "Wild Beat Wood."]

Notes

1. Presumably this is the poem published as "To Satan." SL wrote it before he encountered H. P. Lovecraft, to whom the poem is dedicated in its first published appearance.
2. Edmund Wilson, Jr., "Edward Moore Gresham: Poet and Prose Master," *Nassau Literary Magazine* 71, No. 2 (May 1915): 68–74; rpt. *Vanity Fair* 14, No. 1 (March

1920): 49, 102 (as "The Inevitable Literary Biography"). A "parodic memoir" of a fictitious Pre-Raphaelite poet. See also "Last Remains of Edward Moore Gresham" by T. K. Whipple, A. R. Bellinger, J. P. Bishop, and Edmund Wilson, Jr., *Nassau Literary Magazine* 81, No. 8 (March 1916): 408.

3. William Benjamin Basil King (1859–1928), Canadian-born clergyman who later became a writer after retiring. His novels and nonfiction were spiritually oriented.

4. Probably Pearl Lenore Curran (1883–1937), allegedly contacted by the spirit of Patience Worth.

5. Walter Savage Landor, "Appendix," in *The Hellenics* (1846–59), l. 48 ("me" italicized in Landor).

[200] SL to CAS [nonextant]

[Envelope postmarked Cleveland, Ohio, Mar. 10, 1920.]

[201] [ALS]

East Auburn, Cal.,
March 13th, 1920.

Dear Sam:

My heartiest thanks for "The Renaissance," and "Fantastics." "The Renaissance" is an old love of mine, and I'm glad to have this neat little edition, with Symons' introduction, which is new to me. You couldn't have sent me anything more to my taste than the "Fantastics"—every one of them is a pure delight, though, naturally, I have preferences, such as "Aphrodite and the King's Prisoner." It's interesting—and instructive—to compare the two versions of "A Dead Love," one of the loveliest of all, in its latter form as "L'Amour Apres La Mort." Hearn never wrote anything more beautiful than some of these. The best of them surpass anything of Baudelaire's, at least for pure loveliness.

I'm so glad you liked "The Hashish-Eater" in its entirety. I've done very little in the way of revision, and feel unable to make any important or extensive changes. Here are a few alterations. Read "And take their trailing skies for vestment" in place of "trail / Unsetting noon, etc." Read "Peaks of sharpest adamant" for "pinnacles of adamant.[']" On the second page, read "bubbling grails" for "proffered grails," with "That hide" for "Hiding." None of these changes are of much consequence. I dislike the concluding line of the poem—those "lips of flame" will have to go.[1]

I'll write a sonnet on Solomon, some of these days. I admire him greatly, both as a painter and a poet, and will be glad to give him the honour which is only his due. I never heard of Swinburne's repudiation—it seems incredible. Watts-Dunton has a lot to answer for—including his poetry, which is the most incomparable twaddle written during the reign of Victoria.

I've not heard from George for nearly two months—an unusual lapse in our correspondence.

Another letter shortly.

Your affectionate friend,

Clark.

Notes

1. The phrase remained.

[202] [ALS]

East Auburn, Cal.,
March 16th, 1920.

Dear Sam:

You'll doubtless have received my letter acknowledging the books, by now. The "Fantastics" have given me more pleasure than anything I've read for a blue moon. Yes, you *did* send me the copyright edition of the "Renaissance," several years ago. But I'm glad to have this copy, for its handy size, and the introduction by Symons. I don't know anyone who would appreciate the book, except Dewing, and he already possesses a copy. So I'll keep this one, too.

France is a very great writer, it seems to me. I have three of his books, "Thais," "The Red Lily," and "The Crime of Sylvestre Bonnard." "Thais" is more to my taste than the others, though "The Red Lily" is interesting for its picture of Verlaine, in the character of Choulette.

The letter from your librarian is the sort of thing that one might expect . . . I've not read *all* of Bierce's work, but very much doubt if he ever wrote, or was capable of writing, anything that wouldn't blaze with a crystalline brilliance by comparison with the average output of his contemporaries.

My dear Sam, I don't see why you should speak of your own as a failure! Many a poet is remembered for poems inferior to yours—far, far inferior. One little song of yours (to mention nothing else)[,] the one beginning "I will go back again to my dreams,"[1] is worth trainloads of magazine versification. I wouldn't trade your "Pierrot's Garden" for all the stuff that Louis Untermeyer and Co. could write between now and the freezing of the river Styx . . . I'm eager to see your poem on Debs. I've no especial prepossession in favour of the subject, but I imagine the poem will be good. The scheme you outlined is tremendous.

I saw the article on Saltus.[2] It's good, of course, but might be better,— there are qualities in Saltus' work that Symons neglects to mention. The Wilde epigram is not bad, considered as an epigram, but I'm not enough of a grammarian to appreciate its application. . . . English grammar is largely a matter of taste, anyway, it seems to me.

I know scarcely anything about Flaxman. Blake's admiration of his work certainly recommends it.

Spring is coming with a vengeance; even the peach-trees are beginning to blossom in the orchards below us. I feel incapable of work at present; but the Muse may come when we least expect her. May, June, and July *used* to be my best months for writing, in the "Star-Treader" days. But of late years, my output has depended on the fluctuations of my health.

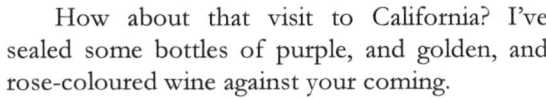

How about that visit to California? I've sealed some bottles of purple, and golden, and rose-coloured wine against your coming.

Affectionately,

Clark.

P.S. "Peter Wilkins" came before I had sealed this letter, so I'll include my thanks. I read the book nearly to the end last night, and was greatly entertained, especially by the Crusoe-like adventures of Wilkins in the former part.[3] The book has some great merits, even though inferior, as a whole, to its models, "Crusoe" and "Gulliver." I wonder if Poe didn't take a few hints from it for the "Narrative of Arthur Gordon Pym?" That device of the underground river has been copied by several latter-day romancers, including Rider Haggard.

Notes

1. "I shall go back to my life of dreams." "Isolation," l. 1.
2. Arthur Symons, "A Note on Edgar Saltus," *Vanity Fair* 14 (March 1920): 71.
3. By Robert Paltock. A fictional account of a European explorer on a fantastic island.

[203] [ALS]

East Auburn, Cal.,
March 20th, 1920

Dear Sam:

Here's a bunch of drawings, in lieu of anything better. Maybe these are some of the demons and monsters in the "Hashish-Eater."

I'd be delighted if you wrote a critique of my work. . . . Oddly enough, I had just mailed a batch of sonnets to "The Nation," one of the papers you mentioned. An acquaintance wanted me to try them.

"Peter Wilkins" is certainly a delightful tale. Its romanticism is phenomenal, considering the age in which it was written.

The German painting you mention is by Arnold Boecklin, is it not?[1] I'm fairly certain that I saw the original at the Panama-Pacific exposition. It is unforgettably weird and beautiful. I used to keep a magazine print of it on the wall above my type-writer-table.

My father and I went for a walk in the canyon yesterday. We saw three deer on the cliffs across the river—a doe and two fauns. [*sic*] They rarely venture so close to "civilization," and doubtless have been driven from the higher hills by the recent snow-fall.

I hear that George has been ill, which explains his long silence. He's quite recovered now, and is booked to introduce Maeterlinck on the lecture-platform in S. F. Maeterlinck is to speak on immortality—in French!

> Affectionately,
>> Clark.

[Envelope postmarked East Auburn, Cal., Mar. 20, 1920.]

Notes

1. CAS refers to *Island of the Dead* (1880) by Arnold Böcklin (1827–1901), Swiss Symbolist painter.

[204] [TLS]

> Sunday.
> [21 March 1920?]

Dear Clark,

I didn't send the books away but will do so tomorrow. In the meantime I await a letter from you.

I mentioned some time ago that I would publish semi-privately some of my things. I expect in a week or two to start the thing going by a paper to be published monthly or every two months or possibly at even longer intervals, and here I would like your advice—which of these two names do you prefer—"The Decadent" or "The Symbolist"—or can you suggest something still better? The first number will contain five of my poems, viz:

> Ode to Dionysos
> Ode to Apollo
> On the Passing of Youth
> Oscar Wilde
> A Chinese Pavilion.[1]

Do you think this a good choice?—the first ode has been revised and I remember that recently you found a good word for it. The second issue I want to devote to an appreciation of your work. If possible a reproduction of one [of] your drawings.

Here are two passages by Arthur Symons that fit either of the above names:

"To fix the last fine shade, the quintessence of things; to fix it fleeting-ly; to be a disembodied voice, and yet the voice of a human soul; that is the ideal of Decadence."[2]

"It is all an attempt to spiritualize literature, to evade the old bondage of rhetoric, the old bondage of exteriority. Description is banished that beautiful things may be evoked magically . . . Mystery is no longer feared, as the great mystery in whose midst we are islanded was feared by those to whom that unknown sea was only a great void. We are coming closer to nature . . ."[3]

I would appreciate any suggestion you care to give. I believe I can get Laukhuff to dispose of a few copies but of course that would not even pay for the printing. Adios.

Affectionately
S L.

1537 East 93 St, Suite 2.

[Envelope postmarked Cleveland, Ohio, Mar. 22, 1920.] [envelope placed here conjecturally]

Notes

1. Indeed, SL published all these, save "A Chinese Pavilion," in his small magazine, *The Saturnian* No. 1.
2. Arthur Symons, "The Decadent Movement in Literature," *Harper's New Monthly Magazine* 87 (November 1893): 862.
3. "Introduction," *The Symbolist Movement in Literature* 8. SL used neither passage in the *Saturnian*.

[205] [ALS]

East Auburn, Cal.,
March 24th, 1920.

Dear Sam:

Here's another batch of my grotesques. Do they still amuse you? I'm afraid there's rather a sameness about most of them—and my knowledge of drawing is rudimentary.

All the books you mention "sound good" to me, particularly that life of Verlaine.[1] . . . I'm overwhelmingly in debt to you for books.

I rather like the little parable you quote from Kahlil Gibran.[2] I'd seen some of Gibran's work before—enough to excite my interest, and set me wondering about him . . . The parable is peculiarly Oriental, and I enjoyed it, though the form is not a favourite one with me.

Thanks for the suggestion about Knopf—I had thought of him, myself. I'll put him second on my list, after John Lane. But I'm in no hurry to submit my work *anywhere*. If I were able, I would print it privately—I hate the thought of competing, or even seeming to compete, with the rabble of poetic hucksters who have set their stalls at the base of Parnassus.

I'd like to see you write an appreciation of Bierce; but I'm doubtful concerning its saleability. The only article (of length) on Bierce that I remember seeing, was in the Bookman a year or so after his disappearance.[3] And this one was by no means the encomium that you or I would write . . . Frank Harris might publish it for you; but why not try some of the English periodicals? Bierce, like Poe and Hawthorne, is more appreciated abroad. Ibanez (the Spanish Harold Bell Wright) found occasion to comment recently on the ignorance and disregard of Poe in America.[4] I don't think Poe will ever be popular in this happy-hunting ground of Methodist parsons.

I have a copy of "Kotto," which, (like everything by Hearn,) contains some fine work. Would you care to read it? I'll be glad to lend you the book, if you would.

I lack even the impulse to write, at present. The monotony of my life is like a stupefying drug. But doubtless the life of cities would be even less tolerable to me; the monotony of utter silence is preferable to that of street-cars and crowds and bravo-bands.

My apologies for this dull letter. Yours are always good.

Affectionately,

Clark.

Notes

1. There were no formal biographies of Verlaine in English at this time. CAS may be referring to Bergen Applegate's *Paul Verlaine, His Absinthe-Tinted Song: A Monograph on the Poet, with Selections from His Work* (Chicago: Alderbrink Press, 1916).

2. Kahlil Gibran (1883–1931), Lebanese-American poet, poet, writer, and artist.

3. Bailey Millard, "Personal Memories of Bierce," *Bookman* (New York) 40 (February 1915): 653–58.

4. Vicente Blasco Ibáñez (1867–1928), Spanish writer and politician who achieved world renown for novels dealing with World War I, the most famous being *Los cuatro jinetes del Apocalipsis* (1916; *The Four Horsemen of the Apocalypse*, 1918). When delivering a speech at the Poe cottage in the Bronx, Blasco Ibáñez exclaimed, "The thing that astonished me beyond all else in my tours around the city of New York was the fact that nowhere could I see a statue or memorial of any kind to that great American— Edgar Allan Poe!" Unsigned, "Poe Not Appreciated in His Own Land," *State Service: An Illustrated Monthly Magazine Devoted to the Government of the State of New York and Its Affairs* 4, No. 5 (May 1920): 411–12. Harold Bell Wright (1872–1944) was a bestselling American novelist held in low esteem by critics.

[206] SL to CAS [nonextant]

[Envelope postmarked Cleveland, Ohio, Mar. 25, 1920.]

[207] [ALS]

East Auburn, Cal.,
March 26th, 1920

Dear Sam:

Bravo! I'm glad indeed to hear that you've resolved to put some of your work, in magazine form. On the whole, I prefer "The Decadent" to the other title you mention. It's as good a name as any, though. I can suggest numerous alternatives, such as "The Satanist," "The Saturnian,['] "The Alexandrian," or even "The Parnassian" or "The Dionysian." "The Alexandrian: A Magazine of Decadence," wouldn't sound bad. I think your selection for the first number a good one, but would suggest that you add a prose-poem or two, such as "The Faun." The two quatrains from Symons are fine; why not use both? If I can do anything to help you, let me know. I might sell a few copies locally, though the title will scarcely make it "popular."

I had a letter from George the other day,—a letter full of good news, apart from the fact that he had been "laid up" for a few weeks, from an injury by no means permanent or serious. He has finished the draught of a new dramatic poem, to be entitled "Rosamund," the plot of which he found in Gibbon's "Decline and Fall of the Roman Empire." Apropos of the title, he remarks "I suppose Swinburne has no patent on that name. It's a proper name. But Rosamund was improper—and a murderess." It sounds very promising, don't you think?

Did you know that there was such a thing as the "American Academy of Arts and Letters?" I did not, till George mentioned it. It seems they elected him to membership, and he refused, after looking over the list of members, "in a letter that Robert Underwood Johnson, (who proposed my name) says contained 'unwarrantable language.' I've written to him in sharper language. Imagine a society that includes Bob Chambers, Will Payne, Ned ('Chimmie Fadden') Townshend, [*sic*] Lafevre, and C. G. Bernald! Mencken is filled with joy at my resignation, and writes, 'The whole episode is rich and stimulating. At one stroke you have accomplished something permanently valuable. Old Johnson is an ass.'"

I transcribe all this, because I know you will enjoy it immensely. I've heard nothing half so good for a coon's age.

I enclose a new lyric that George sends me—a beautiful thing. It **says** very little, but certainly **conveys** a lot.

Do you remember a drawing of mine, entitled "The Flower-Devil?" I've written a little prose-sketch to accompany it, which I enclose. If you care for allegories (I don't) you might find one in this sketch.

Did I tell you that some Canadian professor (a man named Allison) had given me a great send-off in an article syndicated in all the Canadian papers? I've not seen the article—my correspondent, Frank Pollock, said that he was afraid to send it to me, because of its "yellow character." Allison, who is a journalist, it seems, as well as a professor, turned his imagination loose, and worked up a lot of fantastic personal detail, dowering me with the combined misfortunes of Keats, Burns, and Chatterton! This helps to explain (to a certain extent) the letter and poem I received from Francis Lloyd.[1]

I await the books with great interest. Don't hesitate to ask me, if there's anything I can do to help out with "The Decadent." I'll write again very shortly.

Affectionately,

Clark.

Notes

1. Cecil Richard Francis Lloyd (1884-1938) of Manitoba, whose *Collected Poems* appeared in 1935.

[208] [ALS]

East Auburn, Cal.,

March 27th, 1920.

Dear Sam:

On second thought, it seems to me that "The Saturnian" was the best of the titles that I suggested for your magazine. After all, why identify yourself with any "school," even the Symbolist or Decadent? Personally, I'm coming more and more to distrust all critical classifications—they mean either too much or too little, and are used and understood in so many senses, often conflicting. I don't mind being called a "Decadent," but I wouldn't use the word myself, in speaking of my work, though doubtless a lot of it would come under Symons' definition, in a general way. However, you must use your own judgement in this matter . . . Call my poetry and pictures "symbolic," if you like, but don't call them "symbolistic." I distrust the latter word, because a lot of the poetry written under that heading is more or less unintelligible to me. The chief aim of some of the lesser Symbolists was to make their work obscure,—at least, it looks (and sounds) that way. For instance, this sonnet by Paterne Berrichon:[1]

The Orchestra

Weep, O thou pride of fingers deft, that slip
This shameless caprice in that narrow sheath,
Whence die this hollow's lilies underneath

Eros's crackling, unrelenting whip,
While in the centre golden groins vibrate,
And in a womb a noise of silver throbs,
And sucking back his breath that stifles, sobs
The ichoglan on whom young Sultans wait.

With violins of the psychopomp to guide,
Through Lesbian skies your fleeting sorrows glide
In grey flakes into Sodom's yellow blaze,

To rumble through the prolix radiance lit,
Hark! by the red trombone Antinuous plays,
Hidden, and roaring laughter fit by fit.

Perhaps it has a meaning; but I prefer something more direct, more "kinetic." My own ideals (however I may fall short, or seem to wander away from them) are more the ideals of Gautier and Heredia, and the "Parnassians." Bierce, too, it seems to me, held the Parnassian ideal, and Flecker (whom, as you know, I admire greatly,[)] sought to introduce it into British verse . . . Mallarme's method of absolute indirection was surely a dangerous one. After all, what is the use of saying "cat" when you mean "dog?" Too many of the Symbolists did that, or something perilously close to it.

"The Saturnian" seems appropriate, since both you and I were born under the planet Saturn (as were Poe and Verlaine) and our mode of thought certainly has the tinge that its influence is supposed to confer. Do you remember Verlaine's poem on the subject?

I'm wondering what poem of mine you will quote from in your appreciation? "Satan Unrepentant" and "The Hashish-Eater" are by far the most important of the poems, it seems to me. There are many of the shorter things that I shall not care to collect in book-form. I like "The Nereid," ["]Beyond the Great Wall," and the trochaics entitled "Quest," among the lyrics. "Ennui" and "The Traveller," it seems to me, are the best-written of my prose-poems. I care very little now for any of the erotic sonnets and lyrics—"Love is a disgusting subject," as someone remarked to George Moore. I feel like begging you not to quote them. The sensual ones and the elegiacs were the best of the lot!

Excuse all this, won't you?—as you know, I am seldom so critical, and hardly ever so egotistical, as I've been in this letter. I am tremendously interested in your magazine, and want to help all I can. I think I can dispose of at least twenty copies of the first issue, if you will send them to me.

Affectionately,
Clark.

Notes

1. Paterne Berrichon (pseud. of Pierre-Eugène Dufour, 1855–1922), French poet, painter, sculptor, and designer best known as the husband of Isabelle Rimbaud and the brother-in-law and publisher of Arthur Rimbaud. The sonnet is in Bithell, *Contemporary French Poetry* 12.

[209] [ALS]

East Auburn, Cal.,
March 31st, 1920

Dear Sam:

Have you survived the cyclone of which the papers have been full, the last day or so? Amaimon[1] and all his armies are loose in the middle states, it would seem. To-day, there's a terrific norther blowing down our valleys—a wind that I simply can't abide. So I'm staying indoors, turning over the pages of "The French Etchers,"[2] which came yesterday. The book would be worth having for the portrait of Baudelaire alone, and is full of interest to me. Some of Meryon's etchings are truly great ("Le Stryge" is my favourite).[3] I like those of Lalanne,[4] too, for their beauty and clearness, and absolute certainty of line. I have been studying Braquemond's remarkable and rejected frontispiece for the "Flowers of Evil," which is certainly not according to Baudelaire's specifications.[5] Somehow the arrangement of the design reminds me of my "Flower-Devil." I've a notion to tackle the subject sometime, myself—"arborescent skeleton," tiers of potted Fleurs du Mal, and all the rest.

I've done very little with the coloured inks, since the collection I sent you last year. The last bottles I purchased were of very poor quality—adulterated, I suspect. Good ink seems hard to obtain, at least in colours.

Please accept my best thanks for the book. The other will doubtless come to-day—the mails are curiously confused. I hope you've gotten my letters with the pencil grotesques, by this time. I rather fancied some of the last batch, the "imaginary portrait" of Leopardi in especial. I've never seen a picture of him.[6] The female head, and its inscription, referred to one of the most outrageous yarns in the whole Decameron. I am told that the phrase, "putting the devil into hell," is a common proverb in Italy!

Affectionately,
Clark.

[Enclosure? Printed drawing: "Paris, as a gargoyle on the cathedral of Notre Dame sees it."]

Notes

1. A devil in *1 Henry VI*.

2. By William Aspenwall Bradley.

3. Charles Méryon (1821–1868), French artist generally recognized as the most significant etcher of 19th-century France. The first chapter of Bradley's book is on "Meryon [*sic*] and Baudelaire." His etching "Le Stryge" (The Gargoyle) is printed in Bradley's book (facing p. 22).

4. François Antoine Maxime Lalanne (1827–1886), French artist known for his etchings and charcoal drawings.

5. Félix Henri Bracquemond (1833–1914), French painter and etcher. He was married to Marie Bracquemond (1840–1916), a French Impressionist. His unpublished frontispiece is held by the Metropolitan Museum of Art. The frontispiece was to be "an arborescent skeleton, the legs and the ribs forming the trunk, the arms extended in the form of a cross breaking into leave and shoot, and protecting several rows of poisonous plants arranged in rising tiers of pots, as in a greenhouse" (Aspenwall 5).

6. "Leopardi," in *In the Realms of Mystery and Wonder* (n.p.).

[210] [ALS]

East Auburn, Cal.,

April 2nd, 1920

Dear Sam:

Did you mail the "Hindu Myths" at the same time as the other book? It hasn't turned up yet. I'm awfully sorry;—it's the first time that anything you've sent me has gone astray. The book must have been a valuable and expensive one, too. Of course, there's a chance that it may turn up yet; mail is inexplicably delayed at times. Perhaps they've sent it to Burleson for examination, on the suspicion that it contains Bolshevistic propaganda!

I'm still enjoying "The French Etchers." "The Morgue" is very fine and sinister. Meryon's poetry is interesting, too, and I found much of interest in the chapter about the Goncourts and their friends.

Thanks for the clippings; they are all good. I like the poem translated from Duhamel,[1] and was interested by the article about his life and work. The poem by Siegfried Sassoon[2] is well-done, in its way. . . . What a weird name— and such a providential one, for a poet!

I'm sorry to hear that you've been so overworked. What an outrage! No white man should be compelled to work more than six or seven hours a day, at anything whatsoever. If I possessed anything more than a bare competence, I'd get you out of that hell-hole, providing you would come.

"Asia" has accepted my Chinese-Wall poem;[3] but "The Nation" would have none of me. The editor even folded my manuscripts the wrong way, and fastened his rejection-form on to them with a clip,—so that I couldn't possibly miss it, I suppose. I submitted four of my best sonnets, including "Mirrors" and "Eidolon." "What's the use?" I don't know "The Freeman." Give me their address, if you really think it worth while for me to try them. I'm game for anything—once. But I shan't care to trouble "The Nation" again.

None of Beardsley's drawings for "Volpone" are in the B. & L. volume.[4] Nor do I remember to have seen any of them. It's interesting that you should find a resemblance between my drawings and these; there is little enough between my work and the Beardsley drawings that I've seen—at least in style . . . Possibly the spirit is not so dissimilar.

I don't think you have sent me the two translations from Heine that you mention. I should certainly like to see them. . . . If Untermeyer's translations from Heine are at all comparable to yours, I should almost feel like apologizing for some of the things I have said about him. By the way, have you ever seen the picture of Heine that I enclose? It shows a more Jewish type of physiognomy than the usual portraits of him.

I re-read your "Ode to Dionysus lately,"[*sic*] and feel that I have never praised it enough. It is worthy of Keats, and by no means imitative. If Keats had written the poem, it would pass along with the "Psyche" and the "Melancholy."

Have you seen the current "Vanity Fair?" They "nominate" the mulatto anthologist, W. S. Braithwaite, and the Hoosier, George Ade, for their "hall of Fame," on the same page with William Butler Yeats![5] That's the sort of thing one would expect from the "Saturday Evening Post." It disgusted me in "Vanity Fair," a magazine that often contains so much that is really clever and artistic. There are some fine drawings reproduced in this issue, notably those by Rockwell Kent,[6] which remind me of Blake. Also, there are two articles by Symons.[7]

I've mailed a copy of "The Hashish-Eater" to George. He expressed great interest in the subject the last time he wrote, and thought there was "nothing that would afford imagination better excuse for absolute license (if such be needed) than the action of that drug."[8]

You interest me by what you say about your friend Miller. Have you any of his poems?

I read Hardy's "Mayor of Casterbridge" the other day, and feel inclined to agree with all that Lionel Johnson says about it. The book is magnificent, Aeschylean.

Here are some sentimental trifles; I've carried them in memory for a long time without ever writing them down, and feel a bit surprised that I don't forget the stuff. But my memory is like fly-paper, when it comes to verse—even my own.

The sentimental was never my forte; and I trust that I shall not essay it again. . . . I'm developing the Chinese attitude toward love.

Write when you can. But don't force yourself to it, when you are overfatigued. I shall understand.

Affectionately,

Clark.

Notes

1. Georges Duhamel (1884–1966). With Charles Vildrac he founded l'Abbaye de Créteil, an artistic community.
2. Siegfried Sassoon (1886–1967), English poet, writer, and soldier decorated for bravery on the Western Front. One of the leading poets of World War I.
3. "Beyond the Great Wall."
4. *The Art of Aubrey Beardsley* (1918).
5. In the unsigned article "We Nominate for the Hall of Fame," *Vanity Fair* 14, No. 2 (April 1920): 58, W. B. Yeats, Richard Peters, Virginia Gildersleeve, William Stanley Braithwaite (1878–1962; African American editor and critic), and George Ade (1866–1944; American writer best known for writing comic fables in slang) are nominated.
6. Rockwell Kent (1882–1971), American writer, painter, illustrator, printmaker, sailor, and adventurer. See "Rockwell Kent's Visions of Alaska" on p. 38, a reproduction of three of Kent's paintings.
7. Arthur Symons, "The Artistic Circle of Renoir" (pp. 39, 102); "Francis Jammes: The French Poet of Naïvete" (p. 134).
8. GS to CAS, 23 March 1920: "Don't worry about length or incoherence, which are both 'in atmosphere' when it comes to that drug. Nothing, it seems to me, affords imagination a better excuse (if one be needed) for absolute licence" (*SU* 180).

[211] SL to CAS [nonextant]

[Envelope postmarked Cleveland, Ohio, Apr. 5, 1920.]

[212] [ALS]

East Auburn, Cal.,
April 5th, 1920

Dear Sam:

A note to acknowledge the "Mystagogus Poeticus,"[1] and to thank you for it. Where do you find all these "quaint and curious volumes?" I like this one, from what I have read of it. Some of it is beautifully written, apart from the quaintness of the style. . . . There were so many who wrote beautifully in those days; everyone, almost, had a touch of genius. I'm inclined to agree with Henry Adams when he says that human thought and energy reached their apex during the Elizabethan period. Humanity, at least, the western half, has been going down-hill ever since. The worst and surest sign of decadence is the growth of feminism and the increasing dominance of women . . . Look at the history of the ancient peoples, in their periods of decline.

Thanks for the appreciation of Symons, which is well-done, and uncommonly perspicuous. I wish someone would write an appreciation of his poetry; I've never seen one that seemed at all adequate.

Rockwell Kent's drawings are indeed remarkable. "Vanity Fair" reproduced three of them in its last issue. The Blake-like spirit is conspicuous in them; but the mastery of technique is far surer than most of Blake's.

The "Hindu Myths" have not turned up, so far. I'm awfully sorry. . . . I ordered a John Donne months ago, and *that* hasn't come yet. This postal service is a stench to the high heavens.

Here are two unpublished poems of George's that I found in going through some old letters . . . Also, a few more heads in pencil.

> Affectionately,
> Clark.

Notes

1. By Alexander Ross.

[213] [ALS]

> East Auburn, Cal.,
> April 5th, 1920

Dear Sam:

Got the "Hindu Myths" and the copy of the "Dial" to-day, just after I had mailed my letter to you. Query: where has the package been for the past week, if you mailed it with "The French Etchers?" There are some dark mysteries in the U. S. Postal Service.

The illustrations in the book are amazing—I never saw such colours before. The book would be worth having for these pictures alone. My heartiest thanks to you; it is a most valuable collection to my library.

Have been glancing through the "Dial." Some of the stuff in it is simply "fierce"—there seems to be no other word. The sonnet by Edna St. Vincent Millay is good; but I didn't dare read more than one of Sandburg's effusions: I want to retain the little semblance of sanity that I still possess![1]

> Affectionately,
> Clark.

Notes

1. Carl Sandburg, "Four Poems," *Dial* 68, No. 3 (March 1920): 292–94. Edna St. Vincent Millay, "To Love Impuissant," 342.

[214] [ALS]

East Auburn, Cal.,
April 7th, 1920.

Dear Sam:

My best thanks to you for the Mosher reprint of the immortal "Ten O'clock."[1] I am certainly glad to have it, together with Swinburne's essay and the other addenda. It was a delightful idea of Mosher's to collect them in a volume.

Some of the "Hindu Myths" are new to me, and I find the book entrancing. I want to study them at leisure; possibly I may find a theme among them suitable for poetic development. Certain of those I have read are monstrous and grotesque enough to appeal to me! The Greek myths are more beautiful, but the best of them have been handled too often. Then, too, there is really a profounder philosophic significance beneath the grotesquerie of these Eastern fables.

Mr. Pollock finally sent me the Canadian write-up of my work. I enclose it for your delectation. It is not nearly so bad as I had feared, from my past experience of "yellow" journalists. Some of it is quite funny, especially the criticism on the subject-matter of my poems, as being "by no means impressive." Hell, Satan, and Beëlzebub! What does the man want? However, it is all so well-meant, so kindly, and even respectful, that I am loath to take exception, except to the most palpable errors. I have done very little of the farm-work with which Prof. Allison credits me. Also, my poems are not unappreciated in California. They are pretty well known among the few who care for that sort of poetry, and even to some who don't. Some of the lyrics in "The Star-Treader" have been incorporated in the school-readers of the state![2] I'll be occupying the throne of Joaquin Miller in a few years! A live poet, here in the west, is too useful as a real-estate ad. to be passed over entirely.

I'm pretty sure that I can dispose of a few copies of "The Saturnian." If you print anything of mine, it would doubtless be best not to use anything that I have sold to periodicals. I hate to think of your wasting money on my stuff, though. Still, there are many people here who would buy it, if it were put on sale in Auburn. The local news-dealer (there's no real book-shop in the place) could doubtless dispose of a number. So it might not be a dead loss.

I've been looking over some of your prose-poems. "The Flagellant" is a fine thing, and I like also "The One Who Died." But "The Faun" is the plum of the lot—a most beautiful piece of prose-tapestry, if you'll pardon the scrambled metaphor. I hope you print them all.

There's some very clever writing in "The Dial." But I dislike the tone of most of it, and certain of the articles aroused all my antipathies. The thing on Mark Twain must have been written by a man with a total lack of humour.[3] Surely, no one with a sense of humour could swallow all this psycho-analytic rot. I'm sick of hearing about "repressions," and the rest of the horrible rubbish. It's all "German propaganda" to me.

I feel absolutely worthless these days, and lack the faintest sparkle of a poetic impulse. The only real desire I have is to travel—"anywhere out of the world," or, at least, out of the western world, with its demoniacal nightmare of industrialism, and its deification of material force. Of course, I am isolated from it, in a sense; but I cannot help feeling the oppression of its influence. What must it be to you!

Some day (mark my word) I shall disappear, even as Bierce did, "for parts unknown." And very likely I shall not care to return. Certainly, I should not come back for the sake of fame or lucre.

> Affectionately,
>
> Clark.

P.S. No, I haven't a copy of Chatterton. I've read some of the poems. "The Minstrel's Song" is worthy of all praise.

Do you mind returning Professor Allison's article? There are others who will want to read it.

Notes

1. By James A. McNeill Whistler. The lecture (delivered on 20 February 1885 and first published in 1888) was on the nature of art. The Mosher reprint included a reply by A. C. Swinburne, "Mr. Whistler's Lecture on Art," with additional replies by Whistler and Swinburne.
2. See Bibliography under CAS's "The Cherry-Snows."
3. See Van Wyck Brooks, "Mark Twain's Humor," *Dial* 68 (March 1920): 275–91.

[215] [ALS]

> East Auburn, Cal.,
>
> April 8th, 1920.

Dear Sam:

It's raining to-day—a strong, level, wintry downpour, through which the hills and fields are vague as the border-lands of Nirvana; no "April shroud," but a cold, grey veil, much as the latter autumn nears. The rain is needed badly, since the seasonal precipitation is far below normal. Even the wild flowers were beginning to suffer, and wither prematurely—"Half-faded, fiery blossoms, pale with heat."[1]

I read the "Ten O'Clock" last night, together with Swinburne's article. The former is certainly the "last word," at least on pictorial art. Swinburne misunderstood Whistler, but his intentions were of the best; the public letter by Whistler, seems not only ungrateful, but savage to the point of cruelty . . . Strange that Swinburne should have cared so little for Japanese art. However, I suppose Japanese art is an "acquired taste" for most Occidentals. I have always admired it greatly; Dewing says that I like it because I am a Decadent and Japanese art is the perfection of Decadence!

Yesterday was a red-letter day in my calendar: I received a letter from Alice Meynell in regard to "The Star-Treader," a copy of which I had sent to her at Frank Pollock's suggestion. The book seems to have impressed her very favourably, more so than I had expected. She writes: "I think the imagination in your poems very remarkable and wonderfully original. The thoughts on destruction compared with creation for instance, in Nero. I mention this without meaning to distinguish it above many thoughts, many lines, in your poetry. I have read, and am reading it again, with true admiration, and with surprise at a time when most of the young poets have little or nothing to say. You have much to say. I think you have no poem without a thought notably worth thinking." She criticizes me, though, for too much grandiloquence, and goes on to mention Thompson:

"Francis Thompson complained to me once that he had produced too much 'thunder and lightning.' Your vocabulary is not like his, but it has also a 'roaring in the wind.'" She mentions "The Return of Hyperion" and the sonnet, "A Dead City," as being "very beautiful."

Pardon my seeming egotism in quoting all this. But I know it will interest and please you. A letter like this outweighs a world of indiscriminate praise, and the stupid criticism of an army of Braithwaites and Bliss Perrys.[2]

I saw Dewing yesterday. He was much interested in your magazine-project, and remarked, "'The Germ' all over again!" Have you ever seen a copy of "The Germ?"[3] They must be very rare, and of fabulous value now-a-days.

D. has not been writing much of late. . . . I'll send you something of his before long. He has a poem called "The Madman,"[4] which is better than the ones I sent you before.

Wish I had something of my own to send with this letter. But my brain is barren as a seed-plot in the desert.

Affectionately,

Clark.

[Enclosure? Postcard: "American River, Auburn, Cal."]

Notes

1. Algernon Charles Swinburne, "Ave atque Vale (In Memory of Charles Baudelaire)," l. 8.
2. Bliss Perry (1860–1954), American writer, editor, literary critic, and teacher.
3. *The Germ* (1850) was a periodical established by the Pre-Raphaelite Brotherhood. It survived for only four issues (January–April 1850).
4. In *Fantasy Collectors Annual—1974,* ed. Gerry de la Ree (Saddle River, NJ: Gerry de la Ree, 1974), 63–64; it also contains his "A Phantasy" (62).

[216] [ALS]

April 14th, 1920.

Dear Sam:

I'd have written before, but have been suffering from an acute attack of the blues, and saw no reason why I should inflict it upon you. I couldn't **think** anything but pessimism for a few days.

My thanks for the two "Mermaid" volumes, which I'm mighty glad to own. I'm sure that I shall enjoy Dekker—I like what little I have read of him.[1]

The last "Asia" contains my "Palms"—a bit of Oriental colour that I have always fancied. George detests the Alexandrine; but I think the form is capable of fine effect, even in English. It seems to me that I have used it well, as a rule. Dowson and Johnson certainly made good use of it.

I dropped into Peacock's novels the other day, and read "Nightmare Abbey." It is quite clever and amusing, in its way. I felt interested in Scythrop,[2] having read somewhere that the character was founded on Shelley. The similarity is somewhat exiguous, at least to me. But the yarn is clever, for all that.

O'Brien's book must be great stuff. I read a splendid article of his on Kava-drinking, in an old number of "Asia." Perhaps it's included in the book.[3] Dewing has met O'Brien, and gives a fine account of him.

Some-day, we will visit the South Seas together, you and I . . . But how I wish there were still an un-discovered continent, where one could escape beyond the very rumour of Occidental life—a land where the people have never dreamt of newspapers, and steam-whistles, and motor-cars, and all the other impedimenta that make "civilization" a mechanical nightmare . . . A land such as Baudelaire described in "Parfum Exotique." But such a land no longer exists, or exists only on the further strand of the remotest ocean of dream.

I expect a letter from you. Pardon this of mine—it is uncommonly dull.

Affectionately,

Clark.

Notes

1. The Mermaid Series was a major collection of reprints of texts from Elizabethan, Jacobean, and Restoration drama. Some of the plays had not been reprinted in recent editions, and most had dropped out of the stage repertoire.

2. A character in the novel.

3. Frederick O'Brien, *White Shadows in the South Seas*, a book about the author's travels in the South Seas. CAS refers specifically to Chapter XIX, originally published as "The Flowing Kava Bowl," *Asia* 19 (July 1919): 639–44.

[217] [ALS]

April 16th, 1920

Dear Sam:

You'll doubtless have received my acknowledgement of the books by now. My word! That new list sounds good. The Middleton is something I've wanted for a long time past. Also, as I doubtless told you, I am interested in Kahlil Gibran.

Dekker is simply delightful—I heartily concur with all that Swinburne says about him in his sonnet. So fine a combination of romantic beauty with full-blooded "humanism," is rare. The melodious and flexible blank verse impresses me, too; the rhythms are nearly always agreeable to the ear. And there are passages that rival the "mighty line" of Marlowe for pure sonority.

I'll be interested to see your revision of "Dionysus." **I** never noticed anything amiss in the alliterations. The poem seems to me to have very few faults; and none of them are important.

I've received a second letter from Mrs. Meynell, apologizing for her criticism of my poems in the first letter! She had not noticed the date of the "Star-Treader," it seems, and, understanding that I was very young, ventured to offer me the aforesaid critical advice! She says, "I now think it was quite out of plan." How odd that seems! I saw nothing amiss in her criticism, and was totally unoffended by it. Yet it **would** have hurt me, had it been offered seven years ago: at that time, I fiercely resented the attitude of people who took advantage of my extreme youth to offer me advice they would not have offered to an older man. I never relished that rot about "precocity," either. I always wanted my work to stand entirely on its own merits—or de-merits . . . Age is not always a matter of years, anyway. Intellectually, I was old at thirteen, when I began to revel in a mixed diet of Poe, Byron, and Omar Khayyam! I must have been what the French call an "enfant terrible!"

My friend, Albert M. Bender[1] (who was mainly responsible for the publication of my "Odes and Sonnets" by the Book Club) thinks "The Hashish-Eater" is wonderful stuff, but opines that I may have difficulty in finding a publisher for it. . . . Knopf is perhaps the only possibility among American publishers. He has a decided **flair** for the Oriental and the exotic . . . By the way, I want to dedicate the entire collection, "Ebony and Crystal," to you. Many of the poems would scarcely have been written without your encouragement. I owe it to you.

Mrs. Meynell promises to make my work known in London. It is very kind of her; and I am told that her opinion has great influence there, in literary circles.

I enclose a few more pencil sketches. I'll try to send you some poetry before long; several lyrics are beginning to shape themselves in my head. I may tackle some prose, too.

Affectionately,
Clark.

Notes

1. Albert Maurice Bender (1866–1941), San Francisco businessman, leading patron of the arts in San Francisco in the 1920s and 1930s, and also of CAS and GS. CAS dedicated "Memnon at Midnight" to him.

[218] [ALS]

April 20th, 1920

Dear Sam:

     All the books have come safely—the four Mermaid volumes, and the parables and drawings of Gibran. What a glorious book the latter is! The binding is magnificent as the royal robes of Solomon! And some of the drawings are marvellous. They reminded me of Rodin's sculptures at first sight, and at second, of the drawings of Blake. But, all in all, they impress me as being profoundly original. Few artists have such a faculty of getting down to essentials. I like the centaurs in especial. The parables have many similar qualities to the drawings, I think. I enjoy their pithiness, and the power of abysmal suggestion in many of them. Gibran is a genius, beyond question or cavil. . . . Middleton has been on my list of prospective purchases for a long time. But it's not the first time you have forestalled me! You seem to have an uncanny power of divining the lacunae in my book-shelves!

     Prof. Allison's article wasn't so bad. You'd appreciate it more, if you had seen some of the stuff the S. F. journalists wrote about me at the time the "Star-Treader" appeared. That item about my parentage is only half-true: My father is of English birth and blood (he's from Lancashire, Francis Thompson's country) but my mother's people have been in Connecticut since 1630. They were French Huguenots, originally, and fled from France at the time of the revocation of the edict of Nantes, settling in Devonshire for a time—long enough to Anglicize the name, Gaillard, into Gaylord. Oddly enough, some of my father's people (the Ashtons from whom I get my middle name,) were Catholics! I suppose you are right about the English poets. Even Greece never presented any such period of poetic greatness and fecundity as the age of Shakespeare, or the age of Shelley.

     I really had no right to speak of "industrialism." I've never had to work very hard, myself, and feel like a pampered parasite, when I think of you, back in Cleveland. . . . Somehow, it tickled me to know that you had been a bartender—the modern equivalent of Ganymede. . . . But, alas! Ganymede has flown with the gods! You ought to make a book of your experiences, some day.

     Don't worry about my disappearing, tomorrow or the next day. I can't leave my parents, under the circumstances. It may be ten years, or more. And

I shan't go without extending you an invitation to accompany me.

I'll remember that promise of yours, about coming out next winter. If I ever get you here, I'll not want to let you go. . . .

> Aff.,
>> Clark.

P.S. I'm so glad you like the drawings. I feared they might begin to tire you. I make them almost mechanically, at times when I can do nothing else.

[219] [ALS]

> East Auburn, Cal.,
>> April 25th, 1920.

Dear Sam:

Pardon my silence: I have been doing outdoor work for the past few days (wood-cutting, which, I assure you, is real labour) and have gotten horribly tired after a few hours of it each day. However, the exercise ought to be beneficial, in the long run.

I liked the clippings you sent me, with the exception of the article on Gibran's drawings—from which I dissent. Gibran seems original to me. I enjoyed the letter by Yeats, and was greatly interested in the article by Harris on Gladys Cromwell.[1] One of the sonnets quoted from her was really great.

On the whole, I like your alterations in "Dionysus," though one of the rejected phrases, "pouting lips awry," seemed to me to possess a fine graphic value.

I was interested to hear of your dialect-play. If one could only do something of that sort, and make a pile of money! After all, it's no worse than most other modes of money-making.

Auburn is getting to be quite a literary centre—there are half-a-dozen people in the place who write—Jackson Gregory,[2] who writes novels of western life, and moving-picture plays; a Mrs. Sears who writes verse, short-stories, novels, and sociological books; and a cripple, Harold Waldo, who goes in for fiction, and has had stories in the S. E. Post.[3] Also, there are others—(including Dewing and myself.)

Mrs Sears, whom I met a few days ago for the first time, is very interesting. She seems to have met everyone, (including Frank Harris) and has the inside track of the publishing world. She tells me that "The Moon and Sixpence" has been suppressed, along with several other recent novels! The Moral Squad must be uncommonly active—they cinched one of these books a week after publication! I forget its title.

I'll send the "H. E." to Mrs Meynell, some-time. At present, I'm waiting to hear George's verdict. I ought to hear from him pretty soon.

I enclose a rotten sonnet . . . Still, it's no rottener than the subject. It might have pleased Schopenhauer.

That's a great passage you quote, from "The Anatomy of Negation." I have "The Philosophy of Disenchantment."

Another letter very soon.

Aff.,

Clark.

Notes

1. Gladys Cromwell (1885–1919), American poet, who served overseas in the Red Cross during World War I with her sister Dorothea. Both committed suicide on their return home after the war. The article on her by Frank Harris has not been located.

2. Jackson Gregory (1882–1943), American journalist, writer, and teacher.

3. Perhaps Agnes Bertha Sears (1881–1947); Harold William Waldo (1890–1951), "Old Twelve Hundred," *Saturday Evening Post* 192, No. 18 (1 November 1919): 22–23.

[220] [ALS]

April 27th, 1920

Dear Sam:

You'll doubtless have received my acknowledgement of the books by now. Everyone to whom I have shown it, admires the beautiful volume of Gibran's drawings. . . . And, I've told you my opinion of them. There is much in the preface, though, with which I disagree, particularly the references to Rossetti and Watteau. If there's anything more "symbolic" in the true sense, than some of Watteau's paintings, I wish someone would show it to me.

"Noa Noa"[1] is one of the books that I'm most eager to see . . . The Moral Squad seems to be vying with the Prohibition Enforcement Agents, these days. It's a queer phenomenon, this recrudescence of Puritanism. What licks me is that they should object to a little frankness and honesty of speech in books, and yet allow these infernal rotten moving-picture-shows to pass without comment. Some of the stuff in the "movies" would put a Zulu to the blush. Also, the Bible, Rabelais, the Decameron, the Heptameron, etc, are unchallenged, and readily obtainable. I repeat, "It licks me."

Indeed, I'd be greatly interested to see a bit of your collection. What a library you must have! I'm rather proud of my own, though it's of no great extent—five or six hundred volumes altogether. But it would be difficult to duplicate in Auburn.

Please send me "The Sphinx," or whatever you have done of it. I have always felt a peculiar interest in the subject, from your description of it years ago.

I've written nothing, except the bad sonnet I sent you in my last, and the tentative beginning of a poem in terza rima, called "Eros in the Desert." The conception is good, but I seem to lack enthusiasm for it—the conception of Love outcast from birth, and condemned to wander always in a desert land, between the mountains and the sea,—finding, mayhap, in old forsaken cities, the image of some forgotten Venus, or the portrait of an ancient queen, to mock his insatiable hunger. I may tackle something else—I thought of an ode on "The Clouds", among other things, with a quotation from Baudelaire for a heading: "I love the clouds—the clouds that pass—over there—the marvellous clouds." Do you remember that little prose-poem, "The Stranger?"[2] The sentence about the clouds has always haunted me.

Here are a few more drawings. They're not so good, probably, as the last batch I sent you, which included a black Venus, and an ape-like demon with a terrifically corrugated visage; the latter would "go well" for an illustration to the "H. E."

Affectionately,

Clark.

Notes

1. Paul Gauguin's Tahitian journal.
2. "The Stranger," in *The Poems of Charles Baudelaire* 91. For "over there" read "yonder."

[221] [ALS]

May 1st, 1920.

Dear Sam:

By all means, go on with "The Sphinx." What you have done of it is very beautiful, and most fascinating. Many passages are music turned into sculpture—and lapidarian sculpture at that—pagan friezes done in great blocks of sapphire, or chrysolite, or chrysoberyl. In its decorative detail, your prose is far more suggestive of Wilde than of Flaubert. But the whole conception of your "Sphinx" is utterly different from anything else that I have ever seen or dreamed of. By all means finish it: the third you have already done, contains your finest prose . . . I really know so little about dramatic technique, that I feel incapable of any suggestions. But why worry about such things, in a drama concerned with **thought,** rather than action? "The Sphinx" would never "do" on the stage anyway—at least on the American stage.

By all means, avail yourself of Paul Elder's[1] offer—I don't think you will regret it. S. F. ought to prove far more congenial for you than Cleveland, apart from the fact that you will be so much closer to me and to George. Auburn is only a hundred miles from S. F. We certainly ought to "start something," when we all get together! . . . But come early, so you can spend a few weeks (or months) with me before you take up your work!

I am interested in "The Death of Helen"—you outlined the conception to me once. I've mislaid your scene for "Macbeth," but have the impression you sent it to me, in a finished form. I'll hunt it up. I don't remember liking it as well as the "Scene for Lear." The latter is really great work.

I feel absolutely incapable of work, myself. My nerves have "gone bad" again, and existence seems a delirious nightmare. I wonder sometimes, if my nervous trouble isn't a bit similar to Flaubert's. My accursed duality (or multiplicity) of temperament is doubtless at the root of it, though there are aggravations or contributory causes, in the form of astigmatism, bad teeth, and a lonely, monotonous life.

Sinclair is a good writer. I'll certainly be glad to have the book you mention. I've not read very much fiction of late—apart from the daily newspapers! Are you interested at all in the political situation? Wood is the only presidential candidate who appeals to me.[2] Johnson, our California candidate, is the common type of American politician.[3] I can't imagine anything worse.

I'd like to make some drawings for "The Sphinx"—separate heads of the three Satraps, and the Sphinx herself, if possible . . . Oddly enough, drawing often relieves my nervousness.

    Affectionately,

       Clark.

Notes

1. Paul Elder (1872–1948), a longtime independent bookseller and publisher in San Francisco.

2. Leonard Wood (1860–1927), U.S. Army officer, Governor-General of Cuba (1899–1902), Chief of Staff of the U.S. Army (1910–14), and Governor-General of the Philippines (1921–27). He attempted to secure the Republican nomination for president in 1920, but lost to Warren G. Harding, who became president.

3. Hiram Warren Johnson (1866–1945), a leading progressive and isolationist politician from California. He served as governor of California (1911–17) and U.S. senator from California (1917–45). He was Theodore Roosevelt's running mate in the 1912 presidential election on the Progressive ("Bull Moose") party. He too attempted to secure the Republican nomination for president in 1920 (also in 1924).

[222] [ALS]

                 May 2nd, 1920.

Dear Sam:

    You needn't have felt any doubt as to my liking for "The Sphinx." You ought to know, by this time that I'm the last person in the world to object to anything on the score of "paganism." But you certainly have "gone to [the] limit" in certain passages. I can understand how a lot of people will dislike it. But that's beside the point. I don't suppose you are any more concerned about "popularity" than I am . . . Your prose is magnificent. I await the speeches of the Hebrew and the Egyptian with immense interest. There's no limit to the possibilities of the subject.

I've made some pencil sketches of your dramatis personae, and enclose them. I wish they were better. I'll have another "shot" at some of them, when I'm more in the mood. It seems to me that the Sphinx comes out best, in the drawings . . . I enclose some other drawings—a Medusa and a Melancholia among them—"The Melancholia that transcends all wit."[1]

I'm certainly glad to hear that a definitive edition of Clare is to be published . . . I still think that you are the ideal person to write his life. I feel convinced that you would make a fine thing of it. Clare unquestionably had the endowment of a great poet. I wonder, sometimes, if many would have done better, (or as well) if born to the same conditions and misfortunes. Tennyson wouldn't, I am sure, (to take only one instance.)

That's interesting, about your theosophic cousin. I once met a lady adept, who claimed to have known me in a former incarnation, somewhere in India. I never learned the details. Curious: at one time, I was inordinately fascinated by India and its life, and felt a sensation of it so intimate as almost to seem a memory. I was simply mad over Kipling's "Kim" for years; it intensified my sensation of the East more than any other book has ever done. The feeling faded after my seventeenth year, though. I still feel the attraction of the Orient.

I don't think you look very much like Keats, to judge from your pictures. Queer how people will find resemblances of that sort. I've been told that I look like Catullus. Also, that I resemble Upton Sinclair and Francis Thompson! And the Keats comparison has been "sprung" more than once. Verlaine would be nearer the mark, I think! At least, I'm the ugliest of the poetic tribe, with the possible exception of Verlaine.

Affectionately,
Clark.

Notes

1. A line from James Thomson's *The City of Dreadful Night.*

[223] [TLS]

Cleveland, Ohio.
May 8, 1920.

Dear Clark,

I'm sorry to hear of your nervousness and low spirits. I get them venomously myself but I try to walk them off. I believe such a thing is characteristic of all folk who try to use their brain. A doctor once explained it to me in my boyhood and told me not to worry. "You are not going insane—so forget that part of it," he said, "the only difference is that you are a little more complicated in your organization—in other words, a bundle of nerves!" So that I don't worry, come what may. I had it the other evening—it comes in my case from worry over material matters—but I walked seven or eight miles and felt better. No doubt, your teeth and eyes may contribute, but not over-whelmingly so. Don't you see Dewing, very often?

I want to thank you for the two new panels—the "Uranian" is very, very fine and imaginative. I did receive the set containing the black Venus and liked them, one and all.

I left the place I'd been working at last Tuesday noon and have been rus-ticating ever since. I'll probably find something next week as there is work a-plenty. It simply got to be a matter of working from eight in the morning un-til nine at night—and life isn't altogether that. So I told the head of the de-partment to go to Hell at exactly eleven o'clock Tuesday, and left at noon. I received another letter from Kirk[1] urging me to cut the ropes and come out. I can't do it before fall, as I shall want at least three hundred dollars clear, to take with me.

I can't tell you just how relieved I was to know that "The Sphinx" had taken with you—and I appreciate the compliments. I sent you the entire sheet-five early this week and now enclose the sixth. My reason for worrying over it was that Nelson had rather fought shy of it, and Nelson is nothing of a prude. Hence my delay in forwarding. I'll be ever so pleased to have the il-lustrations. Could you manage a "group" drawing of the three with the Sphinx? The Egyptian is the quiet 'un but the turmoil he raises up in the end has it, dogs and all, on the Greek.

Laukhuff asked me yesterday if I would care to translate a drama in blank-verse from the German called "Alcestis."[2] It looks good and is being performed over there to crowded houses. The Playhouse would use it here—but the task seems thankless, and no-doubt the author is second-rate.

This is just a note. More tomorrow.

Affectionately,

Sam

1537 East 93 St., Suite 2.

If mental telepathy does any good it should help you—I think of you very often.

Sheet 5—1st line of the last paragraph (The Sphinx talks) should read "This reminds me of my entry in**to** the **pagan** city," etc. 4th line—"And **their** youngest," etc.

Notes

1. George [Willard] Kirk (1898–1962), a friend of both CAS and SL, published *Twenty-one Letters of Ambrose Bierce* (1922) and ran the Chelsea Bookshop in New York. SL wrote "To George Kirk on His 27th Birthday."

2. Possibly *Alcestis* (1908) by Hugo von Hofmannsthal (1874–1929), derived from the play by Euripides. GS translated his *The Play of Everyman* (1917).

[224] [ALS]

May 11th, 1920

Dear Sam:

I ought to have acknowledged your continuation of "The Sphinx" several days ago, but have been quite busy. I like it all, with the exception of one phrase, "sadly depleted", which seems curiously out of place in the general texture of your simple but gorgeous style. Why not omit the adverb, and use the single word "depleted" or, better still, "decimated?" The speeches of the Hebrew are splendid. I hope you've gone on with the play, and can send me some more. I feel like Oliver Twist.

Hope you got the drawings for "The Sphinx." I enclose another attempt at Athor, this time a wash drawing. I'm coming to fancy the medium—it gives a sort of Japanese-print effect that one can't get with a pencil. I've made a number of drawings lately, some of them in colour, and will send you a batch before long.

I've been expecting a letter from you, and letters from several others; but the past week has been a blank, in regard to correspondence. Curiously enough, I've had an unusual number of visitors, including some very charming ladies. . . . But I'd have preferred the letters. I sent George "The Hashish-Eater" more than a month ago, and he continues "ominously silent." But his correspondence is monumental, and, doubtless, is still increasing.

"The Dial" returned a batch of my best sonnets with a printed rejection-form, expressing the hope that I would send them something more. But it will be a d——d long time before I trouble them again. I'm growing very sick of these continued rejections.

Dekker is certainly "great stuff." I've recently finished reading "The Honest Whore."[1] I've not had time to read much of Middleton as yet. But I feel sure that I will like him.

Affectionately,
Clark.

Notes

1. In *The Best Plays of Thomas Dekker.*

[225] SL to CAS [nonextant]

[Envelope postmarked Cleveland, Ohio, May 12, 1920.]

[226] [ALS]

May 15th, 1920

Dear Sam:

      I like the sixth sheet of "The Sphinx" tremendously. That description of the city of enchantment is marvellous, and reminds me a little of the Arabian Nights (in Burton's translation, of course!) I'm so glad you liked my drawing of the Sphinx. I'll try a group-drawing in colour, if you'll give me a hint as to what colours you would fancy in the costumes. I'd like to do some more drawings; but much of the stuff in "The Sphinx" would overtax what little technique I possess, on account of the architectural detail required.

      I enjoyed all the clippings you sent me, particularly the one about Flecker.

      I hope you'll have gotten the seven drawings I sent you, by now. I took care to register the parcel. One was an "imaginary portrait" of Keats. You'll probably like some, if not all, of them. "Comus" and "The Old Man of the Mountain" were my own favourites.

      I've devoted most of my spare time lately, to making a set of illustrations for "The Hashish-Eater." Most of them are in colour, and some of the effects are as weird as the verbal colouring of the poem. I'll send them on presently. But I want to keep copies of a few, at least.

      Nothing would please me more than that book of O'Brien's. No, I've never seen the rendering of the Rubaiyat you mention. Your quotation from it is most beautiful.

      I don't see any prospect of a trip to S. F. at present. But if I do go, I'll certainly look up your friend. Oddly enough, I've never visited Paul Elder's, though I know nearly all the other bookstores in the vicinity. Elder's is one of the most flourishing of the lot.

      My nervous attack seems to have worn off. Perhaps it was nothing but ennui, after all. No, I don't see Dewing as often as I would like. We live too far apart, and D. is busy most of the time (his people have a fruit ranch.)

      I wish I could sell my drawings. But I fear they're all too weird and uncanny, too much out of the popular style. The obvious and the photographic on the one hand, and the obtrusively rough and queer and formless, on the other, seem to dominate modern art. And my drawings are neither photographic nor formless.

      I do hope you've gone on with "The Sphinx."

      Did you receive a sonnet of mine, entitled "To Love?" It was a "bum" sonnet, but I'd like to be sure that you received it. The mail service here is so rotten, that I tremble every time I post a letter.

      Affectionately,

          Clark.

[227] SL to CAS [nonextant]

[Envelope postmarked Cleveland, Ohio, May 16, 1920.]

[228] [ALS]

May 17th, 1920

Dear Sam:

I like the seventh sheet of "The Sphinx" as well as the others. Ion appeals to me as a subject for an "imaginary portrait," and I'll try him presently. Pardon my stupid question about the costumes of the three satraps—I had forgotten for the moment that you described them as being **naked.** I'll do what I can with the scene, though my anatomy is worse than Blake's, if possible.

I've made twenty-three designs for "H. E.", all but two of them in colour. Some of them are really good, I think, though others are pretty poor. Many are not really illustrative, since I've taken liberties with the text, in certain instances. I'll send you the whole bunch in a week or so.

I enclose a few pencil sketches.

Affectionately,

Clark.

[229] [ALS]

May 21st, 1920

Dear Sam:

I've made a few designs for "The Sphinx," and will forward them next Monday. There are seven in all—a group-drawing of "the bunch," and separate portraits of the Basilisk, the Lamia, the emperor Ion, and the idol Ascheria; also, a line-drawing of the Sphinx and the leper, and a colour-drawing of the isle in the sea of Syme! Don't expect too much of them—none of the lot is very satisfactory.

I'm expecting O'Brien's book with unusual eagerness. I've not read very much of late. I took nearly a week to finish an unpleasant novel drawn from the local library; "Red Pottage" was the title, and Mary Cholmondeley the name of the author. The book is a howling tragedy, and better written than the average.[1]

I've heard of young Maddox,[2] [*sic*] whom you mentioned in a previous letter, but have never come across any of his work. I think Lionel Johnson speaks of him in his book on Hardy.

That volume of Chatterton was certainly a "find." I can imagine what the current reviews of C. must have been!

I'd certainly like a copy of "The Faun" in print, if you have one to spare. I think most highly of "The Faun." And I seem to have mislaid the typescript you sent me.

Why **don't** you send "The Sphinx" to Saltus, when you've finished it? He is one of the very few who are competent to understand and appreciate it.

I can't write at present, and find it difficult to imagine how I ever *could* or *did* write anything,—at least, anything so long and elaborate as "H. E." I can't agree with you that it's the greatest of imaginative poems; but certainly, it's the strangest.

This letter is damnably dull and empty—dull enough and empty enough to represent the way I feel. Our weather has turned uncommonly warm, which accounts, in part, for my lassitude.

There are several people to whom I'd like to give copies of "The Saturni-an." I hope you'll let me pay for them. Have you thought of quoting Ver-laine's poem as a headpiece?[3] I wish there were a decent translation of it. But you could use the original.

      Aff.,
          Clark.

Notes

1. Mary Cholmondeley (1859–1925), English novelist. *Red Pottage*, her best-selling novel, satirized religious hypocrisy.
2. Oliver Madox Brown (1855–1874), an English author and artist, is mentioned briefly in Johnson's book.
3. SL instead used an unattributed passage by Arthur Symons about Gérard de Nerval.

[230] [ALS]

          May 24th, 1920

Dear Sam:

      Received both your letters, but the book hasn't turned up, so far. I'm hoping it will come to-day; the delay is not without precedent.

It's good to know that you liked the imaginary portraits so well. I don't remember caring so much for the "Dionysus"—I thought the colouring ra-ther poor. Reproduce any of them that you like.[1] And command me in regard to "The Saturnian." I shall be overjoyed to do anything and everything that I can, to assist you in its production. That was a good selection you made, for the first number.

I'm mailing you another batch of drawings to-day—the seven for "The Sphinx," and seven miscellaneous ones. The "H. E." designs will follow in a few days. You might as well have the whole lot—I'm thankful that my drawings mean something to you, since they're generally misunderstood and misappreci-ated by people out here. Some day, if ever I am able, I may wish to reproduce the best of the designs for "H. E." I know you'll take good care of them.

Hillier's [*sic*] sonnet is excellent, and very true—terribly true. I don't re-member seeing any of J. A. Symonds' verse.

I've written nothing; but some of the drawings console me, in a measure. They seem creative to say the least. But I hold, and always will hold, that pictorial art is inferior to poetic art.

Another letter shortly.

Aff.,

Clark.

Notes

1. In *Saturnian* No. 1, SL announced: "We hope, in our next number, to present our readers with an appreciation and appraisal of the poetry and drawings of Clark Ashton Smith, the young Californian." In the subsequent issue SL wrote: "It is with regret that we postpone our original intention of dedicating this number to the work of Clark Ashton Smith, until the next issue. This will contain reproductions of two or three of the imaginative drawings, notably the magnificent 'Fear'." The third and final issue did not have any drawings by CAS, nor was any further mention made of them.

[231] [ALS]

May 24th, 1920.

Dear Sam:

Received O'Brien's book this morning, just after I had posted my letter to you. It is a most beautiful and fascinating volume, and I anticipate a world of enjoyment in its pages.

I registered the drawings, which may make them a little late in delivery. Registered mail is slow, but sure. I wish the illustrations for "The Sphinx["] were better; but perhaps you will like some of them.

Hastily,

Clark.

[232] [ALS]

May 26th, 1920.

Dear Sam:

O'Brien's book is a pure delight—I read it through the day it came, with the avidity of a dime-novel fiend. It is far superior to Melville's books; and I know of nothing to compare with it, except the "South-Sea Idylls" of Charles Warren Stoddard. What a wonderful people these Marqueenians [*sic*] must have been! And how it saddens one to read of their decline under the domination of the whites! But perhaps they will have their revenge soon enough: By all signs and reckonings, the star of the Occidental peoples has passed its zenith; and the star of the Japanese (the Prussians of the East) is beginning to ascend.

Hope you'll have gotten the drawings by now. "Ascheria" is something of a curiosity; I set out to draw the figure according to your description, with weird results. What do you think of "The Basilisk" for a decadent colour-scheme?

With the exception of your letters, my correspondence has fallen away to almost nothing, of late. I've received two others in as many weeks—an unpaid bill, and a request for an "occasional" poem! I've no intention of paying the bill, or writing the poem.

I'm expecting "The Saturnian" almost any day. Also, a letter from you.

This is a dull note; but at least, it's brief.

Ever your friend,
Clark.

[233] SL to CAS [nonextant]

[Envelope postmarked Cleveland, Ohio, May 29, 1920.]

[234] [ALS]

May 31st, 1920

Dear Sam:

I hope the two batches of drawings arrived in reasonable time. I took care to register them both. The twenty-three designs in the second batch (many of them rough sketches, as you will notice), are all for "The Hashish-Eater." I feel pretty sure that you will like some of the drawings. Nos. 14 and 15 have somewhat the air of Japanese prints. Tell me what you think of No. 23, the Finis.[1] The scene is really indepictable; I feared to attempt it, but succeeded (it seems to me) in making a presentable design, at least.

My dear Sam, I refuse to quarrel with you about the sale of "The Saturnian." If you insist on distributing it in the manner of Omar's "golden grain," I can easily help you in the distribution. I know a few people who ought to appreciate your poems. . . . Are you sending a copy to W. S. Braithwaite? (!!) Perhaps I mentioned a letter from George, a year or so ago, in which he told me that he had written to Braithwaite requesting the omission of his work from all of B.'s future anthologies? All good poets should declare a similar boycott—that is, if they find themselves in any danger of receiving a merit star from Braithwaite . . . Death, damnation, and a plague of verminous devils, to all such pedagogues as B.

I recur to the "White Shadows" again and again. Some of the photographs are almost as delightful as the text. The chapter on Kava-drinking is wonderful. Have you ever tasted arrack? It's a marvellous drink, and superior even to Scotch or Benedictine—at least for effect. It tastes like hell-fire, though.

"The Sphinx" is a monument of weird and out-of-the-way images. I thought, somehow, that you were "making up" a great deal of the historical stuff—so much of it was entirely new to me. I fear my illustrations were horribly inaccurate in point of costume. I made them from a vague impression or memory, and had no means of verifying them at hand.

I enclose an article on Verlaine, from an ancient copy of "The Forum."[2] The chief part of the prologue to "Poemes Saturnniens" [*sic*] is quoted in the original French. The article is sympathetic, and well-written, though it contains nothing novel. Perhaps it will interest you. At any rate, don't bother to return it.

Affectionately,
Clark.

[Enclosure: Printed article, "Paul Verlaine" by S. C. de Soissons.]

Notes

1. R. H. Barlow sought to obtain these drawings from SL for a proposed illustrated edition of *The Hashish-Eater,* but SL demurred because they were in storage.

2. S. C. de Soissons, "Paul Verlaine," *Forum* 24, No. 2 (October 1897): 246–78.

[235] [ALS]

June 6th, 1920.

Dear Sam:

The eighth sheet of "The Sphinx" is very, very much to my taste. No, I don't find the play monotonous—the range and variety of images is wonderful. In some parts of it, though, I was struck by the preponderance of mineral images. It's possible to overdo that sort of thing, though I'm not saying that you have really overdone it. I am wondering how the play will end; doubtless, there are many possible denouements.

I hope you **do** publish that pamphlet of translations from Heine.[1] Yours are by far the best. I've never seen Untermeyer's. The devil help 'em, if they're anything like his original verse.

I like the "get-up" of "The Saturnian"; and you know my opinion of the poems. The "comments" are good, especially the bit from Heine, which was unfamiliar to me.

I meant to write during the week; but I spent several hours each day in cutting stove-wood, and found myself horribly exhausted by the exercise. I'm not fit for much, it would seem. I've been too tired for drawing, or any but the lightest reading.

The drawings are yours to keep, of course. I should only **borrow** them back for the purpose of reproduction, providing there is ever a chance of their being used. And I see no such chance at present. Few people seem to take them seriously.

I may try a few landscape-sketches during the summer. I should like to render the wild and desolate beauty of these hills; it has never been done before, to my knowledge. The local landscape has many peculiarities; there are hill-tops covered with dark volcanic boulders, where the Indian pines, with their long needles of greyish-green, are moulded into cypress-like forms in the battles of the sea-wind with the wind from the mountains; and there are deep ravines, where the tangles of wild-grape and alder, of syringa and fern, and laurel, and styrax, assume an almost tropical luxuriance.

        Affectionately,

                Clark.

Notes

1. This appeared as the second number of SL's *Saturnian.*

[236] [ALS]

                                    June 8th, 1920.

Dear Sam:

        I am overjoyed to know that the pictures were all so much to your liking. I wasn't sure that you would care for "The Sphinx" illustrations.

        I kept no copies of **any** of the drawings. However, I may attempt to reproduce some of them from memory. When I try to copy anything, the usual result is an entirely new picture! No. 17 of the "H. E." set was one of my own favourites. Also, I liked the two in black and white (for "H. E.['']) I forget their numbers,—and nos. 12, 13, 14, and 23. I'd be interested to hear how they impress your artist-friend. Most artists object to my drawings on the ground that they are too "literary." I don't see the point, myself. Literature is often praised for pictorial qualities (no one objects to Keats being too "pictorial") so why shouldn't art appropriate to itself the qualities—or some of the qualities—of literature?

        I'm expecting "Noa Noa" and the batch of "Saturnians" any day. The postal service is getting slower and less reliable all the time. Have you heard the new slogan of the anti-Wilsonites? "He keeps us out of mail!"[1]

        I don't like the article on Bierce, from "The Freeman."[2] I can't abide these psycho-analysts. It's a pity that there's no living satirist of Bierce's calibre—think what he could (and would) do to such pestilential piss-ants!

        Somehow, that ammunition-escort yarn has a tinny sound to me. It seems improbable that Villa would have wasted a man of Bierce's military knowledge and capacity on duties at once so dangerous and so subordinate as the convoying of munitions . . . It's all a great mystery—as, doubtless, Bierce meant it to be.

        Aff.,

                Clark.

Notes

1. Woodrow Wilson's campaign slogan during the presidential campaign of 1916 was "He kept us out of war." A month after his inauguration, he declared war on Germany.
2. Unsigned, "A Reviewer's Note-Book," *Freeman* 1 (21 April 1920): 143.

[237] [ALS]

June 10th, 1920

Dear Sam:

"Noa Noa," the "Saturnians," "The Playboy,"[1] and "The Vagrant,"[2] have all arrived. I began by re-reading "The Faun," which, (as usual) seems even finer in print. A splendid piece of prose-workmanship, with no faults worth mentioning. I gave the afternoon to that delicious and glorious book of Maugham's.[3] It is sketchier, of course, than O'Brien's volume, but the sketches are those of a master. I see nothing in the book offensive to morality—it is one of the **purest** books I ever read. Of course, its real offense consists in the denial and decryment of "civilization". Nothing is so offensive as truth . . . The paintings are all great—even in black and white. I wish I could see the originals. I like the ones in "The Playboy"; also, the article on Gauguin.

No news—except that the leopard-lilies are in blossom. You would marvel to see them springing from these parched and barren hill-sides—each with a score of orange buds and cinnamon-spotted flowers. I enclose a hasty drawing of one. The colours are poor and crude, but perhaps they will give you an idea of the flower.

Aff.,

Clark.

Notes

1. *Playboy: A Portfolio of Art and Satire* No. 6 (1919). The issue contained black-and-white reproductions of several of Gauguin's paintings and wood carvings, and Egmont Arens's "The Savagery of Gauguin: A Review of Several Current Books" (pp. 3–4, 7).
2. SL had some pieces published in W. Paul Cook's little magazine, the *Vagrant*, including "The Faun."
3. *The Moon and Sixpence.*

[238] SL to CAS [nonextant]

[Enclosure only?—Illustration of "Simeon Solomon: Amor Sacramentum." Envelope postmarked Cleveland, Ohio, June 13, 1920.]

[239] [ALS]

June 15th, 1920.

Dear Sam:

I was glad to get the ninth sheet of "The Sphinx," parts of which are uncommonly fine and imaginative. "The plot thickens!" Pray don't give it up; the play is one of the rarities of literature. You must have put a terrible amount of work into it; and I suspect that your fits of depression are merely the reaction from overstrain. I know that sort of depression all too well.

Robertson is certainly a mystery. One explanation is his failing health. But I can't understand a lot of his actions, even at that. I should think he would put his business into the hands of a competent manager—or else withdraw entirely. . . . I'm not sure that "The Star-Treader" is out of print; at the last accounting, in 1917, half the edition was still lying unbound at the printer's!

Your friend may have difficulty in obtaining a copy of "Lilith." George writes me that he is offering five dollars apiece for copies himself—and can't obtain them!

"Rosamund" will be out before long, and I'll try to make sure that you get a copy of it. It must be a terror; "No hero, no heroine" (to quote George) "but four murders and a rape. Hooray!"[1]

I sent him "The Saturnian," which he praised. He thinks the title is a fine one, and spoke of the contents as being "pure poetry"—which I heartily second.

Here is what he says concerning "The H. E.:"

"'The Hashish-Eater' is indeed an amazing production. My friends will have none of it, saying that it reads like an extension of 'A Wine of Wizardry.' I think there are many differences, and at any rate, it has more imagination in it than any poem I know of. Like the 'Wine,['] it fails on the esthetic side . . . which seems of small moment in a poem of that nature."[2]

I'm sorry that people see nothing in the poem but an "extension" of The Wine of Wizardry. I certainly meant it to be something else; and I think the resemblance is mainly in the first half. Some likeness was inevitable, in any poem dealing with the imagery of delirium. I suppose there'll be a fine old-fashioned row when "The H. E." is published. The unimaginative (which means nearly everyone) will accord it a double share of execration. "But I should worry." It's natural for dogs to howl, and pigs to grunt.

I've been at work on a new set of drawings—fantastic scenes of hunting and warfare, landscapes of stone and poisonous-coloured metals, cities and fanes and castles of unknown architecture. The colour-schemes are all strange; one picture is done in cobalt, copper, and bronze-green. I've worked out some unholy mixtures of colour—tints of crayon ink, and pencil superimposed in a weird chatoyance.[3] I'll divide with you, when I've accumulated a sufficient number (of the drawings) I may try a few additional ones for "The Sphinx."

Aff.,

Clark.

Notes

1. GS to CAS, 10 June 1920: "No heroes nor heroines: only a rape and four murders! Hooray!" (*SU* 183).

2. Ibid.

3. A change in luster, as in a cat's eye.

[240] [ALS]

June 19th, 1920

Dear Sam:

I like your photograph tremendously; also, the verses inscribed—a fine quatrain. I've put the picture on the wall, above my work-table. It's darned good company.

The clippings are all of interest, though I don't think that the review of the Brentano Baudelaire does anything like justice to the poetic qualities of Sturm's translation. The bit on Conrad is good, though I think it underrates him. The critic is evidently one of those people who take the world (and themselves) too seriously. **Is** the universe anything more than "a gorgeous spectacle?" Better that, than a tenebrific tangle of Freudian complexes, etc, etc.

I've made some new designs for "The Sphinx": "The Cappadocian,['] "A Priest of Byblis," "The Kings of Edom," and "The Mad King of the Lestrygonians." The third one is particularly gorgeous,—a room of vermilion marble, with amber, green, blue, and purple in the costumes. I've invested for the first time in a full set of regular drawing-inks, "warranted not to fade." The yellow ink had been so long in stock, (I bought it from a local drug-store) that it had thickened to a lovely amber! I'll send these pictures on in a week or so, with a number of the fantastics I mentioned before.

The drawing by Solomon is supernally beautiful. I thought the drawings in the "Appreciations"[1] wonderful enough. Certainly they are superior to anything by Burne-Jones. Solomon had genius of the first order, it seems to me.

I hope this letter finds you in a happier mood. I'm very nearly due for an attack of hypochondria, myself. I've been drawing like the devil for the past week or ten days, and have produced between thirty and forty pictures, many of them very elaborate.

Ever your friend,
Clark.

Notes

1. See letter 75n1.

[241] [TLS]

Monday.
[21 June 1920]

Dear Clark,

I'd been unwell all day and came home, finding with I can't tell you how much satisfaction, a letter from you. I've had nervous attacks and headaches that play hell with me, altho physically I am probably as well as ever. I figure on saving some two-hundred dollars between now and December which will take me forever away from this accursed place—its commercialism is nothing compared to the climate. People are still wearing overcoats. The wind blows a sickening damp gale all day and all night long. At least ten times a day there is a general downpour of rain—that is undeniably wet.

I want to tell you how much I appreciate the enclosed poems of Sterling's. The one to Untermeyer is a terrible thing.[1] Not Pope ever wrote such burning, such stinging satire. I understand that Untermeyer is a jewelry salesman by profession. Of the "Morning Star" and "Mirage", what can one say excepting that it is the most exalted perfect poetry written by a modern?[2] The sense is as unalterably beautiful as the melody—it seems like the perfume in one of the gardens in Georgia which one can see in the lanes and byways, always at dusk beneath the stars. And there are lines that remind me somehow, of Decatur, where, in the solemnity of the pines, T.H.C. lies buried.

I shall send you the Verlaine as soon as I can get down to Laukhuff's. He's a strange sort, is Laukhuff, very German, but with the melancholy of a poet. He confessed to me not very long ago that there were times when he wished he could fall asleep and never awaken again. He's an organ-maker by profession, lived many years in Florence where he met and knew D'Annunzio, Duse, Verdi, and many other celebrities.

What George says of "The Saturnian" will remain with me for many a day—"pure poetry"—I thank him.

Did I tell you that Blunden the editor of the new Clare sent me a transcript of some new Asylum poems along with an unpublished photograph of Clare in his old age?

The Simeon Solomon photographs are very beautiful. The Book of Ruth and The Song of Songs are like music. Many illustrate the "Vision" and all belong to the early period. One, depicting a Jewish service, is finer than anything I've ever seen. Another is a Greek priest with a face like Christ's. There is a drawing called "The Paranymph", and another with a girl, dying it seems, but nude-breasted with her maiden attendants that seem too beautiful for words. "The Sleeper and one that Waketh" is represented by an earlier version in crayon.

I'll await the drawings with eagerness. *Will* you do some more for "The Sphinx?"—it isn't every creator who has an opportunity to have his work illustrated by drawings such as yours, in the making. Ich danke dir! That means I'm grateful to you.

The Chinese poems are to appear in a Cleveland paper, professional, by the way, called "The Cygnet." I gave it to them gratis. Biehle, one of the editors, is an artist and a friend of Nelson's.[3]

I've done nothing further on "The Sphinx." Maybe. . . .

It matters very little what other folk say about "The H. E." But this I believe—it is a greater poem than Sterling's. There's a great deal of preciosity about the earlier poem. Yours, with its tremendous imagery and its space-wide sweep of effect and sensation, is cyclopean. It is the most imaginative poem written in the English language.

More in a day or two. My best wishes to you, Clark.

Affectionately,

Sam

I've wondered just what you will think of the photograph of myself which should have reached you ere this. Can you read me as I can read myself in it—the weaknesses—and the sensitiveness—I should almost like to say, of the poet?

[Envelope postmarked Cleveland, Ohio, Jun. 22, 1920.]

Notes

1. "To Louis Untermeyer," enclosed in GS's letter to CAS, 10 June 1920 and unpublished in his lifetime.

2. "Mirage," *Nation* No. 2910 (13 April 1921): 552. "The Morning Star," *All's Well* 1, No. 8 (July 1921): 163.

3. *Cygnet: Monthly Arts Magazine* (January–July 1920), edited by August Biehle and others. It published SL's "A Chinese Pavilion."

[242] [ALS]

June 23rd, 1920

Dear Sam:

We've had some hellishly hot weather, the past week. Hence the lapse in my letter-writing. But to-day the heat is no more than purgatorial. Sunday, though, was fit to scorch the skin from the buttocks of a she-devil. The temperature stood at 104!

There's little enough to write. My fit of drawing has worked itself out, for the time, and I feel tired and depressed. I've rather overdone it. But I have to work when the spirit (or the demon!) is with me, or else not at all.

The drawings will go forward as soon as possible. I want Dewing and one or two others to see them, and am holding them over for that purpose.

I gave D. a copy of "The Saturnian" some time ago. I met him again yesterday, and he spoke of it with great enthusiasm. Your odes have quite "bowled" him over. Albert M. Bender (who is secretary of the Book Club) praised your work, too, in his last letter to me.

I hope you've gone on with "The Sphinx." It contains the most elaborate embroideries of "purple prose" that I know. To me, the "apochyral" [*sic*] character of the incidents and imagery, serves to enhance the interest. Ancient history is a mass of vague legends, anyway. "Quien sabe?"

Some of the new drawings are similar in style to "Fear" and "The Rape." Cynicism will out, sooner or later; and I seem to have more of it in me than I thought. One of the drawings ("The Choice") depicts a faun eyeing a couple of nude girls with an expression of mingled lust and perplexity. In another ("The Aphrodisiac") a woman brings a bowl of steaming liquid to a worn-out debauchee seated on a couch. Perhaps these are scarcely suited for "general circulation," at least in America.

> Affectionately,
>
> Clark.

[243] SL to CAS [nonextant]

[Envelope postmarked Cleveland, Ohio, Jun. 25, 1920.]

[244] [ALS]

June 28th, 1920

Dear Sam:

The drawings will go forward in a day or so—pardon the delay. I think you will like some of the new ones for "The Sphinx." I mean to do some more presently. But I'm "worked out" for the time—also, I'm out of drawing paper, and will have to wait till the local dealer gets in a new supply. I've used up all he had!

I'm sorry to hear you've been so unwell. I, too, have had a touch of somewhat the same trouble.

Dewing has given me a copy of one of his best poems for you, which I enclose. It has faults, but, also, great merit. The whole conception is splendid, I think.

Your new photograph is before me as I write. I noticed the sensitiveness to which you refer; also, a touch of the pagan, or the Oriental. I like it tremendously.

I've disposed of nearly all the "Saturnians" you sent me. Dewing took five of them for friends of his. People who really care for poetry are damned scarce, even in California. I'm beginning to realize how few of them I know.

I'm sorry to know that you won't get away till December. I've counted on seeing you some time in the autumn, which is our best season.

Affectionately,

Clark.

[245] [ALS]

June 30th, 1920.

Dear Sam:

I despatched the drawings yesterday, by registered mail. There's a lot of second-rate work in the collection; but perhaps you'll find ideas, even in the failures. I forgot to include several that I meant to send, and will make up another package for you presently. "The Musician" was suggested by the parable from Heine, quoted among your "Comments."[1] Some of the pencil drawings are not meant for "general circulation[']"; "The Fool and the King's Favourite," for example. I began that drawing as an illustration for Baudelaire's "Venus and the Buffoon";[2] but the girl persisted in looking too much alive for a statue, so I reversed the fable, and the expression on the faces of the characters. The result is a bit fescennine,[3] perhaps.

I've been reading "Madeleine," one of the ["]proscribed books." The book is prudish, compared to many. One could hardly deal with such a subject (as prostitution) in more chaste and reticent language than the author uses. I suppose the real offense of the book is its truth-telling. It disposes of the white-slave myth, for one thing.[4]

Affectionately,

Clark.

Notes

1. The passage by Heine is on pp. [7–8] of the *Saturnian* (June–July 1920).
2. "The Buffoon and the Venus." In Merrill 169–70.
3. Vulgar, obscene, scurrilous. From the fescennine verses (*Fescennina carmina*), a form of early Latin poetry that laid the groundwork for Roman satire and comic drama.
4. *Madeleine: An Autobiography* (1910; New York: Harper & Brothers, 1919) by "Madeleine Blair" (actually one Dolly Ogden), with an introduction by Judge Ben B. Lindsey. An account of a prostitute and brothel owner in the Canadian West during the late 19th century, revealing the role prostitutes played in shaping the Canadian frontier.

[246] SL to CAS [nonextant]

[Envelope postmarked Cleveland, Ohio, July 1, 1920.]

[247] [ALS]

July 3rd, 1920

Dear Sam:

I received "The Five Books of Youth"[1] day before yesterday, and meant to acknowledge it immediately. But I've been busy—too busy to give more than a glance at the volume as yet. What I've read of it impressed me as being good stuff, however. I await the Verlaine with enormous interest. Have just read an article on Rimbaud in the current "Dial," in which (of course) Verlaine is mentioned.[2]

You should have the drawings by now. Some of them are unholy mixtures of ink, pencil, pastel, and hard crayon. Latterly, I've confined myself to the regular coloured inks, and have gotten some magnificent effects by mixing and diluting them. I'll send you some more presently. I've gone into costume-designing, among other things, and am trying to rival Bakst.[3] I've drawn the Empress of Cockaigne, among others. Also, there's a head of Pan that you will probably like.

I hardly know what to suggest, as to the reproductions in "The Saturnian." "Fear," and one of the smaller drawings from the last batch of illustrations for "The Sphinx" (such as "The Cappadocian") might not be a bad choice. But really, I'd rather "leave it to you."

Affectionately,
Clark.

Notes

1. By Robert Hillyer.
2. W. C. Blum, "Some Remarks on Rimbaud as Magician," *Dial* 68 (June 1920): 719–32.
3. Léon Bakst (1866–1924), Russian painter and costume designer, most notably for the Ballet Russe.

[248] SL to CAS [nonextant]

[Envelope postmarked Cleveland, Ohio, July 4, 1920.]

[249] [ALS]

July 6th, 1920

Dear Sam:

I've read "The Five Books of Youth" very carefully, with a less favourable impression than at first. Half a dozen things are good, and quite memorable (one or two will haunt me for a long time to come) but the rest seem indifferent, or even poor. However, it's an unusual book, and the thought and spirit appeal to me. Did you notice the echo of Wilde in many of the poems?

Anatole France is a great writer. "Thais" is not unworthy of Flaubert himself. And I found many excellencies in the other two that I've read: "The Crime of Sylvestre Bonnard" and "The Red Lily." I have a great curiosity concerning "The Revolt of the Angels," of which I have heard so much.

Why *don't* you write an elegy on Nora May? You could do it so well. I, too, feel sure of her poetic greatness. She belongs with Sappho and Emily Bronte.

I hope you will like some of the new drawings, particularly the ones for "The Sphinx." I am told that the composite colours I often employ, would be difficult to reproduce in printing.

I've loaned the "H. Eater" to my Canadian correspondent, Pollock. He wrote me the day that it arrived, saying that he had read it through at a sitting, with "a somewhat stunning effect!" I feel sure that many of the images in the poem are more violent and monstrous than anything else in English poetry.

I shall write to George in a day or two, and put in a bid for an extra copy of "Rosamund." The poem should be out before long.

   Aff.,

       Clark.

[250] [ALS]

                Friday.
               [9 July 1920]

Dear Clark,

   Just a few words: I too, have been busy. The journalist club of which I am a member[1] held a convention in Cleveland and the local group entertained. There were some very interesting ladies—one in particular! I sent you 3 An. France books today and will mail you another bundle next week. I was relieved to hear that Hillyer's book came to you. Yes, it is excellent.

The new batch of pictures came three days ago. They are all good but some are superb—Sappho, The Priest of Byblis, The Potion, The Choice— and I admire the precision with which you abstain from prudery. Nudity is not indecent but clothes very often are. I'm eagerly awaiting your experiment in coloured inks and the costuming you speak of—The Priest of Byblis gives a foretaste of that.

Kirk writes me that he succeeded in obtaining four copies of Nora May's book and I asked him to forward one to me as mine is nearly worn to pieces. He is beginning to feel restless in San F. and wants to go to Honolulu— always on, for he says that disillusion follows disillusion. And it does.

A letter Sunday—

      Affectionately

          Sam.

1537 E. 93rd St., Suite 2.

[Envelope postmarked Cleveland, Ohio, July 10, 1920.]

Notes

1. The Colophon Club.

[251] [ALS]

July 12th, 1920.

Dear Sam:

I received the "Ben Johnson," which is certainly a prize.[1] I like Swinburne's attitude—he gives the old bear his just dues, for faults as well as merits. Certainly, Johnson had a surprising number, an astounding measure, of both. I hope the Anatole France books will come to-day or to-morrow—it takes at least a week for second-class mail to get through. I anticipate "The Revolt of the Angels."

Wrote to George yesterday, and asked him to save me an extra copy of "Rosamund." I doubt if the play has been published yet—I've heard nothing about it. The printer (Mrs Morrison, who also printed "Lilith") was ill when George wrote to me.

Albert Bender asked me for some of my manuscripts awhile ago—he wants to present them to Mills College, which is getting up a collection of original mss. I sent him the originals of many of the best things in "The Star-Treader"—written on cheap yellow paper, and fairly illegible with corrections. He intends to put them together in a gorgeous old Venetian book-binding!

I saw the article on Rimbaud—we get the "Dial" fairly often. Thanks for the clippings—as usual, the prose-poems read even better in print. I hope you've gone on with "The Sphinx"; perhaps I can make some more illustrations for it. I thought "The Kings of Edom" the best I had done for it, in point of colour at least. The others in the last batch were negligible. I hope you agree with me about the selection of "Fear" for "The Saturnian." The choice of the second drawing I should like to leave entirely to you. I mentioned "The Cappadocian" in a former letter; but it's not particularly representative.

I'll send you another batch in a week or two. I've worked steadily, and have made a number of fantastics, some of them based upon Poe. I wish I could send you all of them, but some of my work is to be put upon display in S. F., and I am forced to keep a lot of the best ones. There's a faint hope that I may be able to sell them. It's a case of reaching the right people, of whom there are very few. The best chance is with private collectors—they are "impossible" as magazine drawings. Some day, I hope to publish a portfolio, or a set of portfolios. One of them might well be called "The Geography of Saturn." Another could be made up of "Imaginary Portraits."

Affectionately,

Clark.

Notes

1. Swinburne's *A Study of Ben Jonson*.

[252] [ALS]

July 16th, 1920

Dear Sam:

That treasure-trove of books by Anatole France and Havelock El-lis, all came yesterday. I have been reading "At the Sign of the Reine Pedau-que,"[1] which is very rich, and immensely diverting. You've certainly "hit" me with that consignment of France; few living writers could give me as much pleasure. I feel sure that I will like Ellis, too—I nibbled at the articles on Niet-zsche and Huysmans.[2]

I fear there was a lot of second-rate work in that last consignment of drawings. You shall have some better ones before long. The costume-drawings aren't much, except for the harmonies of unusual tints in some of them. I only made a few, of which you shall have your share. Also, there are some more nudes (you shall have them all)—the last that I shall attempt in that genre. Bad drawing shows up so unmercifully in the nude. There are two heads of Dorian Gray that you shall have, also,—a study in transformation.

Another letter shortly.

Aff.,

Clark.

Notes

1. By Anatole France.
2. In *Affirmations*.

[253] [ALS]

July 21st, 1920

Dear Sam:

I've just received a copy of "Heliogabalus" from George Kirk—but not the "Heliogabalus" you mentioned. This one is the very clever and diverting play by Messrs Mencken and Nathan. The mistake is a curious one, but I'm glad to have the book, nevertheless; likely enough, the book by Stuart Hay would be much less amusing. I certainly appreciate the gift; this play must be very difficult to obtain, since only 2000 copies were printed. It was obviously written (as some reviewer remarked) "with the intention of getting Mr. Sumner's[1] goat."

I'll send you another parcel of drawings, to-day, or to-morrow at the latest. Probably I'll not make any more for a while; I begin to feel jaded, with all the work I have done. I can't draw well when I'm tired.

Hope some of these will give you pleasure. Don't take them *too* seriously. Complete mastery of more than one art is seldom (or never) given to anyone; and I am still a pupil in the art of pictorial representation.

Have you seen the current "Vanity Fair["]? It contains two very beautiful and delicate designs for "Atalanta in Calydon."[2]

I should get the ms. of "Ebony and Crystal" together before long, and submit it to Alfred A. Knopf; I suspect he's about the only man in America who would look at the "H. Eater."

> Affectionately,
> Clark.

Notes

1. John Saxton Sumner (1876–1971) succeeded Anthony Comstock as head of the New York Society for the Suppression of Vice.
2. Malcolm Parcell, "Spring in Calydon," *Vanity Fair* 14, No. 5 (July 1920): 60, containing two drawings for Swinburne's verse drama *Atalanta in Calydon*.

[254] SL to CAS [nonextant]

[Envelope postmarked Cleveland, Ohio, Jul. 20, 1920, with note stating "Drawings / Do not fold."]

[255] [ALS]

July 23rd, 1920.

Dear Sam:

I mailed you a batch of drawings—24 in all, several days ago. One of them was a pencil-drawing for "The Sphinx"—"The Sphinx's Dream"; and I included several of the costume-drawings. "The Princess of Faery" was one of the best of these.

All the books you mentioned have come, with the exception of "Francesca di Rimini."[1] "The Revolt of the Angels" is great; the address you have pasted in the back, certainly hits the nail on the head. But the dream of peace is an impossible dream, for hundreds of years to come, and perhaps forever. Germany and Japan are both preparing for world-conquest.

The "Heliogabalus" **was** Mencken's, as I wrote you in my last. It is tremendously clever. Mencken is one of the few bright spots in American "literature"; though he is rotten enough, in some ways. He is also a good friend of Sterling's, and **that** covers a multitude of sins and omissions, at least with me . . . I've written to Kirk, thanking him for the book. It was tremendously kind of him.

Albert Bender has just sent me Houseman's [*sic*] "Tales from the Arabian

Nights," with the gorgeous illustrations by Edmond [*sic*] Dulac.[2] Do you know them? Dulac and Bakst appeal to me more than any others, among the present-day artists.

> Aff.,
>
> > Clark.

Notes

1. By Gabriele D'Annunzio.
2. Edmund Dulac (1882–1953), French illustrator who became a naturalized English citizen.

[256] [ALS]

> July 25th, 1920

Dear Sam:

A note to acknowledge "Lucretius,"[1] "Francesca da Rimini," and the book on "Sex-Worship."[2] I've not had time to read them, as yet, but they all "look good" to me.

Hope the pictures have come by now. They're the last that I'll make for awhile. I may do some more writing, presently.

Pardon the haste. I've no time to write more, to-day. I've been expecting a letter from you for some time past.

> Aff.,
>
> > Clark.

Notes

1. See letter 261.
2. By O. A. Wall.

[257] [ALS]

> July 26th, 1920.

Dear Sam:

Don't worry about the drawings. I've enough left, and to spare, for exhibition-purposes. There's nothing certain about the exhibition, anyway, since no arrangements have been made as yet. Mrs Sears (whom I mentioned in a former letter), thought that some of them **might** be put on display at a certain rare-book shop in S. F.—which, of course, depends on the book-seller. I've small hope of selling the stuff anyway. There are not more than four or five people (including yourself) who take them seriously.

I sent you the two drawings of Dorian Gray. The first, I thought, was more satisfactory than the second. I shan't make any more nudes. The nude has been done so often, and so well, that any repetition of it, even by a master, is a bore and a nuisance.

Yes, I've known Leo Mihan[1] for years. I sent him "The Saturnian," but forgot to mention that it was not for sale. Mihan is a fine fellow, though the poetry he writes is astoundingly bad. He is in very poor health at present—t. b., I fear. He was never strong. He told me (and I agree) that your "Ode to the Passing of Youth" had "the fine touch of Francis Thompson."

The "Lucretius" is magnificent, in spite of the pedantic punctuation. The book on "Sex-Worship" has increased my stock of useful knowledge. I hope that no Christian will start an argument with me henceforth.

The last chapter of "The Revolt of the Angels" is one of the best things I've ever read. The weak point in the book, to me, is the mingling of the angels with men, in Paris, where they plot together like a lot of common anarchists. No one, not even France, could make it seem anything else than grotesquely improbable. But it's a very great book, with more ideas to the chapter than most writers manage to compass in a lifetime of novels.

Yes, I like Havelock Ellis. Learning, intellect, and keen esthetic sense—the combination can be found in every book. Also, he writes admirable English.

Excuse the dullness of my letters. I feel horribly flat. Also, I'm suffering from eye-strain, with occasional head-aches as a result. I've done so much drawing, the past few months. What I've sent you is a scant half of my output.

> Affectionately,
> Clark.

Notes

1. Leo Bergin Mihan (1887–1944) of Berkeley.

[258] [ALS]

Aug 2nd, 1920.

Dear Sam:

Your letter and "Colored Stars"[1] arrived together. I enjoyed the book—most of the poems are beautiful, and many are very perfervid in their colouring.

I'm glad the pictures gave you pleasure. You've named some of my own favourites among them. The exhibition of my drawings is a bit in the air as yet—and will be a very small one, anyway. I've not decided what to send. I'm supposed to name a price on the pictures, and have really no idea as to what I should ask. Some of the heads (for which I care the least) I shall price very cheaply—ten and fifteen dollars apiece, perhaps. Some of them ought to sell readily enough, at such prices. The heads are very easy to draw—far more so than the landscapes, and I do as many as four or five in a day at times, when I feel in the mood.

That's a good idea, to devote the second issue of "The Saturnian" to your Heine translations. Command me as to the article on my own work. As to the reproductions, I think the "City in Ice" might do well enough but I'd advise against the heads of "Dorian Gray," which I think tame and unsatisfactory compared to many others that I have done. I mean to try these again, later on.

I admire your independence in refusing Kirk's offer. But I doubt if I should have had the resolution to refuse such an offer. After all, one shouldn't put an exaggerated value on mere money.

Leo Mihan has had the nerve to ask Frederick O'Brien (who is living near S.F. at present) to help me in the publication of my new book, and O'Brien has generously offered to write me up in the New York Times, or The Nation. I dislike this sort of business—I'm not seeking publicity. But it's very decent of O'Brien to want to be helpful, and the advertisement would undoubtedly be of advantage from a publisher's point of view. I can let him review some of my work, at any rate.

Aff.,
Clark

Notes

1. By Edward Powys Mathers.

[259] [ALS]

Aug. 6th, 1920

Dear Sam:

The past week has been our hottest, so far this summer. I've not felt able to write letters, and have "shelved" my correspondence for the time being. I've done a few drawings, however, in spite of the heat. One of them is a second head of your "mad King" in "The Sphinx"—a really tremendous one this time. You shall have it presently. Have you gone on with "The Sphinx" at all?

I have just selected sixteen of my drawings to put on display next week in S. F. They are mostly heads—a buccaneer, an Oriental beggar, "The Old Man of the Mountains", "The Pirate's Daughter," "Medusa," "A Hassanite," "Mazeppa," "A Priestess of Lemuria," etc. Also, a green devil with copper-coloured hair, and a very fantastic drawing called "The Laboratory," in which a retort of malachite and copper, filled with inflammable acids, flares up in the face of a yellow dwarf. Athanors, alembics, and unknown vessels of bizarre shape and monstrous usage, fill the background, together with a framework of brazen pipes, rusty with verdigris, and intricate as a spider's web. I have set a variety of prices on these drawings,—ranging from five to thirty dollars apiece. The place where they are to go on exhibition—George Hargen's Old Bookshop—is right across the street from Paul Elder's. It is almost the only place in S. F. at which rare books are obtainable.

Affectionately,

Clark.

[260] [TLS]

Tuesday.
[10 August 1920]

Dear Clark,

I'm glad that all the books reached you and I hope that all were to your taste. I am going to mail you some day this week a very beautiful volume containing the work of Condor[1] who was a friend of Beardsley's—and went the way of most of the 1890 group—insanity, although the volume only hints at it. I shall order myself another copy and send you my own. I wondered if the fan designs would be of any use to you—Condor nearly achieved perfection in the limitation of that space. Anyhow—tell me that you like this beautiful book.

I was delighted to hear what Mihan had done with O'Brien—it may all go against your grain—nevertheless, I hope that he makes a review in the NATION. Newspaper writing is all too transient. If you could only sell a few of the drawings—at least it would give you "financial" peace of mind. I've struggled so much that I am sick of it. I face being laid off—concerns are doing that to their employees by the thousands here—and altogether it looks bad. I thought this—that if it came to such a pass—it would hasten my departure for the West.

Before all this happened I sent my second SATURNIAN to the press and will probably be able to mail you a copy by this week end. I'll send you some additional ones to do with as you like. It contains a glowing tribute to George Sterling and his "Lilith".[2] Sixteen pages is the size. The Prefatory Note apotheosises Ambrose Bierce, who incited me to continue the Heine translations.

More Saturday.

Tuissimus,
S L.

1537 East 93 St., Suite 2.

[Envelope postmarked Cleveland, Ohio, August 11, 1920.]

Notes

1. SL means Charles Edward Conder (see letter 158n5). The book in question was probably *Catalogue of a Collection of Silk Fans, Paintings, Pastels, Lithographs, and Drawings by Charles Condor,* introduction by M. Birnbaum ([Buffalo], 1912.
2. The remarks on Sterling's *Lilith* appear in the brief article "Comment" at the end of the issue.

[261] [ALS]

Aug. 16th, 1920.

Dear Sam:

I enjoyed **all** the books, particularly "Francesca" and the prose-translation of Lucretius.[1] I certainly anticipate the volume on Conder; oddly enough, I had been thinking about him just before your letter came. I saw, not long ago, a few reproductions of his paintings on silk, in which I found a suggestion of Watteau, together with much that seemed original.

Our weather has been simply and perfectly hellish, ever since the end of July. Yesterday, the thermometer touched 106; it was 105 on Friday and Saturday. I can't work, or even read; Sunday, I turned over the pages of a big pile of "Hearst's Magazine,"[2] and the "L. H. Journal"; the illustrations served as a counter-irritant to the heat. The best art I could find was in the advertising section!

Send me as many as you can of the second "Saturnian"; I disposed of the others without trouble. I hope you *do* hasten your departure for the west. I believe you will like S. F. much better than Cleveland, though I can't list Paul Elder himself as being among its "leading attractions." The old hypocrite bought up several hundred copies of "Madeleine," and has been selling them at $25.00 each! Anyone who buys that book as a pornographic item, is likely to be disappointed.

I've been reading a borrowed copy of "Jurgen,"[3]—an astounding book! I couldn't have believed there was anyone in America capable of writing it. I'm surprised that a book of that nature should have sold so well; also, I am sorely puzzled to discern its alleged "obscenity" and "salacity." After reading it, I am almost afraid to publish the "H. E." Not understanding it, Mr Sumner might think that the poem conceals some new kind of erotic symbolism! Nothing is safe from the Puritanical imagination!

Affectionately,

Clark.

Notes

1. Recent translations by William Ellery Leonard (1916) and Sir Robert Allison (1919) were in verse. CAS may be referring to the prose translation by H. A. J. Munro (1864), which was reprinted by G. Bell and Sons (London, 1914); or to one by Cyril Bailey from Clarendon Press (Oxford, 1910).

2. *Hearst's Magazine* (1912–14) later became *Hearst's* (1914–21), then *Hearst's International Combined with Cosmopolitan* (1921–25).

3. By James Branch Cabell. The book was the subject of a celebrated trial after accusations of obscenity were brought against it by the New York Society for the Suppression of Vice. The case went on for two years, but the book was finally declared not to be obscene.

[262] [TLS]

[August 1920?]

Dear Clark,

   I am up and about after a three days' attack of what they call the "summer-grippe" here. It comes quickly and leaves equally so, with sort of malignant havoc in its aftermath. I believe that I lost ten pounds in that short space of time.

   I did not have an opportunity to send you the Condor but will do so this week. I did, however, send you a copy of the second "Saturnian", of which more will follow. Should I confess it?—it seems such a poor thing that I have almost decided to withdraw it from the little circulation that it will have. I seem fated to remain an amateur in letters—as in life—to the end of the chapter.

   I have done "nowt" with the "Sphinx." I'll appreciate an opportunity of seeing the drawing you have made. I started a descriptive list of fifty drawings for the next number of my sheet. Is it an "iconography," they call that sort of thing?

   Sherman[1] sent me for inspection a copy of the "London Mercury" a magnificent magazine devoted to literature and criticism which contains a fine essay on John Clare and in it a mention of a certain "Samuel Loveman of Georgia's" discovery of an important Keats–Clare item.[2] If this copy were mine I'd send it on to you, but my Oberlin friend wants it for his files.

   I wish that I could see the exhibition of your work. Kirk is away on a trip to [a] place called Atascadero and wrote me that he intends to see Carmel. Pardon this note, Clark.

Tuissimus

Sam

1537 East 93 St.

The current "Freeman" has a fine appreciation of Ambrose Bierce by Herman Scheffauer.[3] He states Bierce's inability to "keep" friends. He also ventures the supposition that Bierce may be alive. I don't doubt it—never have.

[Envelope postmarked Cleveland, Ohio, Aug. 18, 1920.] [envelope placed here conjecturally]

Notes

1. Philip Darrell Sherman (1881–1957) taught English literature at Ohio Wesleyan and Oberlin College, from which he retired in 1942.

2. The John Clare article is Edmund Blunden, "Manuscripts of John Clare," *London Mercury* 2 (July 1920): 316–26. The mention of SL occurs on p. 317.

3. Herman Scheffauer, "The Satirist in Vacuo," *Freeman* 1 (11 August 1920): 514–16. Scheffauer was a friend and correspondent of Bierce.

[263] [ALS]

Aug. 19th, 1920.

Dear Sam:

Got "The Saturnian" yesterday. I like your foreword as well as the poems. Some of these translations are marvellous, they have a melody and poignance of phrase that no other translator of Heine has attained. I like your notice of "Lilith" also. I forgot to acknowledge "The Sprite," which came some time ago. By the way, I don't care for the phrase, "life of dreams." Formerly you had, "I shall go back again to my dreams," which appears infinitely better to me.[1]

I've not heard from my drawings, directly or indirectly. The silence appears "ominous," but I really had little enough hope. What can one expect from these barbarians? Originality is sure to perplex and offend them.

I wrote to O'Brien yesterday, and sent him a copy of "The Star-Treader" Also, I offered him the loan of "The H. Eater." It would certainly be a great help, if he likes the latter, and cares to "write it up."

The weather has moderated—a few days ago, it was like the climate of a Calvinistic hell.

I've been reading Balzac's "Girl with the Golden Eyes," in the translation by Dowson, with drawings by Charles Conder. The copy belongs to Dewing, who bought it second-hand. It contains James Huneker's bookplate, together with [an] annotation or two in Huneker's own hand! The story itself I found disappointing, except for the description of Paris at the beginning.

Affectionately,
Clark.

Notes

1. SL's revision stands in his poem "Isolation."

[264] [TLS]

Wednesday.
[18? 25? August 1920]

Dear Clark,

I've been fighting a plaguey sick spell for nearly two weeks—it's the chronic bronchial trouble that put me in the hospital in the army. My somewhat melodious (!) voice sounds like a bruiser's and I am fit brother to the crows and magpies. So much for that!

Sent you yesterday twenty-five copies of the "Saturnian", and the Condor— a beautiful volume, I think. Kirk sent me the recently-published Henry James Letters from out your way. Verbiage—verbiage! They contain some of the most marvellous circumlocutions of words and phrases that I've ever read— but the effect is—nothing. He conveys to the reader as much as an autumnal thistle blown into airy seed by the wayside. I like the earlier stories, but what an artist was annihilated in him! Had he a real passion?—I doubt it. The letters imply genuine friendship.

Will you be so good and send me a copy of the original version of "I shall go back again to my dreams"?—I regret, Clark, that the version you preferred the best has been utterly obliterated from my memory. No wonder—it was written in a hospital.

Through some one's good offices here, I was enabled to read Francis Saltus's volume of Sonnets, "Bayedere and Other Poems." This contains the sonnets dedicatory to all the liqueurs known to the avid thirst of man. The book is fine and most undeservedly forgotten. I took copies of two or three of the poems and will mail them later—a sonnet on Satan, for instance, is tremendous, also one on the "Almighty Scoundrel, God." There are tributes to Baudelaire, Gerard De Nerval—beautiful things. I wish that I could procure one for our use! It contains an odd photographic portrait of Saltus by way of frontispiece.

I'm extremely anxious to hear the outcome of your drawings. But after all, what's the difference? I'll do justice to them in the next "Saturnian", which will probably be out before Christmas.

I enclose some interesting clippings from this week's "Freeman." It is, by all odds, the best and most interesting weekly—despite the tendency to "Freudianism" which you (and I also) dislike.

I want to thank you for what you say about the Heine translations—but I've cooled to them considerably. To tell you the truth, it is almost impossible. But this doesn't detract from what I didn't say quite strongly enough about Louis Untermeyer's—whose volume is the most contemptibly commercial and rotten piece of certified muck that any one man has ever perpetrated in the name of literature.[1]

More Friday.

Affectionately

Sam

1537 East 93 St., Suite 2

"Jurgen" is a good book—a very nearly successful attempt at literature. I note by the "Freeman" that Freud's "Leonardo Da Vinci" is the latest to be "deported." It bears (scientifically, of course) on Leonardo's "frailties." You will like the take off on Comstock. I wonder if they would *dare* do anything with the "H. E." What chance have I with the "Sphinx"? I'll have another page ready shortly.

S L

Notes

1. Perhaps *The New Adam* (1920).

[265] [ALS]

Aug. 24th, 1920.

Dear Sam:

Got your letter, and am most sorry to learn that you have been ill. I, too, for more than one reason, have been feeling a bit seedy.

It's cloudy this morning, and the air is filled with the coming of autumn. I feel the melancholy of the season as I have never done before; my vitality is low from overwork, which makes me more susceptible to it, perhaps. Also, the friend of whom I told you is going away, and I shall miss her dreadfully. She is the most congenial woman that I have met in years; and naturally, I have fallen a little in love with her. Did I tell you that she is the author of "Madeleine?" That, of course, is a secret, and you mustn't mention it. I had the pleasure of loaning "Jurgen" to her, when it was in my possession awhile ago!

Frederick O'Brien offered to take my manuscripts east with him (he has gone, or is about to go to New York) and try to find a publisher for them. I sent him "The Hashish-Eater"—I didn't have the others ready. There oughtn't to be any difficulty about my other poems, if he can find a publisher for **that!** It's awfully kind of him to take the trouble.

Send me as many of "The Saturnians" as you can—**I'll** dispose of them!

Affectionately,

Clark.

P.S. I'll send you the drawing before long, and perhaps something else with it. I'm still waiting to hear from my display.

[Enclosure? Drawing of bookshop, with handwritten notation "George Hargens' Old Book Shop San Francisco." Note at top in Loveman's handwriting: "The book-store at which C.A.S.'s drawings were on exhibition."][1]

Notes

1. See letter 306.

[266] [TLS]

Tuesday
[24 August 1920?]

Dear Clark,

I had a little feeling of nausea this evening when I read your account of the treatment of the pictures. Wait! Wait! I've a fine choice of classic Billingsgate, spoken or written, although pretty shy and reserved until I get aroused. I proved that to my full satisfaction today when I told my employer in leaving, what I thought of him. I'm going to give you from twelve to sixteen pages in the "Saturnian"—which means the entire issue. It doesn't make a damn what your technique is—what counts is inspiration, ideas, genius. In the same mail with yours came a letter from George Kirk—he tried to see the pictures but was too late. He also, thinks you were not given a fair deal. I expect that the next "Saturnian" will be out in early December—provided I get work—I shall submit the entire mss. [*sic*] to you before it goes to publication. If you could spare something in prose or poetry, something unpublished—to lead the thing off—well, I'd appreciate it. Also, can you tell me how to go about the copyright—the pictures, for instance, which I want to safeguard in your name.

Kirk let me read Dowson's "Adrian Rome", a beautifully written book. It was done in collaboration with Arthur Moore. I had no very great difficulty in picking out Dowson's share in the thing. Adrian, a somewhat wistful figure, dies by accident in the close.

Clark, I hope that your indisposition is only temporary. Part of mine is mental—I worry excessively over my finances and over my inability to place myself in life. As long's my mother is alive—geht es noch mit—but after that. . . .

I hope that O'Brien comes back this fall—people are so irresponsible in their promises. Maybe he got sick of the thing called "civilization"—sick of human nature, tired of intrigue, of the resolute puritanism here, and fared forth once again in search of elysium. His book is a masterpiece of writing.

I shall write to George this week. I sent him the extra copies he requested. How I look forward to "Rosamund."

I've half-written an "Ode to Satan"—not in competition to your great sonnet and "Satan Triumphant"—but in a minor key. I'll send you a book or two this week. Have you received Condor—and is it not beautiful? More in a day or two. I make my best, smiling face!

> Affectionately,
>> Sam

1537 East 93 St., Suite 2.

[Envelope postmarked Cleveland, Ohio, Aug. 25, 1920.] [envelope placed here conjecturally]

[267] [ALS]

Aug. 29th, 1920.

Dear Sam:

It grieves me to hear of your illness—the more so because I have been half-sick myself. I've lost ten pounds, at least, during the summer, and am beginning to look quite haggard.

I enjoyed the clippings immensely, in especial, the one on Comstock, and Comstockery. I begin to think that psycho-analysis has its good points, after all!

I never could read Henry James, whose "Letters" you mention. Didn't someone say that reading his works was like watching a man who is watching someone else through a keyhole?

I like Saltus—Sterling has the volume you mention, and I remember looking through it. But a man of that sort is bound to be ignored, in this paradise of real-estate promoters, Christian Scientists, and other "cheerful idiots."

The first stanza of your poem ran thus, in the original:

> "I shall go back again to my dreams,
>   Back to my dreams, and bury me deeper;
> And nothing in all the world, it seems,
>   Shall waken again the sleeper."

I don't remember any variations in the second stanza—it seems all right as you have it.

George writes me that "Rosamund" will not make her debut till the 20th of September, at least. The boy printer who had charge of the job, eloped with a married woman! Hence the delay. G. promises to send you a copy when it comes out. . . . He thought your Heine translations very beautiful.

O'Brien departed suddenly for the South Seas, before he could receive "The Hashish-Eater," which (as I must have told you before) I had mailed to him at his own request. He won't be back till October—October a year hence, perhaps! I've not the patience to wait—I shall forward **all** my stuff east in a few days.

There's nothing but bad news about the drawings, though I've not learned the details as yet. The dealers to whom I sent them, called in half the artists in S. F. (there are none but fifth and seventh-raters on the coast!) to get their opinions, and these gentlemen proceeded to turn down their thumbs, with the result that no one in the city will even put my stuff on exhibition! They "decline to handle it." Rather a "raw deal," don't you think? However, I suppose it's really a compliment, that all these artistic termites and pismires should have thought it necessary to "blackball" me! I hope you'll mention this in "The Saturnian"—I'm sure you'll agree with me that such treatment should be put on record. You shall have the rejected drawings, as soon as I get them back.

    Affectionately,
    Clark.

[268] [TLS]

                Tuesday.
             [31 August 1920]

Dear Clark,

    You should have received the book by this time—the Conder, I mean, also the twenty-five copies of the "Saturnian." I had, today, a letter from George Sterling, the first in many years—it was good to get it. He seems to like the "Saturnian" but takes it more seriously than I do. I never was so disgusted with anything of mine as I was with this second number when it came from the press. At least two-hundred and fifty will vanish into one of those pitfalls that Bierce describes so convincingly as existing in the air, in his book, "Can such Things Be?"[1]

I was down to see Sherman at Oberlin Sunday—a beautiful town. Peace—peace, everything seems to say! At dusk one hears the chimes across the campus of elms and oaks, an organ begins to play, the owls hoot in the moonlight. They have a marvellous Persian cat which they call "Count." He seems unlikest a cat that I ever saw—more a dog in fact and gazes at one with eyes unabashed and unblinking. And the books in his library! His latest acquisition is the first 1824 edition of Wells' "Joseph and His Brethren", with the corrections and insertions filling the volume to twice its original size, in the handwriting of Wells for the 1876 edition as published by Swinburne. He gave me another Trelawney letter—this making the second.

I'll send you a book or two next week. You must pardon my little silences, occasionally—things are not going as they should. I envy your knowing the author of "Madeline"—strange, I don't recollect your mentioning her name. Is it actually a human document? I did not read it but glanced through its pages, before it was prohibited.

Sherman gave me some great first hand accounts of the English Literati. Bullen[2] knew them all. Swinburne, very intimately. Swinburne, he told Sherman, inevitably gave the conversation a turn that merged into erotic subjects. It was an obsession with him. It was his habit to tell Bullen his own experiences in that line and he questioned his visitor on the same subject. Concerning Symons, I'll tell you something in my next. He is "batty" part of the time. Sherman visited and had a lot of chumming with Marie Corelli.[3] I'll tell you about her in my next, too. He showed me some letters from her that were outrageously funny—unintentionally, of course.

Good night, Clark!

Affectionately,

Sam

1537 East 93 St., Suite 2.

[Envelope postmarked Cleveland, Ohio, Sep. 1, 1920.]

Notes

1. Probably "The Realm of the Unreal," referring to prestidigitateurs: "by all their common and familiar performances—throwing large objects into the air which never come down."

2. Arthur H. Bullen (1857–1920), leading English authority in his day on Elizabethan and Jacobean literature. Founder of the Shakespeare Head Press.

3. Maria Corelli (1855–1924), popular English novelist.

[269] [ALS]

East Auburn, Cal.,
Sept. 3rd, 1920.

Dear Sam:

I should have acknowledged the Conder and the 20 "Saturnians" before this—they came Tuesday. I like Conder's paintings and fan designs; the colour in many of them is marvellously delicate—an irisated glory from the suns of dreamland. Conder's colour is markedly superior to his drawing; many of the figures, especially the nudes, impress me as being clumsy and unattractive. As a whole, the book is most beautiful, and I value it for the rare poetry in many of these paintings, where something of Watteau seems mingled with a hint of Beardsley, together with individual qualities that elude classification.

I had a letter from George Kirk the other day—he went to see my drawings at the Old Book Shop, and found them gone! He wants to come up to Auburn and look my stuff over, so I've invited him to spend a few days with me. The sixteen rejected drawings are in Los Angeles at present (My friend, Mrs. S.,[1] took them down with her, after failing to place them with any of the S. F. dealers) but I have hundreds of others, both new and old.

My drawings, it seems, **are not Art,** according to the definition current among the artists and articules of S. F. One man accused me of "a total lack of technique"—an amazing charge. I'd like to hear his definition of "technique" . . . One is reminded of Kipling's refrain—"It's striking, but is it *art?*"[2] I begin to think that I have invented something *new* in the way of pictorial representation, since these gentlemen, finding that they can't classify me with Raphael or Whistler or James Montgomery Flagg[3] (or anyone else), flatly deny that my stuff is **Art!** This is the inevitable price—the price one pays for being original, in art, poetry, science, or sewer-digging.

Hope you are feeling better. I was quite seedy for a week or so, but am picking up again.

Affectionately,

Clark.

Notes

1. Apparently Genevieve K. Sully (1880–1970), a resident of Auburn with whom CAS carried on a long-term affair.
2. In Kipling's poem "The Conundrum of the Workshops" (1890), the devil remarks at the end of several stanzas "It's pretty [or clever, or human], but is it Art?"
3. James Montgomery Flagg (1877–1960), American artist and illustrator. His work ranged from fine art painting to cartooning, but he is best remembered for his political posters, such as his Uncle Sam recruiting poster.

[270] [ALS]

[3 September 1920?]

Dear Clark,

I forgot to comment on O'Brien's taking your mss of "The H. E." east for a publisher. It makes me feel that humanity isn't altogether as selfish affair [*sic*] as we crack it up to be. He must be a fine sort—his book shows it—gentle, manly, contemplative.

You are lucky to have work. The concern I am with has practically laid off ⅔ of its help and I leave the 15th. A week's rest (at a metaphorical oasis) and the caravan resumes its wandering over the desert. All life is a pilgrimage. Our faring is only too often, across a desert.

I sent you this morning Ludwig L's[1] "Book of Modern Criticism." You will like it, I think. What it contains of De Gourmont is delicate fare and beautifully coloured. Knopf or Boni have a volume of the essays (translated) for Autumn. The "Dial" translates him, so they advertise, in their September number. Isn't it salutary and comforting to know that such things still find an audience, after much of what gains credence and circulation.

Sterling's letter meant much to me.

We are having fine Autumn weather. I see a little of the country now—or have been this summer. My mother bought a Hudson "Speedster." I don't drive, but take a pleasure in being driven!

More tomorrow.

Affectionately

Sam

1537 E. 93rd St., Suite II

[Envelope postmarked Cleveland, Ohio, Sep. 3, 1920.] [envelope placed here conjecturally]

Notes

1. Ludwig Lewisohn (1882–1955), novelist, translator, and outspoken critic of American Jewish assimilation. The book's actual title is *A Modern Book of Criticism*.

[271] [ALS]

East Auburn, Cal.,
Sept. 10th, 1920.

Dear Sam:

George Kirk has just left, after spending a couple of days with me. I found him very charming, and wished he could have stayed longer. He was much taken with my drawings, and even **bought** a few of them—which is almost the first sale that I have made.

I have been turning over the pages of "The Book of Modern Criticisms" this evening. As you say, there are many good things in it. Those by Symons pleased me as much as any. By the way, I hear that Symons has published a new book of poems.[1] Have you seen it?

Mihan sends me the last "Yale Review," which contains a fine article by Mencken on American "literature."[2] Look it up, if you have not seen it. He wastes no mercy on the democrats and demagogues. The article is a cold and unflinching analysis of the social conditions which cramp and thwart (or distort) any real artistic production in the States.

I'm sorry to hear that you face being "laid off." I can't conceive of anything more disagreeable than hunting for a "job"—unless it's the holding-down of a job when you have procured it! I'm for the wood-pile! I can't make much at wood-cutting, but I have my own hours, and am not super-intended by anyone.

The sixteen rejected drawings are still in Los Angeles. My friend is determined to have them put on exhibition there. I love her perseverance, in the cause of an art so unpopular as mine. But I fear it will be fruitless . . . Los Angeles, I understand, is a city inhabited chiefly by Puritans and moving-picture actors. It's one of the great centres of the "film" industry.

"Madeleine" is exactly what it purports to be—"an autobiography."

I'll send you a few drawings before long.

> Affectionately,
> Clark.

Notes

1. *Lesbia and Other Poems.*
2. "The National Literature," *Yale Review* 9 (July 1920): 804–17.

[272] [ALS]

> Cleveland, Ohio.
> Sept. 14, 1920.

Dear Clark,

Kirk, I suppose, has already visited you and gone. I hope you became friends. There isn't any one just like him that I know of—generous, impulsive, and a lover of beauty. I mailed him an introduction to Sterling but he writes that George is away from San Francisco at present.

I succeeded in getting work this morning. As I wrote, men are being thrown out of employment by the thousands. From now on I am going to bend every energy even to the sacrifice of the few things that I have never denied myself—books—and save enough money to leave this locality. If I get to California, it will mean still further, possibly to satisfy my nostalgia for the South Seas which has become a passion. . . . Artists are leaving this country by the score—not only artists but men of talent and genius. It is easy enough to guess why.

I hope you're well again. I've been wondering lately when some of your poetry will come to me. I miss it and latterly, have been reading and re-reading the unpublished enclosures you sent me from time to time. If only your drawings fare better in Los Angeles!—but human nature is the same world without end. Lately, Clark, I must confess to you that I have been dis-heartened at it. When I used to tell Kirk of my steadfast belief in the regener-ation of mankind to the ideal set forth by all the poets and the prophets of the past, he would say—"Is it worth while? Does it ever change?" I confess that I am less certain of it than before my army experiences—and lately—well, it is best not to go into detail. I don't expect to become Timon of Ath-ens,—ah, no!—but it simply indicates a reversal in my somewhat child-like and ineffable confidence in the general run of humanity.

I *shall* get out the third "Saturnian"—that is certain.

Laukhuff told me a good story today which he had read somewhere in the German: A Jewish Rabbi and a Catholic Priest came together in their travels. Confidences were exchanged and the men of cloth grew reciprocal. Finally the Rabbi turned to the Priest and, apologising for his frankness, ad-mitted that he was puzzled over the fact that anyone with any pretence to ambition would choose the priesthood.

"Well," responded the Priest, "you gauge the situation wrongly. There are unlimited opportunities for us. From the simple priesthood, chance might pave the way to the charge of a flock in a large city. Then, a bishoprick. After that, Cardinal. And then—my dear Rabbi—you are certainly aware that every Cardinal is eligible to become a Pope. To be a Pope, you must understand, is to find oneself next to God. No one has ever aspired to be God, my friend."

The Rabbi gazed at him with a touch of pathos and answered softly—"One of my own race, Father, once aspired to be a God. . . ." He meant Jesus of Nazareth!

Affectionately,
Sam

1537 E 93rd St., Suite II.

[273] [ALS]

Sept. 15th, 1920.

Dear Sam:

Don't take the fate of my drawings to heart; after all, it was what might have been expected. Perhaps they were prejudiced against me because I am a poet! I dare say it's considered immoral (in a country like this) to court two of the Muses—at the same time. Of course, there were plenty of other reasons . . . Personally, I can't see that my technique is so bad.

I don't know very much about copywriting, myself. I believe the usual course is to print "copyrighted by so-and-so" on the book, magazine, or picture in question, and then mail a copy of it to the librarian of Congress, at Washington. Your printer should be able to tell you, if anything else is necessary. I hope you can get out the next "Saturnian" this year; but, please, please, don't make any sacrifices on my account. Why not use the sonnet, "Symbols" to head your article? It has never been published.

"Rosamund" is again delayed in publication. "Next month"—perhaps.

I'm greatly interested in your "Ode to Satan." Pray finish it. I wish I could do something in the way of poetry; but I am desperately worried at present. My troubles (the monetary ones in especial) are beginning to thicken. I've no heart for writing.

Pardon this desultory note. I've had a sleepless night, and am very tired.

Affectionately,

Clark.

P.S. I'll mail you a few drawings to-morrow.

P.P.S. Your letter mentioning Nelson's opinion of my pictures, came before I had sealed this. I am certainly grateful to him; he names the qualities that I have sought to put into my work.

I have heard of Odilon Redon, but have never seen any of his paintings. Someone (perhaps Huneker) once referred to him as "the French Blake."[1]

Don't worry about my loss of weight—it was temporary, and sprang from a complication of causes, work, worry, and the excessive heat. I'm getting back to normal.

Kirk and I seem to have a lot of tastes in common. I enjoyed his visit immensely.

More in a few days.

Notes

1. Odilon Redon (1840–1916), French Symbolist painter. A number of CAS's colleagues compared CAS's own paintings to Redon's. Huneker referred to Redon as "the 'French Blake'" in *Egoists* (281).

[274] [ALS]

Sept. 18th, 1920.

Dear Sam:

I am sending you a few pictures to-day: "The Mad King of the Lestrygonians," "Neobule,"[1] "Endymion," and some grotesques.

"Ephemera" is beautiful—simplicity, grace, and the grief and passion and pathos of a younger and fairer world that will not return. Have you read "The

Songs of Phryne" by the same author?[2] These are even finer,—of a more pregnant, more poignant loveliness, than "Ephemera." They are similar in subject and feeling to "The Songs of Bilitis," by Pierre Luoys. Phryne and Bilitis were both great courtesans.

Yes, Kirk and I became good friends. He has just sent me Flaubert's "Sentimental Education," a book I have been trying to obtain for a long time. It is a great book, particularly at the end, though it lacks the tragic passion and intensity of "Madame Bovary." However, it is tragic enough; I couldn't help finding a bit of myself in Frederick Moreau. The book absorbed me; I read through its eight hundred pages the day it came. Imagine doing that with any two-decker by an English novelist!

I hope things are better with you.

> Affectionately,
>
> Clark.

Notes

1. A woman addressed in the 7th-century B.C.E. Greek poetry of Archilochus.
2. Mitchell S. Buck.

[275] [ALS]

[September 1920]

Dear Clark,

I've just opened the drawings—beautiful! The green-bronze of "Neobule" reminds me of the description of the Greek goddess dug up in Merimee's story by a French antiquarian—"The Venus of Ille." It had the same pale green tint. "Endymion" is the most charming thing you have done. The "Mad King" beats the pen and ink sketch—the night without is vast and overwhelming. For these, Clark, and for the rest—many thanks. Pardon the trite language I've expressed my admiration in—when one works for ten hours adding column after column of figures, perfect phraseology is quite squeezed out of me.

I'm glad Kirk sent you Flaubert's "S. E." These later books of his remind one of a giant playing with sea-shells and "sich-like." But a great book none-theless.

I've sent you so many books in the last few days that I've quite forgotten what they were:

Mary Magdalen	Saltus
Vanity Square	
Crime and Punishment	Dostoieffsky

—something else, but I forget what.

As to the "Saturnian"—it will be published this year. I get letter after letter for spare copies—encouraging, is it not? Sacrifices? It gives me a pleasure to publish anything of yours—and they say that all pleasure is selfish. Ergo . . .

I'll send you the "Ode to Satan" later.

Affectionately

Sam

[Envelope postmarked Cleveland, Ohio, Sep. 24, 1920.] [envelope placed here conjecturally]

[276] [ALS]

Sept. 24th, 1920.

Dear Sam:

There's an absolute dearth of news, but I'll make some sort of attempt at a letter. I've written nothing, done nothing, and thought nothing to any purpose for the past two weeks. I have seldom felt so demoralized; and my isolation preys upon and depresses me more than in years. Perhaps I have more than the normal longing for love and sympathy; at least, I am more conscious of this longing than most others.

You can't say anything that I won't agree with, when it comes to the viciousness and stupidity of mankind in general. I never had many illusions about them—at least about men; and I'm losing, or have already lost, the few that I used to have concerning women.

I read Artzibasheff's notorious novel, "Sanine," last night—a borrowed copy. It's something of a book, I must say—any amount of Russian realism, and no lack of "dramatic interest," either . . . three suicides and two seductions . . . A disproportionate amount of suicide, it seems to me. . . . Lots of people think the book very shocking, I am told. But I didn't find it so. The Nietzschean attitude toward life, typical in Sanine, is the only attitude that will really get you anywhere. To h-ll with all this pettifogging morality!

My poems will begin their search for a publisher next week. Knopf first, and if he fails to come through, Boni and Liveright, or Brentano's. I don't know what I will write next. I think vaguely of a book of erotic poems—"The Book of Eros." Everything in it will be utterly sensual and pagan—a direct challenge to the official suppressors. Everyone else has succumbed to erotomania; after all, love is the core of life, and nothing else is really worth writing about. If one could only treat it with a fresh **nuance!**

Affectionately,

Clark.

[277] [TLS (mutilated)]

[30 September 1920?]

Dear Clark,

I read "Sanine" years ago. I found it interesting and perverse—but somehow I saw no reason for the perversity. Its trend was not artistic—and if, as you say, it is Sanine's attitude toward life itself that counts, I suppose he wins. I talked to a man t'other evening who has charge of the public schools—the publicity part—he vouchsafed the opinion that only about two per cent of the people were worth reckoning—the other ninety-eight being— well, what shall we call them?—I dunno, but he said they were hope[less.] And it is this ninety-eight per cent, the vast majority, with [_____ h]eads and with hearts as responsive as a chunk of lead, who contro[l the] artists and the thinkers. This is also vanity.

Let me warn you about Knopf[. He him]self knows nothing about what is worth while—strange as it may [seem.] But he has a clique about him consisting of Mencken, Hergesheim[er, and Hu]neker, who, I understand, pass in judgement—and it seems to me [that the]ir judgement usually counts in the case of a prior English pu[blication?] I tell you this in confidence—as it was told to me. Can [you imagi]ne a man who was prepared to turn the two volumes of Chinese t[ranslation]s down by Whaley, until assured of their artistic value by s[omeone] who recognised it—and that actually happened. Of course, they [_____] "big." Don't forget the "Seven Seas."[1] They recently printed a litt[le v]olume by Noguchi—that jackass of a Japanese!

I suppose you are right about Love—but I'm a little bewildered over everything. What does it all mean—what's the good of it?—everywhere I see mating and bearing, but somehow it partakes to me the nature of the phantasmagoria on the Brocken in Goethe's "Faust"—where an atom is heard complaining that no sooner does he rise a certain space toward heaven, than an invisible force pulls him netherward. "Immer Hoher—immer hoher!" cries Goethe—"always higher!" I like your plan of an artistic erotic book— but beware!—the world gibbets the man heaven-high who dares to overleap in contradistinction to her stupid morality. I had the same idea in the "Sphinx", but I don't need to tell you what would happen if I should publish it—I should be hounded to death. Beside your copy I gave one to Levison and I worry myself sick lest he should do something with it—or use it for "material." He's a magazine writer you know, and used nearly half of the "Faun" without asking me.[2]

You ought to have some of the books I sent you by this time. One of my acquaintances here, a curio collector—a strange type—gave me a beautiful Florentine terra cotta lamp, perhaps two thousand years old. It is the head of a Satyr with a handle of oak leaves. It may have been that sort of a lamp that Psyche held in her hand when she bent over the sleeping God Eros. . . . that also, was two thousand years ago. Why did they ever come—these Jews and these Christians with their religion? Even the children. . . . the little girl of four or five next door with a celtic face talks quite learnedly about holy water!

I wonder how it will feel to h[ave a] book dedicated to me. Well, Clark—whether my own work brings [me fam]e or not—I shall pass on to immortality in an association with [your gr]eatest volume—for it contains "The Haschich-eater", does it not?

Had a fine letter from Sterl[ing. Ki]rk, I believe, must be in New Orleans. A strange chap—he hates [Clevel]and and yet returns to it.

Affectionately,

Sam

[Envelope postmarked Cleveland, Ohio, Sep. 30, 1920.] [envelope placed here conjecturally]

Notes

1. SL's error for the Four Seas Co., a small press in Boston.
2. How this was done is unknown.

[278] [ALS]

Sept. 30th, 1920

Dear Sam:

Two of the four books you mentioned have come—"The Bayadere, etc", and "Crime and Punishment." Doubtless the others will be here by to-morrow. A few of the sonnets in "The Bayadere" are surprisingly fine; some of them have the bizarre and sinister beauty of black pearls, or the keen, pervasive perfume of nightshade-flowers. Saltus was certainly a real decadent, though many of his sonnets fail to "come off," and only a very few approach perfection. I'd give something to see the reviews he got when his work appeared. But one can imagine them. Think of the holy horror, the bleak and icy consternation, with which he must have been regarded by those who paid any attention to him at all! I am grateful to you for the book; it must be quite rare. Sterling has the only other copy of it that I ever saw.

I read "Crime and Punishment" (a borrowed copy) many years ago, and admired it for its truth and terror. A sublime book, like all of Dostoievsky's. I anticipate re-reading it.

I have spent the afternoon paying visits—adding the boredom of other people's company to the boredom of my own. There is no one in Auburn to whom I can say what I really feel and think—they'd think me the devil himself, if I did. They're all trussed up in strait-jackets of convention and morality, and it's hard to avoid shocking them . . . After an hour or two with such people, I always feel like spending the night in a lupanar . . But even I, perhaps, am poisoned with morality. I shall devote the rest of my life to getting the virus out of my veins.

I sent "Ebony and Crystal" to Knopf yesterday, after winnowing the collection down to less than ninety titles, fifteen of which are prose-poems. I'm not very sanguine. . . . The chief characteristics of the collection are pessimism and exotic beauty—two cardinal crimes in the eyes of the average reader. I do wish I could get "The H. Eater" into print—it ought to start a row, at any rate.

I am quite well again, in the physical sense—indeed, I have never been better. I feel like a mountain-lion, and am looking around for someone to devour.

More in a few days.

Affectionately,

Clark.

[279] [ALS]

Oct. 6th, 1920.

Dear Sam:

The two books by Edgar Saltus have finally arrived. Both of them are clever and readable, and "Magdalene," in especial, is filled with fine bits of mosaic prose. I'd recognize a phrase or sentence by Edgar Saltus, if I found it without quotation-marks in the work of almost any other present-day writer—it would stand out like a crystal in a block of quartz—or a piece of amber in a carrot-heap. A superb and unique style—a style that somehow suggests the splendour of the Borgias, with every now and then a sentence perfect and poisonous as some envenomed ring that they may have used. A style that is made up with segments of gold, ivory, and sard. . . . He is at his best, it seems to me, in "Imperial Purple"—fine as they are, the two present books are inferior.

Don't worry about my volume of erotic verse—I've not written it yet. If I do, I shall probably not care to publish it until I am in a position to leave America for good . . . Don't take me too seriously,—I talk wildly at times; you wouldn't wonder at that, if you knew the sort of frozen hell in which I am condemned to exist. Auburn is to me what Recanati was to Leopardi.[1]

Yes, the collection I sent to Knopf included "The Hashish-Eater." I hope that Huneker will have a chance to pass on my work; it should appeal to him, if to anyone. Mencken seems well-disposed toward me—at least, he has bought more of my work than most other editors.

I wrote to Kirk the other day at his address in Cleveland; I dare say he is home by now.

I must get to work again, if I can. I have done nothing since August. Art seems a mockery to me in my present mood. If love and life are illusions, then art is the illusion of illusions—the subtlest of the veils of Maya . . .

As to love, I really believe that a great passion is the only thing that could make life seem worth while. There is in it an intoxication, an oblivion, that nothing else confers. But I am sure that such passions are rarer than most people think; sexual attraction is almost universal, but love is not. However, I don't believe in marriage as it is constituted; and the bringing of children into the world would seem a horrible business. "Children (as "Madeleine" once said to me) are immoral and unnecessary."

Please send me that "Ode to Satan"; I am eager to see it. In my days of ambition I dreamt of writing a whole book of Satanic psalms and litanies!

Affectionately,

Clark.

Notes

1. Leopardi was born in the town of Recanati, in central Italy, on the Adriatic coast. The area was then controlled by the papacy.

[280] SL to CAS [nonextant]

[Envelope postmarked Cleveland, Ohio, Oct. 9, 1920.]

[281] [TLS]

Wed.

[13 October 1920]

Dear Clark,

I was glad to get your first letter in many days—it does me good to hear from you. I see few people and write to still fewer. Kirk returned last week. I have seen him several times—three, to be definite. He was over last evening, unwell, but we took a long way. He seems to be discouraged over his inability to obtain rooms—which I expected. He seems to have changed—something of his boyishness is gone—but that's the penalty of all marriages. And by the way, he has your letter and will write.

Clark—I know that you will forgive me for even broaching the subject—but we've been friends too long not to allow confidences—but your last few letters lead me to believe that some one person has come into your life who means much to you. Only be careful. . . . it may bring you much joy. . . . it may bring you even more bitterness. . . . and it all depends on the woman, the being to whom you have intrusted your soul. But whatever it is, or whoever she be Clark—you, the artist will profit by it—spiritually, at least—although its drink be that of Marah[1] and the quenching of your thirst, no Lethe. I would like to see you happy, but I know that your temperament like a multitude of others of us, will never enable that to be. You don't object to this frank admonition, do you? I should never have written it, had I thought so.

Talking to George about yourself and your home and your surroundings has made me more than ever nostalgic to get out there. Almost, I pictured you when he described your walks. A few months more . . . I'd like to stay three or four days with you when I get out there.

Following are some of the things I've marked down to send you—some are published, some not yet—but you shall have them within the next month:

Lesbia	Arthur Symons
Ceasare Borgia	Arthur Symons
Seven Men	Max Beerbohm
Philosophic Nights in Paris	De Gourmont
Mademoiselle de Maupin	Gautier
(This is Knopf's marvellous edition, with all the	
additions that have been hitherto expurgated.)	
Verlaine	Lepel[l]ettier

Does it read well?

I wish you had sent your mss to Alice Meynell. I mistrust Knopf and his clique. Huneker and Mencken, in spite of their enormous public, I've always been mistrustful of. Did you know that Boni had the publication of Huneker's new book, "Painted Veils", to be privately printed and said to be decidedly off-colour?

I'll send the Satan lucubration shortly, also another sheet to the perennial Sphinx. This was written some weeks again, and will be resumed shortly and probably to a complete ending. And I'll be glad to get it off my mind.

I was pleased with what you said about Saltus. And Oh!—add to the above list his "Imperial Orgy"—which is shortly to be published—Russia, from the Tzars downward, and the advertisement says, a masterpiece of writing. I believe it. There are four people who have my undivided respect in this country—yourself, Sterling, Saltus, and Sherwood Anderson who wrote "Winesburg, Ohio." Have you it, or have you read it? Please let me know. More Sunday.

Tell your Mother that I have heard from George Kirk concerning the Gaylord book she wants published in Cincinnati.[2] Yes, and I've even heard *of* the book. It was published by Clark and Co. down there. I'll get it for her—tell her for me.

> Affectionately,
>
> Sam

1537 East 93 St., Suite 2.

Notes

1. Ex. 15:23: "When they came to Marah, they could not drink of the waters of Marah, for they were bitter."
2. See Bibliography under William Gaillard.

[282] [ALS]

Oct. 15th, 1920.

Dear Sam:

I've delayed writing, partly because I expected a letter from you; but mainly on account of the paucity of news. Life, with me, seems to have become a blank of absolute boredom. I see no one, and most of my correspondents have been owing me letters for months past. The weather is beastly at present—a perpetual alternation of rain and fog, fog and rain; and I can't even work. I started several prose-poems, got disgusted, and found it impossible to finish or even go on with them; so they went into the stove.

I suppose Kirk is home by now. I wrote him [a] letter at his Cleveland address, some time ago.

I've not learned the fate of "Ebony and Crystal" as yet. I hope to hades I can find a publisher for it; it's hard to go on working in the middle of a desert, with no encouragement beyond that of a few friends whom you never see, face to face. I've come to a full stop at present. It's humiliating to confess, but I feel the need of an outside incentive.

The clippings you sent me are all good reading. Yes, I've heard of Francis Adams. Some of the verses quoted from him in Monahan's article are tremendous.[1]

I've given away my last extra copy of your Heine translations. They were much appreciated, by those qualified to judge. You may have heard from some of the people to whom I gave them—I know that several intended to write you.

How about your "Ode to Satan"? I'm just in the mood for something of that sort!

Aff.,

Clark.

Notes

1. Michael Monahan, "A Poet of the Revolution," in Monahan's *At the Sign of the Van* (New York: Mitchell Kennerley, 1914), 346–56; rpt. *Freeman* 2 (6 October 1920): 84–85, about Adams's *Songs of the Army of the Night* (1887).

[283] SL to CAS [nonextant]

[Envelope postmarked Cleveland, Ohio, Oct. 16, 1920.]

[284] [ALS]

East Auburn, Cal.

Oct. 18th, 1920.

Dear Sam:

Has Sterling sent you a copy of "Rosamund"? He promised to do so. I received mine a few days ago. It lacks the poetic beauty of "Lilith," but here's no dearth of action, to say the least! It ought to make an effective "film"! Rape, murder, and adultery—what more do you want? Seriously, though, it is great work. And "The Hills of Iris"[1] is a beautiful lyric. In the "setting" in which it occurs, it is like a sapphire on a breast-plate of bronze!

Your letter came yesterday, in the same mail with one from Knopf, which I enclose. Quick action! I doubt if they even read my poems. I'll try John Lane for luck, then Boni & L. I thought of Mrs. Meynell, but it seems horribly presumptuous. I'll send her the poems, though, if everything else fails. "The Four Seas Co." is no. 4 on my list of prospectives.

That list of books is tremendous! But I have a "Mademoiselle de Maupin," published in London—a fat book in a scarlet binding . . . Ye gods! If **that** is "expurgated[']! . . .

Don't worry about my love-affairs—none of them has ever lasted more than two years, at the utmost! I fall "in love" with too much facility, if there's a woman around. I can even "love" two or three at the same time! It's a case of erotic temperament . . . Of course, you are right about happiness—there is no such animal. There is only pleasure—and even that is damnably disappointing.

I've never read that book of Anderson's. I believe Kirk mentioned it to me—certainly, I've heard of it before. . . . My mother will certainly be grateful for that book on the Gaylord family. Genealogy interests her—and the family is an old one. . . . Personally, I'd rather not know too much about my ancestors; to me, knowledge of that sort seems to darken, rather than clarify, the mystery of life. But there are many who think otherwise.

"Three or four days" is no visit—I'd keep you for as many months, if I could! I hope you can make it; and I think you will love California.

Give my best to Kirk. Indeed, I will be glad to hear from him.

Aff.,

Clark.

Notes

1. I.e., "The Iris Hills."

[285] [ALS]

Oct. 26th, 1920

Dear Sam:

We've had a spell of warm, bright autumn weather, after much rain and fog, and the orchards are a holocaust of gold and carmine. Here in California, the autumn colour is mostly in the foliage of the fruit-trees, and the cultivated maples and others not indigenous to the country. The native oaks and sycamores show little but browns and pale yellows.

I've spent most of the afternoon in writing letters, leaving yours till the last. One was to Kirk, and another to some collector who wrote asking me for manuscripts. He wanted a hymn, in particular, if I had written anything of that sort! Also, something on the scenic glories of "our great State!"

John Donne, whom I ordered (in the Muses Library) eight or nine months ago, turned up yesterday! There's hope for Thomas Hardy's poems, which I ordered at the same time, and which have not yet come. Why so much delay, I wonder? The books were ordered from a New York firm, who, in turn, sent to England for them.

Have you seen Boni and Liveright's "French Anthology?"[1] I found a number of translations from Verlaine in it, all by Arthur Symons, many of which are new to me. The book is full of astounding misprints, such as "liver" for "river"—and worse!

I began an "Ode to Aphrodite" some time ago, but discarded it as containing too many of the conventional poetic images—"Lesbian eyes" and "beds of shattered rose," for example. I don't want to write in that style any more. Also, I started a fantastic dialogue, "Venus and the Priest." It was to end in the seduction of the priest, but I've done little more than introduce the goddess as yet. She appears in a somewhat peremptory fashion, in place of the crucifix before which the priest is kneeling! But don't ask what happens to the crucifix!

It will mean a lot to me, to have you out here, and within traversable [*sic*] distance. S. F. is only a few hours from Auburn . . . But it seems a long time till spring.

I'm probably due for an avalanche of visitors before long; they usually come in droves, when they come at all. And no one has been here for weeks . . . I expect a girl, among others—a girl with hair the colour of peach-leaves in autumn. She's very ornamental; but I wouldn't care to pay her candy-bills.

Affectionately,
Clark.

[Envelope postmarked Auburn, California, Oct. 27, 1920.]

Notes

1. I.e., *The Modern Book of French Verse,* ed. Albert Boni.

[286] SL to CAS [nonextant]

[Envelope postmarked Cleveland, Ohio, Oct. 29, 1920.]

[287] [ALS]

Nov. 2nd, 1920.

Dear Sam:

I'm writing this in the throes of a fierce cold—the worst one I've had for years. I ought to have written you before; pardon my lapse: it wasn't from forgetfulness.

"Ebony and Crystal" has gone to John Lane. I told them they could consider the prose-poems as a separate volume, if they liked.

Yes, my "Mademoiselle[?]" is the one in the "gaudy red cover." I had forgotten the astericks [*sic*] in the 16th chapter. But why should they have left out a mere rape, after some of the other "doings" in the book? I'd certainly prize a complete translation, though; astericks are never anything but an insult.

I've taken to attending church, the past few Sundays. Not from piety, however . . . Dewing also attends, and I've seen him oftener of late. The rector, Fenton-Smith,[1] is an Englishman—a quite unusual and attractive personality. He paints, as an avocation, and some of his work is surprisingly good, at least in colour.

You are right about women; most of them are mean, timid and mercenary, if nothing worse. I have known some glorious exceptions—or, at least, I *think* I have. But I am so readily victimized by sexual attraction, that it's hard to be sure.

My mother wants to pay you for the Gaylord genealogy, if you can get it for her. It is only right that she should, and I hope you won't say no. You'll *never* get out to California, if you go on buying all the books in the world for me!

Give my best to Kirk.

Affectionately,

Clark.

Notes

1. W[illiam] H[arvey] Fenton-Smith, rector of St. Luke's Episcopal Church in Auburn.

[288] [TLS]

[2 November 1920]

Dear Clark,

There will leave this week for your parts the following:

Seven Men	Max Beerbohm
Zuleika Dobson	"
A Child of the Age	Francis Adams

Three numbers of the "Little Review" (included is the last which has been seized on account of James Joyce's "Ullyses!"[1] [*sic*]

I'll send 'em off as soon as I can get around to it—but let me beg to explain.

In going to work today I fell through a rotten planking into an excavation and very possibly broke or fractured my nose. They took an X Ray today and I'll know tomorrow. The party who is responsible for the said plank has agreed to pay the bill. It may spoil what Mr Abe Potash[2] would call a "classy profile"—but who the hell cares, and I'm beyond the marriagable age anyway.

My copy of Blair's "Grave" came yesterday—1808, a very beautiful thing. You once mentioned Blake's knowledge (or misknowledge) of anatomy . . . . if you could only see this. Kirk sat and looked at it for an hour this afternoon. Also, I've a four volume edition of Lucian printed in 1711, containing most of the dialogues that are usually omitted—the ones between the courtezans, for instance. I've won out on a Samuel Palmer's Virgil—he was a friend of Blake's, and I owe my knowledge of him to Sherman who says he died of whiskey and despair a down-and-outer. Mosher, he tells me, collects him.

Laukhuff has the same difficulty in getting the English books that you have. It is on account of the scarcity of paper in England.

I love your description of the scenery near Auburn.

I cast my vote for the thin, elderly man in Atlanta Prison today.[3] And as I put my cross on the ballot, I remembered the words of Socrates to his accusers: "For if you think that by killing men you can avoid the accuser censoring your lives, you are mistaken. . . ."

Affectionately,
Sam

1537 East 93 St., Suite 2.

You are anxious to see me? . . . . and I to see you.

Notes

1. Joyce's *Ulysses* was serialized in the American journal *The Little Review* from March 1918 to December 1920 prior to its book publication in 1922.
2. Abe Potash was one of a fictional duo with Mawrus Perlmutter in the writings of Montague Glass (1877–1934), a British-American Jewish lawyer and writer of short stories, plays, and film scripts.
3. SL refers to Eugene V. Debs (1855–1926), who ran for president while in prison at the Atlanta Federal Penitentiary. He received 919,799 votes.

[289] [ALS]

Nov. 9th, 1920

Dear Sam:

I'm awfully sorry to hear of your accident, and hope it isn't serious. . . . "Classy profiles" don't count for even as much as you think—if they did,

I would never have a chance!

I'll certainly appreciate the books. I'm at work on some new drawings, of which you shall have your share, in due time. I am combining black and white with pure colour in some of them. Black, in particular, seems to harmonize almost any combination.

This is a note. I'll write you a **letter** in a few days.

Aff.,

Clark.

[290] [ALS]

Nov. 13th, 1920

Dear Sam:

We've had nearly a week of rain, and the autumn leaves are well-nigh ruined. A few remain, on the pear-trees and poplars, like tatters of yellow and scarlet silk. The asters and goldenrod are gone, and I find no wild flowers, with the exception of a few pale and stunted poppies along the railroad track. The native poppy seems to flower at all seasons, though the spring is its time of abundance. But it has second, and even a third, blooming.

I'm sorry that conditions are so bad in the east. They are rotten enough here; I notice more tramps than in many years past . . . I, too, have a peck of worries, chiefly financial ones. . . . I wish you were out here: I feel sure that you would find life easier and pleasanter than in Cleveland, at least on the human side. It will be, if I can do anything to make it so.

My church-going **is** rather funny; I enjoy the piquancy of it. I make eyes at the organist, and recite Baudelaire's "Litany to Satan" under my breath during the psalm-singing. If I had any religious tendencies, the hymns and sermons would cure me of them. I have been attending the Episcopal church, but to-morrow I shall desert to the Congregational. There's a reason, and a very pretty one. Her hair is like a poem by Swinburne! But I'm afraid there's not much underneath it: She thought Swinburne was an American poet, when I asked her if she had read him! But I looked at the hair, and forgave her.

I had visitors last Tuesday—my friend Mrs. Nic[h]ol, and her daughter Margaret.[1] I hadn't seen Margaret since she was ten or twelve, and remembered her as a homely little girl. Now she is seventeen, and looks more like a dryad than anyone I have ever met; she is an artist's model in S. F., and has a heap of admirers. George, I understand, is among them, but she objects to his long list of previous "affinities." I fell as much in love with her as it's possible for me to do, with a young girl. My natural preference (I am like the heroes in Balzac) is for women past thirty.

I hope all this doesn't disgust you too much—this letter seems full of females. Women are my chief interest, aside from art, and their psychologies fascinate me. It is so beautifully primitive, in most instances. They are nearer to nature than men, and are more completely dominated by subconscious impulses.

Kirk has sent me Arthur Ransome's "Aladdin," with some wonderful illustrations by an artist named Mackenzie.[2] Have you seen them? They are much better than those of Dulac, and are full of Chinese and Persian influence. They make my drawings look cheap and tawdry.

My cold was nothing to worry about—I've thrown it off, and feel quite well. Better luck to you! Write again before long.

Affectionately,

Clark.

Notes

1. R. A. and Gertrude Dix Nichol (1855–1952) had two daughters whom CAS knew since their childhood in Auburn: Margaret and Amaryllis. Gertrude Dix was a poet and author of the novels *The Girl from the Farm* (1895) and *The Image Breakers* (1900).
2. Thomas Mackenzie (1887–1944), English artist and illustrator.

[291] [TLS]

Monday.

Dear Clark,

Your very brief note came along today. If you complain of boredom what should I say to this existence of mine? Nothing, not even books, seem to do me any good. I've been reading Conrad's "The Rescue", pagan perfumed with the scent of the tropics, the sunlight on the islets in mid-sea, and I had to lay the volume down—the nostalgia became too great to bear.

There have been no new books that I have read recently—one only, Vincent Starret[t]'s "Ambrose Bierce", practically a pamphlet in size and not much better as to contents in a valuation with literature. Starret[t] is the typical newspaper man with a peculiar adaptation for "Finds"—Arthur Machen, whom he exploits in this country—and Bierce, although he knows less about Bierce than I do. From the odds and ends of a few of Bierce's friends and the few autobiographical passages in the collected works with a purple passage or two of criticism he presents the compilation of the book. Bierce would have given it one burning paragraph—or possibly word—but that would have been enough. The only noteworthy thing in the volume are the two last letters that Bierce wrote to a Mrs McCracken[1] of California. Beautiful, poignant, with a gesture of nobility, Bierce dismisses himself. "Most of what is going on in your own country is exceedingly distasteful to me," he says.

Kirk has just purchased a set of Casanova which is going the rounds hereabouts for one hundred and twenty five dollars for the twelve volumes. Three I have read, but I question whether I'll go further—Casanova seems to have been the transmogrification of the Superman of Niet[z]sche when it came to sexual stimulation, and it gets to be a bore, or to say the least, tiresome. Not that I'm a prude about such matters, but by Priapus—the man had no limitations. I've tried to count the cases of "indisposition" resulting therefrom in the course of the three volumes—and gave it up. His patience as a nurse to himself was marvellous, and he seems to have gloried over the length of the duration of the disease!

I must write Sterling. I haven't even had the heart to write.

I think often of Kirk's account of his visit to you. Bydamn! I shall also be there one of these days. Patience, my soul—if I have any. Did you get "Redemption"?[2] Write oftener—so shall I!

Affectionately,
Sam

1537 East 93 St., Suite 2.

Watch your eyesight. Do I put temptation in the way by sending books?

Notes

1 Josephine Clifford McCracken (1839–1921), a California writer and journalist. Starrett's book contains two letters by Bierce to McCracken.
2. A volume of plays by Leo Tolstoy.

[292] [ALS]

Nov. 23rd, 1920.

Dear Sam:

This is to acknowledge the parcel of books. I've not found time to read them yet; my eyes have been weak and troublesome, so I've been forced to cut down on reading. As to drawing—I've had to give that up entirely.

How are things with you? Better, I hope, than when you wrote me last. No news worth mentioning out here. We've had incessant rain for weeks past—loathsome weather, which keeps me indoors, and makes both work and amusement impossible.

I'll write again, and at greater length, in a day or two.

Affectionately,
Clark

[293] [ALS]

Nov. 29th, 1920

Dear Sam:

I am glad indeed to have "The Garden of Epicurus"; many things in it remind me of the conversations in Remy de Gourmont's "Night in the Luxembourg." I have marked nearly every other page as being especially fine.

"Zuleika Dobson" is an odd sort of farce—more elaborate, it seems to me, than anything of the kind I have ever read. It is brilliantly done, and most original; but one book of it goes a long way.

My eyes are weak, as I probably wrote you before, so I've not found time to read the other books as yet. I've never enjoyed anything of Tolstoi's, with the exception of "Anna Karenina," and a few short stories; his ideas are so utterly antipathetic (or antipodean!) to mine. However, these plays look interesting.

I'm worried a bit over not hearing from you, and hope your next letter will bring better news.

My nerves have bedevilled me of late, which means, doubtless, that I ought to get to work at something or other. I invoke the Muse continually, but she seems loath to return. I've had no word from the John Lane Company, so it looks as if they were **reading** my poems, at any rate. It's nearly a month now since I sent them out.

Mihan writes me that O'Brien is back. He could do something for "The H. E.", if anyone could. Mihan sent him a copy of it.

I've mixed more with the people here, of late, and find some of them more interesting than I had expected. There is a Mrs. Rockwell,[1] who lives across the ridge from me, with whom I talk Epicureanism and smoke cigarettes. Any woman who frankly enjoys "Mademoiselle de Maupin" and "A Night in the Luxembourg", is worth knowing. ... She made a delicious criticism on D'Annunzio—she thought his characters "too fussy!" . . . Also, there are others.

Give my best to Kirk.

As ever, Affectionately,
Clark.

Notes

1. Probably Dorothy H. Rockwell (1885–1944).

[294] [TLS (mutilated)]

Monday.
[6 December 1920?]

Dear Clark,

There's a book on Anatole France leaving for your parts this week.[1] You will like it. Don't feel that you have to read the things I send you in a hurry. They may, some time, save you an hour or two from boredom.

You are fortunate to have a woman whom you can talk Epicureanism to. Strange, women seem to like De Maupin better than men, but it *is* a flawless piece of work.

I went over Swinburne's early "Rosamund" the other night. Wade's Tragedy which I have on the same subject, in mss., is a far finer piece of work.[2] Some day before Spring, I'll quote you the scene, all too brief, of the murder of

Rosamund by Elenor, the Queen. You can't conceive a more girlish piece of flowering beauty than Wade's heroine. Pity is the keynote of the entire scene. But Swinburne makes her as fierce as July sunshine and a bit too passionate.

Here's what I read recently:

Petronius (!!!)	The Satyricon (expurgated)
Conrad	The Rescue
	The Secret Agent
Lucian	Dialogues (early ed.)

Sterling's "Rosamund" is a fine tragedy. He went directly to the Elizabethans for his inspiration and he didn't go in vain.

I have ordered that book on Baudelaire by Gautier and Guy Thorne which we tried to find a few years ago—am I right?—it should come to you in a month unless sold.

I think you are right about Max Beerbohm's work. Somehow, I [do]n't realise the tremendous wit in it that most people see, myself—I suppose it is there, however, rarified to the fourth dimension.

More later.

Tuissimus,

Sam

1537 East 93 St., Suite 2.

Found a copy of "Jurgen"—guess, for how much—two dollars!

P.S. Do you wear glasses. I know what a nuisance they are [but] they would save you a lot of misery. I am very near sighted and have had to wear them half my life. Yet three feet away from me—a blur or twilight.

Do something with O'Brien again.

Notes

1. Lewis Piaget Shanks, *Anatole France* (1919). See further letter 299n1.
2. SL refers to Swinburne's verse drama *Rosamund, Queen of the Lombards* (1899) and Thomas Wade's *Rosamond: A Tragedy* (1830), translated from the German of Theodore Körner.

[295] [ALS, JHL]

Dec. 6th, 1920.

Dear Sam:

The doctor has ordered me to stay in bed for a few days, but I'm disobeying him long enough to write you this letter. I disgraced myself by collapsing in public yesterday, and had to be carried home. I'm better to-day, but still a bit weak. I dare say it's my old nervous trouble,—with a few new and quite unmentionable symptoms.

Fortunately, my eyes are better, and I can read a little. I read Adams' novel, but really didn't care much for it, except in spots. Yes, I received "Resurrection,"[1] and purpose to look it over before long. Conrad's "The Rescue," which you mention, is a fine book.

All I know of Casanova is from Havelock Ellis' essay.[2] The man certainly does seem to have "gone the limit" in sexual matters. But, after all, should one blame him? It's a generous vice. To me, gluttony and avarice are the only intolerable vices.

I've not heard from George for months, and have an intuition that matters are not well with him. Margaret Nic[h]ol hinted as much. Prohibition (and prohibition booze!) is terrible for a man who has drunk heavily for many years. He needs a certain amount of alcohol to keep him normal. And the stuff they sell now is worse than squirrel-poison! (You'd appreciate the comparison if you knew the dope that farmers put in ground squirrel-holes to asphyxiate the creatures.)

Write soon, if you can.

Affectionately,

Clark

Notes

1. By Leo Tolstoy.
2. "Casanova," in *Affirmations* 86–130.

[296] [ALS]

Dec. 9th, 1920

Dear Sam:

I've been laid up, as I wrote you in my last letter, but am better to-day. Perhaps I'd feel quite well, if it weren't for the beastly weather—such incessant, blithering, idiotic rain, day after day, week after week, is new in my experience. No one has come to see me since my break-down, and I don't blame them very much. One can scarcely put his nose outside the door without being drenched.

I had a letter from Mihan yesterday, enclosing O'Brien's report on the "H. E." I am sending it on to you; as you will notice, it requires no comment. I'll mail the poem to Mrs Meynell before long.

Mrs. S. writes me from Los Angeles. There's nothing at all to be done with my drawings. I'll have them back before long, and will divvy up with you.

My eyes are better, but I'm too nervous to read with any pleasure. Helas! what a life!

How are things with you? I suppose our weather isn't a circumstance to the usual winter in Cleveland.

Tell Kirk to write me—I'd like to hear from him.

Aff.,

Clark.

[297] [ALS]

Dec. 19th, 1920.

Dear Sam:

Your two postcards have come. It's just as well you *didn't* send me a telegram—I live outside the town, beyond the regular delivery-limits, and never receive telegrams till they're stale. Besides, there was nothing to worry about. . . . I don't feel very well, it's true; but I'm fairly certain there's no organic malady. I broke down with an accumulation of worries and disappointments; but things are a little better now.

I received a letter from Sterling yesterday. He had heard of my illness, it seems. He tells me there is some possibility of "Rosamund" being made into a "film." Also, "Lilith" may be put on the stage in a modified form. Ruth St. Denis[1] has taken a fancy to it.

No news worth recording—only trivialities. I've had a pretty quiet time—two visitors in the past two weeks! But the ferocious weather is partly to blame. Mrs. Rockwell (whom I mentioned before) was one of my visitors. The other was the Rev. Fenton-Smith. An odd pair of friends for me to have; but both of them are English (Mrs. R., I believe, was born in London.)

Hope you've received the box of mistletoe that I sent you. I included a few manzanita bells—they are coming out months ahead of time this year. We ought to have an early spring; and certainly I look forward to the springtime. I have never loved the winter. Rain is particularly hateful to me—I am like a cat, and don't like to get wet!

I'll write again when I get your letter. I thought I wouldn't wait for it.

Aff.,

Clark.

Notes

1. Ruth Saint Denis (1879–1968), a modern dance pioneer.

[298] [ALS]

East Auburn, Cal.,
Dec. 22nd, 1920.

Dear Sam:

Certainly—send a letter to "The Freeman," if you like. It can do no harm. But I fear that my poetry has as much chance with the public (and the publishers) as a lyre bird would have in the Arctic. . . . However, I shall send a lot of my stuff to London, when the holidays are over. Sterling said he would urge Robertson to publish it, later on . . . But I've had enough of Robertson, and would rather print it myself (or even let you print it, as you so generously offer.) Perhaps I'll have a little money, some day. . . . I might marry a moving-picture actress!

I feel as well as ever, to-day; there was nothing wrong but my nerves . . . Too much virtue, too much temperance, I dare say.

I've heard of that new book by Saltus. Have just been reading Huneker's autobiography, "Steeplejack." There are many good things in it. I remember one bit, where he speaks of Chopin's death. "The combination of consumption and George Sand would have killed Casanova!" . . . I think you told me you had been reading Casanova's Memoirs.

Hope you got the mistletoe I sent you. It is very plentiful here.

  Aff.,

    Clark.

[299] [ALS]

                 Dec. 29th, 1920

Dear Sam:

    I've been enjoying the two books immensely—in especial, the delicate irony and pathos of certain tales in Lemaitre's volume. The first two, "Serenus," and ["]Myrrha," are my favourites so far. "Myrrha," is unforgettable—it haunts me like the memory of some bizarre and mystic dream.

I like the book on France, too—on the whole, it seems a fair summary of his work. The writer seems more than a bit prudish, though—he balks at the mild and harmless fescenninities of "Jacques Tournebroche." I don't understand the attitude.[1]

I am quite well again: my breakdown seems to have done me good, by temporarily easing the strain I was under.

Ye gods! I have another birthday next month! . . . Birthdays are a bore after one is twenty-five; after forty-five, I suppose they are worse than a bore. But perhaps I shall welcome mine . . . The end of one more futile and wasted year.

I don't seem able to write at present; when I write again, it may be something quite different from my past work. I seem to be changing a little—I am growing more observant, more analytical, and find myself studying the people about me as I never did before. I am developing a more positive, more aggressive attitude, though I can't lose, and never will lose, a lurking sense of the universal vanity, the ineluctable boredom and corruption that lie in wait for all beauty and love; and a sense of the horrible readiness with which the thrill of pleasure sharpens to a pang. . . . But one must live, though life be no more than a daily dying.

Pardon the platitudes. They've been sitting on my chest for the last few days. . . . On the whole, I believe I am getting "healthier."

I expect a letter from you any time.

Aff.,

Clark.

[Enclosures? TMSs. of "Le Beau Navire" (Baudelaire), "Les Metamorphoses du Vampire" (Baudelaire), "XXVI" (Baudelaire), "Le Refuge."]

Notes

1. Shanks states that *Les Contes de Jacques Tournebroche* (1909) demonstrates that "even an artistic nature may be swept away by his rollicking humor into a license which ceases to be unconscious and innocent upon the lips of a modern" (202).

[300] [ALS]

Jan. 7th, 1921

Dear Sam:

Things are much as usual here, except that we've had three fair days in succession. Ice and frost, though; but I don't mind a little cold—anything is preferable to the Acheronian murk of the long mid-winter rains.

I am sure that Huysmans' books would interest me greatly, if you can spare them. . . . I shall appreciate "The Imperial Orgy."

I have just ordered a few books—the first I've been able to afford for a long time. Four of them are Modern Library volumes: Loti's "Madame Chrysantheme," ["]Smoke", by Turgenev, "A Bed of Roses", by W. L. George, and "Beyond Good and Evil."[1] Also I'm investing in a two-volume history of Chinese Art.[2] The illustrations ought to be worth the price—there are 240 of them.

A letter from Sterling in to-day's mail. . . . He tells me that Mrs. Meynell is a bigot—she even stopped her subscription to "The Sonnet," because of his (Sterling's) irreligious sonnet "To Science!" I fear I've put my foot in it by sending her *my* stuff . . . Somehow, I had gotten the idea that she was quite liberal, as so many Catholics are. . . . Helas! what a world! I seem to be "getting in bad," whichever way I turn.

A. writes me that she has been offered a fabulous sum for the film-rights of "Madeleine," but will probably refuse the offer: She's afraid the producers would give it a salacious twist. . . . Personally, I think the public deserves all it gets, in that line.

I've a letter from Kirk, also. . . . Tell him I'll write presently.

Aff.,

Clark.

Notes

1. By Nietzsche.

2. Possibly Ernest F. Fenollosa, *Epochs of Chinese and Japanese Art: An Outline History of East Asiatic Design* (London: Heinemann, 1912; rev. ed. 1921; 2 vols.).

[301] [ALS]

East Auburn, Cal.,
Jan. 21st, 1921.

Dear Sam:

Got the parcel of books yesterday, and will write you at length tomorrow. I've been looking for a letter from you, but won't wait any longer.

We've had another week of stormy weather, and I've spent the time indoors with my painting—chiefly water-colours. You will like some of the pictures: I'll send them on in time.

Hastily,

Clark.

[302] [ALS]

Jan. 25th, 1921

Dear Sam:

I enjoyed the "Reminiscences of Tolstoi." Some of the utterances that Gorki records are better than anything I remember from Tolstoi's writings. The book gives me a new, different, and much more favourable impression of T. I never cared much for any of his books, with the exception of "Anna Karenina."

"The Fleece of Gold"[1] is a beautiful story. I am glad to have the translations by Cranmer-Byng—I won't have to borrow Dewing's copies any more!

Have you read "The Chartreuse of Parma?" I got hold of a copy some time ago, and found it excellent, but not extraordinary. Huneker's eulogy of Stendhal[2] had led me to look for too much, I suppose.

I've read some good novels lately—"Of Human Bondage," by Somerset Maugham, and "A Bed of Roses," by W. L. George. I advise you to read these, if you haven't done so already. I'm inclined to prefer George, of these two novelists, though Maugham is tremendously clever. Both are infinitely superior to the Wells–Galsworthy–Bennet[t] school of English novelists.

I feel dull and tired, after a debauch of painting, and I'm afraid it shows in this letter. But, really, there's nothing to write about. . . . I feel bored and unhappy, except when I'm reading, or working out a new colour-scheme.

Mihan (whom you will remember) has sent a copy of "The Hashish-Eater" to James Branch Cabell.[3] C. is one of the few people in America who might appreciate the poem. . . . Mihan, by the way, has experimented with hashish himself, and thinks that I've "hit off" the effect of the drug to perfection!

  I look for a letter from you any day.

Affectionately,

Clark.

Notes

1. By Gautier.

2. "A Sentimental Education: Henry Beyle–Stendhal," in *Egoists* 1–65.

3. The twelve-page typescript, inscribed to Cabell, is among Cabell's papers at the University of Virginia Library in Charlottesville.

[303] [TLS]

[c. 12 February 1921]

Dear Clark,

  Kirk tells me that you are wondering and worrying at my silence. . . . I'll try to remedy matters in the future. This has been the worst winter I've ever experienced financially, and for a time my "nerves" went back on me and I could barely form words on paper. I don't know whether you have ever experienced anything of the sort, but it's hell on earth to have it. After this—look for a letter twice or three times a week, at least. I read "somedel" [*sic*] during my silence.

  I would like to see some of the new pictures you mention, also I'm anxious to know if you have written any poetry. I broke my silence so far as creative work has concerned a week ago when I began an idealistic poem entitled "Hermaphroditus"—it is not obscene but a narration in beautiful words of this creature who was worshipped in the old Greek and Asian cities, buried at Pergamon, then dug up during the Italian Renaissance.[1] . . . and again the recrudescence of the idea during modern times. You will like it and I shall send it on as soon as it is completed.

  Blunden's Book "John Clare: Poems Chiefly from Mss." is out in England and I have it here. A second copy is to come for you which I shall post as soon as it arrives. I am mentioned in the preface and some use has been put of my information in the interesting introduction.[2] This volume contains nearly forty new Asylum poems. Frankly, I think Clare as great an English poet as Blake or Wordsworth, and the English reviewers of the book seem to feel identically so. It took them a long time to find this out. . . . but how many years ago was it my dear friend, Clark, that I first called your attention to it? . . . .

  I've been reading Philostratus' "Life of Apollonius of Tyana," this being the biography in which Keats's Lamia myth occurs. You will find much of Apollonius in Flaubert's "Temptation"—but Anthony is a bit unjust to the man who was Christlike, startlingly so! It (the Life) has, strangely enough, inspired me to finish "The Sphinx."

I would—I can't tell you how much—like to get out to California this Spring!

Kirk sent you or is sending you, Louys' "Aphrodite" . . . I hope that [you li]ke it. I did not read the book but was a bit prejudiced on acc[ount of the] tremendous publicity given to it when it visited Cleveland in drah-mah form. The spectacle of a woman in supposed nudity drew people by the thousands.

Another letter shortly. Will you write? And believe me as always

Affectionately

Sam

1537 East 93 St., Suite 2

Keats died 100 years ago this month, the 23rd.

[Envelope postmarked Cleveland, Ohio, Feb. 12, 1921.]

Notes

1. Hermaphroditus was the two-sexed child of Hermes and Aphrodite. A life-size sculpture of Hermaphroditus from Pergamon stands in the İstanbul Archaeology Museum.
2. "Valuable help, too, has been given by Mr. Samuel Loveman of Cleveland, Ohio, who has placed at our disposal his collection of Clare MSS." (5).

[304] [ALS]

East Auburn,
Feb. 16th, 1921.

Dear Sam:

I was overjoyed to receive your letter yesterday. I knew that something must have gone wrong. I'm sorry to hear of that nervous complaint—I've had similar symptoms, and know the particular hellishness of such.

I might have written you before, but had nothing good to offer. Indeed, I've little news of any sort.

I'm expecting my mss. back any time: Wilfrid Meynell[1] writes me that Mrs. Meynell is a confirmed invalid, and hence is unable to even read my poems. Also, she is not in touch with any publisher to whom she could delegate the task.

I hardly know where to turn next. Is it worth while to try the Four Seas Co? You gave me their address, but I've mislaid it.

I'll send the drawings on next week. I'm keeping them to show to some ladies who are interested in my work.

I've been reading Rabelais, who takes me back to my school-days: No one but a school boy could rival such excessive and gratuitous filth. The effect should be highly moral, to my adult mind. The work of Rabelais is diametrically opposite to such a book as "Aphrodite," which I read many years ago in Sterling's library at Carmel. But I'm afraid that I prefer "Aphrodite"— it's much pleasanter reading.

The Rabelais belongs to Dewing, who, by the way, is to be confirmed as a member of the Episcopal church next Sunday! An amazing step, since he believes as little as I do, and openly avows his disbelief! D. is a queer kid— very much of the same temperament as Verlaine, in some ways.

I'm inclined to agree with you about John Clare. There are poems of his that one could set beside anything of Wordsworth or Blake. But I confess that both of the latter two seem vastly over-rated to me—Wordsworth in particular. However, it's all a matter of taste. Clare certainly had a great endowment, though many of his poems are not great. However, one could say the same of almost any other poet. Clare deserves immortality and a definite place in the hierarchy of English verse.

I've not written anything, but may pitch in and do some prose. I've ideas for several stories—of the "Smart Set" type! My women-friends are all urging me to write prose. Women are certainly practical!

Another letter in a few days.

   Aff.,

     Clark.

Notes

1. Wilfrid Meynell (1852–1948), English newspaper publisher and editor, and husband of Alice Meynell, who sometimes wrote under the pseudonym John Oldcastle.

[305] [TLS]

              [21? February 1921]

Dear Clark,

   Thought you might write this week but no letter came, but I did want to hear from you. I am still out of work, funds very low, and pretty disheartened—myself, not the funds. There are over an hundred thousand people out of work in the city, most of them able-bodied and anxious to work.

I've had an opportunity to read an advance copy of Symons' new work, just published in England: "Baudelaire, A Study", the most amazing of his many books. When it comes here I'll send one to you. . . . I still remember the Saltus! The Baudelaire book, by the way, is the most immoral book ever written concerning a man of great genius by a man of genius. Immoral. . . . in the bourg[e]ois and as directly antagonistic to the Baudelarian [*sic*] sense of averages. The thing is disjointed and in fact merely a grouping of notes—but what notes!

One chapter on the effects of Opium and Hashisch is finer than anything in and out of De Quincey. Your poem alone compares with it, and your poem is a masterpiece. There are passages that make me inclined to believe that Symons has been reading Saltus—with admiration. You will recollect his note on Saltus in Vanity Fair. The volume is heavily illustrated: Baudelaire and Jenny by Baudelaire, Manet, Courbet, facsimiles of the title-pages, of his mss., and an amazing bibliography and note on the portraits. I'm awaiting an early publication here.

Kirk has loaned me Carl Van Vechten "The Merry-go-Round." This contains a fifty-page critical appreciation of Saltus—and did you know—Saltus has written nearly or possibly over, thirty volumes. I remember wondering over your admiration of Saltus many years ago Clark, but I learned since that time that your appreciative leanings were infallibly to be depended upon. And in the past few years the "rare booksellers" seem to have found out just what a treasure-trove his scarce books are. Prices go commandeering and radiantly high.

Clark [*sic*] procured for me some time ago Wade's "The Phrenologist[s]", a farce published in 1830, very slight, but Forman states in his note on Wade that the thing is nearly introuvable.[1] This is Forman's copy. By the way, my mss play of his is mentioned in the Encyclopedia Brittanica.[*sic*]

Please write. I'll do so this middle-week. Don't neglect me. I seem to be enisled in solitariness.

Affectionately,

Sam

1537 East 93 St., Suite 2

[Envelope postmarked Cleveland, Ohio, 21 February 1921.] [envelope placed here conjecturally]

Notes

1. See H. Buxton Forman's essay on Thomas Wade in *Literary Anecdotes of the Nineteenth Century:* "So hard is it to find that Wade's widow was unable to say whether it had ever been printed or not" (51).

[306] [ANS][1]

[Postcard enclosed in envelope:] The statue on the other side is Rodin's "Age of Bronze"—wonderful! but they were afraid to photograph it separately for their series of postcards (I believe) on account of its nudity!

[Envelope postmarked Cleveland, Ohio, Feb. 23, 1921.]

294 ❦ *Born under Saturn*

Notes

1. *Front*: The Cleveland Museum of Art. 19B1304. "The Man of the Age of Bronze."

[307] [ALS]

Feb. 26th, 1921.

Dear Sam:

I wrote you a week ago, and hope my letter has come "to hand" by now. Yours arrived yesterday, but I shouldn't have waited for it. I'll write you twice a week in future.

I'm dreadfully sorry that conditions are so unfavourable with you. Things aren't so bad in California—at least, in small towns like Auburn.

Symon[s]'s book should be the book on Baudelaire. There never was, and never will be, any one better fitted to appreciate B. than Symons. *Is* the book "immoral?" I've almost forgotten what the word means. One must think (and live) beyond good and evil. There is no deadlier slough than the slough of respectability. Save your soul alive—even if you must lose your "reputation!"

Strange that you should be so isolated, in a big city. Things are "picking up" a little for me in that respect—I have at least the nucleus of a "circle," in Dewing and Mrs. Rockwell. There are others—two or three women, at least—whom I mean to cultivate. I encourage people to borrow my books. "The Garden of Epicurus" is in great demand at present—it was borrowed yesterday for the third time . . . This neighborhood will be fit to live in, by the time I am through corrupting it.

I wish you were here—I did hope you would be able to make it this spring. Everything is so lovely now, with the first clear weather, and the coming of the first flowers . . . Helas! if I were only rich!

Auburn (have I told you before?) is quite a "literary" center now. There are several people who write, including Jackson Gregory, a popular novelist, whose books are on the order of Zane Grey and Harold Bell Wright.[1] G. has at least one recommendation—a charming wife![2] The English portrait-painter, Herman Herkomer,[3] lives near Auburn, too. A nice chap, though I don't care greatly for his paintings. Mrs. Herkomer, by the way, is a sister of the actress Mary Anderson.[4] And there is a French actress who has come to live in Auburn—a Madame Jeanne Benedict, late of the Comedie Francaise.[5]

I hope all this doesn't bore you too much. From ennui, if from no other reason, I have begun to study the people about me. Who knows—I may write a realistic novel some day!

Give my best to George Kirk.

Affectionately,

Clark.

Notes

1. Zane Grey (1872–1939), American dentist and author best known for his popular adventure novels and stories associated with the Western genre. For Harold Bell Wright (1872–1944), see letter 205n1.

2. CAS later wrote an introduction to *Shadow of Wings* (1930) by Gregory's sister, Susan Myra Gregory (d. 1939).

3. Herman Gustave Herkomer (1865–1935), Californian painter of portraits and interiors. His wife was Blanch (1872–1961)

4. Mary Anderson (1859–1940), American stage actress.

5. Jeanne Farnes Benedict, French stage actress.

[308] [ALS]

March 1st, 1921

Dear Sam:

I've been reading (or re-reading) "Aphrodite," which seems much less immoral to me than it did when I first read it eight or nine years ago. Indeed, it is not immoral at all, and portions of it are very beautiful. Kirk also sent me the "Dialogues of Lucian," another privately printed book.

I've read my eyes out, during the last few weeks. A lot of stuff from the public library—"Tess of the Durbervilles," "The King in Yellow" (one of R. W. Chambers' earlier and more artistic efforts,) and "Bella Donna," by Robert Hichens, to name only a few. Hichens seems to be obsessed by a particular situation—in several of his books, the heroine is an Englishwoman (usually married) who goes to Italy or Egypt, or Morocco, and gets embroiled with a native. H., however, has written one really great book, "The Garden of Allah" . . . Also, I've tried to read a book of essays by G. E. Woodberry, but found it full of Puritanism and academic dry-rot. I was antagonized by the fol-de-rol about the morality of art in an essay on English poetry—and felt disgusted when I found an unsympathetic reference to Milton's Satan. It's hard to understand an attitude that denies the heroism of Satan.

I'll send you a bunch of drawings before the end of the week. I'm specializing on vampires at present! I want to do some drawings from life—I know several women who would make interesting models.

Aff.,

Clark.

[309] [ALS]

March 7th, 1921

Dear Sam:

Please pardon my delay in sending you the drawings I promised: I've loaned all my best ones to a friend who wishes to exhibit them at an art-club in

Sacramento, the state-capital. I didn't think she would want so many—she called for the drawings while I was out, and fairly looted my collection!

I suppose you've not forgotten my experience with the Hargen's Bookshop. Well, I've some funny news for you: Mrs. Hemphill,[1] the lady to whom I have just loaned my drawings, was in at Hargen's some time ago, and took occasion to rake them over for their treatment of me. So many people have inquired for my drawings, that Mrs Hargens has changed her mind, and wants to know if it is possible to get them back!

What do you think I have been reading? Leo Mihan has loaned me an old, forgotten book, with the same title as my poem, "The Hashish-Eater." It was published by Harpers in 1857, under the pseudonym of "The Pythagorean."[2] It is finely written, with an obvious echo of De Quincey, and contains many tremendous passages. It is evidently a record of personal experience. I'll copy a paragraph or two from it in my next.

I enclose a little appreciation of John Clare, clipped from the "Manchester Guardian." It is significant, don't you think?

　　　Aff.,
　　　　　Clark.

Notes

1. Vivia (Hector) Hemphill (1882–1934).
2. The book is by Fitz Hugh Ludlow.

[310] [ALS]

　　　　　　　　　　　　　　　　　　　March 13th, 1921

Dear Sam:

　　　I'm glad to hear that you are going on with "The Sphinx," and hope you will finish it this time. Wish I had the energy to work; but I feel too discouraged and demoralized at present.

I don't know why G. S. should be shocked by "The Sphinx.["] I don't suppose he'll care for certain phases of the paganism embodied in it; but neither do I, for that matter. Which doesn't prevent me from admiring the play, and thinking it a great thing. I fail to see why any rational being should be shocked by it.

I, too, have the reputation of being shy and unsociable. But I am not really so by nature; ill-health and unfavourable circumstances have made me seem that way in the past. Latterly I've grown afraid of solitude, and am cultivating everyone who seems even half-way congenial.

Most of my neighbors (the Dewings and the Rockwells, at any rate) have been laid up with the "flu" during the past fortnight. I escaped, by some miracle; or perhaps I've developed an immunity to "bugs" of that sort.

I expect a number of visitors next week. . . . I'll send you a batch of the drawings when V. H. returns them.

       Aff.,

           Clark.

[311] [ALS]

                     East Auburn, Cal.

                     March 20th, 1921.

Dear Sam:

      It's good to hear from you again, and to receive the poem ("To Satan".) I like the idea of your ode; but certain lines, especially in the third stanza, seem obscurely expressed. I am curious to see the Debs poem; you quoted a striking stanza from it once.

Mrs Hemphill writes me that the exhibition of my drawings was a great success. The Kingsley Art-Club (a woman's club) wants to keep them for two weeks, in a display open to the public. It's a good idea, and may lead to something. As to the Hargens crowd—I want nothing more to do with them.

The Herkomers dined with us last Thursday, on the fortieth anniversary of my father's departure from England. They have a hundred-acre fruit-ranch seven or eight miles from us. H. seems to have given up his portrait-painting. He likes California, but his wife, I think, merely endures it. H. looks like a German baron, and his wife is somewhat of the Mary Garden type—tall, and statuesque, and with an imposing style of feature.[1]

Friday, I met Madame Benedict—another feminine exile, whom I may have mentioned to you before. She is a Parisian actress who married an American officer. Her husband is now in the real-estate business—the chief industry of Auburn! There are a dozen such, who divide the spoils of the incoming strangers. Madame, of course, is already sighing for Paris, after a month or two of Auburn. She is charming, though not dangerously so—at least, not to me! Or perhaps I am interested in too many others!

Kirk is a royal fellow—I certainly look forward to that book on Baudelaire. I have been designing a book-plate for him—a small return for the treasures he sends me. I wonder if he will like it—it represents a nude woman dancing on a salver upheld by two dog-headed monsters—also nude. It should be appropriate for many books, though not for everything. One ought to have several book-plates, and fit the plate to the book.

You shall have some more drawings as soon as possible.

Cleveland must be a perfect hell-hole, and I wish you could get out of it. But it's been a hard year everywhere—I am told there are bread-lines in S. F., though one sees nothing about it in the papers. Things are not so bad here in the country.

       Aff., Clark.

Notes

1. Mary Garden (1874–1967), Scottish operatic soprano with a substantial career in France and America in the first third of the 20th century.

[312] [TLS]

[March 1921]

Dear Clark,

Spring has come early this year; all the trees and bushes are beginning to bud—somehow one tries to throw off the winter's depression, but not altogether successfully.

I was with Kirk all afternoon. We talked about you, about Sterling. George is going into the rare book business—by mail-order. He is preparing a catalogue which is to contain many of the things he has and after advertising in a few of the papers, expects to get a list of names of prospective purchasers. I think well of the plan, which under ordinary circumstances might go big—nowadays, I dunno. I don't know whether you have followed that particular industry, but it is a big one. People who collect are to be found everywhere. The profits are big. Of late, I've been drifting away from the thing, but I want to see George succeed and am going to help him prepare the catalogue. He mentioned boosting your books and George's. Remember this, Clark—posterity usually does the right thing for men of your type and genius—but it's the rare bookseller who gives them the money and present popularity. Witness Conrad—some of his volumes sell for fifty dollars. Recently, they unearthed a fake forging process on his title-pages in London!

I think you are right about "The Sphinx." Recently, I had a mind to destroy it and was going to ask you to do the same.

I blew myself to a ticket for the great spectacle, "Mecca" tomorrow. It contains the wonderful Russian ballet by Fokine[1]—I love those things, the colour, the rhythm, and the posturing of the performers. I want something to take away my depression. Recently, Clark, I thought of—well, you know what people do when the darkness becomes impenetrable. I am so glad to hear that you meet more folk and take more pleasure in society. I wish I didn't see through people so easily. That also, is vanity!

Affectionately,

Sam

1537 East 93 St., Suite 2.

Notes

1. *Mecca,* a musical set in Egypt a thousand years before, was a musical in two acts,

that opened on Broadway on 4 October 1920 and closed 22 January 1921. SL saw it in Cleveland. Michael Fokine (1880–1942), Russian choreographer who choreographed *The Firebird* (1910) and *Petrushka* (1912) for Igor Stravinsky, along with many other works.

[313] [ALS]

East Auburn, Cal.
March 28th, 1921.

Dear Sam:

Bully for Kirk—I think the rare-book business is just the thing for him. Perhaps I can drum up a little trade. I know a lady who wanted to get the John Martin edition of "Paradise Lost."

I'll mail you some drawings in a day or two—I have them back now. The display in Sacramento was much praised and admired.

I spent yesterday (Easter Sunday) with Mrs. Hemphill, and went with her to Sacramento to get the pictures. They were well-mounted, and hung in a good light, which brought many of them out in a way that surprised me. I didn't think it would make so much difference in the effect.

Mrs. Hemphill (have I told you about her?) is a very unusual type—in fact, I have never known anyone at all like her. She has the features of an Egyptian sorceress—dark hair and eyes, and a long, slender face, slightly flattened in profile, with curious and obliquely-curved eyebrows. She is a true pagan, and we are absolutely congenial. I feel fortunate in having such a friend.

My dear Sam, I never meant to imply any strictures on "The Sphinx," and I have no intention of destroying my copy of it! Few things have been written that mirror the pagan world so well. Of course, it is not the sort of thing to be published broadcast—but neither is that glorious book, "Aphrodite." You should print it privately, some time, when you are able to again.

I hope you've had better luck by now. I, too, am up against it, financially. I think of picking fruit this season, to earn a little money . . . Hell, damnation, and the pitchforks of Satan! What a detestable nuisance it all is.

Dewing took his first communion yesterday, as a member of the Episcopal church. Today, he came and borrowed "Aphrodite." Golly, what a life! I hope you still have a sense of humour. Mine is wonderfully revived, of late.

Affectionately,
Clark.

[314] [ALS]

April 2nd, 1921

Dear Sam:

I am sorry to hear of your continued depression—strange, how our positions have become reversed! Yes, indeed, I remember how you used to remonstrate with me, for my pessimism! But remember that nothing endures, not even pain or melancholia. For years—nay, three years ago, my only desire was the longing for death—all happiness, all success, all good things, seemed impossible to me. Now, (as you surmise) I am healthier and happier than at any previous time in my life. I wish I could help you. At least, I can urge you to stick it out. One never knows what may happen . . . It hurts me unexpressibly to feel that I **can** do nothing to help you. Your idea for "The Hermaphrodite" is a beautiful one, and certainly original. I like it, and am curious to see the poem.

Herkomer *is* a Clevelander, as I discovered recently, but comes of English stock. His father and grandfather were both painters. His work is technically perfect, but he lacks the imagination and insight necessary to a good portrait-painter. I shouldn't care to have him paint me—no ordinary artist could do it well.

I have been doing a little work—some Egyptian heads for Mrs. Hemphill. I have some drawings laid aside for you, and will try to mail them Monday.

      Aff.,

           Clark.

[315] [ALS]

                          April 7th, 1921.

Dear Sam:

      I mailed you a batch of drawings early in the week, and trust they will reach you safely. I'll send Kirk his book-plate in a day or two.

I've looked for a letter from you. I worry about you when I don't hear for such long intervals. I hope that matters are no worse, at any rate.

The Muse is still reluctant—she favours me only when I write illicit love-letters!

The weather is heavenly—the sort of weather they have in Cockaigne—and I never saw so many flowers, of all kinds. My friend from Roseville[1] was here yesterday, and we went out hunting for faun-lilies in the woods. The faun-lily is a delicate white blossom with a yellow center and spotted leaves. They are rare, and one finds them only on sheltered hillsides, among the pines.

I have been reading "Sylvie," a translation from de Nerval, and a book on "Bohemian Paris" by W. C. Morrow,—who also wrote "The Ape, the Idiot, and Other People," a book much in the taste and manner of Bierce. This Paris book is excellent, and moreover, is deliciously illustrated with sketches in pen and ink. Among many others, there is one of Verlaine sitting at a cafe-table with two ladies!

      Affectionately,

           Clark

Notes

1. I.e., Vivia Hemphill.

[316] [ALS]

April 13th, 1921

Dear Sam:

Your letter came last night. It's good to hear of your poetic industry—I particularly want to see that lyric about Lesbos.[1] I, too, have been writing; I may send you something presently, though most of what I am writing is not intended for publication!

I am to have an exhibition of drawings (the sixteen that Mrs. Hargens rejected) at the Art Department of the Public Library in Los Angeles. They are to remain on display for a month. Mrs. L., who is managing the exhibition, says that she is also going to "toot my horn" by lecturing on my poetry before several women's clubs.

"The Star-Treader" is likely to be a "rare book"! I have ordered some copies from my publisher, but can't get any response out of him. Possibly the book is out of print . . . Robertson reminds me of a paralyzed snail! I wish I could get someone else to bring out a new collection of the "S. T."

I have been trying to fight off a bad cold ever since Sunday. It's better today, but I am suffering from indigestion, and have had a beastly attack of heart-palpitation. Probably I'll feel all right in a couple more days—I'm planning to spend the week-end with my sorceress in Roseville; and go with her on Monday to a reception at the Kingsley Art Club, to which I am invited.

I mailed three drawings to George Kirk this forenoon. Hope you got the batch that I sent you last week.

Affectionately,
Clark.

Notes

1. Probably "Lineage."

[317] [TLS]

[April 1921?]

Dear Clark,

The drawings came—I was delighted with them. I feel at times, that I'm not worthy of the kindnesses and the way you single me out for these gifts. An awkward way of putting it—is it not?—yes. But I am going through a vast amount of buffeting these days. . . . Still up against it. This is now nearly three months in which I have not done a stroke of work, and as to my finances—O God! I sold my set of Burton's "Arabian Nights", 17 volumes, for twenty-five dollars, ten days ago. One must live, must one not? Kirk is cataloguing some of the folios. He has offered me money—but pride forbids. You see, Clark, added to my poetic temperament, there is this other curse—and curse it is!

There is an exhibition of original Mantegna engravings at the Museum which would do your soul good to see; included are some of the contemporary artists.[1] Two (one by Mantegna) represent a procession of Bacchus—but here is the most marvellous part. A Hermaphrodite follows them pouring the wine for the god. His breasts are globed like a woman's, wine seems to be pouring from them; the genitals are "half". But so marvellous is the artist's representation that the thing achieves itself simply as a thing of beauty. The other by a contemporary, shows the unveiling of Bacchus. Beautiful—the vine-leaves, the grapes, the significant gesture of the god. I mention these because I seem instinctively to have done the thing in poetry without consciously knowing why.

I hope you return to the writing of creative work again. I miss it. Don't—Clark—give it up for a mess of pottage. True, you have done enough to make the reputation of ten men—but how much more there is still in you!

I see Kirk nearly every day. We were down to Warren Ohio, together, a week ago Monday—but I was in one of my sulky, moody spells and probably spoilt the occasion. He went to see a bookseller there who has an immense stock. His catalogue went to press today. His advertisements have brought him a flood of correspondence, but whether the business will prove successful commercially, I know not. I'm a hell of a temperamental guy and ill indeed when it comes to business matters but I believe I gave him a great deal of assistance in the compilation of the catalogue.

Write soon. Morris (or Maurice Hewlett) quotes my Keats–Clare documents in the "Cornhill."[2]

Affectionately,
Sam

1537 East 93 St., Suite 2.

Notes

1. Andrea Mantegna (1431?–1506), Italian painter. The painting SL refers to is now titled *Bacchanal with a Wine Vat* (c. 1475).
2. Maurice Hewlett, "Clare's Derivations," *Cornhill Magazine* NS 50 (March 1921): 274–81; rpt. in *Wiltshire Essays* (London: Oxford University Press, 1921), 58–68. The article doesn't mention SL specifically, but it does mention the book *John Clare: Poems, Chiefly from Manuscript*, to which SL contributed material, as acknowledged on p. 5 therein.

[318] [ALS]

East Auburn, Cal.,
April 25th, 1921

Dear Sam:

It's good to know that you liked the pictures, and I wish that I could have spared you more of them. But I have not been producing so many of late.

I spent four days in Roseville last week, with the Hemphills, who are the most hospitable people I know. I even had breakfast in bed—think of it! I had a few adventures, too—I went to a reception at the Kingsley Art-Club, where I was the only man present, among forty or fifty women! . . . Also, I encountered several new varieties of home-brew, made friends with a ferocious black bull-dog, and met some curious people. Among the latter was a man at Rocklin—a repulsive old rouè, [*sic*] who owns a fine house, crammed like a museum with old furniture, paintings, vases, carpets, statuary, etc. The room that I liked best was devoted to Templewhite chairs and tables. He treated us to some rare old Marsala, and induced his pet peacock (the only one that I know of in this region) to perform,—vocally and otherwise—for our benefit. Personally, the man reminded me of an over-fed buzzard—he is one of the most repulsive beings I have ever met. But Mrs. H. insists that he has his good points—and he admires my poetry! . . . Does all this interest you? . . . I hope to have the material for a novel, some day, out of my own experiences, some of which are extremely curious,—and madly romantic.

As to selling out for a mess of pottage—I'm not likely to do that! Anyway, the pottage is not forthcoming, as yet. I'm poorer than ever, and will probably have to pick fruit, canvass for magazines, and do other odd jobs to scrape along . . . I hope the exhibition of my drawings in Los Angeles will lead to something—but you know what I'm up against in the way of a public. "The many-headed beast," will be suspicious of my smell for a long time to come.

But things are pleasanter for me than they have been, since, (as I told you before) I have made some new and devoted friends. It makes a difference.

Certainly, I shall go on writing—I may produce several more books before I decide to open my veins or quaff the hemlock . . . I'll have something for you in my next.

Why don't you let Kirk help you—money, it seems to me, is such a little thing compared with friendship . . . **I** have taken money from my friends. I lived on the bounty of a rich woman[1] for years, at the time my health failed—much as Francis Thompson did . . . But I understand your pride—and I suppose one can't argue with an instinct.

Good luck to you, and to George! Tell George to send me several copies (at least five) of his catalogue. I'll distribute them properly.

Aff.,

Clark.

P.S. Pardon the writing—I'm out of pens, and could find nothing but a superannuated stub!

Notes

1. Celia Tobin Clark (1874–1965), second wife of Charles Walker Clark (1871–1933). See *SU*157.

[319] [ALS]

Sunday
[2 May 1921?]

Dear Sam:

I meant to acknowledge the books before, but have been laid up with a severe cold—the second that I've caught within the month, after a winter of immunity!

Rockwell Kent's drawings are most remarkable—I think they impress me more every time I look at them. There are some that I don't care for—they seem repulsively formless and uncouth—but most of them are instinct with a novel power and beauty, together with a sense of the stark and the primitive that one seldom finds in art. The resemblance to Blake is obvious; but there is more "nature" in them than in Blake, it seems to me . . . I don't care so much for the journal, though it is undoubtedly a document of much interest and value.[1] Some of the Creole proverbs in "Ghombo [*sic*] Zhebes"[2] are delicious, and all of them are quaint. I am glad to have the book.

I've been writing a bit, and will try to enclose something with this— perhaps "The Litany of the Seven Kisses" (a somewhat inadequate number!) I have begun a series of "Psalms" in the Bible manner; but the context is nearer to that of the "Song of Solomon." I have also started a blank verse poem ("Antony to Cleopatra") and have numerous other projects.

I like some of the lyrics you send me. You have a delicate touch—like that of Heine, in some ways.

I have not read much, of late. I picked up Symons' poems this morning, and was much taken with "Rosa Alba,"[3] though it is no better than hundreds of others he has written . . . Different moods, different poems.

How are you? I've looked for a letter.

Give my best to George.

Aff.,

Clark.

Notes

1. *Wilderness: A Journal of Quiet Adventure in Alaska.*
2. I.e., *Gombo Zhèbes* by Lafcadio Hearn.

3. *Poems* 1.117.

[320] [ALS]

May 10th, 1921

Dear Sam:

I have been unwell—hence my delay in writing. My cold—a head-and-throat affair—, still hangs on.

I received the life of Apollonius, and am reading it with interest. I remember his appearance, together with Damis, in "The Temptation of St. Anthony." A strange and remarkable being, though I've no great enthusiasm for ascetics.

Kirk has sent me some of his catalogues, several of which I have distributed. His list is a select one, and I'd buy many of the items in it, if I had the money. I gave one of the catalogues to a woman whose favourite book is "Aphrodite!" I notice there is something by Luoys in the list.

I'll try to send you some more poetry before long. I feel demoralized at present—in every sense of the word.

Aff.,

Clark.

[321] [ALS]

May 14th, 1921

Dear Sam;

I am very sorry to hear that Kirk has been ill. I received the catalogues, and thought the list an admirable one.

I haven't written much, but hope to begin work seriously before long. My cold has helped to set me back—and I have had other distractions. I'll try to enclose something with this.

A. writes me that my pictures "are raising a riot" in Los Angeles. People are asking questions about them—and about the artist! Hell knows if it will lead to anything substantial, though; the professional art-critics (as might be expected) are ignoring the exhibition.

I have sent my new book to Boni & Liveright. One chance in many thousand, I suppose I've not much hope.

Am I right in inferring that things are a little better with you? I hope so.

This is no letter. I've had a run of restless nights, and feel about as lively and brilliant as a stuffed owl. I'll try to write you a real letter before long.

Aff.,

Clark.

[322] [ALS]

May 21st, 1921

Dear Sam:

Forgive my silence—I am still a bit unwell. The weather has been cold and wet—a most phenomenal thing for this time of year—and I don't seem to get rid of my cold. Nothing to worry about, though,—everybody has been having one.

Here are some verses for you. I have been scribbling, and have others that I'll send later—You'll remember that I once threatened to write a volume of erotic verse. I'll fulfill the threat, if I keep on at the present rate!

Had a letter from Sterling the other day. He seems happy,—and is writing love-poems, too.

This is a note: I seem capable of nothing more. Apart from the cold, I have been under a heavy nervous strain—and I collapse at times.

All my friends here have had colds! Mrs. Hemphill was coming down with one when she last wrote me . . . D—n this weather!!!

Tell Kirk to write me—I'd love to hear from him. I, too am so glad that we met. He is unique, I think at least, I have never met anyone at all like him.

Good luck to you, my friend! I've looked for a letter from you.

Aff.,

Clark.

[323] [ALS]

June 9th, 1921

Dear Sam:

I've not heard from you for over a month, and am beginning to wonder (and worry) about your silence. Have you written me? The mail-service here is none too reliable.

There isn't much news—at least, nothing sensational. I am in splendid health (physically, at least) and am writing a little. But boredom has me by the throat at present—all my affairs are "hung up"—and nothing seems to happen . . . How is it with you? I shall feel anxious till I hear . . . I have not heard from Kirk, either.

Sterling asked about you in his last letter. He had not heard from you for a long time.

Here are some of my new verses . . . "Ebony and Crystal" *will* be published, sooner or later: I have a friend who will either put up the money herself, or find someone else who can . . . Boni and Liveright rejected the book without reading it, and I shan't bother to send it out any more.

The tiger-lilies are coming out—gorgeous and barbaric as the flame of yellow torches, on the dead hill-sides. I wish you could see them.

A new magazine, "The Lyric West," devoted entirely to verse, has been started in Los Angeles. I *gave* them a few poems; they can't afford to pay at present.

>Affectionately,
>Clark.

[324] [TLS]

[Summer 1921?]

Dear Clark,

After nearly two months of inaction I've taken my typewriter out again, dusted it off and proceed to write my first letter to you. If only you knew the tragedy behind this first sentence!

Will you, Clark, agree to take up the thread where we dropped it so many weeks ago and forgive—as well as forget. For six months I've done only ten days of work, sold many of my books, and those that I retain have barely looked into. Recently, I borrowed a bunch of Beethoven records, and lo! the apathy of so many months is beginning to disappear—I believe I want to do things again. Something in the music, as beautiful as anything in the old Greek world brought me back again.[1]

I'll write you two or three times a week after this—only do you also write to me and tell me that you bear no offence against my silence.

Sunday I want to mail you a thing or two that I did before that period, also to write a letter to George Sterling. I've had a desire recently to review his two plays for "The Double Dealer" of New Orleans, also your poems for that periodical—they seem to be fair in their acceptance of mss.

This has been the hottest and most disagreeable summer since I can recollect and for two or three weeks I was ill with desperate nervous attacks. Kirk, I see—he took me out rowing yesterday in a terrific gale on the lake. His business has been coming on in dribbles, but nothing noticeably prosperous as yet. He has some fine things, however for the next catalogue. A Swinburne first of the Poems and Ballads, Simeon Solomon's "Vision" inscribed to Swinburne, etc.

I read "Oscar Wilde: Three Times Tried",[2] a complete stenographic report of the proceedings recently. He seems to have been completely in the hands of a group of blackmailers. O these beautiful laws! Here in Cleveland, a marvellous murderess who fits far better in the Renaissance than in her present surroundings is being tried for the murder of her husband, a wealthy man. First, a connivance with a local fortune teller to have the spirits do away with him, failed. Then came strychnine, with equal results—the man refused to attend his own funeral—after that two Italian braves were hired and he was stabbed twenty times. So, they torture the poor thing when her only outlet had been a remarkable display of originality in making away with a brute who probably deserved it.

I'll have a package of books for you by early next week—promised, I believe, a long time ago. Write soon. More in a day or two. With best wishes to you all from

Affectionately

Sam

Cleopatra is beautiful. The H.E. still stands supreme.

Notes

1. See "Comment," *Saturnian* No. 3.
2. By Christopher Sclater Millard.

[325] [ALS]

July 23rd, 1921

Dear Sam:

There is absolutely nothing to forgive—on my part, at least. I thought of writing you several times, in the past six weeks, and regret now that I kept putting it off: I feared that matters were not well with you.

I, too, have been unwell—a desperate cold, to mention nothing else. It's the third one I have caught this year; I must be run down, or I wouldn't get them so easily.

I was in San Francisco for a week early in the month, and saw Sterling several times. He writes a poem every morning! He asked about you, and said he had not heard from you for a long time. . . . Liquor is still obtainable in S. F.—for those who have the price,—and the courage! Cocktails are 75¢ apiece. I didn't buy very many! They were bad, anyway: The best stuff that I remember drinking was some South American absinth[e],—which is very different from the French absinth.

I spent another week in Roseville, after my return from San Francisco. Mrs Hemphill has charge of the local Water Co's office; I took the place of the typist (who was ill) for a few days. I expect to go back in September, and work there indefinitely.

Poetry and art have both gone "by the board"—for the present, at least. I have done nothing at all; one needs a little peace of mind for creative effort; and I have had none.

The president of a local woman's college[1] has offered to recommend my poems and prose poems to the Houghton Mifflin Co. I am told that she has considerable influence with them; and they can do no worse than refuse.

Don't forget to send me the new poems you mention! . . . .

You can't say anything that I won't agree with, when it comes to "law"—and morality! . . . I wish I could get hold of an indetectable poison—I should make excellent use of it!

I am sorry you have had trouble with your nerves. Everything of that sort is traceable to the unnatural restraints and inhibitions of "civilization." Life is becoming impossible, now-a-days. . . .

I am always hoping that your luck will change. It must—sooner or later. Give my best to Kirk. I'll write again, before long.

Aff.,

Clark.

Notes

1. Aurelia Henry Reinhardt, president of Mills College (1916–43) in Oakland.

[326] [ALS]

July 24th, 1921

Dear Sam:

Your second letter came yesterday. I am sorry you thought I could be offended at your silence,—I never dreamt of such a thing!

It must be hell in Cleveland. We've had a little hot weather, too; but I dare say it's not like the devastating heat of the Middle States. And the conditions of life are not so bad out here,—at least, in the country.

I feel ashamed of having neglected you so! But everything has gone "to pot" the last few months,—including my correspondence. I have not felt like writing, and have had little enough that was fit to write! Life is a sorry mess: Everyone that I care about is unfortunate and unhappy. I have more troubles than I can tell you.

No, I have not heard of the "Double-Dealer"—an interesting name. Is it worth while for me to try them with my verse?[1] I'd like to sell something. I read "Main Street"[2] some time ago, and can testify that the realism of the book, as a depiction of small-town life, is more than photographic! The satire is ferocious—and horribly true to life!

Barbey D'Aurevilly's little shocker, "The Story Without a Name", is among the latest accretions of my library. The diabolism of the tale is perfect. I also bought a novel by Bourget ("A Tragic Idyll.") The plot resembles that of "The Red Lily;" but the book is totally destitute of merit. It represents the popular idea of a French novel.

Please don't put yourself to any further expense in sending me books at present! The little pleasure that they give me is not worth it; and my conscience troubles me about you. I feel that you can't afford it; and books mean less to me now than they ever did. I require a stronger narcotic! I have never read so little as during the past few months.

I'll write again in a few days. Perhaps there'll be a little news by that time. I expect some visitors next week. I've seen no one lately, except Dewing, who took me for a long motor-trip the other day. Mrs. Hemphill is in Berkeley for the summer. She was almost in a state of breakdown when I left Roseville. . . . Overwork, worry, etc.

I am trying not to break down; but I have a rotten cold, in addition to my "nerves." Oh, hell!!!! . . . .

Write me when you can.

Affectionately,

Clark.

Notes

1. It is unlikely CAS submitted anything to the magazine, which favored Southern, modernist writers. It was meant to combat the stereotype of Southern literature as provincial and second-rate, as in H. L. Mencken's "The Sahara of the Bozart" (1917).

2. By Sinclair Lewis.

[327] [ANS postcard][1]

[Postmarked Cleveland, Ohio,
1 October 1921.]

Dear Clark,

Your 1st letter came today. I'm so glad to have heard from you again. If you could have seen my delight when I opened the envelope. Thanks for the lovely sonnet of George's. Will write in the morning—a little news I have to tell you.

P.S. Sending you a parcel this week. Sam

Notes

1. *Front:* Blank.

[328] [ALS]

East Auburn, Cal.,
Oct. 6th, 1921

Dear Sam:

Forgive me for not having written before. I surmised the reason for **your** silence; but things have not been overwell with me, either.

I am dreadfully sorry that you and George are still "up against it." *My* plans for going to work fell through, for more reasons than one; but I have a small income—enough to starve on respectably. Conditions are "tight," even here in California; they say there are long bread-lines in San Francisco.

I wish I had some good news for you; but there's little except trivialities. I've actually sold two of my drawings; but I've not written anything lately. I confess to a sense of disillusionment and discouragement, through my repeated failure to find a hearing. Even Robertson is unwilling to assume the risk of publishing my new volume. I shall have to wait till I can print it myself; and hell knows when **that** will be.

I am grieved to hear about Nelson's illness. I remember his praise of my drawings with gratitude—no other painter ever said as much for them. . . . Helas! Life is a dirty mess! Death, at least, can be no worse.

I am glad that you are still writing. Send me all that you do; perhaps I'll be able to send something in return presently.

I have a new friend—a lady from Stockton who is coming here to live. Life is a little brighter,—but not bright enough. However, I've no right to complain, when I think of you and Kirk. I am still desperately poor; but my loneliness is becoming a thing of the past.

Dewing has just returned from a week in San Francisco. He saw G. S. several times.

I wish I could say something to cheer you up;—at any rate, I'll write oftener in the future. Try to "hold on"; one never knows what will happen. "It's a long lane, etc"[1]—and I really believe there **is** something in the old platitude!

Tell Kirk to write.

Affectionately,
Clark.

Notes

1. The line "It's a long lane, a crooked lane . . ." occurs four times in "The Long Lane" by Agnes Lockhart Hughes.

[329] [ALS]

East Auburn, Cal.
Oct. 12th, 1921.

Dear Sam:

Your two letters are both ["]at hand," to use the argot of the business world. I am sorry that conditions are still so desperate. Is there really no way you could get out of Cleveland?

As usual, I haven't much news for you. "The Lyric West," published in Los Angeles, has just paid me five dollars for my sonnet "The Absence of the Muse." Why don't you try them? The address is 1139 W. 27th St., Los Angeles, Cal. They don't pay till publication, however.

As to love-affairs—I have a new one now! The old one fell through, because of a jealous husband. The latest love is a voluptuous blonde, who smokes, drinks, and recites fescennine doggerel. She also has a jealous husband! . . . You are right—all is vanity; but one must have a little amusement.

I have done very little reading of late—mainly because I could find nothing to tempt me. My new friend, however, has some books that I mean to borrow. I noticed two volumes by F. W. Bain[1] on her shelves—"A Digit of the Moon," and "The Substance of a Dream." Have you read them? I am told they are beautifully written and very erotic . . . This lady (she hates the word "lady!") owns a number of my favourite books, and is the only woman I have met with a taste for Edgar Saltus and Ernest Dowson.

I am very, very idle at present, but find myself observing and analyzing much. I wonder if I will take to fiction-writing some day. I am rapidly acquiring the material for a novel—or an autobiography!

Here are some more of Sterling's new poems. Keep them, if you care to. My best regards to George Kirk.

Affectionately,
Clark.

Notes

1. A writer of fantasy stories that he claimed were translated from Sanskrit.

[330] [ALS]

East Auburn, Cal.,
Nov. 15th, 1921.

Dear Sam:

I haven't heard from you for a month, and am beginning to feel worried. Have you written me? Your silence makes me fear that conditions are still bad with you,—if not worse. If I had the money, I'd come to Cleveland, and carry you away with me! But my own circumstances are precarious enough.

Did I tell you that "The Lyric West," had accepted my "Ode to Omar?" I've heard nothing from the Houghton Mifflin Co., but can't persuade myself that their hesitation is very hopeful.

I may go to San Francisco next week—and possibly I'll stay there for a month or two, if I can find anything at which to earn expenses. I need a change badly: I am stifling here in Auburn, and need to be stirred up and stimulated.

Here are some of Sterling's new poems—also, two or three of my own that I may not have sent you before.

Give my best to George Kirk. Good luck!

Affectionately,
Clark.

[331] [ALS]

[10 December 1921]

Dear Sam:

I like some of your Baudelaire translations immensely—"Ciel Brouille," "Le Lethe," "Chaunt D'Automne" in particular. They are much more literal—are they not—than those of E. P. Sturm and the others?

Your pardon for not writing before: I've had a bout of the beastly "flu," and spent several days in bed. I intended to visit S. F. early this month, but am still too unwell.

I've done a few paintings lately—nothing else. I may sell some of them.

There's nothing new. My last "love-affair" was only a flirtation to begin with; and it seems to be turning into a platonic friendship now. Women are queer animals; but they lend a little variety to existence.

Have you read anything of F. W. Bain's? I borrowed "The Substance of a Dream" from Mrs L. It is very lovely and colourful; but I am told that "A Digit of the Moon" is better. I haven't read it yet.

Give my best regards to Kirk and Ernest Nelson. I have never forgotten Nelson's appraisal of my drawings. Forgive this scratchy note. I'll try to write you a real letter before long.

Affectionately,
Clark.

P.S. Have you done anything more from Baudelaire? Send it along, if you have. There's certainly a flavour to some of these!

[332] [ALS]

[24 December 1921]

Dear Sam:

Your note came this afternoon. I am dreadfully sorry to hear of Nelson's death,[1] since I can well understand what he meant to you and Kirk. There are so few of our kind in this world. Humanity as a whole is worse than anything that Leopardi or Baudelaire ever said about it.

You shouldn't have worried about my illness—it was only a cold, and I'm as well as ever now. I shall run down to San Francisco after Christmas, if the weather is half-way decent. I'd like to be there on New Year's eve, when the carnival spirit reigns as it does nowhere else in America. Dewing—lucky dog—goes down to-morrow.

G. S. sends me his new book, "Sails and Mirage." I've ordered a copy for you. There are many lovely things in it—it is superior, I think, to either of his lyrical collections since "The House of Orchids."[2]

I painted for awhile, but have fallen into a mood of disgust and depression that makes it impossible for me to work to any purpose. I've had too much of Auburn at a stretch. The people here are all addicted to money-making and the seven deadly virtues.

I've been reading and dissecting magazine-stories lately. Some day, in an extra-cynical mood, I'll sit down and write something that will sell to "Smart Set" or the "Cosmopolitan." The story ought to deal with harlots and whoremasters!

                Affectionately,
                    Clark.

Notes

1. Nelson had recently been killed by a reckless driver.
2. I.e., *Beyond the Breakers* and *The Caged Eagle.*

[333] [ALS]

                          East Auburn, Cal.
                              Jan. 18th, 1922

Dear Sam:

        The beautiful volume of Verlaine[1] came yesterday. Many of the poems in this translation are new to me. . . . No translation that I've seen, however, comes anywhere near to Symons, considered as English poetry . . . Please tell Kirk that I received the book. I'll write to him before long.

I'm ashamed of not having written you before. But I'm still in a state of demoralization, following a week's visit to S. F. I'm glad I went, however—I received some fresh encouragement on the score of my drawings (several artists praised them highly!) and was given a clean bill by my doctor. I acquired some new books, among them "The Anatomy of Negation," which seems to be quite rare. G. S. told me that he was weaned from entering the Catholic priesthood by reading this book at the age of twenty or thereabouts!

My birthday (the 13th) fell on Friday this year! Truly, an unlucky day! I celebrated it by having a row with one of my sweet-hearts. . . . Fortunately, perhaps, I am still in love with the other (the Roseville lady) who can't see me any more without defying her husband. A nice mess, is it not? Don't ever fall in love with anybody, if you can help it—one always has to suffer. G. S. (who ought to know) once told me that he didn't wish anybody any worse luck than to be really in love. My own experience bears it out.

I am so sorry that you continue to be unwell . . . Physically, at least, I was never better than I am now. Hell knows why:—everything has gone wrong with me. I suppose the Lord delights in giving good teeth to those who have no nuts to crack.

        My best regards to G. K.
          Aff.,
                Clark.

Have you done any more translations from Baudelaire?

Notes

1. See letter 205n1.

[334] [ALS]

> Auburn, Cal.
> Feb. 22nd, 1922.

Dear Sam:

       How is it with you? I wrote in January, but have had nothing from you except the beautiful card which came yesterday.

       Things are very slack here—one reason why I have not written oftener. I have been re-typing a lot of my poems, preparatory to a fresh assault on the publishing houses. But I have not done anything new, except a few drawings. And I have never read so little, either, as during the past few months. Boredom and malaise—malaise and boredom!—I seem to know all that Baudelaire suffered. . . . Ill-luck pursues me so relentlessly, that I almost begin to believe in Karma, and the doctrine of expiatory incarnations. . . .

       Are you better? I fear not—since you have not written . . . I scarcely hear from anyone, of late—even Sterling has not written since I was in S. F. But, I, too, have neglected to answer letters.

       The weather has been simply abominable for the past two months— nothing but frost, ice, fog and snow in January, and continuous rain during the present month. I don't remember such a winter before. Everyone is more or less ill—there's a "flu" epidemic, of a secondary type. I've escaped, so far. We're entitled to an early spring, this year.

       It is very much on my conscience that I have not written to Kirk. But I intend to write very soon. . . . One shouldn't let everything slide, as I have done lately. I owe half-a-dozen letters.

       Have you done anything more from Baudelaire? I'd like to see them, if you have.

> Affectionately,
> Clark.

[335] [ALS]

> Auburn, Cal.
> April 12th, 1922.

Dear Sam:

       I was surprised and delighted to get your letter from New York . . . No, I don't imagine you would like the place. Sterling once spoke of it as a "stone inferno."[1]

You ask for news: The only news fit to tell, is, that my poems are likely to be in print before summer. One of the local printers has promised to do the job for me—on credit! The cost is appalling—I'll be in debt for the rest of my life, if I can't unload three hundred out of the five hundred copies in the proposed edition. Do you think Laukhuff could handle a few copies in Cleveland?

The "Baudelaire" came, and I enjoyed it thoroughly. B. has left d——d little for any poet who wants to be original—at least, in regard to the treatment of human life and emotion. They call *me* "the new Baudelaire" in S. F.; but the best of *my* "Flowers of Evil" were plucked in the outer constellations!

Life is a desert of boredom. Perhaps things will be livelier—for a little when my book comes out. The "H. E." ought to start a row. Some people look on the poem as a "mere extension" of "The Wine of Wizardry!" Women seem to like my poem, however—everyone that I've shown it to has been more or less enthusiastic over it. I suppose the violence appeals to them.

Our spring is uncertain and delayed. Rain—and sleet—to-day, though many of the fruit-trees are in blossom.

I plan some new books: A collection of prose-fantasies of the Poe–Dunsany order, and one of love-poems with an Oriental colouring. "Sandal-wood" ought to be a good title for the latter. It won't be my best work; but it might help to bring me "to the front." God knows when these books will be written, though: My present state of mind is very similar to the one that Symons describes in the last poem of "Mundi Victima."[2]

George's last book is selling very well, I hear. Robertson doesn't publish for *anyone* now, except G.

My sonnet "Symbols," was taken by "The London Mercury."

Good luck, my dear friend.

Aff., Clark.

I wrote to G. K. the other day.

Notes

1. GS to CAS, 6 May 1914 (*SU* 107).
2. *Poems* 2.63–67.

[336] [TLS]

Cleveland, Ohio.
[April 1922?]

Dear Clark,

I promised to write you again from N.Y. but the world was too much with me.[1] It was one continual round of museums, theatres and sight-seeing—without a chance for employment—and I got home minus about ten pounds with enough cynicism to start a cyanide factory, and eyes that were full of forfeited sleep. It's a hell of a fine place, but the people are impossible. The women paint like hetaira's,[2] [*sic*] one and all. The men carry canes. Both sexes lead poodles and bulls, although it would better become them to raise families and trundle baby-carriages. But I know that this idea would be abhorrent to you, my dear friend, as you would rather see an extermination of the cosmic vermin. I hope you got my letter from that Sodom.

"The Saturnian" containing the French translations is out and I'll send you a copy. This issue was a gift made to me and one of the conditions was that I publish these translations. The next one—I promise by everything sacred will be yours—only I must have the money.

Dear Clark, life has been a hideous nightmare for me for the last year. I've been on the point of throwing it up at least three times and once made active preparations to do so. There is nothing for me to live for and I've been in such misery over my finances that even that one hope slid by aghast. George has become so hide-bound commercial that you would marvel at the change. The huge joke of it all lies in the fact that all his efforts have come to naught—he has lost money and is now on the point of embarking into a venture that will probably complete his Fool's paradise—or the ruins of it. Advice which he used to take from me seems to be of no avail—only, I happen, as previously, to know the end of it. When he really is up against it, the good friend will be reinstated.

I wish you could have seen the Met. Museum. All the beauty of all the ages seems to be centred there. The Egyptian collection is so rich and magnificent that in it alone, one could spend a week. Entire tombs have been transferred, mummies, sphinxes, canopic jars of loveliest alabaster. In the Greek rooms are the red and black vases, beautiful fragments of sculpture, Roman busts. More than once I said to myself—if only Clark were here.

Tell me about yourself and your work. I feel certain that if ever you got to N.Y. you would have no difficulty in placing your poetry. I seriously think of going there next winter—would you come along and try pot-luck with me. Live for it—why not? More in a day or two.

> Affectionately
>
> Sam

1537 East 93 St., Suite 2.

I send one copy of "Sat."—more later.

Notes

1. Alluding to "The World Is Too Much with Us" by William Wordsworth. SL had gone to New York to look for work. It was on this trip that he first met H. P. Lovecraft.
2. Courtesans or mistresses, especially those in ancient Greece akin to the modern geisha.

[337] [ALS]

Auburn, Cal.
April 23rd, 1922

Dear Sam:

I received your letter and the new "Saturnian." Hope you got my last letter—I wrote in answer to yours from N. Y.

There's little to write, just at present. I told you that I was to have a book published; but I don't know just when the printer will get to work on it: The local High-school annual has to take precedence!

I have already told you what I thought of your Baudelaire translations. Those from Verlaine are new to me, and I like some of them very well. The "Saturnian" isn't at hand; so I can't comment on them in detail. "Il Bacio" and "Vert" are the ones I remember best. I enjoyed the finely polished satire of your note on modern poetry![1] There ought to be a market for prose like that—it's damn good stuff, if you don't mind my lapsing into profanity.

I've been very much alone of late. One of my friends used her claws on me once too often, and I've stopped calling for the present. I've not seen Andrew for several weeks, either, and am beginning to wonder if he is vexed with me about anything. My mother met some people from Cleveland who were here awhile ago. Their name was Griggs, I believe. They had heard of you, or seen some of your work.

I was surprised to get a letter from the editor of "The Bookman,"[2] asking me to submit some of my poems. "The winds whisper that you can write," quoth he. At this rate, I'll be famous yet, from San Bernadino to Boston Common!

Thanks for the proposition about going to New York next year. But I dunno—one can't tell what may happen by that time. The trouble is, I couldn't endure city life for very long. No doubt I could place my poems more readily, if I were on the ground; but I wouldn't be able to live very long on the proceeds. However, there's no telling—I might come for the experience, if no deterrent casualties occur—such as death, marriage, or a new and urgent adultery.

Remember me to Kirk, when you see him. I'll send you some verse with my next; but there's no time to type them this morning.

Aff.,
Clark.

Notes

1. "Modern Poetry (An Exorcism)."
2. John Chipman Farrar (1896–1974), editor of *Bookman* until 1927.

[338] [TLS]

[c. 24 April 1922]

Dear Clark,

George got your note the same day I did and we were both damn glad to hear from you. We are going to do everything in our power to make your book sell. I can assure you of at least ten copies among the folk I know and George will exploit it through his book-business. I would like to know what the title is that you have finally decided on. I think your move is a wise one—Robertson never did do justice to your first output and I believe with all my heart that he deters the sale of Sterling's. Be sure and reserve a few to send out to the reviews—as no doubt, you will. This is imperative and greases the wheels of everyman's chariot.

"The Hermaphrodite" is still incomplete but is promised for publication by July. I'll send you a copy as soon as I make one—at present I have simply the one original.

As to the originality of the "H.E." it makes me laugh. When any of the people you have shown it to tell you it apes Sterling, it would be wise to inquire in what respect. The poem is the biggest piece of imaginative work I've ever read. Things like Coleridge's "Kubla Khan" are child's play in comparison. I don't think I over-exaggerate. Think of the few things in Coleridge and the terrific number of images and incubi in your poem. The worst of it is that when people once make a classic they do so hate to upset their idols.

I would like to have copies of anything you have written that I have so far failed to receive.

George gave me a copy of Petronius, absolutely unexpurgated and printed in Paris, which I would like to send you through the mails to read, but the risk is too great—at present, at least. It's marvellous. I'd like to have mine bound in green with doublure's of gold and with tiny satyrs grinning from each corner. Also, he gave me Symonds' "Dante", a book that deserves to be far better known than the innumerable tomes written for and published by erudite elderly gentlemen of Harvard University.

Did I tell you that when I visited N.Y. I went to the apartment house on E. 278th St., where Edgar Saltus used to live all by himself and interviewed a colored porter who knew him well. "Nevah did know he was aroun'—'peared so quiet," he said, and—"a nice, kin' ol' gentleman!" So they live and die, these geniuses—and we both agree that Saltus was one. George had a marvellous collection of his work. Mss of two of his novels, an inscribed copy of Imperial Purple/The Garden of Aphrodite of which only 68 copies were issued—O, and what not! I saw a mss (orig.) of Chivers "Lily Adair", in N.Y.C. Also visited the Poe cottage at Fordham, a lovely little toy-house, with much of what must have been the old charm. There are apartment houses all around but it still has an air of being away from the multitude. More later.

Affectionately,

Sam

Give my best to your father and mother.

[Envelope postmarked Cleveland, Ohio, Apr. 24, 1922.]

[339] [ALS]

May 10th, 1922.

Dear Sam:

Here are some of the verses that I promised you. I've not written much of late—partly from lack of inspiration, partly because I have put most of my time and energy into clearing land for a vineyard.

The printer can't get to work on my book before the end of the month. "Ebony and Crystal" remains the best title I have been able to find. It will be a marvellous relief to get the volume off my hands—and off my nerves.

Not much news that's fit to tell. I went to a bacchanalian party last Sunday, and acquired a "hang-over" that lasted for two days. This morning, I woke up with a cold; so I'm trying to write you this letter before I'm laid out entirely!

I hope you've had, or will have, a little luck. My own finances are worse than ever: I shall have to cut wood, and pick fruit in order to keep things going. But wait till the vineyard begins to bear!

Give my best to George . . . And pardon the brevity of this: My head feels like a rotten cabbage.

Aff.,

Clark.

[340] [ALS]

Auburn, Cal.,
May 23rd, 1922.

Dear Sam:

Here are some more of my stray verses. I've written very little this Spring—the effort of composition literally tears me to pieces—"Satiety" is much the best of the lot.

"Smart Set" has just taken a lyric ("Requiescat.") Mencken "gets my goat"—he'll always take something if G. S. sends it in with a letter of commendation; but he won't look at my stuff when *I* submit it! It shows how much the personal factor counts.

I'm glad you've "landed" a job. As for me, I'm planning to pick fruit this summer; the cherry season begins in another week. My finances are more desperate than they have been for years; and I don't imagine that my new book will improve matters. The printer hasn't begun work on it yet; but I dare say he will, sometime. It was his own proposition. . . . I'll have to leave out several poems of the "Secret Love" type,—unfortunately.[1] The printer might boggle at them; or if he didn't, some ass would be sure to make trouble . . . What a country!! ***+0!! . . . . . .

Certainly, I'll save the proof-sheets for you. They're likely to be a sad mess; typesetters, as a class, seem to be possessed of even less intelligence than publishers or magazine-editors—if such a thing be possible—or credible.

I hope and pray that you *can* come out next winter. It will do you good to get away from Cleveland; and it goes, or should go, without saying, that you will be welcome to share whatever we have for as long a period as you care to stay. You may find me a dull companion, though: Burnt-out nerves and a broken heart make a hopeless sort of combination.

I think I understand your nervous trouble thoroughly, from what I know about my own. I have lived too much in some ways, not enough in others. The result is altogether disastrous.

I've been terribly alone, of late. I never had many friendships; and two of them have gone to smash within the year—the first, because it became too dangerous for the woman; and the second, through incompatibility. I have two friends left (here in Auburn) but they're so much in love with each other that I hardly count.

A letter from G. S. the other day. I'll enclose the poems he sent me.

Remember me to Kirk. I often think of him, and remember his visit as a rare pleasure.

    Affectionately,
     Clark.

Notes

1. CAS included such poems in *SP* as translations of the fictitious Christophe des Laurières.

[341] [ALS]

            Auburn, Cal.,
            Aug. 6th, 1922.
Dear Sam:

   I received your card months ago, and have waited for the promised letter, thinking that it might come any day. Your silence makes me fear that matters are still unwell with you. Anyhow, I've decided to "take the law into my own hands," and write.

The chief news—almost the only news—is that "Ebony and Crystal," after a series of idiotic delays, is being "set up" by the printers at the "Journal" office. I'm reading galley-proofs for "The H. E." at present—it comes in the middle of the book. The volume ought to be ready by September.

I've had to work pretty hard this summer—mostly at fruit-picking—and poetry and art have gone by the board. One **must** have leisure and surplus energy for any serious creative effort. . . . However, the work seems to be beneficial, from a physical stand-point. I have gained in weight and strength.

"Symbols" came out in the July issue of "The London Mercury." They sent me a copy of the magazine, and a cheque for two pounds, which is more than any American periodical has ever paid me for a sonnet. "Poplars" sold to "Snappy Stories," much to my surprise. They *pay* better than "Smart Set." Mencken ought to be ashamed of the pittance that he doles out for verse . . . But, oh, hell, what's the diff.? No one can possibly make a living, or the ghost of a living, out of **poetry.** I am not speaking of Edgar Lee Masters, Sara Teasdale, Louis Untermeyer, Robert Frost, Alfred Noyes, Walt Mason, Edgar Guest, Amy Lowell, et cie.[1]

Give my best to Kirk. And write me when you feel like it. I hope things are not **too** rotten.

Aff.,

Clark.

Notes

1. All popular poets. Walt Mason (1862–1939) was a Canadian-American humorist and poet famous for his "Rippling Rhymes" column (written mostly in prose).

[342] [ALS]

Auburn, Cal.,

Sept. 11th, 1922.

Dear Sam:

I have been abominably tired and depressed for weeks, from overwork and the usual accursed monotony;—otherwise, I'd have answered your last with a little more promptness.

Sorry you've had another bout of "nerves"; the God of the Calvinists could not devise a more atrocious torture. One is tempted to believe in a malevolent principle of things—only, it's better not to believe at all, save in the Oriental concept that pain, as well as pleasure, is a form of the Manifold Illusion.

What you have done of "The Hermaphrodite" is very beautiful, I think. It is more to my taste than "The Sphinx," and contains many of the loveliest verses that you have written. I could pick them out by scores. Yes, you are a poet—no one but the squalor-blinded mob of ver-libreists [*sic*] and modernists would deny it. Their eyelids are gummed together with hog-wash!

My book is coming on slowly. I have just received proofs for "Satan Unrepentant," and "The Ghoul & Seraph." My linotyper was much taken with the former! I suppose the book will be out before the Millennium or the second Ice Age.

I was greatly pleased by what your friend Sommer[1] said about my drawings. Both your guests—Galpin[2] and Lovecraft—have written me letters in a most laudatory vein. The latter seemed particularly impressed by my drawings. He has just sent me a short story, which like the one you showed me, indicates a weird and fantastic genius. The stuff is strangely like, and unlike, Poe. It is worth tons of the usual magazine fiction. Galpin seemed an amazing youngster; but I suppose he might get to be a nuisance.

I may go to S. F. for a few months, when this new volume is off my hands. "A short life and a merry one." The compulsory asceticism of life in the local Thebaid is driving me nearly crazy.

Your affectionate friend, Clark.

Notes

1. William Sommer (1867–1949), American Modernist painter.
2. Alfred Galpin (1901–1983), American literary academic and composer of classical music. Now known chiefly as a close friend, protégé, and correspondent of Lovecraft.

[343] [ALS]

Auburn, Cal.,
Nov. 2nd, 1922.

Dear Sam:

Many thanks to you and to George for the volume of Bierce's letters! I am glad you have put these in evidence for reasons apart from the light they throw on Bierce's disappearance. They are all beautifully written, full of insight and irony; and the history of "Pierrot's" rejection by the magazines is put "on the stand" in the most effective manner. . . . Oh! "The moronic editors," as G. S. puts it! Incidentally, the book is finely printed and bound. And I like your preface.

G. S. has written a little preface for my book—very brief, but a model of its kind . . . "Here are neither kindergartens nor skyscrapers," as he says toward the end.

"Ebony and Crystal" goes on at the conventional snail's pace. I mailed you some of the first pages awhile ago. My printer swears it will be ready by the 20th of November. I think he's too optimistic, myself. Anyway, the binding (a dark green cloth) has been selected and ordered. I've had one hell of a time with the proofs. The first set was so rotten that the linotyper destroyed them out of shame! The second set is bad enough, but I'll see that they're saved for you. The book will have a number of misprints, but most of them are not *my* fault.

I have been laid up with a fierce cold, and was just able to crawl around when your book came . . . Life remains a mixture of pain and boredom, for the most part. I think I shall simply "go to hell" by way of S. F. and Bohemia when this new book is off my hands.

My girl is writing a book on "Life!" A disgusting theme, and fit only for doctors—or contraceptionists! Someone ought to write a book entitled "Life: Its Cause, Cure, and Prevention."

Your friend Lovecraft sent me a bunch of genuine thrillers sometime ago. The man is a genius, beyond doubt. The fact that his work is unpublished—and unpublishable—is the most decisive indictment that one could wish, of American life, intellect, civilization, and letters. The whole situation is enough to turn the stomach of a Hottentot.

Here are some new drawings.

    Aff.,

        Clark.

[344] [ALS]

                      Auburn, Cal.,

                         Dec. 27th, 1922.

Dear Sam:

    Got both your letters—the last one to-day. Glad you got the book, and that it gave you a little pleasure. I have had the galley-proofs (which you wanted) saved for you, and will mail them pretty soon. I sent you five copies of the book by express this afternoon. I appreciate your kindness in offering to dispose of them. I wish all of the five hundred copies could fall into the hands of people who would appreciate them; but I fear that so many of them won't. Quite a few have sold locally, and you can imagine the effect on the more stupid and more narrow-minded readers.

I feel infinitely tired, and immeasurably bored . . . Even if one does have a "gaudy day" once in a while, it only serves to make all the succeeding ones worse by contrast. I have a girl—of sorts—(since you ask me!) but she's anything but "steady," and there isn't the slightest danger of my marrying her—since she's already married, and her husband shows no indication of a premature demise. Anyhow, I've always held that marriage was an immoral institution; and its very legality is disgusting.

I sent G. S. a copy of your Bierce letters (I obtained several from Kirk for various people[)]; but I dare say he'd appreciate a copy from you: he seems to think you have taken offense at something, or other . . . I don't think he minded anything that Bierce said about the small fry at Carmel. He expressed surprise at the number of times that Bierce referred to him (G. S.) in the letters. I don't see any rhyme or reason to Mencken's treatment of the book, after the respect that he accorded Bierce.[1] I wouldn't let it worry me, if I were you: Mencken is a d——d poor judge of poetry, though he may be able to distinguish an epigram from an after-dinner speech.

I'll try to dig up some of the S. F. press-notices of my book for you.[2] They all mention Poe and Baudelaire—though I can't see why the former should be thrown at my head. I am sure Galpin will make a good job of his review: he is very clever, and appreciative, and is certainly more than kind to me.[3] And so is Lovecraft—who is a genius if there ever was one.

Have you seen Lytton Strachey's "Books and Characters?" There is a fine appreciation of Beddoes in it.

> Aff.,
> Clark.

Notes

1. Mencken had written: "The Bierce book, a thin pamphlet in boards, obviously put out to tempt collectors, is a piece of unmitigated impudence. A circular used to advertise it says that it discloses 'the secret of his (Bierce's) startling disappearance.' It discloses nothing of the sort. At the end there is a brief and formal note in which Bierce says that he is 'going away to South America,' but is it seriously to be argued that Bierce would tell the truth about his plans to a relative stranger, and yet conceal it from his oldest and most intimate friends? The appearance of such volumes adds a new terror to the ordinary pains of hell. The editor, Loveman, is a poet who apparently asked Bierce to help him sell his wares. The result was a polite exchange of letters, but there is scarcely a word in any of them that justifies printing them. To them the editor prefixes a bombastic preface containing some gratuitous and nonsensical criticism of Hergesheimer and Cabell." "Confidences," *Smart Set* 70, No. 1 (January 1923): 142.
2. [GS], "Recent Books of Fact and Fiction," *San Francisco Bulletin* (19 December 1922): 8 (as by "George Douglas"); Morton Todd, "Clark Ashton Smith's New Volume," *Argonaut* (16 December 1922): 387–88 (in Connors, *The Freedom of Fantastic Things* 53–58); [Unsigned], "Boy Publishes Poems," *San Francisco Examiner* (17 December 1922): 20; [Unsigned], "San Francisco Poet Treads New Worlds: Earth Fetters Cast Off by Star Rover," *San Francisco Chronicle* (10 December 1922): 59.
3. "Echoes from Beyond Space," *United Amateur* 24, No. 1 (July 1925): 3–4. A review of *The Star-Treader* and *Ebony and Crystal*.

[345] [ALS]

> Auburn, Cal.,
> Jan. 25th, 1923

Dear Sam:

I hope you received the galley-proofs of my book, which I sent you several weeks ago. I haven't heard from you since then, nor from George, either. By the way, I wrote to George before Christmas, asking him to send a copy of the Bierce letters to Albert M. Bender, 311 California st., S. F. Bender says that he hasn't received the book. I wish you'd ask George if he received my letter, and filled the order. Bender wants **two** copies now, and I wish you'd send them to him, or have G. send them, as quickly as possible. I'll pay for them—and B. will pay me.

Galpin, as you doubtless know, has been writing some reviews of my book. I hope he puts them over—but it's very doubtful.

I've done no work lately, except a series of pen-drawings for a shocker by Lovecraft which is appearing in "Home-Brew!"[1] I'm afraid they'll disappoint L.—the mechanical requirements cramped me a great deal.

Not much news. My book is quite "successful," at least in Auburn— mainly because of one or two highly-coloured erotic images! I daresay that's all the average reader could understand in it! "Between thy thighs is a valley of delight,"[2] seems to have tickled their fancy. Many people praise the book—but praise doesn't cost them much, or commit them to much: all it requires is a little hot air!

I hope you'll write me soon. I miss your letters. Here are some pen-drawings, which you can add to your collection.

Remember me kindly to George.

  Aff.,

   Clark.

P.S. By the way, how is Bill Sommer, whom you mentioned once? Tell me more about him.

[Envelope postmarked Auburn, Cal., Jan. 25, 1923.]

Notes

1. "The Lurking Fear," *Home Brew* (January–April 1923).
2. "A Psalm to the Best Beloved," l. 20.

[346] [ALS]

[CLARK ASHTON SMITH
AUBURN, CALIFORNIA]

July 25th, 1923

Dear Sam:

  I am taking the law into my own hands again, after this age-long silence of yours. I presume you have not written because of illness or despondency. I **hope** you weren't afraid to write because the copies of "E. and C." proved unsaleable. It wouldn't matter—I've sold more than I expected to, anyway, though San Francisco gave the book a frosty reception. The main sale has been local: the S. F. booksellers have disposed of 38 copies, all told!

Here are some recent verses. The local newspaper gives me a "column" every week,—so I can depend (for once) on getting my stuff into print![1]

I have not done any drawing for a long time. My paintings seem more hopeless of an audience than my poetry . . . Anyway, I have suffered a great deal from eye-strain,—so much so that I have had to limit my reading.

Do you remember a sonnet of mine that began "My soul is like a secret garden-close?"[2] A new magazine called "Weird tales" [*sic*] has accepted it for publication! They are also buying some of Lovecraft's work.

I have been picking fruit this summer, and am hellishly tired. I may have a chance to go to Carmel later on. That would be preferable to dodging street-cars and drinking bad cocktails in S. F.

Remember me kindly to George.

With affection, as ever,

Clark.

Notes

1. "Clark Ashton Smith's Column" ran in the *Auburn Journal* for 41 installments from 4 October 1923 to 11 June 1925. It included poems, translations, epigrams, and other matter.
2. "Duality."

[347] [ALS]

[CLARK ASHTON SMITH
AUBURN, CALIFORNIA]

Sept. 20th, 1923.

Dear Sam:

It was good to hear from you again, after so long a time; and I am glad indeed that conditions have improved for you . . . The books came, and I have been glancing through them. Machen is a genius, though possibly a bit overrated at the present time. Still, I really haven't read enough of his work to decide. I have "Hieroglyphics"; and someone loaned me "The Hill of Dreams" many years ago. Apart from these I have never read anything of Machen's.

Everything is at sixes and sevens with me. I have done no painting for a long time, and very little writing. For one thing, my eyes have been giving me more trouble than ever, and I am forced to conserve them.

I haven't heard from Galpin for a long time. He owes me a letter. And I've not answered Lovecraft's last, which has been lying on my table for a month or six weeks. But no one else has fared any better. I've been in a state of mental slump, and the weather has been uncommonly hellish, with excessive heat and high winds. A goodly portion of the country has gone up in flames lately. There were forest fires (five or six at least) all about us the other day,—though none of them approached very close to Auburn. And there were fires all over the state, one of which consumed a large portion of Berkeley, where Kirk formerly lived.

I enclose some unpublished poems by G. S., which you are at liberty to keep. I know you will like them. Sorry I've nothing more of my own—I think I sent you all of my late productions.

Look up the little notice of my book by Benjamin de Casseres, in the August number of "Arts and Decoration."[1] It is brief, but highly complimentary.

I'm sorry Kirk has been having trouble. Remember me to him kindly.

This letter sounds perfunctory; but it is not meant to be. I am suffering from excessive brain-fog.

My mother sends her regards to you and George.

Ever your friend,
        Clark.

Notes

1. See Appendix.

[348] [ALS]

[CLARK ASHTON SMITH
AUBURN, CALIFORNIA]

Sept. 27th, 1925.

Dear Sam:

I was indeed glad to receive your letter, enclosed with Lovecraft's. I've thought of you very often, and wondered over your silence; but I never took it unkindly . . . As to questions,—well, I'm not good at asking them, since I've always followed the good old policy of minding my own business. (I only wish the people of Auburn would do as much!)

It is good news that you are to have a book out. Saltus is a worthy subject—I told you my opinion of his best work years ago.[1] I wish something could be done about issuing your poems in book form. But publishers are all slaves of fashion, more or less—usually more. . . . G. S. told me that he had talked Seymour, of the Chicago Bookfellows, into promising to bring out "Sandalwood."[2] But when I submitted the typescript, it was returned to me with an intimation that they could do nothing with it till next year. I don't like their putting me off, so I'm printing a small edition (250 copies) myself, through the financial assistance of a new admirer.[3] The book—or pamphlet—ought to be ready by November. Of course, I'll send you a copy of it. The poems are mostly lyrical, apart from the 19 Baudelaires in the tail.

I don't suppose there's much news that you haven't heard through H. P. L. Doubtless he told you about my being laid up for nearly six months, with a bruised toe. A hellish ordeal; but I might never have made a beginning on the B. translations, had it not been for the enforced leisure. I am inclined to think well of some of them. Half of them, perhaps, are more or less unsatisfactory; but then, nearly *all* of the Sturm and Robertson versions are unsatisfactory. In time, I hope to accumulate enough successful ones for a sizeable volume.

I enclose several that I am not including in "Sandalwood." "L'Irreparable" is more faithful to the original text than Sturm's version—he sacrificed the "caterpillar" and "courtezan" images, not to mention anything else. However, some of my phrases could be improved, from a poetic standpoint . . . The sestet of "Les Hiboux" is more literal—and successful—than verse-translation usually succeeds in being. However, I'm more anxious to reproduce the spirit than the exact letter, of Baudelaire. I merely want to conserve enough of the latter to give a fair equivalent of the style.

Life goes on quite monotonously, as usual. My worst complaint is, that I can't give all my time and energy to writing. But doubtless, I should be thankful that I don't have to drudge every day, and all day.

I'll ask G. S. about the Bierce letters. Have you seen his article on Bierce—"The Shadow-Maker"—in the last "American Mercury?"[4] I haven't seen it myself, since the local newsstand does not carry the "A. M." In fact, they don't carry anything much, except a full array of wild-west magazines, and sex-slush of the types of "Hot Dog" and "True Confessions." (They also have the "S. E. Post," the "Police Gazette," and the "Family Journal"—the old-time housemaid's favourite!)

Your saying that "the last two years have been alternately hell and heaven—but mostly the former"—sounds like a love-affair! But perhaps you mean something quite different. As for me, I have no entanglements; but I nearly got into a divorce-case some months back, through a platonic friendship.

Please send me some of your new poems. I think there is more true Hellenism in work like "The Hermaphrodite" than in anything since Keats and Landor. The note is rare—and becoming rarer—in modern verse.

Have you seen the symposium of "great" poetic lines that has been running in the "Literary Review" of the New York Evening Post? I was quoted twice—by a Mrs Chauncey Juday, and by Edwin Markham.[5] Markham also wrote me a letter of encouragement, in which he ended by saying: "I can assure you that your circle of admirers will continue to widen, for your distinguished poetry will be admired by all the discriminating and intelligent readers who come in contact with it." That is rather neat, n'est-ce pas?

Tell Howard that I will write in a few days.

Aff., as ever—

Clark.

[Envelope postmarked Auburn, Cal., Sept. 27, 1925.]

Notes

1. SL had written a critical study of the work of Saltus in 1924, but the publisher (the Centaur Book Shop in Philadelphia) abandoned plans to publish the book after the manuscript had been prepared. A subsequent plan with Brentano's also came to naught.
2. George Steele Seymour (1878–1945), head of a literary and publishing club in Chicago called The Bookfellows, had issued GS's verse drama *Truth* in 1923.

3. Donald Wandrei (1908–1987) of St. Paul, MN, offered to pay half the cost to print the booklet.

4. GS, "The Shadow Maker," *American Mercury* 6, No. 1 (September 1925): 10–19.

5. From "The Judgment of Mr. Markham," *Literary Review (New York Evening Post)* (12 September 1925): 6.

[349] [ALS]

Auburn, Cal.,

Dec. 4th, 1926.

Dear Sam:

I am so glad that you have finished and printed your master-piece, "The Hermaphrodite." I think (as I may have said before) that it contains more of "the indestructible pagan delirium"[1] than anything else in modern literature. You ought to be proud, for such inspiration has been given to few—and to no-one else in the present age, as far as I know. Your poem should add laurels to any poet, living or dead. I shall re-read it many times, and treasure it as something beyond praise. Ben's preface is admirable, too, like everything that he writes. He will not have his due, or a tithe of his due, in this hell-bemerded age.

I have often thought of you. But I've no questions to ask. I hope life is not too intolerable for you. As for me, after much suffering, I seem to have attained a condition of comparative indifference. The mystic strain is growing in me, and I am less subject to external influences than formerly.

George's death shook me up,[2] but I feel that he took the best way out. He seems closer to me now than during the past few years, and I feel that he is more truly alive than most of the people one meets in the flesh. Most Americans are dead and damned, without knowing it, and I feel like Dante in hell when I enter a town or city.

Ben and Bio[3] are very good to go on bothering about my pictures, and I hope their faith will be justified before we are all dead. But picture-dealers, like the rest of the world, are not looking for original genius. They want stuff that is obviously safe, sane—and saleable. I have recently gone through Muther's four-volume "History of Modern Art." It's a disgusting record— nearly everyone with the faintest spark of originality has been howled down, hooted, hissed, bepissed, execrated and contumeliated at every step of the way. One Rousseau, back in the 1830's, drew the indignation of his contemporaries by painting green trees! It all goes to justify my epigram: "The real objection to the Darwinian theory is that man has not yet evolved from the ape."[4]

The current "Overland" contains a little appreciation of your "Hermaphrodite" by George.[5] It must have been one of the last things that he wrote. I will send you a copy next week. The same issue contains a long article on my

work by D. A. Wandrei of St. Paul.[6] Both articles, as is usual with the "Overland," are marred by abominable misprints.

Good luck to you, Sam. Your poem is glorious, glorious. I don't know
what kind of a reception it will get; but,—since you printed only three hundred and fifty,—few will have a chance to spit on it. Some day you will have a
place all to yourself in English (I don't say American) literature. There is a
touch, a breath (I don't know what) in your poem that is not in Keats or Shelley. I salute an immortal.

> Believe me always your affectionate friend,
>
> Clark.

My best to George Kirk, and to Ben and Bio.

Notes

1. Benjamin De Casseres, "The Unearthly Imagination," *Shadowland* 8, No. 2 (April
1923): 20, 69.

2. GS committed suicide on 17 November.

3. Bio De Casseres (née Adella Mary Terrill) was born in 1875. She died c. 1963.

4. First published in "The Epigrams of Alastor," *Dragon-Fly* No. 1 (October 1935): [10].

5. GS, "Rhymes and Reactions," *Overland Monthly,* 84, No. 12 (December 1926): 395.
Possibly because the column had been submitted as a handwritten ms., the typesetter
rendered SL's name as *Tweman.*

6. "The Emperor of Dreams." *Overland Monthly* 84, No. 12 (December 1926): 380–81,
407, 409; rpt. *Klarkash-Ton: The Journal of Smith Studies* No. 1 (1988): 3–8, 25.

[350] [TLS]

[DAUBER & PINE BOOKSHOPS, *Inc.*
64–66 FIFTH AVENUE
NEW YORK CITY

———

PHONE CHELSEA 5670]

[Postmarked New York City,
14 December 1926]

Dear Clark,

If I were to write you an apology for not writing it would needs
have to be a history of my stay in New York. I half-starved here for a while
on a salary of fifteen dollars a week, then came a nightmare or a holoca[u]st
of work, work and nothing but work. After New Years I'll get a weekly wage
of fifty dollars a week. I came to New York because I could no longer obtain
work in Cleveland; office helpers had long been supplanted by women;
bookstores were few—I broke away, and while New York has a million

pleasures to distract one from the things that hurt one in solitude, here I am, here I have been, but I continually hope that it will not be to stay. These people I am with are kind and agreeable—two Jews who started in on less than nothing four years ago and now have one of the most fl[o]urishing book stores in N.Y.[1] I'm a sort of straw boss. I do all the cataloguing. Supposedly, I'm an expert on rare books.

Isn't it strange to be writing to you once again after all these months and years?

I've seen a great deal of Ben and Bio De Casseres here, both fine and loyal-hearted folk. Bio is a Shaksperian type of woman, hearted, it has always seemed to me, like Hermione, in a Winter's Tale. Both still struggle against finances but when the shadow falls they take to work even more indomitably than before.

George wrote me a wonderful letter about "The Hermaphrodite" before he died. Your letter and his constitute the only appreciations I've had. I'd appreciate a copy of the review in the "Overland."

I want to take the thread of our correspondence up again—only, believe me that it has not been anything personal—simply incessant brainweariness, almost an entire or complete subjugation of myself to the need that forced me at last to succumb to the making of a livelihood. I'll write more, honestly, in a few days. I'll begin to send you books, on and off, since I can really afford to do so again. George is here, a little the worse for wear. He was divorced in Cleveland but has, I believe, engaged himself once again.[2]

Howard, as you probably know, is back in Providence.[3] He would have gone insane had he continued here. He is very wonderful and has a mind that belongs to a giant.

I appreciate what you say about my book. Write soon. My best to you and yours. You'll hear from me in a few days.

Faithfully
Sam

78 Columbia Hts.,
Brooklyn, N. Y.

Notes

1. Samuel Dauber and Nathan S. Pine operated a bookstore at 66 Fifth Avenue, New York City.
2. In 1927 Kirk married Lucile Dvorak (1898–1994), later an associate editor of *Parents Magazine,* with whom he was involved since 1924. His first wife was Harriet Louise Brooks (1895–?), whom he married on 31 January 1920. She remarried in 1924.
3. H. P. Lovecraft, who lived most of his life in Providence, RI, lived in New York City from March 1924 to May 1926.

[351] [ALS]

Auburn, Cal.,
Dec. 23rd, 1926.

Dear Sam:

It was certainly good to hear from you again, and to know that things were picking up a little with you. The "berth" you have sounds like a good one; though I can readily imagine that you don't find the N. Y. atmosphere very congenial. Lovecraft (from whom I hear quite often) was obviously more than glad to escape from it. I can't endure cities at all, and have not even visited San Francisco for the past four years. Crowds oppress me— Baudelaire's "bath of multitude"[1] involves an actual suffocation in my case. Probably my sense of psychic smell is too keen.

Hope you got "The Overland" that I mailed you. The editor, Miss Lee,[2] is a good girl; but the linotyper ought to be taken out and ganched from the parapet of the nearest frotteur-du-ciel; his typographical errors are simply heinous! George "did you proud" in his little write-up. I am sorry you have not found more appreciation, but what can you expect from swine—except a grunt? Anyhow, as Bierce once said, you have the experts in your favour— G. S. and De Casseres are a quorum by themselves.

I have been asked to write an article on G. S. for "The Overland," and will get to work on it after Christmas. I have never done anything of the kind, and have the most horrible misgivings as to my abilities in that line. I have already written an elegiac poem,[3] but it seems uncommonly rotten. I've done nothing but paint for the past year, and am out of practice as far as literature goes. But I want to do another book—"Incantations" will be the title, and there will be few madrigals in it, and much of the trans-Hyperborean ultra-zodiacal. Of course, it won't get a hearing. To receive attention from the "young intellectuals", I should do something ala Sandburg or Robinson Jeffers. But I don't want a public badly enough for **that.**

If you send me any books, make sure that you **can** afford it. The ones that you sent from Cleveland are a library in themselves! There are no volumes on my shelves that I prize more.

I am expecting Symons' translation of Baudelaire. Symons *ought* to be the ideal translator.

Remember me to George Kirk. He's certainly "in the swim," if he has been divorced.

Will try to send you some verses when I write again. Hope to hear from you before long.

My parents join me in the best holiday wishes.

Yours, in the name of the Dive Bouteille,[4]

Clark.

You are lucky to have friends like the De Casseres. I like Ben's essays better than those of Emerson.

Notes

1. From Baudelaire's prose poem "Clouds."
2. B. Virginia Lee, editor of the *Overland Monthly*.
3. "George Sterling—An Appreciation" and "To George Sterling: A Valediction."
4. "The divine bottle."

[352]   [ALS, JHL; enclosed with letter from Donald Wandrei]

[Postmarked New York City,
9 July 1927]
[7 July 1927]

Dear Clark:

I can only add that I think of you often—very often—and that I am physically and mentally worked to death. I'll write at length soon. Wandrei is very fine and charming.

Your friend
Sam

78 Columbia Hts.,
Brooklyn N.Y.

[353]   [ANS postcard][1]

[Postmarked Boston, Mass.,
5 January 1929]

Greetings from a section of the gang! Loveman is making a business trip to New England, & I am showing him the sights & antiquities of Providence, Boston, & other historic sights. Tomorrow we go to Salem & Marblehead—the old town of the witchcraft, & the best preserved Colonial village in America.

Best wishes—
Yr obt Servt H P L

Dear Clark

I am here on business and having a marvellous time. Marblehead and Salem tomorrow! Much affection to you—Sam

Notes

1. *Front:* Old South Church.

[354] [ALS]

Auburn, Cal.
March 21st, 1929.

Dear Sam:

Somehow, my thoughts have turned to you even oftener than usual, of late. You are never really forgotten . . . and I find myself wondering
about many things.

The poems enclosed with this are all quite recent. I felt that I should like
you to have them. I have put the typescript of a new volume, "The Jasmine
Girdle and Other Poems," in the hands of a N. Y. literary agent who thinks
she might do something with it.[1]

Many things have happened (my life would make a strange tale if it could
be told) and at present I am far from unhappy. But . . . to-morrow? To deprecate the wrath of the gods, let it be said that I never forget the frailty and
brevity and bitterness and imperfection that is inherent in all things. I am
haunted by "Le Gouffre"; and some day, sooner or later, I shall fare as Bierce
did, "au fond de l'inconnu."[2]

Is there any chance that you might come to California some time?

As ever,
Clark

Notes

1. The book never appeared. In 1938, R. H. Barlow was to include poems from *The
Jasmine Girdle* in his edition of CAS's *Incantations,* but the book never materialized. A
section of *SP* is titled "The Jasmine Girdle."
2. From Baudelaire's "Le Voyage": "in the depth of the unknown."

[355] [ALS]

Auburn, Calif.
April 14th, 1929.

Dear Sam:

It was like old times to receive your letter and the book, and it
meant more to me than you will probably realize. I hope you will keep your
resolution this time. **Not** writing can get to be a habit, I think, like anything
else. I know how it is.

Thanks for "Perversity,"[1] which is well and inevitably named. The psychological horror of the thing compelled me to read it through at a sitting, the
day it came. One who admires Baudelaire as I do, could not help being fascinated by such subterranean *fleurs du mal.* I've had a little experience of sadism
(not in myself) and can see that the book is veridical.

I hope you will send me the two poems you mention. I enclose some of my own recent verse, including a French sonnet with a word-for-word version in English.[2]

Lovecraft must be a wonderful person. I admire his unique genius tremendously. He is a more faithful correspondent than I deserve to have, since I have been guilty—quite inexcusably—of more than one protracted lapse.

I can well understand how you feel toward New York—indeed, the marvel to me is, how you can endure such a place or such a life at all. I, personally, find **any** city impossible—a sort of nightmare sensation takes possession of me the moment I am among crowds, clangour and big buildings, and away from the woods and fields. Evidently, "civilization" is not for me; nor I for it. The whole thing seems inconceivably futile, and I can't even conceive pleasure in the terms that you mention—"people, theatres, dance-recitals." My conception of pleasure is one that that [*sic*] the modern world would doubtless think hopelessly bucolic, idyllic and antiquated, since there is nothing that I like better than to wander in the vernal or autumnal woods with a beloved mistress, or to lie with her on a couch of grain or ivy beneath the stars and meteors of summer. Civilization hasn't invented anything that I care for—with the exception of a few perfumes. I could weep to think of a Greek spirit like you in the welter of it.

Adios. Write soon, and believe me, as always,

Your faithful friend,

Clark.

Notes

1. By Francis Carco.
2. I.e., "L'Amour supreme."

[356] [ALS]

Auburn, Calif.
April 15th, 1929.

Dear Sam:

I found your letter, with the supplement by H. P. L., in my mailbox just after I had mailed mine to you. It was more than welcome, and I think the poems are beautiful. I don't know which of the two I like best. Both remind me of Greek vases.

I can't remember just what poems and translations I sent you, but am glad you liked them. De Casseres wants me to do the whole of "Les Fleurs du Mal" into English prose, and has offered to write a preface and try to market the book for me. The work has all been blocked out, more or less roughly, but I find the polishing of some of them a formidable task, and there is much yet to be done.[1] Perhaps a hundred or more are fit for publication as they stand.

. . . The Symons translation, in regard to verse at least, was inconceivably rotten. My private theory is, that he did it under the influence of hashish—nothing else, it seems to me, could account for the vile and inconceivable twistings and per- versions of Baudelaire's actual thought and imagery.

You ask for an account of my life during the past few years—a thing that is difficult to give, in a way. I seem to have drifted along, half-idle, lazy, negli- gent, as I have always been, alas! and my grand literary projects have resolved themselves into a few slight lyrics and translations (I think I mentioned the new book, "The Jasmine Girdle and Other Poems," for which I am now try- ing to find a publisher.) As for my personal life, there **has** been much loneli- ness and sadness, a few friendships, and a little—or much—romance and glamour. Life has been pleasanter, and far less lonely, for the past two years.

I have just received a letter from Miss Virginia Lee, former editress of the "Overland Monthly," who is now on the staff of a new magazine, "Main Street," which is to be issued in N. Y. as a sort of counterblast to "The Amer- ican Mercury." Among other things, they are planning to print or reprint an entire book of poems in each issue, and there is talk of using my "Star- Treader." Certainly this, if done, should give me a little circulation.[2]

I do hope your idea of coming out here will crystallize into a genuine resolution. The climate should be better for you than that of the East, and I think you will find other merits and attractions, too.

Another letter soon.

As ever, Clark.

[P. S.] I enjoyed H. P. L.'s jeu d'esprit[3]—the two of you must have had a great time!

[P.P.S. (top of letter):] "Alexandrins" is an attempt to gallicize the poem of that name in "E. & C." There's a loss of force, concision and plangency, I fear.

Notes

1. From 1925 to 1929, CAS worked on translating *Les Fleurs du mal*. His method was to first make a literal prose translation, then to recast it into verse. Many of his trans- lations did not get past the prose stage. It does not seem that CAS ever contemplated an entire prose translation as he describes. Few of the translations were published. The presumed entirety of *Les Fleurs du mal* appears in vol. 3 of *CP*. In the absence of verse, CAS's prose version is provided.
2. It does not appear that any such magazine as *Main Street* was published at this time.
3. Unidentified.

[357] [ALS]

Auburn, Cal.,

July 25th, 1929.

Dear Sam:

Your card and the book have both arrived and both are tremendously welcome. Thanks—*mille remerciements!* Ye booke makes me think of the drawings of Hogarth, though of course it is more *naive* and roisterous, [*sic*] and without satiric or moralistic bias.

I am looking intently for that promised letter. There isn't so much news with me. I have been a little under the weather of late, and was accused of looking like a t. b. patient a few days ago, which, to please and placate some friends, has put me to the bother of visiting a doctor. The dr. says that my lungs are in perfect condition, which is no news to me—I had diagnosed that myself . . . But I wish you could have seen the damn lollipop who told my friends that I looked tubercular: I haven't told anyone what I think **he** looks like.

I have recently discovered a fellow-artist here in Auburn, one Jerome [*sic*] Rollin.[1] He is probably about 26 yrs. of age, was born near here, and has lived and studied in S. F. and Paris. I don't care much for his oils and watercolours, most of which are somewhat muddy Parisian street-corners, but some of his black-and-white drawings are quite powerful—sufficiently so, I should think, to be highly unpopular. There is a taste of Rops and Goya in some of them: a quite Satanic treatment of the female form, which is always nude, poisonous—and undepilitated. He has some drawings of devils also; one of them is gouging out the eyes of another with Chinese finger-nails, while Satan looks on and grins.

My late verses are mostly in French. De Casseres thinks that "Une Vie Spectrale" reaches the heights. Anyway, I enjoy the irony of having written it. It is probably an addition to French literature.

I think of you often. Write me soon, dear Sam, and believe me always your faithful friend,

Clark.

"Gusto" is the one word for the quality of "The English Rogue."[2]

Notes

1. CAS refers to the painter Gerome Darrell De Rollin (1905–1986).
2. By Richard Head (1637–1686). The first work of English prose fiction to be translated into a continental language.

[358] [ALS]

Auburn, Cal.,
May 12th, 1930.

Dear Sam:

I was indeed glad to receive the card which you wrote conjointly with H. P. L. And the promised letter will be extremely welcome . . . No period of silence, however, could make any difference in my friendship. I understand everything.

I would send you some poems, if I had any new ones; but I have taken exclusively to prose-writing in my old age.[1] I had stories in the May and June issues of "Weird Tales";[2] and seven more are slated for publication in the same medium. Another story, "A Murder in the Fourth Dimension," has been accepted for one of the Gernsback Magazines, "Amazing Detective tales." It is an ingenious little horror, about a man who took his rival into the fourth dimension to dispose of him without future detection, and then found that he himself couldn't get out; also that he and the corpse were subject to some very peculiar laws of time and space. These fantastic stories amuse me—in fact, they're the only sort of thing that does, just at present. The market is limited; but I simply can't write the usual magazine junk. I am now writing a fantastic novelette, about some mutineers on a space-flier, who have been marooned on a world of Delta Andromedae.[3] They have been picked up by a great bird, something between a pterodactyl and a pelican, which has stowed them away in its pouch, and is carrying them half across the world to a terrible forest of semi-animate carnivorous vegetation. Here, after escaping from the bird, which has gotten into the coils of a vegetable anaconda, one of the mutineers is partially devoured by the narcophagous plants. Human flesh, however, doesn't agree with the digestion of these plants; and the other mutineers are shoved away by the intelligent growths that are holding them captive. I don't know just what the rest of the story will be; but there are infinite possibilities, in the line of the grotesque and monstrous.

Let me hear from you; soon—

As ever,

Clark.

Notes

1. CAS almost exclusively wrote fiction from 1928 to 1938, then very little thereafter.
2. "The End of the Story" and "The Last Incantation."
3. "Marooned in Andromeda."

[359] [ALS]

Auburn, Calif.

June 16th, 1932.

Dear Sam:

      Would any of the enclosures be of interest for "Trend?"[1] The Baudelaires, as you well observe, are literal prose renderings from "Les Fleurs du Mal." "The Mirror in the Hall of Ebony" is one of my own prose poems.

      I've written nothing in verse for a long time, but have become heavily addicted to prose in my old age. Most of it sells, rather surprisingly. I sent in a little fantastic tale, "A Night in Malnéant," to "Trend" not long ago; but probably it won't be suitable. It was too plotless for the commercial mediums of fantasy.[2]

      Lovecraft spoke of seeing you, in his last letter. He seems to be having a great time in New Orleans.

As ever,

Clark.

[Typed note (by Loveman?) at bottom of letter: "This came enclosed with some manuscripts."]

Notes

1. A little magazine that SL helped establish. SL is listed as on the editorial board for only the first issue (March–April–May 1932). He contributed poems, essays, and reviews to the first several issues.

2. Nothing by CAS appeared in *Trend*.

[360] [ANS postcard][1]   [Donald Wandrei and CAS to SL]

[Postmarked Auburn, Cal.,

21 November 1934]

Dear Sam—The picture fails utterly to convey the quiet beauty of Auburn and the hills that sweep into mountains— Would that you had been present on the sessions with Clark. You would immensely enjoy talking to him, and perhaps he may yet adopt my suggestion that he investigate the wiles of Manhattan.

Donald

Sometime I shall adopt the suggestion of the Wanderer! Till then, my best to you.

Clark.

Notes

1. *Front:* Auburn, Calif.

[361] [TLS]

[January 1935?]

Dear Sam:

Your letter, enclosing the round robin from the gang (and what a gang!) was most warmly welcomed. Never, at any time, be it said, had I misunderstood your silence; for I know too well how hard it is to write letters under conditions of grinding work, worry, struggle, and general infelicity. Too much of my own correspondence, for such reasons, has been sorely neglected or late; so that no one in the world should—or could—be more lenient than I toward a long epistolatory gap.

I hope that the concern with which you work is not *too* hardly hit; or that, if you are forced to make a change, the change will be for the better. Certainly these are parlous times; and your simile of "a civilization oozing away like a gas balloon" certainly expresses it. As for me, I have, for several years, been able to peck out some sort of living for myself and my parents from the writing of fantastic fiction. Nothing gaudy; but most of the bills have been paid, so far. Of late, work has been terribly slow and difficult; not, I think, because of any failure of power, but because of circumstances that form a sort of deadlock. I have not done any drawings (other than a few pencil grotesques, and illustrations in ink for Weird Tales[)], for a longer period than I like to realize; and poetry has also gone by the board.

Donald Wandrei, whose visit here was prodigiously enjoyed by all who met him, has doubtless told you something of my life. I am glad that he has been able to give so good an account of Auburn and its denizens! I hope to God that your western visit will materialize some time—the sooner the better. You can rest assured of a welcome which, if not royal from the material standpoint, will be such in all other ways. As for my coming to New York, I am inclined to think that such an event is impossible till my present responsibilities come to an end. I should like tremendously to come there for a visit; though, being country-born and having spent half a lifetime amid sylvan surroundings, I cannot quite imagine myself wanting to live for any period of time in a metropolitan center.

I hope that a volume of your poems can be brought out, including the beautiful "Hermaphrodite." There is a certain one of your lyrics—beginning, "I shall go back again to my dreams,"[1] which recurs in my memory about as often as anything that I know.

There has been for some time past, on the [p]art of an admirer in S. F.[2] who has English connections and influence, a project to submit a selection of my best poems to publishers in Great Britain. But I do not know that anything has been done about it yet. The aforesaid admirer, a lawyer and novelist, is sadly overworked. Perhaps something may yet eventuate.

I shall try to find something to enclose with this. Here's hoping that you will write again soon, and that Fate will repent of her everlasting perverseness and at last enable us to meet.

> A double health—sherry and then whisky—to you!
>> Faithfully, Clark.

Tell me more about Hart Crane—I know so little of him.[3]

[Enclosure? Clipping from *Fantasy Fan*, December 1934: "Prose Pastels 5. The Passing of Aphrodite." Handwritten note on top: "For Sam."]

Notes

1. "Isolation," l. 1: "I shall go back to my life of dreams,"; see letter 202.
2. George Work.
3. Harold Hart Crane (1899–1932) was an American poet and friend of SL. He wrote Modernist poetry that was highly stylized and ambitious in scope. His most significant work, *The Bridge* (1930), was an epic poem in the vein of Eliot's *The Waste Land*. He committed suicide at the age of 32. SL was his literary executor.

[362] [TLS]

> Auburn, Calif.,
>> March 5th, 1936.

Dear Sam:

I was mightily pleased to receive your volume of poems, and this not alone for the sake of the book itself. My opinion of your work you have long known: it has been confirmed by a re-reading of the pieces familiar to me, and a delighted perusal of the ones I had not seen before. The Hermaphrodite (maybe I have said this: but it will bear repeating) has in it more of the nostalgia of ancient beauty, the nympholepsy and "the indestructible pagan delirium,"[1] than anything written since Keats. The earlier poems, in [*sic*] Pierrot's Garden, To Dionysus, to [*sic*] Apollo, and others, have lost nothing of their dewy loveliness. I found an old favorite in Isolation—a lyric that I have long remembered and often quoted to friends. Palingenesis is new to me; it seems one of the most perfect of the shorter pieces.

The Caxton Printers have done an admirable job, and I hope the book will receive something of its proper meed of appreciation. I do not see how it could fail to delight any true lover of poetry. But such lovers, as we know, have never figured prominently in the census returns.

It seems the natural resumption of an old habit to be writing to you again. I had meant to write, long before your book arrived: but my vice of procrastination seems to have grown upon me damnably. I have never written so few letters as during the past year; but this has been due to a complex of troubles, duties and sorrows, together with a sort of nervous exhaustion. My mother's death[2] last autumn was a heavy blow to me; and there have been many other things to depress and wear me down. Writing of any kind has been difficult. I completed only four stories, and perhaps five or six new poems, in the whole of 1935. I am now making a systematic attempt to resume my fiction, on which I must depend almost entirely for a livelihood; but I find the concentration, so far, abominably hard and thankless. If it weren't for the money angle, I'd paint and carve for a few months. I haven't made any paintings in years (only small grotesque drawings) but during the past year have experimented considerably with carvings done in local minerals, and have found a vast fascination in an art which, heretofore, I never even thought of attempting.[3]

These carvings, I believe, will interest you, since you found so much in my pictorial efforts. In a day or two, I shall express you a box containing twelve or thirteen of them. From this lot, I should like you to select one as a gift for yourself. Wandrei, Long, Koenig,[4] perhaps others, should see the exhibit while it is in your possession. Benjamin and Bio deCasseres [*sic*], with whom I am somewhat out of touch through my neglect in writing to them, would also be interested.

At your leisure, you can forward the box to Lovecraft, who is next on the circulation list. I am very eager to learn your opinion of the carvings, and trust that they will not be a disappointment to you. The subject-matter is similar to that of my drawings; fantastic and monstrous entities, for the most part. You will find among them a harpy who departs from the classic conception in having a horny carapace in lieu of wings; a primordial cat-goddess; beings from Venus and a world of Algol; a cameo of Proserpine after many ages in hell; a medallion showing a blossom such as she might have plucked in the fields of Enna; several beings from pre-glacial Hyperborea; and perhaps others of equally fabulous origin. I'll number them on the base and enclose a list of titles with notations as to the materials. Some of these materials, by the way, were taken from the carcass of a dinosaur. Technically speaking, they are fossils; though the dinosaur's remains had all been converted into talcs and clays which I am not enough of a mineralogist to identify precisely. All have the property common to the other minerals I use: they harden more or less when burnt in an open fire after carving.

Here's hoping (I don't mean this in any flippant sense!) that you are able to obey Baudelaire's injunction concerning inebriety,[5] whether with wine, poetry, prose, the body's beauty, the soul's beauty, or what you will. I can think of no better advice. To this I add my sincerest good wishes for the success of the new bookshop. Sometime I hope to see you face to face: it seems highly probable that I shall come to New York, at least for a visit, when my present responsibilities are at an end. I dream of a one-way journey to Acheron; but, having deferred this through all my past miseries, perhaps I shall unwind the thread of mortality to its dark spindle!

Yours, with fraternal affection, as always,

Clark.

Notes

1. Benjamin De Casseres, "The Unearthly Imagination," *Shadowland* 8, No. 2 (April 1923): 20.

2. Mary Frances (Gaylord) Smith (b. 1850) died on 9 September 1935, age 85.

3. CAS worked longer and more steadily on carving (1935–59?) than he did in other media.

4. Frank Belknap Long (1901–1994) and Herman Charles Koenig (1893–1950), members of Lovecraft's circle of friends.

5. See letter 43n2.

[363] [TLS]

Auburn, Cal.,

April 21st., 1936.

Dear Sam:

      Have you received the box of carvings which I expressed to you at 17 Middagh St., on March 9th? Not having heard from you, I am beginning to wonder if some mishap could have befallen the box. If you did receive it, could you set my mind at rest with a postcard; if you did not, I suggest that you make some inquiry at the Brooklyn office of the Railway Express Agency. I am holding the receipt of the local office for the box. It was very carefully packed and marked **Fragile.**

    I hope things are better with you than with me.

      As ever,

        Clark

[364] [TLS]

[BODLEY BOOK SHOP
104 FIFTH AVENUE
ROOM 1705
NEW YORK, N. Y.]

[June 1941]

Dear Clark,

      Eric Barker[1] has just dropped into my office, and there has been much discussion as to your intended visit to New York. I hope you can, and I fervently believe you will. Eric tells me that he and Madeleyne intend to stay until after Christmas. I believe that a Christmas or New Year[']s spent in the company of the three of you, would be a high-point in my own, somewhat careless career. So what say you? Can you—will you? Don't take this for a letter. I'll get down to the business of writing you a real one soon. This is the eve of Madeleyne's recital, and I am going uptown to see it to-night. I wish

her a lot of luck—lots of it. Eric wants to say a few words. With kind and affectionate regards from your since[re] and oldtime friend

Sam Loveman

Dear Ashton:

I'm writing in Sam's private sanctum on the 17th floor high up above the teeming antheap. Tonight we are all going to Madelynne's recital; she has been nervous, naturally, with all the thousand and one things there is to do, but now everything is looking promising. Our one regret is that you are not here, but after your last letter, perhaps you will be ere long. I only hope you can carry this zestful mood of yours through to a successful conclusion, and join us before long. Madelynne has prevailed upon me to stay until after Christmas; after that our finances will be at such a low ebb that something will have to pop, one way or another. I'm still as homesick as hell for the warm hills of home. Sam has just presented us with a copy of his unequalled "The Hermaphrodite." Will write a real letter in a day or two. In haste. Fraternally and affectionately

Eric

Notes

1. Eric Barker (1905–1973), American poet born in England. He was the husband of dancer Madelynne F. Greene (d. 1970; her tombstone gives no birth date). Both were good friends of CAS. Their friendship inspired CAS's poetry cycle *The Hill of Dionysus*.

[365] [TLS]

Auburn, Calif.,
June 17th, 1941.

Dear Sam:

I was glad to hear from my friends, Eric and Madelynne, that they had called on you; but I regret most abominably that I could not have been with them! However, I am still hoping to raise the cash that will enable me to make an eastward trip.

I believe you will find the Barkers very congenial; they, like you and I, are pagans haunted by the nostalgia of antique beauty. I owe them many of my happiest days, and have found something of the Golden Age in their company.

Eric is a true poet, especially in his feeling for the more inward and mystic springs of nature. Madelynne has imaginative talent both as a dancer and sculptress, together with energy, ambition, untiring application. I am delighted to learn that you can give her so many introductions in New York dancing circles. She deserves a recognition she has not yet had out here in the west.

How is it with you nowadays, Sam? It is so long since I have heard from you. But I have become a most errant correspondent myself and am hopelessly in arrears to almost everyone.

No doubt the Barkers will have told you as much about me as I could tell in a letter. I write an occasional poem, and will type some of the recent ones for enclosure. One or two pieces, such as *Witch-Dance*, have been suggested by Madelynne's dancing: she once did her *Witches' Sabbat* for me by firelight and moonlight here on the ridge, as described in the poem. She has created a dance to interpret my poem, *The Phoenix*, and has made dances for two of Eric's poems.

May the old, the true gods be with you. I hope we shall meet before many moons.

                    Faithfully,
                         Clark

[366] [ALS]

                                        Auburn, Cal.,
                                      Nov. 25th, 1941.

Dear Sam:

I can't make N. Y. this Christmas but may do it by Xmas 1942.

Note enclosed clipping from local paper. I've started a little publicity for myself and am beginning to get results.[1]

I'm looking for that promised letter.

                    Faithfully, yr. old friend, Clark.

Notes

1. Probably "Local Boy Makes Good" [unsigned, but by CAS], *Auburn Journal* (3 November 1941): 1, 4; *WT* 36, No. 4 (March 1942): 119–21 (under heading "The Eyrie"; as "Clark Ashton Smith—His Life and Letters"). This was followed in December by an article by Eleanor Fait. Both are reprinted in *Eccentric, Impractical Devils.*

[367] [ANS postcard][1]

                            [Postmarked Venice, Italy,
                                date undecipherable]

Dear Clark—Its impossible to describe all the magnificence & splendor of this city. Have come here after a week in Paris. I go from here to Florence, Rome, Naples, Capri, Amalfi and Sorrento—then back to Venice again & a week more in Paris. I'll write you at great length when I return. I may be in California later this year. I will surely be

        Your old friend
            Sam Loveman

Notes

1. *Front:* Venezia—Basilica di S. Marco.

Appendix

Samuel Loveman's Letters to Carol Smith

[1] [ALS]

Jan. 15 / 69 [i.e. 1970]

Dear Mrs. Smith—

       If I have been amiss in writing to you, forgive me. I am old, as years go—83—and in abominable health. I hope to leave New York before the end of the year and return to my home-town, Cleveland, where I still have a brother and sister.[1] New York has become a city of terror to me, and so utterly different from what it was when I came here in 1924. Apart from all this, I was happy to hear from you.

       Now as to Clark and my material. Some time ago, I catalogued two sets of his letters—five in each, at $50.00. One set sold; the other remained. I am sending the remaining batch of five for the check that you have enclosed. If you dissent I will gladly return that amount.

       The remainder of Clark's material is in storage—safely. It is a tremendous collection. I have not counted the letters, but there are upwards of 500—many of great length. Included in them are many mss. of his poetry—much, unpublished. Clark was very young when I began to correspond with him. It began with "The Star-Treader"—a volume as great, if not greater, than anything by Keats or Shelley. I have several hundred (I believe) of his drawings, proofs, etc. I had intended to offer this material, at a price, to either the University of California or the Huntington Library. I shall be glad to make some arrangement to sell all of this to you. Its biographical and critical value to foster a claim or appraisal of Clark's great station as an American poet (over the pygmies who function now) would be inestimable.

       I was a close friend of George Sterling and a protege of Ambrose Bierce, whom I visited in 1913, just before his disappearance.

       Believe me, with kind regards

Sincerely
Samuel Loveman

1486 Second Ave.,
New York, N.Y. 10021

[Envelope postmarked New York, N.Y., Jan. 16, 1970.]

Notes

1. Hermine R. Vodička (1889–1974) and Isadore Loveman (1892–1984). His brother Alfred (b. 1895) died in 1964.

[2]   [ALS]

Jan. 25 / 70

Dear Mrs. Smith,

It was good to hear from you; your letter brings the happy relationship of Clark in happier times, closer to me.

I am extremely old now—83, to be exact, mentally alert, but in bad health, chiefly among the ailments being angina, not to mention other things, including cataracts.

It is my intention to go back to Cleveland where I stem from, and live with my sister, who is 80. I have a brother there, 75. My youngest brother lies buried in a military cemetery in L.A. I visited there with my sister two years ago; I would love to live in California, where I have a niece and many relatives.

All of this prefatory matter leads me to this. I must sell all my possessions. I believe that you should acquire Clark's material. If a biography is to be done, and it should be—this early period in his career of writing would be invaluable. I have hesitated to reread it—the past is poignant.

I am asking $1200 for everything. The letters include many manuscripts of his poems. I do not want to parcel it off into payments, as I want to make short shrift and leave N.Y., which I abominate. I believe that with your assistance, Clark should become recognised as a great American poet—greater, I believe, than George Sterling. I am the literary executor of Hart Crane, my closest friend. I sold all of his letters for $5000, including all the mss. of his poems—15 years ago. The collection is now worth from $75,000 upwards. Single letters bring $350. I hope you can make a speedy decision. What I ask is not through greed—but emergency.

There is a massive biography of Hart just published by Farrar, Straus, by Prof. John Unterecker; it is dedicated to me and I figure (happily) in the text concerning Hart's calamitous life. Incidentally, I was a protege of Ambrose Bierce whom I visited in 1913; he was outspoken in his praise of Clark's poetry; antagonistic toward Sterling.

I would so much like to know about Clark's later life. My own has had its catastrophes—too many, as a matter of fact.

Permit me to hear from you and believe me

Sincerely and Cordially

Sam Loveman

1486 2nd Ave.,
      N.Y.C. 10021
         N.Y.

[P.S.] I hope you can decipher this letter. My typewriter is in need of repair.

And a Little Book Shall Lead Them

Benjamin De Casseres

SELECTED POEMS. *By George Sterling.* Henry Holt & Company.
EBONY AND CRYSTAL. *By Clark Ashton Smith.* Printed by the *Auburn Journal,* Auburn, Cal.

I bunch these two books together because they came together and because George Sterling wrote the preface to the Ashton Smith poems.

It is hard for me to review books of poetry. In the first place, I am a poet myself; in the second place, I have so saturated my life since boyhood with the great poets and the great prose writers, that I have gone stale on poetry. In a word, I am simply tired of it—at least to-day. I prefer to take my poetry, now, in prose or music or the curves of women's bodies. The poets writing to-day in America are mere echoes. After Whitman and Poe, Swinburne and Francis Thompson, Verlaine, Hugo, and D'Annunzio, what is there to be said? Nothing. And there is no new way of saying the old things.

I have always been an admirer of George Sterling since that day he burst upon us in the old *Cosmopolitan* yahooed by Ambrose Bierce. But his was never great poetry. No rebellion, no real terror, too much rhyming, too much perfection, too much artistry—no real personality. No one would necessarily want to know Sterling after reading his poetry. No one would be curious about him. And the test of all great art is personality. But I have known no better poetry of its kind being written in the present-day America than Sterling writes.

The poetry of Ashton Smith is out of an unearthly imagination. It is morphinated, hallucinated poetry. It is gemmed and jeweled stuff. Some of it is as ethereal as Poe's. It is a book I am always picking up and finding in it gorgeous adventures.

But, gentleman, poetry is dead the world around.

[*Arts and Decoration* 19, No. 4 (August 1923): 47, 50.]

Preface [*to* The Hermaphrodite]

Benjamin De Casseres

Maybe it was more than a coincidence, for there is a profound courage in certain forms of credulity. And so, on second thought, I will call it literary, or psychic magnetism.

I was deep in a second reading, after a quarter of century, of Balzac's "Seraphita," that amazing imaginative flight of the French writer into the realms of the occult. Seraphita–Seraphitus, the hero–heroine of Balzac's book, is a hermaphrodite, a mysterious and divinely beautiful boy–girl of the Norse Mountains, who is loved by both a girl and a man. She is an epiphany, an incarnation, the final evolution of the human being before its evanescence into a super-dimension, where male and female are one, a union in one body of eternal mates lost to one another for kalpas of time before the Fall into duality, a myth that is universal and which is the basis of profoundest mystical thought.

It was while deeply absorbed in the philosophy of "Seraphita" that Samuel Loveman, a poet whom I knew only vaguely by name, brought to my house casually a poem called "The Hermaphrodite." I had not read the first four lines of it when I was completely under the spell of Loveman's magic—for there is in this poem a magic as authentic as Keats and a contained and sustained lyrical frenzy for the "Supreme Loveliness" that sets it apart from all other poetic fads, fancies and transparent fakery that is yowled and yawped abroad as the "Ultra Modern note."

No, there is quite another "note" in Loveman's "The Hermaphrodite." It is the note of the Eternal. There is in his work the breath of Ineffable Beauty that soars and shudders and flashes and blazes in the souls of Spencer, Herrick, Marlowe, Keats, Swinburne, Baudelaire, Poe and Verlaine. The footprints of the phantom Helena are in every line of "The Hermaphrodite."

Passion, sensuousness and spontaneity are inherent in this poem. In art there cannot be illusion without spontaneity. It is implicit. Because of this spontaneousness—this unfettered parade of vision and image from brain to paper—I received this rare blessing (rare in poetry nowadays) of perfect illusion. Samuel Loveman is Prospero.

His style is simple and chaste. One can easily see he is not a poet by profession. He is a poet by election, "whose footfall loosed Olympian splendor."

[Samuel Loveman, *The Hermaphrodite: A Poem* (Athol, MA: W. Paul Cook/The Recluse Press, 1926), n.p.]

Rhymes and Reactions

George Sterling

Long Island is the terminal moraine of the great glacier of the last Ice Age, and on some of its eastern beaches one may find beautifully lucid quartz crystal, eternal dews that the sun and wind of Time have not effaced.

Thinking of them, I am reminded of a remarkable poem that has just reached me, "The Hermaphrodite," by the young poet Samuel Loveman.* It is from The Recluse Press of Athol, Mass., which has printed three hundred and fifty copies of the small book—in a true civilization thirty-five million would be required.

If you expect to find in it any tale of erotic aberration or stimulus, you would better leave this splendid poem unread. It has none of that: it is "only" poetry, pure poetry of as marvelous a translucence as any crystal polished by the sand and waves of lonely beaches. Here indeed Mr. Loveman has taken all the loveliness and tragedy of the great Past, and distilled from them his necklace of immutable dews. The poem is coherent and mournfully beautiful, and the lament of the hermaphrodite over the perished splendor of old years is, as De Casseres points out in his all-too-brief preface, of "a magic as authentic as Keats and a contained and sustained lyrical frenzy for the 'Supreme Loveliness' that sets it apart from all other fads, fancies and transparent fakery that are yawled and yawped abroad as the 'ultra modern note.'"

One can more than echo all that De Casseres says in praise of the poem. Reading his preface I feared that it must prove extravagant, but the lyric outburst in the pages that followed gave rest to my apprehensions. Here is an unforgettable and almost perfect poem, as authentically the work of genius as "The Eve of St. Agnes." Whether or not Mr. Loveman can follow it up with others of the same amazing quality I do not know. Even if he fail to, his fame should be assured by this single triumph of sheer art and inspiration. No reader of "The Hermaphrodite" will forget it, for

> "Beautiful was this god and tender,
> Whose footfall loosed Olympian splendour,
> Where on the golden hair were set
> Wind flower for a coronet."

[*Overland Monthly* 84, No. 12 (December 1926): 395.]

---

*The typographer misspelled Loveman's name as *Tweman* throughout, and *footfall* as *football*.

Bibliography

A. Works by Clark Ashton Smith

Books

The Abominations of Yondo. Sauk City, WI: Arkham House, 1960.

The Black Book of Clark Ashton Smith. Edited by Donald Sidney-Fryer and Rah Hoffman. Sauk City, WI: Arkham House, 1979.

The Complete Poetry and Translations. Edited by S. T. Joshi and David E. Schultz. New York: Hippocampus Press, 2007–08. 3 vols.

The Devil's Notebook: Collected Epigrams and Pensées. Edited by Donald Sidney-Fryer and Don Herron. Mercer Island, WA: Starmont House, 1990.

Ebony and Crystal: Poems in Verse and Prose. Auburn, CA: Auburn Journal, 1922.

Eccentric, Impractical Devils: The Letters of August Derleth and Clark Ashton Smith. Edited by David E. Schultz and S. T. Joshi. New York: Hippocampus Press, 2020.

Grotesques and Fantastiques. Saddle River, NJ: Gerry de La Ree. 1973.

In the Realms of Mystery and Wonder: Collected Prose Poems and Artwork of Clark Ashton Smith. Edited by Scott Connors. Lakewood, CO: Centipede Press, 2017.

The Lure of the Grotesque and Monstrous: Three Letters. Edited by D. S. Black. [Berkeley, CA:] Bancroft Library Press, 2004. *Contents:* "Introduction" by D. S. Black ([3–4]); Letter to Samuel Loveman (19 June 1915) ([5–6]); Letter to Samuel Loveman (16 February 1921) ([7–8]); Letter to Samuel Loveman (12 May 1930) ([9–10]).

Nero and Other Poems. Lakeport, CA: Futile Press, 1937.

Odes and Sonnets. San Francisco: Book Club of California, 1918. *Contents:* "Preface," by George Sterling (iii–iv); "Nero" (1–5); "Ode to the Abyss" (6–9); "To the Darkness" (10–12); "The Retribution" (13); "Satan Unrepentant" (14–18); "Alexandrines" (19); "Exotique" (20); "Ave atque Vale" (21); "The Ministers of Law" (22); "The Refuge of Beauty" (23); "The Crucifixion of Eros" (24); "The Harlot of the World" (25); "Belated Love" (26); "The Medusa of Despair" (27); "Memnon at Midnight" (28).

Planets and Dimensions: Collected Essays of Clark Ashton Smith. Edited by Charles K. Wolfe. Baltimore: Mirage Press, 1973.

Poems in Prose. Sauk City, WI: Arkham House, 1965.

Sandalwood. Auburn, CA: Auburn Journal, 1925.

Selected Letters. Edited by David E. Schultz and Scott Connors. Sauk City, WI: Arkham House, 2003.

Selected Poems. Sauk City, WI: Arkham House, 1971. Prepared 1944–49.

The Shadow of the Unattained: Letters of George Sterling and Clark Ashton Smith. Edited
   by David E. Schultz and S. T. Joshi. New York: Hippocampus Press, 2005.
Spells and Philtres. Sauk City, WI: Arkham House, 1958.
The Star-Treader and Other Poems. San Francisco: A. M. Robertson, 1912.
Strange Shadows: The Uncollected Fiction and Essays of Clark Ashton Smith. Edited
   by Steve Behrends, Donald Sidney-Fryer, and Rah Hoffman. Westport,
   CT: Greenwood Press, 1989.

Poems

All extant works noted by Smith in verse are gathered in *The Complete Poetry
and Translations.*

"The Absence of the Muse." *Lyric West* 1, No. 6 (October 1921): 14. In *EC, SP.*
"The Abyss Triumphant." *Town Talk* No. 1041 (3 August 1912): 8. *Current
   Literature* 53, No. 4 (October 1912): 473. In *EC, SP.*
"Alexandrines." In *OS, EC, SP.*
"Alexandrins." In *SP.*
"Alien Memory." See "Exotic Memory."
"Amor Aeternalis." In *SP.* In *Fire and Sleet and Candlelight,* ed. August Derleth.
   Sauk City, WI: Arkham House. 186. First title: "To Love."
"L'Amour suprême." In *Grotesques and Fantastiques.*
"Antony to Cleopatra."
"Arabesque." In *EC, SP.*
"Autumnal." In *EC.*
"Ave atque Vale." In *OS, EC. Step Ladder* 13, No. 5 (May 1927): 136. In *SP.*
"Belated Love." In *OS, EC. Step Ladder* 13, No. 5 (May 1927): 132. In *SP.*
"Beyond the Great Wall." In *EC. Asia* 24, No. 5 (May 1924): 359. In *SP.*
"The Blindness of Orion." *Arkham Sampler* 1, No. 1 (Spring 1948): 20. In *SP.*
"The Cherry-Snows." In *ST.* In *California State Series: Sixth Year Literature Read-
   er,* ed. LeRoy E. Armstrong. Sacramento: Robert L. Telfer, Superinten-
   dent State Publishing, 1916 (11th ed. 1928). 86. In *SP.*
"The City in the Desert." In *EC, SP.*
"The Clouds."
"Coldness." In *EC, SP.* It did not appear in *Bohemia* (letter 66).
"Crepuscule." In *EC* (as "Crepuscle"), *SP.*
"The Crucifixion of Eros." In *OS, EC. Step Ladder* 13, No. 5 (May 1927): 132.
   In *SP.*
"The Desert Garden." See "Song of Sappho's Arabian Daughter."
"A Dead City." In *ST, SP.*
"Dissonance." *Thrill Book* 2, No. 6 (15 September 1919): 149. In *EC, SP.*
"A Dream of Beauty." *Academy* 81 (12 August 1911): 196. In *ST.* In *A
   Collection of Verse by California Poets: From 1849 to 1915,* ed. Augustin S.
   Macdonald. San Francisco: A. M. Robertson, 1914. 54. *Golden Atom* 1,

No. 8 (May 1940): 3. In *SP*. In *Unseen Wings: The Living Poetry of Man's Immortality*, ed. Stanton A. Coblentz. New York: Beechhurst Press, 1949. 261–62.

"Duality." *WT* 2, No. 1 (July–August 1923): 69 (as "The Garden of Evil"). *AJ* 24, No. 20 (28 February 1924): 6. In *S*, *SP*.

"Eidolon." In *EC*, *SP*.

"Ennui." *Weird Tales* 27, No. 5 (May 1936): 547. In *SP*,

"Eros in the Desert."

"Exotic Memory." In *SP* (as a translation from "Christophe des Laurières").

"Exotique." In *OS*, *EC*, *SP*.

"Fire of Snow." *Poetry* 6, No. 4 (July 1915): 178. In *SP*.

"The Flight of Azrael." *Fantastic Worlds* 1, No. 1 (Summer 1952): 15. In *SP*.

"Flamingoes." *Asia* 19, No. 11 (November 1919): 1134. In *EC*, *SP*.

"For a Wine-Jar."

"Forgetfulness." *Sonnet* 4, No. 2 (May–June 1919): 2. In *EC*, *SP*.

"The Garden of Dreams." In *Grotesques and Fantastiques*.

"The Ghoul and the Seraph." In *EC*, *SP*.

"Give Me Your Lips." *Live Stories* 10, No. 1 (February 1917): 48.

"The Harlot of the World." *Town Talk* No. 1115 (27 March 1915): 5. In *OS*. *Town Talk* No. 1361 (21 September 1918): [15] ("Golden Gate Literary Number"). In *EC*, *SP*.

The Hashish-Eater; or, The Apocalypse of Evil. In *EC*, *SP*.

"Heliogabalus." In *SP* (as a translation from "Christophe des Laurières").

"In Saturn." *Sonnet* 2, No. 2 (January–February 1919): 2. In *EC*, *SP*.

"In the Wind." *Poetry* 6, No. 4 (July 1915): 178. In *SP*.

"Inferno." In *EC*, *SP*.

"Inheritance." In *EC*, *SP*.

"The Kingdom of Shadows." In *EC*, *SP*. "The Kingdom of Madness" is probably an alternate title.

"Laus Mortis." *Pearson's Magazine* 47, No. 3 (September 1921): 100. In *EC*, *SP*.

"Love Malevolent." *Live Stories* (1916) [not seen]. In *EC*. *Step Ladder* 13, No. 5 (May 1927): 134.

"The Medusa of Despair." *Town Talk* No. 1113 (20 December 1913): 8. In *OS*, *EC*, *SP*.

"Mirrors." In *EC*, *SP*.

"The Mummy." *Sonnet* 4, No. 2 (May–June 1919): 3. In *EC*.

"Nero." In *ST*, *OS*, *SP*.

"Ode to Aphrodite."

"Ode to Beauty." See "To Beauty."

"The Orchid of Beauty." In *EC* (as "The Orchid"), *SP*.

"Orion." See "The Blindness of Orion."

"Palms." *Asia* 20, No. 3 (April 1920): 330. In *EC.* In *Songs and Stories,* ed. Edwin Markham. Los Angeles: Powell Publishing Co., 1931; Freeport, NY: Books for Libraries Press, 1974. 424. In *SP.*

"The Phoenix." *WT* 35, No. 3 (May 1940): 94. In *SP.*

"Poplars." *Snappy Stories* 70, No. 2 (5 November 1922): 46 (12 lines only). In *Grotesques and Fantastiques.*

"A Prayer." *Snappy Stories* 24, No. 3 (4 February 1917): 23.

"Psalm to the Desert."

"Quest." *AJ* 22, No. 10 (22 December 1921): 4. In *EC. Step Ladder* 13, No. 5 (May 1927): 133. In *SP.*

"Le Refuge" [French].

"The Refuge of Beauty." In *OS, EC. L'Alouette* 1, No. 3 (May 1924): 66. In *SP.* It did not appear in *Town Talk* (letter 66).

"Remembered Light." *Poetry* 1, No. 3 (December 1912): 78. In *EC, SP.*

"Requiescat" (What was Love's worth,). *Smart Set* 68, No. 4 (August 1922): 102. In *EC, SP.*

"Requiescat in Pace." *Midland* 5, No. 5 (May 1920): 46–47. In *EC, SP.*

"Retrospect and Forecast." *San Francisco Call* (1 December 1912): 6. In *ST. Current Opinion* 54, No. 2 (February 1913): 150. In *SP.*

"The Return of Hyperion." In *ST, SP.*

"Satan Unrepentant." In *OS, EC, SP.*

"Satiety" (Dear you were as is the tree of being). In *EC, SP.*

"Saturn." In *ST, SP.*

"Secret Love." In *SP* (as a translation from "Christophe des Laurières").

"Sepulture." *Smart Set* 57, No. 2 (October 1922): 122. In *EC.* In *California Poets: An Anthology of 224 Contemporaries.* New York: Henry Harrison, 1932. 664. In *SP.*

"Song of Sappho's Arabian Daughter." *Ainslee's* 43, No. 1 (February 1919): 80 (as "The Desert Garden"). In *EC* (as "The Desert Garden"), *SP.*

"The Sorrow of the Winds." *Poetry* 1, No. 3 (December 1912): 80 (as "Sorrowing of Winds"). In *EC, SP.*

"Strangeness." *Bohemia* 2, No. 4 ([May] 1917): 3. In *EC, SP.*

"Symbols." *London Mercury* No. 33 (July 1922): 245 (as by "A. Clark Ashton Smith"). In *EC.* In *California Poets: An Anthology of 224 Contemporaries.* New York: Henry Harrison, 1932. 664. In *SP.*

"To Beauty." In *SP.*

"To George Sterling: A Valediction." *Overland Monthly* 85, No. 11 (November 1927): 338. In *SP* (both as "A Valediction to George Sterling").

"To Love." See "Amor Aeternalis."

"To Nora May French." In *EC, SP.*

"To Omar Khayyam." In *EC. Lyric West* 5, No. 8 (May–June 1926): 216–17. In *SP.*

"To the Darkness." In *ST, OS, SP.*

"To the Sun." In *ST, SP.*
"Une Vie spectrale." In *SP.*
"A Vision of Lucifer." In *EC, SP.* Alternate title: "To Satan."
"Winter Moonlight" (The silence of the silver night). In *EC, SP.*
"Witch-Dance." *WT* 36, No. 1 (September 1941): 104–5. In *SP.*
"The Witch in the Graveyard." In *EC, SP.*

Translations from Baudelaire. All in CP 3.
"Le Beau Navire."
"Le Gouffre."
"Les Hiboux." *AJ* 25, No. 51 (1 October 1925): 4 (as "Les Hiboux"). *Step Ladder* 13, No. 5 (May 1927): 138 (as "Les Hiboux"). *WT* 36, No. 2 (November 1941): 120 (as translated by "Timeus Gaylord"). In *Dark of the Moon,* ed. August Derleth (Sauk City, WI: Arkham House, 1947), pp. 346–47 (as by [not translated by] "Timeus Gaylord"). In *SP.*
"The Irreparable." *WT* 12, No. 2 (August 1928): 261 (as "L'Irreparable"; as one of "Three Poems in Prose"). In *Grotesques and Fantastiques* (as "L'Irreparable"). [Some mss. as "L'Irréparable."]
"Les Metamorphoses du Vampire." In *Spells and Philtres, SP.*
"Parfum Exotique." *Measure* No. 50 (April 1925): 9. In *S.*
"XXVI." [Untitled.]

Fiction. All in CF 1.

"The End of the Story." *WT* 15, No. 5 (May 1930): 637–48.
"The Last Incantation." *WT* 15, No. 6 (June 1930): 783–86.
"Marooned in Andromeda." *Wonder Stories* 2, No. 5 (October 1930): 390–401.
  "Murder in the Fourth Dimension." *Amazing Detective Tales* 1, No. 10 (October 1930): 908–37.
"A Night in Malnéant." In *The Double Shadow and Other Fantasies.* Auburn, CA: [Auburn Journal Print], [June] 1933. *WT* 34, No. 3 (September 1939): 102–5.

Other Works

All prose poems are gathered in *In the Realms of Mystery and Wonder.*

"The Black Lake." In *EC.*
"The Crystals."
"The Demon, the Angel, and Beauty." In *EC.*
"Ennui." *Smart Set* 56, No. 1 (September 1918): 32. In *EC.*
"The Flower-Devil." In *EC.*
"From the Crypts of Memory." *Bohemia* 2, No. 3 (April 1917): 27. In *EC.*
"George Sterling—An Appreciation." *Overland Monthly* 85, No. 3 (March 1927): 79–80. In *Planets and Dimensions.* In *SU.*

"Gray Sorrow." Nonextant?

"The Litany of the Seven Kisses." In *EC. Laughing Horse* No. 6 (1923): [19].

"The Memnons of the Night." *Bohemia* 2, No. 1 (1 February 1917): 27 (as "Memnons of the Night").

"The Mirror in the Hall of Ebony." *Fantasy Fan* 1, No. 9 (May 1934): 140, 144. *Acolyte* 1, No. 4 (Summer 1943): 3–4. In *The Abominations of Yondo*.

"The Mortuary."

"A Phantasy." *Bohemia* 1, No. 5 (15 November 1916): 157. In *EC*.

"The Princess Almeena." *Smart Set* 61, No. 2 (February 1920): 1. In *EC*.

"Remoteness." In *EC*.

"The Shadows." In *EC*.

"The Sun and the Sepulchre."

"The Traveller." In *EC*.

"Venus and the Priest." Nonextant (probably never completed).

B. Works by Samuel Loveman

All extant works noted by Loveman in verse and prose are gathered in *Out of the Immortal Night.*

Books

The Hermaphrodite: A Poem. Preface by Benjamin De Casseres. Athol, MA: Published by W. Paul Cook/The Recluse Press, [July] 1926.

The Hermaphrodite and Other Poems. Caldwell, ID: Caxton Printers, [January] 1936.

Out of the Immortal Night: Selected Works by Samuel Loveman. Edited by S. T. Joshi and David E. Schultz. New York: Hippocampus Press, 2004; revised and expanded ed. 2021.

Poems. Cleveland: Published for the Author, 1911. 24 pp. *Contents:* In Pierrote's Garden (3–5); Ode to Dionysus (5–7); Ode to Ceres (7–8); Fra Angelico (9–10); Song (10); Dirge (11); To P. G. (12–13); Lines (13); A Twenty-Second Birthday (14–15); From Heine (15–18); Oedipus at Colonus (18–24).

A Round-Table in Poictesme: A Symposium (co-edited with Don [Marshall] Bregenzer). Cleveland: Colophon Club, 1924. New York: Gordian Press, 1975.

The Sphinx: A Conversation. [North Montpelier, VT]: W. Paul Cook, 1944.

Twenty-One Letters of Ambrose Bierce. Cleveland: George Kirk, 1922. Norwood, PA: Norwood Editions, 1976. West Warwick, RI: Necronomicon Press, 1991 (with introduction by Donald R. Burleson).

Poems

"Adventure." *United Amateur* 21, No. 4 (March 1922): 42.

"A Burden." *Sprite* 9, No. 1 (March 1919): [3] (under heading "Five Poems").

"Chaunt d'Automne." See "Translations from Baudelaire."

"A Chinese Pavilion." *Sprite* 10, No. 2 (May 1920): 6–8. *Cygnet: A Quarterly Journal of Arts and Letters* 1, No. 3 (July 1920): 6. *Clevelander* 2, No. 1 (April 1923): 8 (as "Six Chinese Poems"). *H.*

"Ciel Brouillé." See "Translations from Baudelaire."

"Debs in Prison."

"Five Poems" [5 poems: "Resurgam"; "Shadow-Love"; "Euthanasia"; "Ecce Homo"; "A Burden"]. *Sprite* 9, No. 1 (March 1919): [2–3].

The Hermaphrodite. 1926. *H.*

"In Pierrot's Garden." *Cartoons* 2, No. 3 (November 1907): [18–19] [3 stanzas]. *Cartoons* 2, No. 5 (May 1908): [78][stanza IV only]. *National Amateur* 31, No. 3 (January 1909): 33 [3 stanzas]. *Poems* [5 stanzas]. In *Mon Ami Pierrot: Songs and Fantasies,* ed. Kendall Banning. Chicago: Brothers of the Book, 1917. 59. In *The Younger Choir,* ed. Edwin Markham. New York: Moods Publishing Co., 1910. 61–62 [3 stanzas]. *National Amateur* 41, No. 6 (July 1919): 232–3 [3 stanzas]. In *Twenty-one Letters to Ambrose Bierce* [in all editions][4 stanzas]. *L'Alouette* 1, No. 1 (January 1924): 16–17 [3 stanzas]. *H* [4 stanzas]. In *Threads in Tapestry* ed. Charles A. A. Parker, Rachel Hall, and Marcia A. Taylor. Medford, MA: C. A. A. Parker, 1935. 90–91 [Stanzas II, III, and V numbered as I, II, and III]. In *The Ancient Wood and Other Poems.* Ysleta, TX: Edwin B. Hill, 1942. [12–13] [omits stanza I].

"Isolation." *Sprite* 10, No. 2 (May 1920): 12 (under heading "Five More Poems"). *H.*

"John Clare in a Madhouse." *Sprite* 8, No. 1 (January 1917): [1–2]. *H.*

"Le Lethé." A translation from Baudelaire. Nonextant.

"Lineage." *United Co-operative.* No. 3 (April 1921): 15. *H.*

"Memoralia." *Vagrant* No. 10 (October 1919): 5. *H.*

"Nepenthe." *Crypt of Cthulhu* No. 20 (Eastertide 1984): 16.

"Ode to Apollo." See "To Apollo."

"Ode to Dionysus." See "To Dionysus."

"Oedipus at Colonus" [verse drama]. *Poems.*

"On the Passing of Youth." *Sprite* 10, No. 2 (May 1920): 3–6 (as "Ode on the Passing of Youth"). *Saturnian* 1 No. 1 (June–July [1920]): 1–4. Alternate title: "Ode on the Departure of Youth."

"Oscar Wilde." *Saturnian* 1, No. 1 (June–July [1920]): 6–7. *H.* In *Fear and Other Poems,* ed. Tom Collins (with EOD mailing 21, 1977), 1.

"Palingenesis." *National Amateur* 50, No. 5–6 (May–July 1928): 7. *H.*

"Shadow-Love." *Sprite* 9, No. 1 (March 1919): [2] (under heading "Five Poems").

"Simeon Solomon." *Californian* 3, No. 1 (Summer 1935): 14 (under heading "Contemporary Verse"). *H* (under heading "Quatrains").

"Song" [6 lines, beginning "Blossoms, blossoms, pink and white"]. *Poems* (1911).

"Song" [8 lines, beginning "In the Spring of the year, in the silver rain"]. *Conservative* 5, No. 1 (July 1919): 1. *H.* In Lovecraft's *The Conservative: Complete.*

Ed. Marc A. Michaud. West Warwick, RI: Necronomicon Press, 1976.

"A Song of Chamisso's." *Dowdell's Bearcat* No. 19 (December 1919): 5.

"Thomas Dermody 1775–1802." *Adelphian* 1, No. 2 (September 1917): [4-5]. *National Amateur* 61, No. 4 (March 1919): [121]. In Bodley Book Shop. *A Summer Catalogue of Unusually Desirable Books* . . . No. 30, n.d. [July 1939]: [2].

"Thomas Holley Chivers." *Conservative* No. 12 (March 1923): 1. *H.* In Lovecraft's *The Conservative: Complete.* Ed. Marc A. Michaud. West Warwick, RI: Necronomicon Press, 1976.

"To Apollo." *Sprite* 8, No. 1 (January 1917): [5] (as "Ode to Apollo"). *Saturnian* 1, No. 1 (June–July [1920]): 4–5. *H. Yawning Vortex* 3, No. 1 (October–November 1996): 38.

"To Dionysus." *Poems* (1911) [as "Ode to Dionysus"]. *Cartoons* 3, No. 1 (October 1909): 10–12 [as "Ode to Dionysus"]. *Saturnian* 1, No. 1 (June–July [1920]): 5–6. *H. Yawning Vortex* 3, No. 2 (July–August 1997): 16.

"To Satan." *Conservative* No. 13 (July 1923): 1–2. *Miskatonic* No. 15 (August 1976): [25–26]. In Lovecraft's *The Conservative: Complete.* Ed. Marc A. Michaud. West Warwick, RI: Necronomicon Press, 1976. In *The Miskatonic: Lovecraft Centenary Edition.* Glenview, IL: Moshassuck Press, 1991. In Lovecraft's *Letters to Samuel Loveman & Vincent Starrett.* Ed. S. T. Joshi and David E. Schultz. West Warwick, RI: Necronomicon Press, 1994. 41–42. *Yawning Vortex* 2, No. 1 (July 1995): 13–14.

"Translations from Baudelaire." *Saturnian* 1, No. 3 (March 1922): 3–11. *Contains:* "1. La Musique"; "2. Parfum Exotique"; "3. Horreur Sympathique"; "4. De Profundis Clamavi"; "5. La Beauté"; "6. Causerie"; "7. Chant d'Automne"; "8. La Couvercle"; "9. Le Chat"; "10. La Fontaine de Sang"; "11. Sonnet d'Automne"; "12. Ciel Brouillé."

"Translations from Verlaine." *Saturnian* 1, No. 3 (March 1922): 12–15. *Contains:* "1. Sagesse"; "2. Bruxelles"; "3. Romances sans Paroles"; "4. Il Bacio"; "5. La Bonne Chanson"; "6. Vert"; "7. Sappho."

"A Triumph of Anarchy." Alternate title: "The Mask of Anarchy." Nonextant.

"Twenty-four Translations from Heine." *Saturnian* 1, No. 2 (August–September [1920]): [2–13].

"Two Poems for Book Marks." Printed on bookmarks distributed by SL.

"Understanding." *H.* In *Masquerade: Queer Poetry in America to the End of World War II,* ed. Jim Elledge. Bloomington: Indiana University Press, 2004. 160.

Other Works

"Comment." *Saturnian* 1, No. 1 (June–July [1920]): 7–8; 1, No. 2 (August–September 1920): [13–15]; *Saturnian* 1, No. 3 (March 1922): 18–19.

The Death of Helen. One-act play. Nonextant.

"The Departed." Nonextant.

"Ernest Nelson: In Memoriam." *Saturnian* 1, No. 3 (March 1922): 18.

"The Faun" [story]. *Vagrant* No. 12 (December 1919): 4–12. *Leaves* No. 2 (1938): 102–6.

"The Flagellant." Nonextant.

"A Hopeless Love." *National Amateur* 45, No. 6 (July 1923): 1–3.

"Hubert Crackanthorpe: A Realist of the Nineties." *Recluse* No. 1 (1927): 71–75.

"A Keats Discovery." *Dial* 63 (19 July 1917): 77–78.

"Modern Poetry (An Exorcism)." *Saturnian* 1, No. 3 (March 1922): [1]–[3].

"The One Who Found Pity" [story]. *United Amateur* 24, No. 1 (July 1925): 5–6 (alternate titles: "He Who Found Pity" and "The One Who Died").

Philip Heather. A novel. Probably not completed. Nonextant.

"Preface" [dated 24 September 1922] to a scene, translated by George Borrow, from *Hakon Jarl,* by Adam Gottlob Oehlenschläger.

"A Scene for *King Lear*" [prose/verse drama]. *Sprite* 8, No. 3 (August 1917): [2–10]. (Introductory note by Harry Edward Martin, pp. [1–2].)

"A Scene for *Macbeth*" [prose/verse drama]. *United Amateur* 20, No. 2 (November 1920): 17–19. ("Editor's Note" by H. P. Lovecraft, p. 20.)

The Sphinx [one-act play]. *Ghost* No. 2 (July 1944): 19–41.

"A Triumph of Anarchy" (alternate title "The Mask of Anarchy"). Nonextant.

C. Works by Others

Adams, Francis William Lauderdale (1862–1893). *A Child of the Age.* London & Boston: John Lane/Roberts Bros., 1894.

Anderson, Sherwood (1876–1941). *Winesburg, Ohio: A Group of Tales of Ohio Small Town Life.* New York: B. W. Huebsch, 1919.

Andreyev, Leonid (1871–1919), with Ivan Bunin. *Lazarus and The Gentleman from San Francisco.* Tr. Abraham Yarmolinsky. Boston: Stratford Co., 1918.

Artsybashev, Mikhail (1878–1927). *Sanine.* Tr. Percy Pinkerton. New York: B. W. Huebsch, 1919. [Trans. of *Sanine* (1907).]

Bain, Francis William (1863–1940). *A Digit of the Moon: A Hindoo Love Story.* London: Methuen, 1911.

―――. *The Substance of a Dream.* London: Methuen, 1919.

Balzac, Honoré de (1799–1850). *Beatrix.* Tr. James Waring. London: J. M. Dent; Philadelphia: Gebbie, 1896. [Trans. of *Béatrix* (1839).]

―――. *The Girl with the Golden Eyes.* Tr. Ernest Dowson. With six illustrations engraved on wood by Charles Conder. London: Ernest Smithers, 1896. [Trans. of *La Fille aux yeux d'or* (1835).]

―――. *A Harlot's Progress.* Tr. James Waring. London: J. M. Dent; Philadelphia: Gebbie, 1896. 2 vols. [Tr. of *Splendeurs et misères de courtisanes* (1845).]

―――. *The Lily of the Valley.* Tr. Katharine Prescott Wormeley. Boston: Roberts Brothers, 1891. [Trans. of *Le Lyx dans la vallée* (1835–36).]

―――. *Lost Illusions: A Distinguished Provincial in Paris.* [Tr. anon.] Introduction by George Saintsbury. Boston: C. T. Brainerd, 1901. [Trans. of *Un Grand Homme de province à Paris* (1839).]

———. *A Passion in the Desert; An Episode under the Reign of Terror; A Dark Affair.* Tr. J. Alfred Burgan and Peter P. Breen. Philadelphia: G. Barrie, 1898. [Trans. of "Une Passion dans le désert" and other stories.]

———. *The Wild Ass's Skin.* Tr. Ellen Marriage. London: J. M. Dent; New York: E. P. Dutton (Everyman's Library), 1906. [Trans. of *Le Peau de chagrin* (1831).]

Barbey d'Aurevilly, J. (1808–1889). *The Story without a Name.* Tr. Edgar Saltus. <1891> New York: Brentano's, 1919. [Trans. of *Une Histoire sans nom* (1882).]

Bashkirtseff, Marie (1858–1884). *Journal of Marie Bashkirtseff.* Tr. A. D. Hall and G. B. Heckel. New York: Rand McNally, 1890. [Trans. of *Journal de Marie Bashkirtseff* (1887).]

Baudelaire, Charles Pierre (1821–1867). *Baudelaire: His Prose and Poetry.* Ed. T. R. Smith. New York: Boni & Liveright (Modern Library), 1919.

———. *Baudelaire: His Prose and Poetry.* Tr. Arthur Symons. New York: Albert & Charles Boni, 1926.

———. *Poems in Prose from Charles Baudelaire.* Tr. Arthur Symons. Portland, ME: Thomas Bird Mosher, 1909.

———. *The Poems of Charles Baudelaire.* Selected and translated from the French, with an introductory study, by F. P. Sturm. London: Walter Scott Publishing Co., 1906.

———. *The Poems and Prose Poems of Charles Baudelaire.* With an introductory preface by James Huneker. New York: Brentano's, 1919. [A reprint of the previous, but Strum is not acknowledged as the translator.]

Beaumont, Francis (1584–1616), and John Fletcher (1579–1625). *Beaumont and Fletcher's Plays.* Ed. George Philip Baker. London: J. M. Dent; New York: E. P. Dutton (Everyman's Library), 1911.

Beardsley, Aubrey (1872–1898). *The Art of Aubrey Beardsley.* Introduction by Arthur Symons. New York: Boni & Liveright (Modern Library), 1918.

Beerbohm, Max (1872–1956). *Seven Men.* London: Heinemann, 1919.

———. *Zuleika Dobson; or, An Oxford Love Story.* London: Heinemann, 1911.

Bennett, Arnold (1867–1931). *Anna of the Five Towns: A Novel.* <1902> New York: George H. Doran Co., 1915.

Bierce, Ambrose (1842–1914?). *Can Such Things Be?* New York: Cassell Publishing Co., 1893. Washington, DC: Neale Publishing Co., 1903.

———. *Collected Works.* New York & Washington, DC: Neale Publishing Co., 1909–12. 12 vols.

———. *The Shadow on the Dial and Other Essays.* Ed. S. O. Howes. San Francisco: A. M. Robertson, 1909.

Bisland, Elizabeth (1861–1929). *The Life and Letters of Lafcadio Hearn.* Boston: Houghton, Mifflin, 1906. 2 vols.

Bithell, Jethro (1878–1962), ed. *Contemporary Belgian Poetry.* London: Walter Scott Publishing Co., 1911.

———, ed. *Contemporary French Poetry.* London: Walter Scott Publishing Co., 1912.

Blair, Robert (1699–1746). *The Grave: A Poem.* <1743> Etchings executed from original design by William Blake and engraved by Louis Schiavonetti. London: Printed by T. Bensley, Bolt Court, for the proprietor, R. H. Cromek, 1808.

Boccaccio, Giovanni (1313–1375). *The Decameron.* <1349–52> Cincinnati: Stewart & Kidd Co, 1920. "India paper edition."

Boni, Albert (1892–1981), ed. *The Modern Book of French Verse: In English Translations by Chaucer, Francis Thompson, Swinburne, Arthur Symons, Robert Bridges, John Payne and Others.* New York: Boni & Liveright, 1920.

Borrow, George Henry (1803–1881). *The Bible in Spain; or, The Journeys, Adventures, and Imprisonments of an Englishman, in an Attempt to Circulate the Scriptures on the Peninsula.* <1843> London: J. M. Dent; New York: E. P. Dutton (Everyman's Library), 1907.

———. *Lavengro: The Scholar—the Gypsy—the Priest.* <1851> Introduction by Augustine Birrell. London: John Lane, 1902.

Bourget, Paul Charles Joseph (1852–1935). *A Tragic Idyl.* New York: Charles Scribner's Sons, 1896.

Bradley, William Aspenwall (1878–1939). *French Etchers of the Second Empire.* Boston: Houghton Mifflin, 1916.

Bridges, Robert Seymour (1844–1930). *Poetical Works of Robert Bridges Excluding the Eight Dramas.* Oxford: Oxford University Press, 1913.

Brooke, Rupert (1887–1915). *1914 & Other Poems.* London: Sidgwick & Jackson, 1915.

Brown, Horatio F. (1854–1926). *John Addington Symonds: A Biography Compiled from His Papers and Correspondence.* London: Smith, Elder, 1903.

Browning, Robert (1812–1889). *The Complete Poetic and Dramatic Works of Robert Browning.* Boston: Houghton, Mifflin, 1895.

Buck, Mitchell S. (1887–1959). *Ephemera: Greek Prose Poems.* Philadelphia: N. L. Brown, 1916.

———. *The Songs of Phryne.* Philadelphia: N. L. Brown, 1917.

Burke, Thomas (1886–1945). *Limehouse Nights.* <1916> New York: Robert M. McBride, 1917.

Burton, Sir Richard Francis (1821–1890). *A Plain and Literal Translation of the Arabian Nights Entertainments, Now Entituled [sic] The Book of the Thousand Nights and a Night, with Introduction, Explanatory Notes on the Manners and Customs of Moslem Men and a Terminal Essay upon the History of the Nights [Volumes I–X, Complete] + Supplemental Nights to the Book of the Thousand Nights and a Night.* N.p.: Printed by the Burton Club for Private Subscribers, 1886. 17 vols.

————. *The Kasidah*. Portland, ME: Thomas Bird Mosher, 1905.

Butler, Samuel (1835–1902). *The Way of All Flesh*. <1902> New York: E. P. Dutton, 1916.

Bynner, Witter (1881–1968). *The Beloved Stranger: Two Books of Song and a Divertisement for the Unknown Lover*. Preface by William Marion Reedy. New York: Alfred A. Knopf, 1919.

Cabell, James Branch (1879–1958). *Jurgen: A Comedy of Justice*. New York: Robert M. McBride & Co., 1919.

Carco, Francis (1886–1958). *Perversity*. Tr. Jean Rhys (though attributed in this edition to Ford Madox Ford). New York: Pascal Covici, 1928.

Casanova, Giacomo Girolamo (1725–1798). *Memoirs of Jacques Casanova de Seingalt: An Autobiography*. Tr. Arthur Machen. London: Venetian Society, 1894. 12 vols. [Trans. of *Histoire de ma vie* (1826–38).]

Chambers, Robert W. (1865–1933). *The King in Yellow*. <1895> London: Constable, 1919.

Cherry, John Law (1832–1911). *Life and Remains of John Clare, the "Northhamptonshire Peasant Poet."* London: Frederick Warne; New York: Scribner, Welford & Armstrong, 1873.

Cholmondeley, Mary (1859–1925). *Red Pottage*. New York: Harper & Brothers, 1900.

Clare, John (1793–1864). *Poems, Chiefly from Manuscript*. Ed. Edmund Blunden and Alan Porter. London: R. Cobden-Sanderson, 1920.

————. *The Rural Muse: Poems*. London: Whittaker, 1835.

Colvin, Sir Sidney (1845–1927). *Keats*. London: Macmillan, 1887. New York: Harper & Brothers, 1887.

Connors, Scott, ed. *The Freedom of Fantastic Things: Selected Criticism on Clark Ashton Smith*. New York: Hippocampus Press, 2006.

Conrad, Joseph (1857–1924). *Falk, Amy Foster, and To-morrow*. New York: McClure, Phillips, 1903.

————. *The Rescue: A Romance of the Shallows*. Garden City, NY: Doubleday, Page, 1919.

————. *The Secret Agent: A Simple Tale*. New York: Harper & Brothers, 1907.

————. *Tales of Unrest*. New York: Charles Scribner's Sons, 1898. [Contains "Karain: A Memory" and "The Idiots."]

————. *Youth: A Narrative and Two Other Stories (Heart of Darkness and The End of the Tether)*. London: William Blackwood & Sons, 1902.

————, and Ford Madox Ford. *Romance: A Novel*. New York: McClure, Phillips, 1903.

Crackanthorpe, Hubert (1870–1896). *Sentimental Studies, and a Set of Village Tales*. London: Heinemann, 1895.

Cranmer-Byng, Launcelot (1872–1945). *A Feast of Lanterns*. New York: E. P. Dutton, 1916.

————. *The Lute of Jade: Being Selections from the Classical Poets of China.* New York: E. P. Dutton, 1913.

D'Annunzio, Gabriele (1863–1938). *The Flame of Life.* [No translator identified.] New York: Boni & Liveright (Modern Library), 1918. [Translation of *Il fuoco* (1900).]

————. *Francesca da Rimini.* <1901> Tr. Arthur Symons. New York: Frederick A. Stokes, 1902.

Darley, George (1795–1846). *Nepenthe: A Poem in Two Cantos.* Introduction by R. A. Streatfeild. London: Elkin Mathews, 1897.

————. *Selections from the Poems of George Darley.* With an introduction and notes by R. A. Streatfeild. London: Methuen, 1904.

————. *Sylvia; or, The May Queen: A Lyrical Drama.* London: John Taylor, 1827.

Davidson, John (1857–1909). *Selected Poems.* London: John Lane, 1904.

Dekker, Thomas (1572?–1632). *The Best Plays of Thomas Dekker.* Notes by Ernest Rhys. The Mermaid Series. London: Vizetelly, 1887.

De la Mare, Walter (1873–1956). *Songs of Childhood.* As by Walter Ramal. London: Longmans, Green, 1902.

Donne, John (1572–1631). *Poems of John Donne.* The Muses' Library. Ed. E. K. Chambers. London: A. H. Bullen, 1901. 2 vols.

Dostoyevsky, Fyodor (1821–1881). *Crime and Punishment.* <1866> Tr. Constance Garnett. New York: F. Collier & Son, 1917.

————. *Pages from the Journal of an Author.* Tr. S. Koteliansky and J. Middleton Murry. Boston: John W. Luce, 1916.

Dowson, Ernest Christopher (1867–1900). *Cynara: A Little Book of Verse.* Portland, ME: Thomas Bird Mosher, 1907.

————. *Dilemmas: Stories and Studies in Sentiment.* London: Elkin Mathews, 1913.

————. *The Poems of Ernest Dowson.* With a memoir of Dowson by Arthur Symons, four illustrations by Aubrey Beardsley, and a portrait by William Rothenstein. London: John Lane, 1906.

————. *Studies in Sentiment.* Portland, ME: Thomas Bird Mosher, 1915.

[————, tr.] *Story of Beauty and the Beast: The Complete Fairy Story Translated from the French.* With Plates in Colour by Charles Condor [*sic*]. London: John Lane, 1908.

————, and Arthur Moore (1866–1952). *Adrian Rome.* London: Methuen, 1899.

Dunsany, Lord (1878–1957). *The Book of Wonder* [with *The Sword of Welleran*]. <1912, 1908> New York: Boni & Liveright (Modern Library), 1918.

————. *A Dreamer's Tales and Other Stories.* New York: Boni & Liveright (Modern Library), 1917.

————. *Fifty-One Tales.* <1915> Boston: Little, Brown, 1917.

————. *The Gods of Pegāna.* <1905> Boston: John W. Luce, 1916.

Ellis, Havelock (1859–1939). *Affirmations.* <1898> Boston: Houghton Mifflin, 1915.

FitzGerald, Edward (1809–1883), tr. *Rubaiyat of Omar Khayyam.* <1859> New York: Century Co., 1915.

Flaubert, Gustave (1821–1880). *Madame Bovary.* <1857> Tr. Eleanore Marx Aveling. New York: Modern Library, 1918.

———. *Salammbô: A Realistic Romance of Ancient Carthage.* <1862> Tr. J. S. Chartres. London: Vizetelly, 1886. *Salammbô of Gustave Flaubert.* Englished by M. French Sheldon. London: Saxon, 1886.

———. *Sentimental Education or the History of a Young Man.* London: Vizetelly & Co., 1886. Cleveland: St. Dunstan Society, 1904. [Trans. of *L'Éducation sentimentale* (1869).]

———. *The Temptation of St. Anthony.* Tr. Lafcadio Hearn. New York: Alice Harriman, 1910. Tr. G. F. Monkshood ([W. J. Clarke] 1872–?). London: Greening, 1910. [Trans. of *La Tentation de Saint Antoine* (1874).]

Flecker, James Elroy (1884–1915). *The Collected Poems.* Ed. J. C. Squire. New York: Alfred A. Knopf, 1914.

———. *Forty-two Poems.* London: J. M. Dent, 1911.

———. *The Golden Journey to Samarcand.* London: Martin Secker, 1913 (rev. ed. 1915).

Forman, H. Buxton (1842–1917). "Thomas Wade: The Poet and His Surroundings." In *Literary Anecdotes of the Nineteenth Century,* ed. W. Robertson Nicoll and Thomas J. Wise. London: Hodder & Stoughton, 1895. 1.43–67.

France, Anatole (1844–1924). *At the Sign of the Reine Pédauque.* Tr. Mrs. Wilfrid S. Jackson (Wilfrid Scarborough). New York: Dodd, Mead, 1920. [Trans. of *La Rôtisserie de la reine Pédauque* (1892).]

———. *The Crime of Sylvestre Bonnard.* Tr. Lafcadio Hearn. New York: Boni & Liveright, 1917. [Trans. of *Le Crime de Sylvestre Bonnard* (1881).]

———. *The Garden of Epicurus.* Tr. A. R. Allinson. New York: Parke, Austin & Lipscomb, 1914? [Trans. of *Le Jardin d'Épicure* (1895).]

———. *The Merrie Tales of Jacques Tournebroche and Child Life in Town and Country.* Tr. Alfred Allinson. London: John Lane/The Bodley Head, 1919. [Trans. of *Les Contes de Jacques Tournebroche* (1908).]

———. *The Red Lily.* Tr. Winifred Stephens. New York: Boni & Liveright, 1919. [Trans. of *Le Lys rouge* (1894).]

———. *The Revolt of the Angels.* Tr. Wilfrid Jackson. New York: John Lane, 1919. [Trans. of *La Révolte des anges* (1914).]

———. *Thaïs.* <1890> [No translator given.] London & New York: John Lane, 1909.

French, Nora May (1881–1907). *Poems.* San Francisco: Strange Company, 1910.

Freud, Sigmund (1856–1939). *Leonardo da Vinci: A Psychosexual Study of an Infantile Reminiscence.* Tr. A. A. Brill. New York: Moffat, Yard, 1916? [Translation of *Eine Kindheitserinnerung des Leonardo da Vinci* (1910).]

Gaillard, William (1807–?). *The History and Pedigrees of the House of Gaillard or GAYLORD in France, England and the United States, with a view of Chateau Gaillard, in Normandy; a view of Gaylordsville in Connecticut; a portrait of the author with the family arms, and other portraits.* Cincinnati: Caleb Clark, 1872.

Gauguin, Paul (1848–1903). *Noa Noa.* <1901> Tr. O. H. Theis. New York: Nicholas L. Brown, 1920.

Gautier, Judith (1845–1917), tr. *Chinese Lyrics: From the Book of Jade.* New York: B. W. Huebsch, 1918.

Gautier, Théophile (1811–1872). *Baudelaire: His Life.* Tr. Guy Thorne (pseud. of Cyril Arthur Edward Ranger Gull, 1875–1923). London: Greening, 1915. [Trans. of *Charles Baudelaire* (1868).]

———. *Mademoiselle de Maupin: A Romance of Love and Passion.* <1835> Illustrated by Toudouze. Paris: Société des Beaux-Arts, 1905. Tr. Burton Rascoe. New York: Alfred A. Knopf, 1920.

———. *One of Cleopatra's Nights and Other Fantastic Romances.* Tr. Lafcadio Hearn. New York: Worthington, 1882.

———. *Théophile Gautier's Short Stories: The Fleece of Gold, The Dead Leman, Poems, etc.* Tr. George Burnham Ives. New York: G. P. Putnam's Sons, 1909.

George, W. L. (1882–1926). *A Bed of Roses.* New York: Boni & Liveright, 1919.

Gérard de Nerval (pseud. of Gérard Labrunie, 1808–1855). *Sylvie: Souvenirs du Valois.* <1877> Tr. Lucie Page. Portland, ME: Thomas Bird Mosher, 1896.

Gibran, Kahlil (1883–1931). *The Madman: His Parables and Poems.* New York: Alfred A. Knopf. 1918.

———. *Twenty Drawings.* With an introductory essay by Alice Raphael. New York: Alfred A. Knopf, 1919.

Gissing, George (1857–1903). *The Private Papers of Henry Ryecroft.* London: Constable, 1903. New York: E. P. Dutton, 1903.

Goncourt, Edmond de (1822–1896), and Jules de Goncourt (1830–1870). *Renée Mauperin.* <1864> New York: Boni & Liveright (Modern Library), 1919.

Gorky, Maxim (1868–1936). *Reminiscences of Leo Nicolayevitch Tolstoi.* Tr. S. S. Koteliansky and Leonard Woolf. Richmond, UK: Hogarth Press, 1920.

Gourmont, Remy de (1858–1915). *A Night in the Luxembourg.* Tr. Arthur Ransome. Boston: John W. Luce, 1912. [Trans. of *Une Nuit au Luxembourg* (1906).]

———. *Philosophic Nights in Paris.* Tr. Isaac Goldberg. Boston: John W. Luce, 1920. [Trans. of *Promenades philosophiques* (1905).]

Hall, Mark. "Clark Ashton Smith Collections in the San Francisco Bay Area, Pt. 1: Letters to Samuel Loveman." *Lost Worlds: The Journal of Clark Ashton Smith Studies* No. 2 (March 2005). 31–38.

Hardy, Thomas (1840–1928). *The Mayor of Casterbridge.* <1886> New York: Modern Library, 1920.

———. *Tess of the d'Urbervilles.* <1891> New York: Harper & Brothers, 1921.

Harris, Frank (1855–1931). *Contemporary Portraits.* London: Methuen, 1915. New York: Mitchell Kennerley, 1915.

———. *Oscar Wilde: His Life and Confessions.* New York: Frank Harris, 1908.

Hay, John Stuart (1875–1949?). *The Amazing Emperor Heliogabalus.* London: Macmillan, 1911.

Head, Richard (1637?–1686?). *The English Rogue, Described in the Life of Meriton Latroon, a Witty Extravagant: Being a Complete History of the Most Eminent Cheats of Both Sexes.* <1665> New York: Dodd, Mead, 1928.

Hearn, Lafcadio (1850–1904). *Chita: A Memory of Last Island. Harper's New Monthly Magazine* (April 1888). New York: Harper & Brothers, 1889.

———. *Fantastics and Other Fancies.* <1914> Boston: Houghton Mifflin, 1919.

———. *"Gombo Zhèbes": Little Dictionary of Creole Proverbs, Selected from Six Creole Dialects.* New York: Coleman, 1895.

———. *In Ghostly Japan.* Boston: Little, Brown, 1919.

———. *Japan: An Attempt at Interpretation.* New York: Macmillan, 1905.

———. *Japanese Fairy Tales.* <1899> New York: Boni & Liveright, 1918.

———. *A Japanese Miscellany.* Boston: Little, Brown, 1916.

———. *Karma.* New York: Boni & Liveright, 1918.

———. *Kotto: Being Japanese Curios, with Sundry Cobwebs.* New York: Macmillan, 1910.

———. *Kwaidan: Stories and Studies of Strange Things.* Boston: Houghton Mifflin, 1914.

———. *Leaves from the Diary of an Impressionist: Early Writings.* Introduction by Ferris Greenslet. Boston: Houghton Mifflin, 1911.

———. *Letters from the Raven: Being the Correspondence of Lafcadio Hearn with Henry Watkin.* Ed. Milton Bronner. New York: Brentano's, 1907.

———. *Out of the East: Reveries and Studies in New Japan.* <1895> Boston: Houghton Mifflin, 1919.

———. *Some Chinese Ghosts.* Boston: Little, Brown, 1917.

———. *Stray Leaves from Strange Literature.* New York: James R. Osgood, 1884.

———. *Two Years in the French West Indies.* New York: Harper & Brothers, 1890.

———. *Youma: The Story of a West-Indian Slave.* New York: Harper & Brothers, 1890.

——— and others [Grace James, Basil Hall Chamberlain, et al.]. *Japanese Fairy Tales.* <1898> New York: Boni & Liveright, 1918.

Heine, Heinrich (1797–1856). *Poems of Heinrich Heine: Three Hundred and Twenty-five Poems.* Tr. Louis Untermeyer. New York: Henry Holt, 1917.

Hichens, Robert (1864–1950). *Bella Donna.* Philadelphia: J. B. Lippincott, 1909.

————. *The Garden of Allah.* <1904> London: Methuen, 1920.

Hillyer, Robert (1895–1961). *The Five Books of Youth.* New York: Brentano's, 1920.

Housman, Clemence (1861–1955). *The Were-Wolf.* Illustrated by Laurence Housman. London: John Lane at the Bodley Head; Chicago: Way & Williams, 1896.

Housman, Laurence (1865–1959). *Stories from the Arabian Nights.* Retold by Laurence Houseman [*sic*]. Illustrated by Edmund Dulac. London: Hodder & Stoughton, 1919.

Hugo, Victor (1802–1885). *History of a Crime.* New York: Athenaeum Society, 1909. 2 vols. [Trans. of *Histoire d'un crime* (1877–78).]

Huneker, James Gibbons (1857–1921). *Egoists: A Book of Supermen.* New York: Charles Scribner's Sons, 1910.

————. *Ivory, Apes and Peacocks.* New York: Charles Scribner's Sons, 1915.

————. *Painted Veils.* New York: Horace Liveright, 1920.

————. *Promenades of an Impressionist.* New York: Charles Scribner's Sons, 1910.

————. *Steeplejack.* New York: Charles Scribner's Sons, 1920.

Jackson, Holbrook (1874–1948). *The Eighteen Nineties: A Review of Art and Ideas at the Close of the Nineteenth Century.* London: Grant Richards, 1913.

James, Henry (1843–1916). *The Letters of Henry James.* Ed. Percy Lubbock. New York: Charles Scribner's Sons, 1920. 2 vols.

Johnson, Lionel (1867–1902). *The Art of Thomas Hardy.* London: Elkin Mathews/John Lane; New York: Dodd, Mead, 1894.

————. *Poetical Works of Lionel Johnson.* Preface by Ezra Pound. London: Elkin Mathews, 1915.

Kent, Rockwell (1882–1971). *Wilderness: A Journal of Quiet Adventure in Alaska.* New York: G. P. Putnam's Sons, 1920.

Kingsley, Charles (1819–1875). *Westward Ho! or, The Voyage and Adventures of Sir Amyas Leigh, Knight, of Burrough, in the County of Devon, in the Reign of Her Most Glorious Majesty Queen Elizabeth.* London: J. M. Dent, 1906.

Kipling, Rudyard (1865–1936). *The Day's Work.* <1898> Garden City, NY: Doubleday, Page, 1916.

————. *Kim.* New York: Doubleday, Page, 1901.

La Fontaine, Jean de (1621–1695). *The Original Fables of La Fontaine.* Translated and illustrated by Frederick Colin Tilney. London: J. M. Dent; New York: E. P. Dutton (Everyman's Library), 1913.

La Jeunesse, Ernest (1874–1917); Gide, André (1869–1951); and Blei, Blei (1871–1942). *Recollections of Oscar Wilde.* Tr. Percival Pollard. Boston: John W. Luce, 1906.

Le Gallienne, Richard (1866–1947). *English Poems.* <1892> London: John Lane/The Bodley Head, 1912.

Lemaître, Jules (1853–1914). *Serenus and Other Stories of the Past and Present.* Tr. A. W. Evans. London: Elkin Mathews & Marrot, 1920.

Leonardo da Vinci (1452–1519). *The Thoughts of Leonardo da Vinci as Recorded in His "Note-Books."* Tr. Edward McCurdy. London: Duckworth, 1907.

Leopardi, Giacomo (1793–1837). *Essays, Dialogues and Thoughts (Operette Morali and Pensieri) of Giacomo Leopardi.* Tr. James Thomson. Ed. Bertram Dobell. London: George Routledge & Sons; New York, E. P. Dutton, 1905.

———. *Essays, Dialogues, and Thoughts of Count Giacomo Leopardi.* Tr. Major-General Patrick Maxwell. Camelot Series. London: Walter Scott, [1893?].

Lepelletier, Edmond (1846–1913). *Paul Verlaine: His Life—His Work.* <1907> Tr. E. M. Lang. London: T. Werner Laurie, 1909. New York: Duffield, 1909.

Lewisohn, Ludwig (1882–1955). *A Modern Book of Criticism.* New York: Boni & Liveright, 1919.

Loti, Pierre (1850–1923). *From Lands of Exile.* Tr. Clara Bell. New York: W. S. Gottsberger, 1888. [Trans. of *Propos d'exil* (1887).]

———. *Madame Chrysantheme.* <1887> Tr. Laura Ensor. New York: Boni & Liveright, 1920.

———. *The Romance of a Spahi.* New York: Brentano's, 1914. [Trans. of *Le Roman d'un Spahi* (1881).]

Louÿs, Pierre (1870–1925). *Aphrodite.* n.p.: Privately printed, 1913. [Trans. of *Aphrodite* (1899).]

———. *The Songs of Bilitis.* Tr. Mitchell S. Buck. n.p.: Privately printed for the Parnassian Society, 1920. [Trans. of *Les Chansons de Bilitis* (1894).]

Lowell, Amy (1874–1925). *Sword Blades and Poppy Seed.* Boston: Houghton Mifflin, 1914.

Lowes, John Livingston (1867–1945). *Convention and Revolt in Poetry.* Boston: Houghton Mifflin, 1919.

Lucian of Samosata. (125?–180? C.E.). *Lucian's Dialogues of the Hetaerai.* Tr. Mitchell S. Buck. Philadelphia: Privately printed, 1916.

———. *The Works of Lucian: Translated from the Greek, by Several Eminent Hands.* With the Life of Lucian . . . by John Dryden. London: Printed for Sam. Briscoe, and sold by J. Woodward in Scalding-Alley against Stocks-Market, and J. Morphew near Stationers-Hall., 1710–11. 4 vols.

Lucretius (T. Lucretius Carus, 99?–55? B.C.E.). *Lucretius on Life and Death, in the Metre of Omar Khayyam to Which are Appended Parallel Passages from the Original.* Tr. W. H. Mallock. London: Adam & Charles Black, 1900. [Book 3 of *De Rerum Naturae.*]

Ludlow, Fitz Hugh (1836–1870). *The Hasheesh Eater: Being Passages from the Life of a Pythagorean.* New York: Harper & Brothers, 1857.

Machen, Arthur (1863–1947). *Hieroglyphics: A Note upon Ecstasy in Literature.* <1902> New York: Alfred A. Knopf, 1923.

———. *The Hill of Dreams.* <1907> New York: Alfred A. Knopf, 1923.

Macleod, Fiona (pseud. of William Sharp, 1855–1905). *Diedrê and the Sons of Usna*. Portland, ME: Thomas Bird Mosher, 1903.

Maeterlinck, Maurice (1862–1949). *Mary Magdalene: A Play in Three Acts*. Tr. Alexander Teixeira de Mattos. London: Methuen, 1911. [Trans. of *Marie-Magdeleine* (1910).]

———. *A Miracle of Saint Antony and Five Other Plays*. New York: Boni & Liveright (Modern Library), 1917.

Majid, Syed Abdul (1868–?). *The Rubáiyat of Háfíz*. Rendered into English verse by L. Cranmer-Byng. London: John Murray, 1910.

Mandeville, John. *The Voyages and Travels of Sir John Maundeville, Kt*. London: Gorge Bell & Sons, 1914.

Marguerite of Navarre (1492–1549). *The Heptameron: Tales and Novels of Marguerite, Queen of Navarre*. Tr. Arthur Machen <1886>. London: George Routledge, 1911.

Marsh, Edward (1872–1953). *Rupert Brooke: A Memoir*. New York: John Lane, 1918.

Marston, John (1575?–1634). *The Workes of Mr. Iohn Marston: Being Tragedies and Comedies, Collected into One Volume*. London: Printed [by Augustine Mathewes] for William Sheares, at the Harrowe in Britaines Bursse, 1633.

Martin, Frederick W. (1830–1883). *The Life of John Clare*. London: Macmillan, 1865.

Masefield, John (1878–1967). *Dauber: A Poem*. London: Heinemann, 1913.

Mathers, Edward Powys (1892–1939). *Coloured Stars: Versions of Fifty Asiatic Love Poems*. Boston: Houghton Mifflin, 1919.

Maugham, W. Somerset (1874–1965). *The Moon and Sixpence*. New York: Modern Library, 1919.

———. *Of Human Bondage*. Garden City, NY: Garden City Publishing, 1915.

Maupassant, Guy de (1850–1893). *Love and Other Stories*. Tr. Michael Monahan. New York: Boni & Liveright (Modern Library), 1919.

———. *Mademoiselle Fifi and Twelve Other Stories*. [No translator identified.] New York: Boni & Liveright, 1917.

———. *Une Vie*. <1883> Introduction by Henry James. New York: Boni & Liveright (Modern Library), 1918.

Melville, Herman (1819–1891). *Omoo: A Real Romance of the South Seas*. Boston: Page, 1919

———. *Typee: A Narrative of a Four Months' Residence among the Natives of a Valley of the Marquesas Islands, or a Peep at Polynesian Life*. New York: Lincoln MacVeagh/The Dial Press, 1910.

Mencken, H. L. (1880–1956), and George Jean Nathan (1882–1958). *Heliogabalus: A Buffoonery in Three Acts*. New York: Alfred A. Knopf, 1920.

Meredith, George (1828–1909). *The Egoist: A Comedy in Narrative*. <1879> New York: Charles Scribner's Sons, 1911.

————. *Love in the Valley.* <1851–78> Portland, ME: Thomas Bird Mosher, 1910.

————. *The Shaving of Shagpat: An Arabian Entertainment.* <1856> New York: Charles Scribner's Sons, 1917.

Merrill, Stuart (1863–1915), tr. *Pastels in Prose.* New York: Harper & Brothers, 1890.

Meynell, Everard (1882–1926). *The Life of Francis Thompson.* London: Burns & Oates, 1913.

Middleton, Richard (1882–1911). *Poems and Songs.* Introduction by Henry Savage. New York: Mitchell Kennerley, 1913.

Mighels, Ella Sterling (1853–1934). *Literary California.* San Francisco: Harr Wagner Publishing Co., 1918.

Millard, Christopher Sclater (1872–1927). *Oscar Wilde: Three Times Tried.* London: Ferrestone Press, 1912.

Milton, John (1608–1674). *Paradise Lost.* Illustrated by John Martin. London: Septimus Prowett, 1827. 2 vols.

Mitchell, S. Weir (1829–1914). *Characteristics.* New York: Century Co., 1910.

Montaigne, Michel de (1533–1592). *The Essayes; or, Morall, Politike, and Militarie Discourses of Lord Michael de Montaigne.* Tr. John Florio. London: Printed by M. Flesher, for R. Royston, 1632.

————. *The Essayes of Michel, Lord Montaigne.* Tr. John Florio. (The Temple Classics.) London: J. M. Dent, 1897. 6 vols.

Moore, George (1852–1933). *Impressions and Opinions.* <1891> New York: Brentano's, 1913.

Morley, Christopher (1890–1957). *The Haunted Bookshop.* Garden City, NY: Doubleday, Page, 1919.

————. *Shandygaff: A Number of Most Agreeable Inquirendoes upon Life and Letters, Interspersed with Short Stories and Skitts, the Whole Most Diverting to the Reader; Accompanied also by Some Notes for Teachers Whereby the Booke may be Made Usefull in Class-Room or for Private Improvement.* Garden City, NY: Doubleday, Page, 1918.

Morrow, W[illiam] C[hambers] (1854–1923). *The Ape, the Idiot and Other People.* Philadelphia: J. B. Lippincott, 1897.

————. *Bohemian Paris of To-day.* From notes by Edouard Cucuel. Philadelphia: J. B. Lippincott, 1901; London: Dent, 1907. 4 vols.

Muther, Richard (1860–1909). *The History of Modern Painting.* <1896? Rev. ed. London: J. M. Dent; New York: E. P. Dutton, 1907. 4 vols. [Trans. of *Geschichte der Malerei im XIX. Jahrhundert* (1894).]

Nietzsche, Friedrich (1844–1900). *The Antichrist.* Tr. H. L. Mencken. New York: Alfred A. Knopf, 1920. [Trans. of *Der Antichrist* (1895).]

————. *Beyond Good and Evil.* Tr. Helen Zimmern. New York: Boni & Liveright (Modern Library), 1918. [Trans. of *Jenseits von Gut und Böse* (1886).]

————. *Thus Spake Zarathustra.* <1883> Tr. Thomas Common. New York: Boni & Liveright (Modern Library), 1917.

Nivedita, Sister (pseud. of Margaret E. Noble, 1867–1911), and Ananda K. Coomaraswamy (1877–1947). *Myths of the Hindus and Buddhists.* New York: Henry Holt, 1914.

Noguchi, Yonejirō (Yone) (1875–1947). *Japanese Hokkus.* Boston: Four Seas Co., 1920.

O'Brien, Frederick (1869–1932). *White Shadows in the South Seas.* New York: Century Co., 1919.

Paltock, Robert (1697–1767). *The Life and Adventures of Peter Wilkins.* <1751> New York: E. P. Dutton, 1914.

Pater, Walter (1839–1894). *Appreciations: With an Essay on Style.* <1889> London: Macmillan, 1918.

————. *Imaginary Portraits.* <1887> London: Macmillan, 1912.

————. *Marius the Epicurean: His Sensations and Ideas.* <1885> New York: Macmillan, 1908.

————. *The Renaissance: Studies in Art and Poetry.* <1873> Portland, ME: Thomas Bird Mosher, 1912.

————. *The Renaissance.* Introduction by Arthur Symons. New York: Boni & Liveright (Modern Library), 1919.

————. *Sketches and Reviews.* New York: Boni & Liveright, 1919.

Peacock, Thomas Love (1785–1866). *Headlong Hall, Melincourt, Nightmare Abbey, Maid Marian.* London: George Routledge, 1910.

Petronius (T. Petronius Arbiter, 27?–66 C.E.). *The Satyricon.* Paris: n.p., 1889.

Philostratus, the Athenian (170?–250?). *The Life of Apollonius of Tyana, the Epistles of Apollonius and the Treatise of Eusebius.* Tr. F. C. Conybeare. London: Heinemann; New York: Macmillan, 1912. 2 vols.

Plarr, Victor (1863–1929). *Ernest Dowson: 1888–1897—Reminiscences, Unpublished Letters and Marginalia.* With a bibliography prepared by H. Guy Harrison. London: Elkin Mathews, 1914.

Poe, Edgar Allan (1809–1949). *The Works of the Late Edgar Allan Poe.* With Notices of His Life and Genius by N. P. Willis, J. R. Lowell, and R. W. Griswold. New York: J. S. Redfield, 1858. 4 vols.

Pollard, Percival (1869–1911). *Their Day in Court.* New York: Neale Publishing Company, 1909.

Polo, Marco (1254–1324). *The Travels of Marco Polo the Venetian.* Introduction by John Masefield. London: J. M. Dent; New York: E. P. Dutton (Everyman's Library), 1911.

Ransome, Arthur (1884–1967). *Aladdin and His Wonderful Lamp in Rhyme.* Illustrated by Thomas Mackenzie. New York: Brentano's, 1920.

————. *Oscar Wilde: A Critical Study.* New York: Mitchell Kennerley, 1912.

Rittenhouse, Jessie B. (1869–1948), ed. *The Little Book of Modern Verse: A Selection from the Work of Contemporaneous American Poets.* Boston: Houghton Mifflin, 1913, 1917.

Ross, Alexander (1591–1654). *Mystagogus Poeticus; or, The Muses Interpreter: Explaining the Historicall Mysteries, and Mysticall Histories of the Ancient Greek and Latine Poets.* London: Printed for Richard Whitaker, 1647.

Rossetti, Dante Gabriel (1828–1882). *The Collected Works of Dante Gabriel Rossetti.* Ed. William M. Rossetti. London: Ellis & Scrutton, 1886.

———. *Hand and Soul.* Portland, ME: Thomas Bird Mosher, 1900.

Sa'di, Shaikh (1210?–1292?). *The Gulistan: Being the Rose Garden of Shaikh Sa'di.* Tr. Sir Edwin Arnold. New York: Harper & Brothers, 1899.

Saltus, Edgar (1855–1921). *The Anatomy of Negation.* New York: Scribner & Welford, 1886.

———. *The Gardens of Aphrodite.* Philadelphia: Privately printed for the Pennell Club, 1920.

———. *The Imperial Orgy: An Account of the Tsars from the First to the Last.* New York: Boni & Liveright, 1920.

———. *Imperial Purple.* New York: Brentano's, 1906.

———. *Mary Magdelene: A Chronicle.* New York: Brentano's, 1919.

———. *The Philosophy of Disenchantment.* Boston: Houghton, Mifflin, 1885.

———. *Vanity Square.* Philadelphia: J. B. Lippincott, 1906.

Saltus, Francis S. (1848–1889). *The Bayadere and Other Sonnets.* New York: G. P. Putnam's Sons, 1894.

———. *Flasks and Flagons: Pastels and Profiles, Vistas and Landscapes.* Buffalo: C. W. Moulton, 1892.

Sandys, George (1578–1644). *A Relation of a Journey Begun An. Dom. 1610. Foure Bookes. Containing a description of the Turkish Empire, of Ægypt, of the Holy Land, of the remote parts of Italy, and ilands adjoyning.* London: Printed for W. Barrell, 1615.

Sappho (630/612–570? B.C.E.). *Memoir, Text, Selected Renderings, and a Literal Translation.* Tr. Henry Thornton Wharton. London: Stott, 1887.

Schedel, Hartmann (1440–1514). *Das Buch der Chroniken.* Nuremberg: A. Koberger, 1493.

Schopenhauer, Arthur (1788–1860). *Studies in Pessimism.* Tr. T. Bailey Saunders. London: S. Sonnenschein, 1890.

Seltzer, Thomas (1875–1943), ed. *Best Russian Short Stories.* New York: Boni & Liveright (Modern Library), 1917.

Shanks, Louis Piaget (1878–1935). *Anatole France.* Chicago: Open Court Pub. Co., 1919.

[Solomon, Simeon (1840–1905).] *A Vision of Love Revealed in Sleep.* London: Printed for the author, 1871.

———. *A Vision of Love Revealed in Sleep.* <1871> With a "review" by John Addington Symonds. Portland, ME: Thomas Bird Mosher, 1909.

Sorley, Charles Hamilton (1895–1915). *Marlborough and Other Poems*. Cambridge: Cambridge University Press, 1919.

Starrett, Vincent (1886–1974). *Ambrose Bierce*. Chicago: W. M. Hill, 1920.

Stedman, Edmund Clarence (1833–1908), ed. *An American Anthology 1787–1900; Selections Illustrating the Critical Review of American Poetry in the Nineteenth Century*. Boston: Houghton, Mifflin, 1900.

———, ed. *A Victorian Anthology, 1837–1895: Selections Illustrating the Editor's Critical Review of British Poetry in the Reign of Victoria*. Boston: Houghton Mifflin, 1895.

Stendhal (pseud. of Marie-Henri Beyle, 1783–1842). *The Chartreuse of Parma*. Tr. Maurice Hewlett. London: London Book Co., 1908. [Trans. of *La Chartreuse de Parme* (1839).]

Sterling, George (1869–1926). *Beyond the Breakers and Other Poems*. San Francisco: A. M. Robertson, 1914.

———. *The Binding of the Beast and Other War Verse*. San Francisco: A. M. Robertson, 1917.

———. *The Caged Eagle and Other Poems*. San Francisco: A. M. Robertson, 1916.

———. *The House of Orchids and Other Poems*. San Francisco: A. M. Robertson, 1911.

———. *Lilith: A Dramatic Poem*. San Francisco: A. M. Robertson, 1919. San Francisco: Book Club of California, 1920. New York: Macmillan, 1926 (introduction by Theodore Dreiser).

———. *Ode on the Opening of the Panama-Pacific International Exposition*. San Francisco: A. M. Robertson, 1915. Also in *San Francisco Examiner* (20 February 1915): 65.

———. *Rosamund: A Dramatic Poem*. San Francisco: A. M. Robertson, 1920.

———. *Sails and Mirage and Other Poems*. San Francisco: A. M. Robertson, 1921.

———. "A Wine of Wizardry." *Cosmopolitan Magazine* 43, No. 5 (September 1907): 551–56. In *A Wine of Wizardry and Other Poems*. San Francisco: A. M. Robertson, 1909.

———. *Yosemite: An Ode*. San Francisco: A. M. Robertson, 1916. Also in *San Francisco Call and Post* (22 October 1915): 13.

Stevenson, Robert Louis (1850–1894). *Kidnapped: Being Memoirs of the Adventures of David Balfour in the Year 1751*. London: Cassell, 1886.

———. *Travels with a Donkey in the Cévennes*. Boston: Roberts Brothers, 1879.

———. *Treasure Island*. London: Cassell, 1883.

———. *Vailima Letters: Being Correspondence Addressed by Robert Louis Stevenson to Sidney Colvin, November 1890–October 1894*. <1895> London: Methuen, 1913.

———. *Virginibus Puerisque, and Other Papers*. London: C. K. Paul & Co., 1881.

Stoddard, Charles Warren (1843–1909). *South Sea Idylls*. <1873> New York: Charles Scribner's Sons, 1892.

Strachey, Lytton (1880–1932). *Books and Characters: French and English*. New York: Harcourt, Brace, 1922.

Swinburne, Algernon Charles (1837–1909). *A Pilgrimage of Pleasure: Essays and Studies*. With a bibliography by E. J. O'Brien. Boston: R. G. Badger, 1913.

———. *Poems and Ballads*. London: John Camden Hotten, 1866.

———. *A Study of Ben Jonson*. London: Chatto & Windus, 1889.

Symonds, John Addington (1840–1893). *An Introduction to the Study of Dante*. <1872> London: Adam & Charles Black, 1906.

———. *Percy Bysshe Shelley*. <1878> London: Macmillan, 1918.

Symons, Arthur (1865–1945). *Cesare Borgia, Iseult of Brittany, The Toy Cart*. New York: Brentano's, 1920.

———. *Charles Baudelaire: A Study*. London: Elkin Mathews, 1920.

———. *Dante Gabriel Rossetti*. New York: Brentano's, 1909.

———. *Days and Nights*. London, New York: Macmillan, 1889.

———. *Lesbia and Other Poems*. New York: E. P. Dutton, 1920.

———. *Poems*. New York: John Lane, 1919. 2 vols.

———. *Studies in Seven Arts*. <1906> New York: E. P. Dutton, 1913.

———. *The Symbolist Movement in Literature*. New York: E. P. Dutton, 1919.

———. *Tristan and Iseult: A Play in Four Acts*. New York: Brentano's, 1917.

Synge, John Millington (1871–1909). *The Playboy of the Western World*. <1907> Boston: John W. Luce, 1911.

Thompson, Francis (1859–1907). *The Collected Works of Francis Thompson*. London: Burns & Oates, 1913. 3 vols.

Thompson, Vance (1863–1925). *Drink and Be Sober*. New York: Moffat, Yard, 1915.

———. *Eat and Grow Thin: The Madha Menus*. New York: E. P. Dutton, 1914.

———. *French Portraits: Being Appreciations of the Writers of Young France*. <1899> New York: Mitchell Kennerley, 1913.

Thomson, James (1834–1882). *The City of Dreadful Night and Other Poems*. London: Reeves & Turner, 1875.

Thorne, Guy (pseud. of C. Ranger Gull, 1875–1923). *When It Was Dark: A Story*. London: Greening, 1903. [Later editions use the subtitle *A Story of a Great Conspiracy*.]

Tolstoy, Leo (1828–1910). *Anna Karenina*. <1878> Tr. Rochelle S. Townsend. London: J. M. Dent, 1912.

———. *Redemption and Two Other Plays*. Introduction by Arthur Hopkins. New York: Modern Library, 1919.

———. *Resurrection*. <1899> Tr. Archibald J. Wolfe. New York: International Book Pub. Co., 1920.

[Trelawny, Edward John (1792–1881).] *Adventures of a Younger Son*. London: Henry Colburn & Richard Bentley, 1831. 3 vols.

———. *Adventures of a Younger Son*. A new edition, with an introduction by Edward Garnett. London: T. Fisher Unwin; New York: Macmillan, 1890.

Turgenev, Ivan (1818–1893). *Smoke.* Tr. Constance Garnett. New York: Boni & Liveright, 1919.

——. *Virgin Soil.* <1877> Tr. Rochelle S. Townsend. London: J. M. Dent, 1914.

Unterecker, John (1922–1989). *Voyager: A Life of Hart Crane.* New York: Farrar, Straus & Giroux, 1969.

Untermeyer, Louis (1885–1977). *The New Adam.* New York: Harcourt, Brace & Howe, 1920.

——, tr. *Poems of Heinrich Heine: Three Hundred and Twenty-five Poems.* New York: Henry Holt, 1917.

Van Vechten, Carl (1880–1964). *The Merry-Go-Round.* New York: Alfred A. Knopf, 1918.

Verlaine, Paul (1844–1896). *Poems.* Selected and translated, with an introduction by Ashmore Wingate. London: Walter Scott Publishing Co., 1904.

——. *Poems of Paul Verlaine.* Tr. Gertrude Hall. <1895> New York: Duffield, 1906.

Villon, François (c. 1431–1464). *Poems.* Tr. John Payne <1878>. New York: Boni & Liveright (Modern Library), 1918.

Virgil (P. Vergilius Maro, 70–19 B.C.E.). *An English Version of the Eclogues of Virgil.* Tr. Samuel Palmer. London: Seeley, 1883.

Visiak, E. H. (1878–1972). *The Phantom Ship and Other Poems.* London: Mathews, 1912.

Voltaire (François Marie Arouet, 1694–1778). *Candide.* <1759> [No translator indicated.] New York: Boni & Liveright (Modern Library), 1918.

Wade, Thomas (1805–1875). *The Phrenologists: A Farce in Two Acts.* London: J. Onwhyn, 1830.

Waddell, Helen (1889–1965), tr. *Lyrics from the Chinese.* Boston: Houghton Mifflin, 1913.

Waley, Arthur (1889–1966), tr. *A Hundred and Seventy Chinese Poems.* London: Constable, 1918.

——. *More Translations from the Chinese.* London: Allen & Unwin, 1919.

Wall, O. A. (1846–1922). *Sex ad Sex-Worship (Phallic Worship): A Scientific Treatise on Sex, Its Nature and Function, and Its Influence on Art, Science, Architecture, and Religion—with Special Reference to Sex Worship and Symbolism.* St. Louis: C. V. Mosby, 1919.

Wandrei, Donald (1908–1987). "The Emperor of Dreams." *Overland Monthly* 84, No. 12 (December 1926): 380–81, 407, 409. *Klarkash-Ton: The Journal of Smith Studies* No. 1 (1988): 3–8, 25.

Webster, John (1580?–1634?), and Cyril Tourneur (1575?–1626). *Webster and Tourneur.* Ed. John Addington Symonds. The Mermaid Series. London: Vizetelly & Co., 1888.

Wells, Charles (1798–1879). *Joseph and His Brethren: A Dramatic Poem.* London, 1824. London: Chatto & Windus, 1876.

————. *Stories After Nature*. London: Lawrence & Bullen, 1891.

Whistler, James A. McNeill (1834–1903). *Mr. Whistler's Ten O'Clock—A Lecture*. <1888> Portland, ME: Thomas Bird Mosher, 1920.

Wilde, Oscar (1854–1900). *De Profundis*. London: Methuen, 1916.

————. *Novels and Fairy Tales of Oscar Wilde*. New York: Cosmopolitan Book Corp., 1915.

————. *Intentions*. <1891> New York: Brentano's, 1905.

————. *The Picture of Dorian Gray*. <1890> New York: Brentano's, 1906.

————. *The Plays of Oscar Wilde*. New York: Cosmopolitan Book Corp., 1914.

————. *The Prose of Oscar Wilde*. Designed by Frederic W. Goudy. New York: Cosmopolitan Book Corp., J. J. Little & Ives Company, 1916.

Woodberry, George Edward (1855–1930). *Literary Essays*. New York: Harcourt Brace & Howe, 1920.

Younghusband, Francis Edward (1863–1942). *Kashmir*. London: Adam & Charles Black, 1909.

Index